BERYL IVEY LIBRARY

Shakespeare's
Lyricized Drama

Shakespeare's
Lyricized Drama

Alexander Shurbanov

Newark: University of Delaware Press

Associated University Presses
2010 Eastpark Boulevard
Cranbury, NJ 08512

The paper used in this publication meets the requirements of the American National Standard for Permanence of Paper for Printed Library Materials Z39.48–1984.

Library of Congress Cataloging-in-Publication Data

Shurbanov, Aleksandur.
    Shakespeare's lyricized drama / Alexander Shurbanov.
        p. cm.
    Includes bibliographical references and index.
    ISBN 978-0-87413-086-7 (alk. paper)
  1. Shakespeare, William, 1564–1616—Technique. 2. Drama—Technique. I. Title.
    PR2995.S58 2010
    822.3'3—dc22
                                                        2009030479

PRINTED IN THE UNITED STATES OF AMERICA

Contents

Acknowledgments

THE TOPIC OF THIS BOOK HAS OCCUPIED MY STUDIES AND MY TEACHing for at least the last fifteen years. All along I have shared my growing interest in Shakespeare's manifold intricate uses of the lyric in his dramatic work with many colleagues and have received from them valuable suggestions, which I am unfortunately unable to acknowledge in detail. In the early 1990s I first started discussing these problems with groups of graduate students at the English Department of Sofia University. For a couple of years we were coteaching such classes with Evgenia Pancheva, whose contribution to the initial shaping of my ideas is hard to exaggerate. I am also grateful for the insights of a number of brilliant students, which inevitably directed my thinking on the subject in important ways that I find impossible to fully gauge and express my thanks for. It has been especially beneficial for me to be offered the opportunity of teaching graduate and postgraduate courses on the lyric element in Shakespeare's plays at other universities in Europe and the USA, including the University of Zaragoza (1994) and the State University of New York at Albany (2004). I am particularly indebted to the library of SUNY for letting me use its resources during the full year I spent there. It would have been difficult to complete my project if I had not had this good luck. My thanks would have to go first of all to the late Kay Shaffer, senior librarian at SUNY and a generous friend, whose bibliographical help I had learned to rely on for a number of years.

It has also been very useful for my work on the topic to be able to discuss its progress with colleagues from the international Shakespeare and English literature academic community. I would like to thank the organizers of two of the European Society for English Studies conferences—in Glasgow (1995) and in Helsinki (2000)— for inviting me to give papers related to my interests. Last but not least, I have received invaluable advice and encouragement from Professor Jay L. Halio, who kindly agreed to read the manuscript of this book and made many helpful suggestions. The anonymous readers of the UDP have also helped me a great deal to improve the text with a number of general and concrete remarks. For reasons of space, I must leave similarly anonymous many other friends at home and abroad, though I should single out for special thanks those nearest to me in both kin and kind, my wife and my sons, whose understanding, patience and cheerful assistance have been unstinting as always.

Author's Note

ALL QUOTATIONS FROM SHAKESPEARE'S PLAYS IN THIS BOOK ARE taken from the latest Arden Shakespeare editions, to wit: *Love's Labour's Lost,* edited by H. R. Woudhuysen, 1998; *Romeo and Juliet,* edited by Brian Gibbons, 1980; *King Richard II,* edited by Charles R. Forker, 2002; *As You Like It,* edited by Juliet Dusinberre, 2006; *Hamlet,* edited by Ann Thompson and Neil Taylor, 2006; *Othello,* edited by E. A. Honigmann, 1997; *King Lear,* edited by R. A. Foakes, 1997; and *Macbeth,* edited by Kenneth Muir, Ninth edition, 1962. All line references are to these editions.

Shakespeare's sonnets are quoted from Helen Vendler's 1997 edition in her book *The Art of Shakespeare's Sonnets.* The sources of other quotations are specified in the text.

Shakespeare's
Lyricized Drama

1
Introduction

WE ARE SO USED TO CALLING SHAKESPEARE'S PLAYS "POETIC DRAMA" that we hardly ever stop to think about the more specifically generic meaning of the term implying a set of distinctive features that separate them as a class. What makes a drama poetic is not the mere fact that it is (mainly) written in verse, but rather its preference for a type of language we associate with poetry and, even more importantly, its dealing with its material in a way that would be considered poetic. It is therefore fair to see poetic drama—and, in particular, its variety characteristic of the English Renaissance—as a kind profoundly molded by the methods and techniques of poetry. How this combination is effected in its details is a question that might help us to understand better the specificity of Shakespeare's artistic achievement and the power of its impact. Such is the task that the present study sets for itself.

The Renaissance was an age particularly prone to the interplay and hybridization of genres. It created such crossbreeds as the romantic epic, the pastoral romance, the epigrammatic sonnet, the tragicomedy, even the "tragic farce."[1] But none of these can compare to the marriage this period effected between two of the most basic types of literature, drama and poetry. While it is true that Shakespeare was neither the first nor the only begetter of English poetic drama, it can hardly be disputed that it "grew to maturity in his lifetime and that Shakespeare was a major fashioner of its growth."[2] It would therefore be interesting to see how he introduced the poetic element into his plays and, further, how gradually he perfected the generic blend by making it less local and mechanical, more pervasive and organic. In order to study this development as a process, I have chosen to examine a few of Shakespeare's dramas leading to his own and the period's aesthetic maturity in their chronological order.

Before coming to the concrete discussion of the plays, however, we must make sure that we know exactly what we mean by the two components of the composite "poetic drama," namely by *poetry* and *drama*. This will necessarily take us away from our immediate concern with Shakespeare, into the more abstract regions of literary theory, but it will provide the framework for the analysis in the subsequent chapters. Though both terms appear to be transparent, they are far from being so and can be confusingly ambiguous even in the specialized discourse of literary criticism. To start with, when we use the words "poetry" or "poetic" in a fairly loose way, we most frequently have in mind not poetry in general (a notion that tends to be so broad as to become almost synonymous with literature) but one of its varieties, lyrical poetry—"the only pure poetry," as it has been called, supposed to contain and foreground all the essential poetic features.[3]

Thus we find ourselves face to face with the formidable Triad, overarching in traditional European criticism the whole of literature and dividing it into three great kinds: epos, drama, and lyric. Lately this inherited classificatory model has been subjected to a good deal of theoretical animosity. Ever since Croce's wholesale attack on the idea of genre, the imposition of any order in the vast and unruly economy of literature has been viewed with suspicion and irritation.[4] The Triad as the apex of the entire generic pyramid is singled out for particular opprobrium. It has been revealed that this trinity is both unholy and illegitimate: though the construct was long ascribed to the reverend authorities of classical poetics, Plato and Aristotle, their theoretical constructions do not appear to make any provision for lyrical poetry.[5] The fourth-century grammaticus Diomedes is credited with the first attempt to introduce the tripartite division of literature with a slot comfortable enough for lyric, but the express introduction of the Triad did not in fact occur until the Renaissance. In 1559 the Italian theorist Minturno divided all poets into epic, scenic, and melic/ lyric, and during the next couple of centuries most of his colleagues in Europe took the same position, which eventually received the sanction of an extensive philosophical discussion in Hegel's *Aesthetics* (published in the 1830s).[6]

The triadoclasts may have a point in claiming that too much intellectual effort has been wasted since the Romantic Age on fruitless disquisitions about such great and notoriously elusive abstractions. It has been argued persuasively that the basis of the Triad is very uncertain, the criteria underlying its formation being mixed and heterogeneous. There is not even a generally accepted term by which we could refer to its members. Goethe called them *Naturformen* to differentiate them from the more concrete genres they would encompass, and later theorists have tried to veer away from the essentialist connotations of his term by supplying a number of questionable substitutes: *universals, megagenres, theoretical genres, fundamental attitudes, representational modes*, etc.[7] Various definitions have been offered for these categories from rhetorical, linguistic and philosophical perspectives. Some influential authors have even proposed that we should leave the generic trinity behind and replace it with an attitudinal one, denoted not by nouns but by adjectives: epic (narrative), dramatic, and lyric.[8]

If we extend to the Triad Alastair Fowler's distinction between two categories in the genre system of literature—the *kinds*, representing a unity of substantive and formal features, and the *modes*, produced from them through the shedding of the latter—we may attempt a solution of this vexed question.[9] It would be difficult to argue that the Triad does not exist in its generic definitiveness, and very few of its detractors would go as far as to suggest that it is an entirely imaginary construct. A play by Ibsen is certainly above all an example of drama, no matter what historical variety of this kind it may represent, and, by the same token, any of Keats's odes would be classed as a lyrical poem by the vast majority of professional or amateur readers. It is hard to deny that the traditional Triad is formed by the most capacious genre groupings at so high a level of abstraction as to be the least subject to historical change and to appear immutable—"Naturformen." At the same time, their less definite, bodiless emanations—the epic, dramatic, and lyrical modes—spread across the whole generic field, molding the formalized kinds (genres) in a variety of characteristic ways. Thus, according to Eduard von Hartmann, we arrive at a triad of kinds multiplied by its modal projection and producing nine instead of the three basic forms sanctified by tradition: pure lyric work, epic lyric, dramatic lyric; pure dramatic work, lyrical drama, epic drama; pure epic work, lyrical epic, dramatic epic.[10] The specific focus of the present study indeed falls on one of Hartmann's nine modulated supergenres, that of lyrical drama and, particularly, on its remarkable historical avatar at the peak of the English Renaissance.

And, once again, what are the distinctive features of drama and lyric, which we have to look for in their combination underscoring lyrical drama? Let us first, very briefly, consider the repertoire of features attributed to drama. Although there is a good deal of disagreement on this point, the majority of authors seem to concur in associating the members of the Triad with the three dimensions of time and most of them allocate the past to epic, the present to lyric, and the future to drama.[11] Admittedly, everything that happens in drama takes place in front of our eyes, at the present moment, but the drive is always toward some goal in the future. The present of drama, as Susanne K. Langer writes, is "filled with its own future."[12] Etymologically, the very word "drama" means action, and action is certainly the essence of this kind. While physical action is presupposed in its presentation, the text of a play itself is made of action. Its basic form is dialogue and it is in dialogue that the insistent directional pulls of different wills toward their (often conflicting) futures take place. Dialogue stems from one plot situation and gradually transforms it into another. So there can be little doubt that dialogue is a kind of action, verbal action, or "azione parlata," as Pirandello called it.[13]

Character is also an important component of drama, but character has no existence outside its action.[14] And yet, we know from Hegel that action in drama does not only issue from one plot situation in order to produce another one—it similarly issues from character and is finally absorbed in character.[15] The soliloquies, these monologic retreats from dramatic dialogue are usually the places where this happens. It is incidentally at such junctures, when we are allowed to get a glimpse of the characters' inner life, that drama most often seems to come in direct contact with the lyric.

The definition of lyric will of necessity take much longer and remain less satisfactory than that of drama, due to the considerable margin of theoretical disagreement about the parameters of this younger member of the Triad. René Wellek advises against even attempting to define the lyric, for, he fears, "nothing beyond generalities of the tritest kind can result from it."[16] Elder Olson seems to agree—yet with a difference: he deems it possible, if not to define lyric as such, "to delineate its boundaries, so that we may at least know where it begins and where it leaves off."[17] We could try to do this charting of lyric's territory by summing up the variety of ideas expressed at different times and from different points of view but contributing to our understanding of it.

First of all, as has just been hinted, lyric, in contrast to drama, is primarily monologic. More often than not there is in it a single speaker, sometimes referred to as "persona." In the bulk of lyric poetry predominant in Europe since the Renaissance, this speaker is a private individual who may empathize with the community or some of its sections but, above all, expresses his or her own personal attitudes. Moreover, the monologic utterances of the lyrical poet resemble the dramatic soliloquy: they are self-addressed and do not seem to presuppose an audience. Even in cases when the utterance is expressly addressed to somebody else, the addressee is absent or unable to enter into actual conversation with the speaker, for that is a deity, a spirit, an inarticulate or deceased being, an inanimate thing, a natural phenomenon, a person who is out of reach, etc. In the words of Osip Mandelstam, "Normally, when a person has something to say, he goes to people, he seeks out an audience. Yet, a poet does the opposite: he runs 'to the shores of desert waves, to broad and resonant oaks'."[18] Lyric has been called "the art of solitude."[19] But, paradoxically, the solitude of the poet can be opened to an imaginative communication with the whole of the universe.

The speaker of lyrical poetry is a very subjective presence, the voice of intense and uncompromising individualism. At the same time, however, it expresses something that tends to be "universally human," something with which we in the audience can identify.[20] For the mind of the lyric poet, according to Shelley, "is itself the image of all other minds."[21] As Emil Staiger argues, "in the lyric 'I' am not a 'moi' that consciously maintains its identity, but a 'je' that does not maintain itself, but dissolves in every moment of existence."[22] And, again in his words, "'inner' and 'outer,' 'subjective' and 'objective' are absolutely not divorced from one another in lyric poetry."[23] There is no distance between "the poet and what he speaks about" and, similarly, "between the poetic creation and the listener."[24]

The actual audience of lyrical poetry is usually not directly addressed. The addressee—when an addressee is invoked—is no more than a character in the fictive world of the poem. It is Mandelstam again who observes that "appealing to an actual addressee dismembers poetry, plucks its wings, deprives it of air, of the freedom of flight."[25] In such cases a poetic utterance is robbed of its imaginative

latitude and is reduced to a cue in an act of practical communication—a mere letter or a memo. The audience of poetry is always "a
third party," of whose existence the poet seems to be unaware or
heedless. As theorists have put it, in lyric the audience is hidden from
the poet. His is therefore an utterance that is *overheard*—a word first
used by John Stuart Mill and expressing eloquently the peculiar relation between the solipsistic lyrical poet and the audience.[26]

The corollary of this peculiar communicative situation—overhearing something that is not addressed to you—is that the lyric
is inherently averse to persuasive rhetoric, to pathos. For pathos, as
Staiger observes, devours individuality, the very element from which
the lyric grows and in which it moves.[27] Pathos always needs for its
unfolding a stage, for which the lyric has no use, because as soon as
it finds itself face to face with an actual audience it ceases to be itself
and is transformed into one of the other, less introvert, members of
the generic Triad. To various extents, pathos is not particularly welcome in any kind of imaginative literature.

Not only does the lyrical poet speak to himself, but he also speaks
about himself. His inner state is what chiefly interests him, and anything from the outer world that happens to come into his poem can
only be admitted there if it is relevant to that inner state. An object,
a circumstance or an event external to the poet cannot be of central
importance for the poem—it is no more than an occasion, a prop for
the expression of what is going on inside, in the heart and the mind
of its author.

The main focus of lyric is usually an emotion that would out. "Lyricism," says Paul Valéry, "is the development of an exclamation."[28] But a
mere exclamation, however passionate, is not yet a lyrical poem. What
is conveyed in lyrical poetry, as Herbert Read observes, is not just an
emotion but "the imaginative prehension of emotional states."[29] This
is achieved by the complex interplay of emotion and thought. In the
words of Barbara Hardy, "Feeling is part of an argument, warming,
sustaining, and generating fresh poetic ideas. A poetic idea is a passionate idea, warming, sustaining, and generating fresh feeling."[30]
Hegel deems it possible that ideas, even philosophical thoughts, be
drawn into the heart of lyric, "so far as these are accommodated to the
form of imagination and intuition and enabled to enter the sphere
of feeling."[31] Yet he remarks that thought as a purely mental process
of logical operations is unable to create a lyrical utterance. The true
poet finds himself in a state very different from that of rational delib-

eration—he "appears to be possessed by a power and a 'pathos' which rules him and carries him away against his will."[32] Some poems, such as those of Donne and his followers in seventeenth-century English literature, can imitate intricate logical discussions to the point of becoming exercises in casuistry, but this form is nothing more than what Susanne Langer calls "the semblance of reasoning."[33] The actual goal of the poet even in such cases is not to validate a thesis in an argumentative way but to come as close as possible to the expression of the inarticulate aspects of feeling.[34] To Staiger, what sustains the lyric is unity of mood and not logical coherence.[35]

It is this unity of mood, this specific state of mind, rather than information or philosophical views, that lyric endeavors to impart. And the act of imparting it, unlike the act of persuasive rhetoric, is unpremeditated. Therefore it appears to be happening at the very moment of the poem's reception, which can recur an infinite number of times, reproducing again and again the moment of its composition. Thus the lyric creates the impression that we are listening to "a voice striving to verbalize," to formulate something that is going on in the inner world of the speaker *now*.[36] And this *now*, unlike the present of drama, is not fraught with future, not focused on what should happen next but on itself alone. The lyric present is a state of mind that exists at the moment and does not lead to any immediate action.[37]

The lyric time, therefore, can be said to be the present moment. Yet it is not exactly the same as other moments. Like them, it contains a transitory state of mind, but, unlike them, would not let it go. The lyric tries to capture this particular state of mind and put it into words. And in doing so the lyric plunges into the moment, losing its bearings in the ongoing flow of actual time. In the words of Manfred Kridl, the lyric represents "a unique moment detached from the current of phenomena and crystallised in a special form (phase)."[38] As Hegel writes, "the whole gamut of feeling is seized here in its momentary movements, or in its single fancies about all sorts of things, and made permanent by its expression."[39] This is the peculiar characteristic of the lyric moment: it is both fleeting and "crystallized," permanent, a quality that has made some theorists conceive of lyric time as a total departure from time, as "timelessness" or eternity. Susanne Langer believes that "the lyric poet creates a sense of concrete reality from which the time element has been removed, leaving a Platonic sense of 'eternity'"; she calls this phenomenon "timeless present."[40] Jonathan Culler would rather see it as "a temporality of discourse."[41] A recent dictionary of literary genres and notions states that "the privileged lyric time is a problematic present 'suspended' in language."[42]

No matter how we choose to consider it, the lyric takes off from the subjective emotional reality of the present moment and departs into a dimension that has very little to do with the continuing flow of time. In this sense the lyric moment becomes timeless, "eternal." The emotion that has brought the lyrical utterance into existence, however, can never be timeless. It is rooted in a concrete experience that has taken place in time. Only after that can the lyric afford to turn its back on time and embrace eternity. The alternative, i.e. the absolute emancipation from the flow of time, is what breeds not poetry but philosophy.

Since, by departing from public time, it necessarily absents itself from the never ending business of the "real" world, whatever inner activity the lyric may plunge into, from the perspective of that real world it is bound to be seen as static. Of course, the other two members of the Triad also withdraw from the activities of their social environment to enter another, imaginary sphere of existence, but, unlike the lyric, they depict or represent an evolving action. More than two centuries ago Charles Batteux drew the following useful distinction: "As long as there is an ongoing action in it, poetry is epic or dramatic; as soon as that action stops and nothing else is depicted but the state of mind, the pure experienced emotion, it is of itself lyric."[43] More recently, James Calderwood has argued that lyric discovers "a retreat from the hurly-burly of action and consequences where thought and feeling crystallise in an expressive stasis."[44] In a discussion of a Wordsworth sonnet, Kenneth Burke coins a somewhat oxymoronic and therefore perfectly appropriate phrase to describe the lyrical time in such a poem: "a moment of stasis."[45] It can be used to denote the nature of all lyrical poetry as a literary kind fusing the fleeting moment into a state of eternal immutability.

The word *stasis* may be misleading. Lyric is static only in so far as it does not participate in the actions that surround it and, perhaps more importantly, though it may spring up from some action, it does not normally lead to another—instead, it is content to plunge as deep into its own element of inner reality as possible. However, this does not mean that a lyrical poem is inherently immutable. Susanne Langer believes that, though it works in momentary glimpses, lyric is not entirely static, for "feeling is a process, and may have not only successive phases, but several simultaneous developments."[46] Elder

Olson makes room in the lyric kind for sequences or accumulations of moments building up into suites.[47] And then, as Hegel reminds us, even the simplest poem, giving vent to an uncomplicated ephemeral emotion, "portrays the momentary emergence of feelings and ideas in the temporal succession of their origin and development and therefore has to give proper artistic shape to the varied kinds of temporal movement."[48] This inner time of the lyric is not the same as Culler's time of discourse, but can coincide with it. Whatever the inner time may be, it is not that of a narrative, for a poem does not relate an event, it tries to be it.[49]

Since the lyric has neither a narrative nor a representative structure, which are characteristic of the other two members of the Triad, its interplay of emotion and thought can find some stability only in a thematic framework. On the example of a Thomas Wyatt poem, Northrop Frye shows how in the lyric "we are circling around a defined theme instead of having our attention thrown forward to see what comes next."[50] Some theorists are even tempted to chart out the ideational scope of lyric poetry, though the predominant opinion is that at the highest level of generic grouping it is absurd to talk about content. Still, the example of Ronsard, set as early as the sixteenth century, has proved infectious. The leader of the Pléiade held that the lyric deals with the following matters: "love, wine, dissolute banquets, dances, masques, victorious horses, fencing, jousts and tournaments, and some little argument of philosophy."[51] Four centuries later, the already quoted dictionary of literary genres and notions follows suit: "The lyrical themes are not numerous but rich in nuances. Love, time, nature and death, these archetypes are spread out in innumerable figures: the inebriation of wine, the charm and the transience of beauty, the variety of flowers or of the animal kingdom, the relish of dusks, autumns or river banks."[52] R. S. Crane listed as specifically lyrical the following oppositions: life and death, good and evil, love and hate, harmony and strife, order and disorder, eternity and time, reality and appearance, truth and falsity, emotion and reason, complexity and simplicity, nature and art.[53] When it comes to such formulations, Paul Fussell is the most succinct of all. For him the "essential poemly theme" has always—until quite recently—been "the menace of mutability."[54]

Thus far we have ascertained that the lyrical utterance departs from the flow of public experience into a world of private inner life, and that it turns its back on any kind of actual audience, so that the speaker confers with himself and the emanations of this private inner world. We have also found out that the framework of such utterance does not depend on the unfolding of an imaginary action with fictional characters placed in fictional circumstances but on the interplay of emotion and thought within a (more or less predictable) thematic circle. The word "circle" is quite appropriate here, for, as has been observed by a number of commentators, the natural movement of the lyric, if allowed at all, is circular rather than linear and its form, as some theorists have established, is concentric rather than kinetic.[55]

Let us see how this general orientation affects the textual parameters of the lyric. In his brief synopsis concerning some typical views of this literary kind, Kenneth Burke refers to it "as an ordered summation of emotional experience otherwise fragmentary, inarticulate, and unsimplified."[56] The notion can be traced back to Coleridge, who defined poetry as "a more than usual state of emotion, with more than usual order."[57] Similar assessments of the relationship between content and form in lyrical poetry have been made more recently in the study of literature. The specific structuring of the lyric has been said to be ambivalent in its role of giving a full expression to an emotion and at the same time endeavoring to curb and contain it within a recognizable aesthetical shape.[58] An important question to ask at this point would be: what kind of order does the lyric impose on emotion and how is this order created?

Northrop Frye suggests that "as a verbal structure, literature presents a *lexis* which combines two other elements: *melos*, an element analogous to or otherwise connected with music, and *opsis*, which has a similar connection with the plastic arts."[59] This scheme may be indebted to Aristotle's set of similar concepts revived by Ezra Pound under the names of *logopoeia* and its constitutive elements, *melopoeia* and *phanopoeia*.[60] Frye recognizes the fact that the operation of these principles in their conjunction is especially important for poetry, which is understandable in view of the fact that lyric is the quintessentially verbal art—it is the kind that turns away from the reality of the outside world and focuses on an inner reality that is difficult to express. Language does not seem to have developed the same kind of dependable instruments for the representation of this inner sphere of experience as it has for the outer, much more palpable and publicly recognized one. Hence the unusual concentration on language in lyric, the intent delving into its hidden resources, the search among their multitude for attitudinal shades of meaning and suggestive sound that might come closer to the expression of that apparently inexpressible part of life, imprisoned in the hidden recesses of the individual soul and informing our being.

For Jan Mukařovský, lyric is specifically "the poetry of language, and it is also the main vehicle of the development of poetic language."[61] And for E. D. Hirsch, "what we call lyric poetry is by purpose and convention language-bound."[62] It is this inextricable link between lyric and language, he argues, that makes the translation of poetic texts next to impossible. For: "the things that count most in a great deal of poetry are word associations that are endemic to a particular language, plus the rhythmical and phonetic aspects of those words."[63] The material with which the lyrical poet grapples then is not the words of a language as just so many dictionary entries, i.e. units of meaning, but the full corporeality of these words, their complexity of meaning and sound, which gives rise to multiple intralinguistic associations. By stirring these latent powers of language into action, the poet problematizes the relation of language to reality. By focusing on the sign and its place in the semiotic system, he questions the conventionally accepted principle of one-to-one referentiality in our thinking of the world. His mission is therefore to tear a curtain of opaque hackneyed language that we are used to having in front of us and to reveal the ineffable richness of life that it has veiled away from us. The act is somewhat paradoxical, because it achieves the overthrow of the tyranny of words through an utmost infatuation with words.

To return now to Northrop Frye's *melos* and *opsis* molding the lexis of poetry, we may try first to look into the functions of these twin principles in the ordering of lyrical expression. In Frye's understanding, melos is rooted in the hypnotic incantation of magic (charm), while opsis can be derived from the riddle as the knot of sensation and reflection.[64] The principle of melos has been universally recognized as present in poetry in the form of the phonetic patterning of its language, the "musicality" of its intonation, and the harmonious and rhythmical diction associated with it. Mukařovský considers rhythm and lyric "an inevitable pair, which to a certain extent governs the fate of poetic language in its entire scope," and Susanne Langer tends to agree: "The fullest exploitation of language sound and rhythm, assonance and sensuous associations, is made in lyric poetry."[65] Robert Scholes calls poetry "a kind of musical word game."[66]

The opsis counterpart can have as many different manifestations as there are levels in the structuring of a text, but its most common form is that of poetic imagery, which is so closely associated with the lyric. In Frye's words, "Much more frequently than any other genre does the lyric depend for its main effect on the fresh or surprising image."[67] Andrew Welsh makes the following important point about the formative effect of imagery on the nature of lyrical poetry: "The sense of an image or picture, the sense of intellectual patterning, and the sense of time caught in space form a complex which lies at the roots of lyric poetry."[68] Welsh, obviously, sees the poetic image as the mechanism through which time in lyric is spatialized and the moment of stasis is achieved. But Kenneth Burke discovers a dynamic force in "the progression or development of the poem's imagery," which he views as an "analogue of plot," an inner kinetic structure that can sustain this allegedly static kind.[69]

Finally, we should not ignore Rene Wellek's caveat that poetry's dependence on imagery is not absolute.[70] The opsis principle can indeed be discovered at different levels of lyric structuring. Witness the closing couplet of Shakespeare's sonnet 65, where the anxious question about who can champion the fragile materialization of beauty in this mutable world is answered with a subtly qualified assurance:

> O none, unless this miracle have might,
> That in black ink my love may still shine bright.

As I have tried to argue elsewhere, the last line of the sonnet seems to perform in an emblematic way the poetic miracle envisaged by the poet.[71] The word *love*, referring as it does in the majority of the sonnets both to the speaker's feeling and to its human object, is placed safely in the middle of the line and encased—like King Tut's mummy—in a triple sarcophagus, though not of precious materials but of phonetic echoes, the innermost one made up of the almost identical monosyllabics *my* and *may*, the middle one consisting of the assonantal pair *ink* and *still*, and the outermost resting triumphantly on the two poles of the antithetical paradox—*black* and *bright*—knit together by plosive alliteration. The usual temporal flow of poetic locution has thus been spatialized into a static pattern.

Or, to go even further afield, the concluding lines of sonnet 74, attempting to reconcile the young friend to the prospect of his having to part with the aging poet, whose death is imminent, offer the following encrypted promise:

> The worth of that is that which it contains,
> And that is this, and this with thee remains.

Here the first *that* clearly refers to the speaker's body, on which the preceding lines focus, while the second and third repetitions of the same pronoun point to the soul contained in the body. Then comes the *this*, referring to the poem itself and, by inference, to the sum of love poetry dedicated to the friend. The pivotal argument of the sonnet about the identity of all three notions—body, soul, poetry—is underpinned by the full or near identity of the words by which they are denoted. And the whole series culminates in the last pronoun that alliterates with them and is evidently of the same kin: *thee.* Thus the poet's central idea about the possibility of an ultimate conquest over mortality through the magic union of poetry and love is not only stated but mimetically realized through the offices of morphological categorization and sound echoes.

On the above example we can actually see how melos and opsis come together in lexis producing the specific lyric effect of the logopoeia. Andrew Welsh concludes his study of the roots of lyric by focusing on the pun as the tightest knot in which the essential lyrical impulses come together in a kind of symbiosis. He views it as "a metaphor that unites melopoeia and phanopoeia in a single word."[72] This is the crux in which the near or complete identity of sound discloses an unexpected relation of two hitherto separate elements of vision; the screen of automatized language is removed and we experience the lyric revelation. But at the same time, a pun is quite overtly a kind of game. It grants us its revelation in the form of a joke, the form characteristic of the speech of the jester, of Lear's Fool for instance. As C. L. Barber observes in his analysis of the language used in Shakespeare's festive comedies, "In such exploitation of the physical qualities of words, there are no hard and fast lines between wit and eloquence and poetry, a fact which is reflected in the broad Renaissance usage of the word wit."[73] Lyric locution and wit are of one family, for they both rely on the interplay of a variety of meanings and on the resulting provocatively revealing ambiguity. One step further will take us to Northrop Frye's discovery of the close proximity between the lyric and the ironic, in both of which the writer turns his back on the audience.[74]

The lyrical poet's lack of concern for the audience is expressed above all in the lack of logical coherence in his production. A number of commentators have noticed the dream-like inconsequentiality of lyric language, the "sudden and almost violent transitions" in the argument, occasioned by the leaps between ideas far removed from one another.[75] This approach is not a whimsical act of defiance on the part of the poet but his only way to render mimetically the uneven and jerky movement of passionate feeling, which, as we have seen, is at the roots of lyric. The result is logical fragmentariness, resolved in the unity of theme and mood.

The formal ascendancy over the fragmentariness or discontinuity of expression can be discovered in another characteristic aspect of lyric, the imposition of a variety of patterning schemes on its utterance.[76] These patterns organize the melos and opsis factors and provide an overall framework for their operation within the poem. If we wish to oversimplify the matter, however varied, they can all be subsumed under the general heading of repetition. Emil Staiger declares that "only repetition saves lyrical poetry from disintegration," and Barbara Herrnstein Smith has no doubts that "[r]epetition is the fundamental phenomenon of poetic form."[77] Repetition in poetry can be observed at a number of levels, as Cecil Day Lewis makes clear: "Repetition of some kind is integral to poetry. Rhyme is a form of it; so is alliteration; so are the balanced reiterations we hear in the Psalms, and the balanced antitheses of Pope; so is the image which reminds us of an earlier image in the poem. But refrain is the form of repetition special to lyric poetry, whether it comes in story-lyric (ballads), in popular song, or in art-songs."[78] A similar list, confined to the phonetic level, but a little more detailed in the consideration of this particular section, can be found in a more recent publication by Timothy Bahti: here we get references to meter, ictus, caesura, rhyme, alliteration, assonance, consonance, anaphora, and a few other devices whose inclusion in this category could be disputed.[79]

Repetition is universally recognized as a staple principle of lyric structuring. The end result of its imposition on the logical fragmentariness of lyrical texts is the imposition of a circular order on the disturbing linear disorder. The final effect is that of a concentric form defying directional movement, a spatialization of time creating a sense of timelessness. The poem is self-enclosed. It is a system centered in itself. Coleridge's succinct definition of it as a whole "the parts of which mutually support and explain each other" has had a long line of followers, among whom are Paul Zumthor and Jonathan Culler.[80] The latter has actually succeeded in coining another infectious phrase by calling this intrasystemic principle in the construction of lyric "totality of coherence."[81]

In a word, due to the specific organization of its material, the lyric poem becomes self-contained and therefore self-sufficient. We have returned to the observation that lyric turns its back both on the exigencies of life's time flow and on its own audience. It does not appear to be straining to communicate, but rather, encased in itself like an "impersonal object," it is content to *be*.[82] Any interest in what it has to offer is rooted not in a particular rhetorical appeal that it makes to an addressee but in the appreciation of its inherent worth by a chance passerby. The corollary of this is that lyric, as Susanne Langer states, "is not genuine discourse at all," constituting, in effect, what Mathieu-Castellani calls "anti-discourse" ("un anti-discours").[83]

But if lyrical poetry is a nondiscourse, then its language is nondiscursive. It is, as Paul Valéry says, "freed from all its burden of immediate utility" or, in Culler's phrase, liberated "from the constraints which discursive order imposes on it."[84] Thus emancipated, the word "sparkles with infinite freedom and is ready to radiate toward a thousand uncertain and possible relations."[85] Not only is the entire polysemous potential of the word in lyric unfettered, but so are also its innumerable and unpredictable sound associations with other words. The great carnival of language, within which all established order and hierarchy, all rules and conventions have for awhile been suspended, is now in full swing. Reason has been momentarily demoted from its position as absolute ruler of all life to a mere footman in the service of our sensuous nature.

A curious corollary of the word's liberation in lyric poetry is its striving toward the critical minimum of linguistic material that would contain an explosive maximum of suggestion. The lyric therefore is materially reductive or extremely compressive in its dealing with language, a quality that seems to lead eventually to the paradoxical goal of an all-expressive absolute silence. Barbara Hardy has formulated this in a memorable way: "Perhaps most lyrics end in a reverberation of words, but some can move out of vibrant stillness into that familiar silence of strong feeling where words fail us."[86] The end result of this tendency in most cases is condensed brevity, a feature of lyric poetry that is often seen as its hallmark.

So far lyric has, admittedly, been presented from the point of view of our own time, and although such perspectival distortion is inescapable, we should try to take cognizance of the problem in its legitimate historical context. Gérard Genette makes it clear that the Triad is not in any sense a privileged group. In his words, "The great ideal 'types,' which, since Goethe, have so often been opposed to small forms and middle genres, are but vaster and less specified classes, whose cultural extension, because of this, has some greater possibilities of existing but whose principle is neither more nor less ahistorical."[87] The three "supergenres," as we have already had occasion to notice, are indeed the most capacious and, of necessity, the most abstractly defined of all literary kinds, and therefore they are the least subject to change, which makes them appear almost eternal, immutable. And yet, being as historical as the rest, they also evolve, though not as quickly as those at the lower levels of genre typology. As a matter of fact, lyric seems to be the least stable of the three, possibly because of its rootedness in subjectivity. To quote Hegel, "in scarcely any other art is the determining factor for its form and content to the same extent a particular period and nationality and the individuality of the poet's genius."[88] In his overview of the lyric, David Lindley makes the following important point: "What constitutes a lyric now is different from what did in the past, and from what will in the future. As critics we can only attempt to be scrupulous in always using a generic term like 'lyric' with the fullest possible historical awareness.[89]

P. A. Miller is the author who offers a most comprehensive and succinct account of the emergence of lyric from its "prehistory." He makes it clear that in our present-day understanding lyric is the kind that "separates the individual from his or her communal ties and responsibilities, and examines his or her most intimate thoughts and feelings, in the process lifting a corner of that veil of socially useful repression which allows us to interact with one another in a reasonably civilized manner."[90] The long historical process leading to this state of affairs is then shown to contain the following stages.

In the Ancient Greek period no real lyric poetry was possible, for, even when Sappho or Pindar made their utterances in the first person, they remained the spokespersons of communal conventions. The polis was such a compact phenomenon that it did not make room for any independent individuality and the poets were an integral part of its entity. It was only in the Hellenistic Age that the conditions were created for the social and political emancipation of artistic voices, but the separation between poets and community at this stage became so absolute that the poems ceased to have any relevance to the latter.

The poets of Augustan Rome from Catullus to Horace changed the tradition by making poetry the expression of individual emotional states and points of view placed in the context of communal life. Miller explains this new departure, which he sees as the actual emergence of true lyric poetry, by reference to two significant changes in public life that took place in that period: (a) the formation of a group of educated people independent of and unassociated with the political establishment, and (b) the transition from oral to written literature. The latter led to the creation of the poetry collection, capable of projecting "an image of a complex, highly interiorized subjectivity, which is only secondarily social."[91]

The Middle Ages saw a return to a predominantly oral culture and prelyric communally oriented poetry. J. A. Burrow's estimate of the English tradition largely complies with this view: "Indeed, one might argue that the poet's own thoughts and sentiments found direct expression *less* often in lyrics than in other kinds of writing. . . . In many medieval first-person poems, the 'I' speaks not for an individual but for a type. The speaker is to be understood not as the poet himself, nor as any other individual speaker, but as a lover, a penitent sinner, or a devotee of the Virgin."[92]

Paul Zumthor offers a similar picture on the basis of the French tradition, especially during the early period up to 1100. Even in the later centuries poetic texts were most frequently "the synthesis of signs used by successive 'authors' (singers, reciters, scribes) and of the text's own existence in the letter."[93] In effect, all poetry up to the fourteenth century seems to belong to folklore by virtue of at least some of its characteristics. The subsequent separation of poetry from music resulting in the elaboration of poetic form plus the creation of collections of poems led gradually to the rise of the lyric as we know it now. An especially important step is that of Villon, who explodes the usual rational smoothness of poetry and replaces it with an invigorating discontinuity. "The poem," Zumthor concludes, "no longer reflects cosmic order but, in intention at least, expresses personal awareness."[94]

Lyric proper (or lyric as we nowadays understand it) in post-classical Europe, then, appears to be essentially the creation of the Renaissance or its immediate prelude. Philip Sidney celebrates its triumph with the injunction he hears from his Muse in the opening sonnet of *Astrophil and Stella*: "look in thy heart and write!" And it is indicative that, as Genette has amply shown, the notion of lyric as a major genre itself belongs to the Renaissance.[95]

We should not be surprised by the fact that this particular kind of literature came to a head and enjoyed its full flowering in that particular age. Miller notes that the precedent of Augustan Rome was repeated in the Renaissance, the Romantic and the Modern periods, when poets were "people with sufficient standing in the community to be able to claim a right to speak, but not so identified with the ruling elite as to appear to speak for the state itself."[96] While this consideration is irrefutable, there are, I feel, some more important and deeper-lying factors that ensured the preeminence of lyric in the said four periods and most of all in the Renaissance. With the Age of Romanticism in mind, Hegel maintains that lyric, the quintessential art of individual expression, "is especially opportune in modern times when every individual claims the right of having his own personal point of view and mode of feeling."[97] And, indeed, what Miller's ages of lyricism share in common above all is the daring thrust of individualism—a characteristic particularly central to the Renaissance.

There is also an important corollary to the replacement of traditional theocentricity with anthropocentricity in the humanist period. Man was now viewed as agent rather than patient of history. Vita activa was elevated above vita contemplativa, action became worthier than resigned expectation of what fate might hold in store. The interaction of a multiplicity of individual wills in a world that had become so vigorous and bustling was the only true element of man's realization. The present moment was charged with endless possibilities for the future, and at the same time its own worth had increased tremendously. Eternity, which had occupied the thoughts and anxieties of Christendom for centuries, lost its centrality.

In a book significantly entitled *The Renaissance Discovery of Time*, Ricardo Quinones writes: "Time is not an element that one divines in the men of the Renaissance: it is a force of their consciousness by which they themselves indicate the differences that set apart their new awareness of the world and their place in it from an older one. Time itself and temporal response are factors in distinguishing Renaissance from medieval."[98]

A further pertinent observation of Quinones's focuses on an apparent paradox in the Weltanschauung of the Renaissance and its aesthetic reflections: "the growth of the myth of the golden age was coincidental with the Renaissance discovery of time. Neither of these themes was a critical force in the Middle Ages, yet in the Renaissance they seem to coexist, the one almost necessarily provoking the other. The pressures of the temporal world of history produce the need to escape from time."[99] For a striking illustration of this preoccupation one should read Shakespeare's *Sonnets*. The return of the classical carpe-diem theme in the poetry of the new age (e.g. Daniel's *Delia*) is also indicative.

What Quinones outlines in the above passage is indeed the complex and contradictory mental setup that can best find expression in the two literary arts that the Renaissance is above all associated with: drama and lyric—singly or (why not?) in lively interaction. The one draws its energies from the incessant flow of time, the other endeavors to overcome the tyranny of time. In their conjunction they reflect the dialectics of pluralistic society and individuality, the thesis and antithesis of emergent modern culture.

Since the Renaissance, European and, more generally, Western lyric poetry has drifted toward an ever starker subjectivism, which has perhaps reached its climax in our day. This accumulated experience cannot but color our idea of lyric in a particular manner. In the Renaissance, poetic utterances were certainly less discontinuous than they have become since. The chief function of "poesy" then was "to teach and delight."[100] Most literature was construed as not only aesthetically gratifying but also as didactic in its purpose and therefore rationally structured, stemming from the concerns of the community and addressed to the community in a language that it could readily understand. This orientation conditioned the choice of expression. As Robert O. Evans reminds us, "In the Renaissance there was no reason why rhetoric and poetry should not make good bedfellows; in fact they were inseparable."[101] The system of conventions informing the Petrarchan tradition is a case in point—it is an established supraindividual code of communication between poets and their public. Turning its back on the audience, disowning the uses of rhetoric was not a pose that the poetry of that period would consciously and gladly adopt until the Mannerist revolt. The new age was still too close to its medieval roots for such a "decadent" stance to be unreservedly embraced. And yet, most of the developments that took place in the lyric in subsequent ages can be traced back to the Renaissance. Mutatis mutandis, it would not be anachronistic to approach the poetry of Shakespeare's age with our own expectations for the lyric. Modern atemporal theoretical approaches, based largely on recent material, can thus be tapped for what they offer, not, of course, without some caution vis-à-vis the inevitable developments that have taken place over the last few centuries.

The variability of lyric is not just diachronic but synchronic too. It has been argued that historically lyric emerged from the epic only to flow into drama.[102] Many theorists consider the diversity of lyric forms in any given period of time taken in isolation as representing a similar relatedness between the members of the Triad. Hartmann's model of the nine hybrid supergenres produced through the cross-fertilization between the original three in every possible combination seems to express a view embraced by the majority of authors. Hegel maintains that the expression of general views as well as the concern with epic events of different kinds are all in the purlieu of lyric poetry, given that the poet "shall entirely assimilate and make his own the objective subject matter," so that the focus is not on his outer frame of reference but on his mode of apprehending and feeling.[103] Thus, though we do come across plot and character elements in some lyric poems, these are no more than occasions for their inner message, something like the objective correlate of the mental state expressed in them.

Manfred Kridl argues that the lyric can exist in a relatively pure form as a "direct eruption" of feeling, but more often it manifests itself in an indirect way through the mediation of various phenomena permeated to a greater or lesser extent by a certain emotion. Thus the lyric invites into its territory epic, descriptive and even dramatic elements, which interpenetrate and fuse into a common medium. Accordingly, we have two principal kinds of lyric poetry: pure or direct and descriptive or indirect.[104] One may justly ask why a poem containing epic or dramatic components should be called "descriptive," but Kridl's general outline is perspicuous enough. Emil Staiger doubts the very existence of "pure lyric" and offers an interesting explanation of the tendency of this kind toward hybridization: "the concept 'lyric' is a concept that can never be fully realised as poetry—not because of human weakness on the part of the poet but because of the very nature of the lyric. Therefore the lyric needs to be complemented by an epic or a dramatic element. For an inspirational mood lasts only a moment: it is a single resounding chord that fades away or else is followed by a new chord."[105]

Paul Hernadi prefers to classify the lyric in a more comprehensive and logically consistent way than most of his precursors in this field. His main types of lyric structure are four: (1) quasi-thematic poems, stressing the speaker's vision; (2) quasi-dramatic monologues, emphasizing the speaker's situation and actions in relation to other fictive characters; (3) songlike poems, focusing on the private experience of the very act of vision; and (4) quasi-narrative enactments of vision through the objective correlate of a theme or mood.[106] So, in Hernadi's view, each of the different lyric types is associated with one of the members of the Triad—(2) drama, (3) lyric, (4) epic,—which it chooses as a model to imitate. Only the affiliation of the first type (1), which is obviously extratriadic, is in need of a separate discussion, and we will return to it shortly.

In his survey of the sixteenth-century lyrical modes of discourse, G. Mathieu-Castellani singles out three major discursive schemes: narrative, descriptive, and argumentative. He claims that, although all three are recurrent in the poetry of the period, they provide no more than a surface to be disrupted by the underlying lyric impulse, for "the nature of lyric . . . is to transgress the order of discourse and, necessarily, at the next moment to discern the system of gaps and tensions which tend to disorganize the surface structure for the benefit of a 'profound rhetoric,' particular to each text."[107]

A fairly neat distribution of logically based types is offered by Käte Hamburger. If the statement-object is ideal, she argues, we have didactic, epigrammatic, and philosophical poetry. But when the statement-object is figurative, we have to do with the ballad, the picture poem (Bildgedicht), and the role poem (Rollengedicht), which last includes Browning's "dramatic monologues."[108] Hamburger's first group seems to have a lot in common with Hernadi's quasi-thematic and Mathieu-Castellani's argumentative type, while her second group embraces most of their remaining categories.

Some different principles of typology have been adopted by such influential theorists as Jonathan Culler and Elder Olson. Culler divides lyric poetry into apostrophic and narrative/allegorical but makes no bones about the preeminence of the first kind as more genuinely lyrical.[109] Olson isolates three forms of lyric poetry in an ascending order of complexity which eventually reaches the intergeneric border dividing it from plot-based kinds: "We have three basic lyrical phases: that of the private sphere, which involves the continuity of expression; that of the verbal act, which involves the continuity of address; and that of the colloquy, which involves the continuity of inter-action. All of these may entail the momentary (or elementary) or the sequential . . . In the lyric of mental experience or activity, that experience or activity is primary. In the lyric of the verbal act, it is no longer primary but merely a factor of the act. In the lyric of colloquy, the verbal act is no longer primary but a factor in the colloquy. And so on: each is sublated in the next."[110] Thus Olson posits a continuity of generic transcendence from one type to another which does not respect any borderline, even that between one supergenre and another.

Gémino Abad takes his cue from Olson's crystal clear scheme and some accompanying suggestions and proceeds to elaborate on this basis a detailed, though not always sufficiently neat classification.[111] First of all, he divides the lyric of expression (Olson's simplest kind) into lyric of thought (or noetic lyric) and lyric of emotion (or pathetical lyric), though he then concedes that these two types are often mixed. Next Abad develops a system of types and subtypes, in which he seems to be trying to include almost all previously suggested varieties of the lyric. With some oversimplification his detailed taxonomy could be represented in the following graphic way:

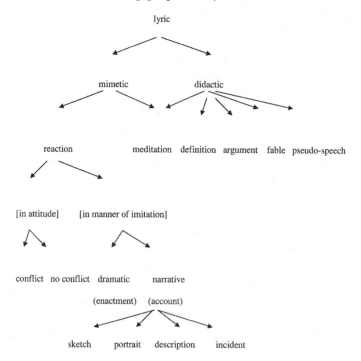

Most of this seems in one way or another to reflect the critical consensus about the lyric and its generic forms, which I have tried to outline. The lowest level in both the mimetic and the didactic halves is debatable. The left-hand side of our graph seems to be taking care of all the three basic lyric varieties affiliated to the members of the Triad: the pure lyric being subsumed under the meditation type and the dramatic and epic lyric figuring as the two main types of the lyric of reaction according to the manner of imitation. The right-hand side, however, suggests a different model, which is obviously outside the Triad. Many theorists are aware of the existence of this fourth basic type of lyric poetry and more often than not they refer to it as *didactic*. Is this type—like the remaining three—based on imitation of manner, and if so, what is its model? We must tackle this problem in our next section.

First of all, the very term "didactic" does not seem to be applicable to lyric poetry. This type of discourse with its obvious reliance on pathos is external to it, if not external to literature in general. In his discussion of the problems of medieval poetics, Paul Zumthor states that the nonnarrative mode of literary expression falls into two kinds, depending on whether the discourse is personal or not. If it is personal, he prefers to call it "lyric," if impersonal, "didactic."[112] Didacticism, as well as its close relative, persuasive rhetoric, do make their inroads into the sphere of the aesthetic, but their denizenship in these territories will always be questioned. And yet, it cannot be denied that an important part of lyric poetry—and its importance grows the further back we go in the history of literature—imitates a didactic kind of writing just as other parts imitate the epic and dramatic ones. Is the said didactic kind wholly external to literature, or has it established any more or less recognizable representation within its domain?

A tentative answer to this question can be attempted if we consider the status of a still disputable addition to the Triad, the essay and its relation to the long established members of the group, especially to the lyric. This is what the influential genre theorist Claudio Guillén has to say on the subject in fairly unambiguous terms: "Even within the bounds of Western literature, the tripartite division into narrative, drama, and lyric has been insufficient for several centuries now. The rise of the essay as a genuine—certainly, since Montaigne, not spurious or marginal—literary genre has made the point quite clear."[113] Many subsequent writers concur with Guillén in one way or another. In his *Die Seele und die Formen*, Georg Lucács was similarly inclined to consider the essay a bona fide literary genre "emerging from the emotive experience of conceptual thinking,"[114] though he did not necessarily rank it together with the three traditional "supergenres." Later Lucács recanted and excluded it altogether from literature as a conceptual rather than aesthetically reflective kind. Paul Hernadi is also doubtful about the essay's literary credentials: "Certain 'essays'—most newspaper editorials as well as a good deal of published research, even in the humanities—are examples of non-artistic, purely utilitarian verbal communication; as such, they are not works of imaginative literature at all."[115] But then he concedes that, "whenever an individual persuader's voice becomes enjoyably audible in artistic, 'personal' essays, . . . such essays approach the lyric poet's 'enactment' of vision" (ibid.).

The theoretical problem seems to lie exactly in the extraordinary heterogeneity of the essay as a type of writing. In *Elements of the Essay*, Robert Scholes and Carl H. Klaus, to whose taxonomic endeavors in this area we will be obliged to return more than once, contend that the essay—rather like the lyric—camouflages as one of the supergenres unless it chooses to be itself. This is how they define the four chief varieties of essayistic writings:

> An essay is poetic to the extent that its author or speaker appears to be talking to himself rather than to others. A poetic essay takes the form of a meditation "overheard" by the reader. A dramatic essay takes the form of a dialogue between two or more characters. The author is present, if at all, only to perform the minimal duties of a director: to set the scene and identify the characters whose words and actions are witnessed by the reader. In a narrative essay the author becomes a narrator who reports directly to us on persons and events. A narrative essay sees its subject in time and presents it in the form of history. An essay is most essayistic when it comes to us as an argument, an explicit attempt to persuade, in which the author addresses us directly, much as any public speaker would address an audience.[116]

Persuasion, the authors maintain, is at the heart of all essays, though some of them acknowledge it while others conceal it and go about their business in a roundabout way. Thus, we get overtly essayistic essays side by side with others that could be categorized as narrative, dramatic, or poetic. This generic variability of the essay is due to the modulation already noticed as a universal phenomenon in the sphere of literature and it need not worry us. Its heavy rhetorical leanings, however, make us wonder about the right of the essay to membership in the club of imaginative writing.

Still, it would seem that, before the modulations come into play, the specifically literary (not narrowly pragmatic) essay exists as a legitimate genre. Scholes and Klaus trace its pedigree back to public oratory and debate. "The literary essay," they point out . . . offers us a persuasive experience which we want to repeat for the sake of the intellectual stimulation it affords us and the truth it offers us. It does not merely stir us or move us to some action of the moment. It makes the moment permanent."[117] The literary essay, then, imitates oratory just as the other literary genres may imitate recognizable genres of speech, but it has shed the practical purposefulness of its model, thus earning admission into the realm of literature.[118] Rosalie L. Colie suggests some alternative ancestors for this mongrel kind: she says that the essay is "in part a fulfillment of the implications of adage-making; by working from adages into new context, it developed into a form of its own."[119] This, in her opinion, happened in the Renaissance, when, as a matter of fact, the Erasmian adage gave birth to yet another immensely popular genre, the poetic emblem.

The recent dictionary of genre, to which I have referred earlier, agrees that the essay takes its origins from some Renaissance precedents and declares an absolute certainty in "the paternity of the genre, which must be irrefutably attributed to Montaigne."[120] While few would disagree with this ascription of paternity, one wonders if the genre's inherent variability did not make itself known from the time of its inception with the establishment—not so long after Montaigne—of alternative and equally viable models, such as that of Francis Bacon, or the early seventeenth-century character writers, or, why not, Donne's earlier *Paradoxes and Problems*. Other possible Renaissance starting points, like the Machiavellian discourse, the philosophical treatise, and the "anatomy," should also be considered.[121] Lastly, we must not overlook the religious writings of the period. Their international spread during the Reformation is impressive indeed, but even if we confine ourselves to England, Richard Hooker's *Ecclesiastical Politie* or the plethora of protestant sermons and religious meditations of the kind the reformed Dr. Donne became famous for, are vastly relevant.

Thus, both lyric in its modern sense and the essay could be seen as types of writing established largely during Shakespeare's age. Genre theorists and commentators have in fact shown that the distinctive features of the literary essay are very similar above all to those of the meditative lyric. Austrian novelist Robert Musil defines the essay as "the unique and unalterable form that a man's inner life assumes in a decisive thought."[122] The above-mentioned genre dictionary specifies that the essay gives expression to subjective thought and that it is marked by precision, brevity, and intelligence.[123] According to another encyclopedic survey, for the essay "all subjects are good: from the most fantastic to the most serious, the most learned and the most eternal."[124] What essays share in common are "the wealth of the language, the precision of style, the density of thought coupled with a natural expression, which can assure the longevity of texts, while assuming a variety of forms."[125]

These are all traits that we have already associated with the lyric. Both kinds are predominantly subjective and focused on language. The only important difference seems to lie in that while the lyric is centered in a complex of emotion and thought in which emotion takes precedence, the essay opts for thought capable of generating emotion. In our discussion of Shakespeare's plays we are going to notice again and again how difficult it is to draw a line between lyrical and essayistic elements and how the two feed into each other. It is with this proximity in mind that we are obliged to go a little further into their relationship.[126]

The entire genre of the essay has been defined as lyric of prose. Scholes and Klaus make this case for the variety of essayistic writing that is closest to poetry: "In reading a meditative essay our attention must shift from structure to texture. Instead of a causal network running through time (a plot), we are likely to find in meditation an associative movement of the mind. Not the persuasive relation of point and support, but a poetic connection of image and idea, is the formal pattern of meditation."[127]

Besides the intimate relation between imagery and subject matter, Scholes and Klaus point out yet another "lyrical" characteristic of the meditative essay: unlike its persuasive counterpart, it is self-centered and pays little attention to a possible audience. Moreover, they argue that the remaining types of modulated essays, the narrative and the dramatic, are similarly focused not on the plots and characters they display but rather on the ideas that can be extracted from these structures or that they overtly illustrate.[128] Here again we are reminded of the almost identical principle discovered in the lyric poems of "indirect expression," which works through an imitation of epic or dramatic genre specifics to convey a poetic idea.

Given the central place the essay has occupied in modern European literature, its immense variability and its give-and-take relationships with the members of the Triad of supergenres, it would be very difficult to exclude this type of writing from the sphere of interest of literary history and criticism. Guillén's conviction that it is high time to consider the addition of the essay to the distinguished group of most capacious genre categories has not lost its urgency. It was indeed as early as the 1950s that Northrop Frye unhesitatingly confirmed the essay in this position when he wrote: "In such genres as novels and plays the internal fiction is usually of primary interest; in essays and in lyrics the primary interest is in *dianoia*, the idea or poetic thought (something quite different, of course, from other kinds of thought) that the reader gets from the writer. The best translation of *dianoia* is, perhaps, 'theme,' and literature with this ideal or conceptual interest may be called thematic."[129]

On the basis of the opposition between two of the Aristotelian aspects of poetry, *mythos* (or plot) and *dianoia* (or idea, theme), Frye establishes a strikingly balanced typology of all literature, in which two *fictional* supergenres, novels and plays (or the modern forms of epic and drama) are juxtaposed to two *thematic* ones, lyrics and essays. Of course, Frye hastens to warn us that there is no hard and fast division between these two pairs, for the *mythos* and *dianoia* principles mix in different proportions to produce a variety of in-between cases:

> When a reader of a novel asks, "How is this story going to turn out?" he is asking a question about the plot, specifically about that crucial aspect of the plot which Aristotle calls discovery or *anagnorisis*. But he is equally likely to ask, "What's the *point* of this story?" This question relates to *dianoia*, and indicates that themes have their elements of discovery just as plots.
>
> It is easy to say that some literary works are fictional and others thematic in their main emphasis. But clearly there is no such thing as *a* fictional or *a* thematic work of literature, for all four ethical

elements (ethical in the sense of relating to character), the hero, the hero's society, the poet and the poet's readers, are always at least potentially present.[130]

Such caveat is familiar. In one way or another it is made by all thoughtful genre theorists, for they all agree that the categories of their field of investigation form typologies rather than strict classifications. Let us agree then that when, in our further discussion, we designate a text as fictional or thematic that will be but short for "primarily fictional" or "primarily thematic."

Frye's division of literary types is comprehensive and enlightening. It takes stock of the actual situation in modern European literature in a way similar to that in which Plato's and Aristotle's precedents did for classical antiquity. Unsurprisingly, his scheme is more revealing than theirs when we have to deal with the literary production of the last five centuries or so. As a matter of fact, it has been represented by Scholes and Klaus in the following symmetrically graphic way:

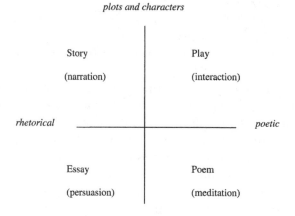

plots and characters

Story	Play
(narration)	(interaction)

rhetorical ———————————————— *poetic*

Essay	Poem
(persuasion)	(meditation)

ideas and feelings

The authors explain that in stories and plays (the upper row of the chart) words are used to create plots and characters, whereas in essays and poems (the lower row) they express ideas and feelings. In the "rhetorical situation" of stories and essays (the left-hand column) words are directly addressed to the audience, whereas in the "poetical situation" of plays and poems they are overheard by it.[131]

Notwithstanding the endemic tendencies of generic hybridization, the typological distinctions between fictional and thematic kinds are

clearly defined. On one side of the theoretical divide are the epic
and dramatic works, and on the other the lyrical and essayistic. This
seems to be the main division in spite of the care Scholes and Klaus
take to show that alternative cross-pairings, based on criteria of representation, are also possible. The distinction between the members
of the upper row does not require much discussion. The opposition
narration versus interaction is plain enough. The lower row, however,
is more problematic, for we have seen that overt persuasion is not the
radical of all essays, least of all of the literary ones.

The first important difference between the lyric and the essay is
that the former seems to spring up from a concrete personal experience, with which it remains closely associated throughout, while the
latter's pivot is an abstract idea that may or may not be illustrated with
concrete examples. Even when the illustration precedes the statement,
the order of importance remains unchanged. This substantive opposition between the two thematic kinds necessarily entails a procedural
one: while ratiocination reigns supreme in the development of the
essay, in lyric poetry thought is triggered by emotion and merges into
it. Hence the markedly different ways in which the two kinds treat
the system of logical thinking. Frye notes that poetic creation is "an
associative rhetorical process, most of it below the threshold of consciousness, a chaos of paronomasia, sound-links, ambiguous sense-
links, and memory-links very like that of the dream."[132] By contrast,
it might be argued, the rhetoric of the essay, however concealed and
mediated, relies on the firm rational discipline of the waking mind.
Its orientation is entirely purposeful rather than immersed in the
puzzled contemplation of a present experience. And, in spite of its
occasional recourse to poetic imagery, the essay never allows an image
to take the upper hand and let loose the dreamlike chaos of associations. Consequently, its tone is primarily rational and only secondarily
emotional, its language is primarily conceptual and only secondarily
figurative, while the case of the lyric is diametrically opposite.

A corollary of the above oppositions is yet another one, which
has to do with the way time is treated by each of these kinds. On the
face of it, the essay is dynamic whereas the lyric is static. This impression is due to the fact that the essay is usually based on the linear
development of an argument, which proceeds from the statement of
a problem through illustrations of its complexities and their discussion toward a logical conclusion. The lyric, conversely, even when it
imitates a logical discussion, tends to revolve in a whirl of repetitions

leading back to the starting point and thus drawing the reader or listener to its fixed center.

In the depth of the two kinds, however, this relation is reversed. Hernadi's definition of the difference between the lyric and the essay's likely ancestor, the adage, can be extended to refer to its progeny too. He argues that the lyric principle is that of "integrating the 'timeless' quality of thematic vision with the intersubjective temporal progress of dramatic action into the private time and perspective of enacted vision. In this respect the contrast between proverbial and lyric texts is very illuminating. While adages merely imply a mind that has arrived at clearly evoked insights, the lyric poet evokes the inner voice of a man now striving to verbalize whatever may emerge from the 'existential depth' of his conscious or subconscious psyche," though not without imposing an aesthetic thematic order on it.[133] While the lyric is the process of eternalizing a fleeting present moment in the full vigor of its actuality, the essay is timeless and its observation of the current of time is performed from a vantage point that appears to be external to that current.

No doubt, the two thematic kinds influence each other continually. We have already seen how the essay is infinitely modulated by the other supergenres and, naturally, by the lyric, which is substantively closest to it. The lyric, however, is also open not only to dramatic and epic elements but to the intimations of its more rational sibling, the essay, too. Although the Italian Renaissance humanist Pomponio Torelli was convinced that scientific and philosophical conceptions, "intelligible things," are excluded from lyrical poetry, his French contemporary Jacques Peletier du Mans observed that the sixteenth-century sonnet was "as if fully philosophical in its conceptions."[134] It has been already pointed out that Hegel was not averse to the adoption of philosophical topics by lyric poetry, if only under certain conditions. Rosalie L. Colie supports this view by referring to the work of Drayton, Davies of Hereford, and also of Chapman, whose sonnets were dedicated "To his Mistresse Philosophie." "Necessarily in such poems, figures of thought were very important," she concludes, "pushing into second place the figures of speech so important in the Petrarchan tradition. Merely by its concentration on a particular subject matter, the sonnet (or quasi-sonnets) became the ground for the celebrated 'intellectual' or metaphysical style of the early seventeenth century."[135] We could therefore consider Alastair Fowler's note on twentieth-century poetry that "essayistic poems are common enough to suggest an emergent mode" as doing less than justice to the actual spread of this modulated form for some five centuries now.[136]

In the preceding pages we have discussed possible generic interaction within the thematic group of literary kinds. The phenomenon, however, is universal and it pervades the entire system of literature. In view of our further analysis it would be useful to survey its basic mechanisms. As Adrian Marino writes, "The latent movement of the genres being considered the recovery of primary solidarity, their intrinsic logic rejects strict divisions of stagnation in an excessive specialization. This feature explains the permanent aspiration toward regrouping, the tendency to remove barriers between genres, the insistence upon intermediary, graduated nuances and tinges."[137]

Alastair Fowler is the theorist who has perhaps done more than any other to formulate the variety of ways in which this ongoing process is realized.[138] The simplest and most mechanical method is what he calls *inclusion*, an operation by which one literary work enters another in its entirety thus becoming an inset form. An illustration of this would be the masque enclosed in an Elizabethan tragedy. If such an intrusion becomes a more or less permanent feature of the host genre, we can speak of generic transformation. Larger literary kinds, such as epic and drama, tend to encourage inclusion and provide sufficient space for it. Inclusion, however, does not necessarily bring about generic change; if it is not persistent, it may remain occasional and inconsequential. Generic *mixture* of various kinds, of which *hybridization* is probably the most important, is the next variety. It occurs when two or more genres coexist in a single literary work with their complete repertoires. Such is the case of the merger of sonnet and epigram in European Renaissance poetry, discovered and discussed by Rosalie Colie.[139] The interweaving of tragic and comic plots in English drama of the same age is another. For a generic hybrid to emerge, the component genres usually have to be qualitatively commensurate. The most widespread kind of generic "interinanimation," however, is something that could be categorized as *modulation*—here a genre is not coupled with another one as fully-fledged as itself but is pervaded by a mode, i.e. by the formally unspecified emanation of another. It is usually by this mechanism that established genres are transformed and invigorated for a new lease of life.[140]

Genre interaction in its different forms is endemic in literature, which could hardly exist and evolve without it. But, as already pointed out, the Renaissance was exceptionally prone to experimentation with genre combinations and alterations. And there was no one during that period who could rival Shakespeare in his innovative daring, for, as Colie puts it, "his interest in the traditional aspects of his art lay precisely in their problematic nature, not in their stereotypical force."[141] Heather Dubrow explains this propensity of the age and its major representatives through reference to its extraordinary social mobility, which had come to replace the former fixedness of status—features of life and thinking that had their reflection in the structuring of literary forms.[142] While I find her view acceptable, a number of other, no less important accompanying factors could also be adduced, including the problematization of the traditional static world picture, the unyielding secularization of literature, depriving all genres of their canonical status, etc.

Further, Dubrow points out that theoretical interest in generic matters made a noticeable leap in the postmedieval world: whereas genre is barely mentioned in Bede's treatise, Renaissance discussions of poetics treat it as a subject of primary importance.[143] Both Zumthor and Colie concur on that, and Claudio Guillén sees the intellectual ferment of the age as essential for its artistic verve.[144] An interesting distinction of Renaissance attitudes to genre from the classical ones is that most authors of treatises dealing with the problems of poetics no longer champion the purity of kind but are ready to accept generic mixtures without qualms. From Minturno through Scaliger to Sidney we invariably come across this attitude. In the *Defence of Poesy* the point is made clearly: "Now in his parts, kinds, or species (as you list to term them), it is to be noted that some poesies have coupled together two or three kinds, as the tragical and comical, whereupon is risen the tragi-comical. Some, in the manner, have mingled prose and verse, as Sannazaro and Boethius. Some have mingled matters heroical and pastoral. But that cometh all to one in this question, for, if severed they be good, the conjunction cannot be hurtful."[145] A few years later Guarini would spring up to the defense of his own bold experiment in *Pastor Fido*, arguing that Aristotle "did not forbid us from making new graftings on the trunk of natural poetry."[146]

According to Ireneusz Opacki, every age has its dominant literary genre, which infiltrates and molds the remaining ones in its characteristic way.[147] In Renaissance England—and, perhaps, in other West

European countries too—there seem to have been a duumvirate of supergenres, drama and lyric, which left their mark on everything else but also penetrated each other to such an extent that at times it is difficult to analyze them apart. Again—as in so many other aspects of this inherently dialogical age—there are two foci rather than a single center of generic power in literature, and they interact in a vigorous way, introducing a strong dramatic element into most lyrical works and, vice versa, modulating drama in a distinctly lyrical manner.[148] These mutual influences of one genre over the other are often due, as Jan Mukařovský has contended, to authors carrying their artistic habits from one kind of writing over to another.[149]

And as the Elizabethan and Jacobean professional writers, usually excelling in both dominant genres of their age, switched back and forth from the one to the other, this intergeneric "contamination" was inevitable. Shakespeare's nature was perhaps "subdued" more than anybody else's to what it worked in, "like the dyer's hand," and what it was steeped in, especially in the last decade of the sixteenth century, were exactly these two supergenres, lyric and drama, practiced by him alternatively and concurrently—most probably during the period when the plays of my selection were composed. The dramatic propensity of his lyric poetry, especially of *The Sonnets*, has received more critical attention than have the lyrical features of his plays. As the latter is the topic of this study, before turning to the texts, let us consider briefly the usual ways in which the lyric can enter drama in principle, and Renaissance plays in particular.

One of the three methods of generic interaction formulated by Alastair Fowler, that of overall hybridization, seems to be ruled out a priori, since the two kinds under consideration are incommensurable, the one being defined by condensed brevity and the other by extension. Even so, the application of hybridizing techniques to considerable sections of the dramatic text, as we are going to see, is not impossible. Of the remaining two, inclusion is conspicuously present in the bulk of Renaissance drama, while modulation would require a greater analytical effort to discover because of the organic and often uncircumscribed fusion of component elements on which it is based.

The lyrical insets as the chief forms of inclusion in plays of the age belong to three main categories: songs, poems (usually sonnets or sonnet-related forms), and soliloquies. They provide a short pause in the ongoing action of the play. As Francis Berry argues in a book wholly devoted to insertions of various sorts in Shakespeare's plays, "The Inset time can be a kind of pocket within the dramatic time."[150] The functions of the inset may vary. Berry focuses his attention on two of them—character building and conflict between what we see and hear while watching the performance and hence between appearance and reality—but, of course, the list can be extended to include amplification of meanings, creation of atmosphere, etc. Rosalie Colie, for instance, maintains that the insertion of sonnets into Shakespeare's love plays infuses into them the high idealistic seriousness of this genre.[151] The ensuing chapters will probe into, among other things, the variety of uses to which lyric insets are put in Shakespeare's drama and will attempt to offer a fuller account of them.

An important point has to be made right away: although the inset seems to be fairly isolated from the host text, its incorporation in the latter affects its own nature in a marked way. Elder Olson defines this phenomenon in his usual succinct manner: "Obviously private happenings in the mind, verbal acts, and colloquy or dialogue are not peculiar to the lyric forms; they may be found everywhere in the longer and more complex narrative and dramatic forms. But here they are parts, not wholes; they are subservient to some more comprehensive principle, such as *plot*; and, serving a function beyond themselves, they are seldom intelligible by themselves (a speech from a play is not intelligible by itself) or developed as they would be in lyrical treatment."[152]

Thematically, as Nicholas Brooke has shown on the example of Shakespeare's tragedies, the inset is relativized and molded in a particular way by its dramatic context.[153] In this sense, its independence is only partial. Songs, perhaps more categorically than other kinds of insets, seem to be introduced into a play primarily in order to ensure a break in the action, a brief respite amidst the rush of the chain of events.[154] And Cecil Day Lewis is right that they can indeed often be detached from their environment without being deprived of their luster. Yet, as he himself has noticed, "a [Renaissance] dramatist wished the songs not merely to entertain but to have some dramatic relevance."[155] The detachability of inset poems is even more problematic, since these are usually composed by one character or another and form an aspect of his part in the play.

As for the soliloquy, it is a section of Renaissance drama that is particularly hospitable to the lyric, as noticed already by Batteux, but recently put in the following eloquent way by W. R. Johnson: "Even

when Elizabethan characters seem almost to be conversing or arguing with one another, even when the dramatic demand for dialogue
seems about to be honoured, suddenly one of the characters soars off
into lyric flight, talking now no longer to other characters and talking not so much to himself as to some other self, to a vast darkness
of unreality, some black, wordless place both inside him and outside
him, neither inside nor outside him."[156]

When this happens, Manfred Pfister points out, time is suspended—just as it is in lyric.[157] And again, as in lyric, the Jakobsonian
expressive function of language dominates the utterance to such an
extent that the referential and appellative functions, inherent in dialogue, are obliterated.[158] Monologic sections are characterized by a
flow of speech independent of the immediate reactions of interlocutors. They are usually longer and organized in a more complex way
than dialogic cues. This brings them close to lyrical poetry, to which
they are related both structurally and functionally. According to Una
Ellis-Fermor, what distinguishes the Elizabethan soliloquies from the
surrounding dialogue and approximates them to narrative or lyric is
the fact that they render thought rather than speech and so belong
to "a kind of communication differing from that of strict drama and
more nearly akin to that of narrative or lyric."[159] This association with
the "subconversational or even subconscious depths" of the characters' minds, Hernadi agrees, makes their medium "almost entirely
lyric."[160]

Drama, as the host genre, is indeed hospitable to lyric, but not
altruistically so: it needs this idiosyncratic and self-centered lodger
for its own purposes and it hastens to reform it accordingly. In the
soliloquy, as a more integral part of the dramatic work than the inset songs and poems, this transformation of the lyric is considerably
more intense and thorough. We have all come across publications of
excerpts from great drama presenting famous soliloquies, such as the
Shakespearean "To be, or not to be" or "To-morrow and to-morrow
and to-morrow," as autonomous texts, sometimes indistinguishable
from actual lyric poems. Yet they are essentially different.[161] Being
unable to provide resolution for its problem through action, the lyric
outside drama is content to gauge it in a strongly emotional way, and
its emotional temperature is the higher for its perceived inability to
transcend it. In contrast, the lyric state occurring in the midst of
drama is most often generated by some action and clamoring for
another, though, as we shall see, this interrelation is not always direct

and obvious. Whatever the concrete case may be, soliloquies, for the most part, are concentrations of energy that make subsequent action possible or even inevitable. So their withdrawal from the exigencies of immediate activity into the inner recesses of the soul can be likened to the athlete's taking a step back before the jump. Further, as Olson points out, any speech in a play is there only because it contributes to the total unfolding of the action and revelation of character; therefore it does not strive for "completeness."[162]

Drama also endeavors to change the inner essence of the lyric principle invading its monologic sections by infusing its characteristic urgency into them and by drawing them away from the thematic toward the fictional pole of literature. Th. A. Meyer comes near to making this point when he differentiates the lyric from the dramatic attitude: "Although the lyric poet, at least dramatically, identifies himself with the 'lyric I' (lyrisches Subjekt), the reader of his poem does not experience a strong mimic impulse because, unlike the reader of drama, he is not made to witness the actual emergence of emotions; the emotions appear to have been there before the speaker of the poem begins to talk."[163]

A Renaissance soliloquy, unlike the typical lyric poem, often mimics the emergence of an emotional state and its turbulent evolution, rather than trying to grasp and express it a posteriori. This inner dynamism, particularly characteristic of Shakespeare's tragedies, which prefer to present "the image of a mind as yet in chaos, not of the resultant that we shall find when the forces have come into equilibrium" is the perfect blend of the lyric and the dramatic principle, achieved in the poet's mature work.[164] The interpenetration of the two modes becomes conspicuous in soliloquies based on what Manfred Pfister calls "interior dialogue" expressing strife or conflict in the speaker's soul "by apostrophizing the self in the second person."[165] At such points we may contend that a certain form of modal hybridization is achieved between the dramatic and the lyric.

Pfister suggests several different ways of ordering the endless variety of soliloquies, one of which may take care of the dynamic kinds mentioned above: first of all, they are *spontaneous* as opposed to the *premeditated,* rhetorically orientated ones.[166] Another of his typologies, however, seems to me to be especially important for our further discussion of the place of the lyric in Shakespeare's drama, for it is based on the soliloquy's relation to the encompassing dramatic action. On this basis all soliloquies are divided into *actional* or *reflective.*

The first of these two types constitutes in itself an act that changes the situation due to the decisive choice of action made by the speaker. The second falls into two subtypes: *informative* and *commentative*.[167] In the former the audience is offered some necessary information about an event or a situation, while in the latter an event or a situation already known to the audience is interpreted from the point of view of the particular speaker. If we want to be even more precise, we could further split the commentative soliloquies into *lyrical* (primarily emotional) and *essayistic* (primarily rational). The following chart should make this typology clearer:

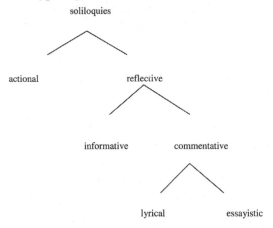

soliloquies

actional   reflective

informative   commentative

lyrical   essayistic

These, like all categories in the field of genre theory, are types rather than classes: they can freely overlap and combine at every level, producing mixed forms, in which the different models either merge or alternate.

Soliloquies are perhaps the area of transition from lyrical inclusion to a kind of local (modal) hybridization of lyric and drama. The phenomenon of thorough modulation occurs in those cases when the entire dramatic work is permeated by the lyrical mode at every level of its composition. This permeation is easiest to observe in the stylistic crust of the work, where the factors of melos and opsis take precedence to such an extent that they draw the reader's / listener's attention to themselves. The poetic rhythm based on the subtle handling of metrical schemes, the intricate phonetic patterning of the text and the systematic use of imagery are the clearest signs of such modulation. It has been amply shown that imagery provides the material for a thematic organization of Shakespeare's mature plays over and above their plot structure.[168]

But the penetration of the lyrical mode into drama does not stop there. It can go as far as to mold the very structure of action in a similarly repetitive or circular way, which all but cancels the inherently dramatic progression of plot development. The concentric (static) structure, as we are going to observe, can be superimposed over the kinetic (dynamic) one to an extent at which the latter is partly or fully suppressed.

Especially interesting are the workings of lyric at the level of character. Emil Staiger insists on "the rule that the hero of a drama must be active, that a passive hero is supposedly undramatic. The point of this rule lies in the realization that the future must be anticipated."[169] And Susanne Langer entirely concurs when she says that personages in drama are "purely agents—whether consciously or blindly, makers of the future."[170] But we know that "undramatic" dramatis personae also exist. These figures are more prone to meditation than to action; they are apt to withdraw into their inner world at the exact moment when the outer world requires their decisive participation. In a word, these characters are lyrical rather than dramatic.

Tzvetan Todorov draws attention to the following amply relevant formulation of two psychological types of people, found in Novalis's book *Heinrich von Ofterdingen*. The first type is that of people "born to carry on trade and business." Such men do not give in to the lures of quiet contemplation. "Their soul may not indulge in introspective reverie; it must be steadily directed outward and be an industrious, swiftly-deciding servant of their mind. They are heroes, and around them throng the events that need to be guided and solved. All occurrences turn into history under their influence, and their lives form an unbroken chain of remarkable and splendid, intricate, and strange events." The second type, conversely, is represented by those "whose activity is contemplation, whose life is a gradual development of their inner powers. No restlessness exerts an outward drive. . . . The vast drama around them does not tempt them to play a role in it themselves, but it does seem to them important and marvelous enough to devote their leisure to its contemplation. . . . They will never take a step without making the most surprising discoveries within themselves about the nature and significance of these phenomena." These are Novalis's poets.[171]

On this basis Todorov schematizes the opposition between the two types in the following table:

Heroes	Poets
experience	contemplation
action	reflection
worldly affairs	essence and meaning of the world
striking and memorable events	existence reduced to utmost simplicity
involvement of the person himself	interest in the world as spectacle
learning spread over time	immediate knowledge
passage from one thing to another by deduction	intuitive grasp of each thing taken separately, then compared
uninterrupted chain of events	increase of inner strengths
maintenance of diversity and singularity	secret identity of things (microcosm and macrocosm)[172]

The first category clearly accommodates the truly dramatic characters, the agents and propellers of action, while the second comprises those resembling the lyrical persona, through whom the perspective of poetic contemplation is introduced into drama. *Richard II*, as I will have occasion to argue, provides a perfect illustration of this opposition in the figures of the King and Henry Bolingbroke, but other Shakespearean plays are also interesting to explore.

None of the above-formulated features of lyrical modulation at every level of dramatic structure is foreign to the poetic drama of Shakespeare's age, and we will be looking for them in the subsequent study of his plays. However, it is important to remember that this Renaissance generic merger is not absolutely unique. Precedents of or parallels to it can be found in other periods of the history of European literature and culture, and they are worth bearing in mind in our further analysis. The lyrical drama of Romanticism, whose most prominent examples are Shelley's *Prometheus Unbound* and Byron's *Manfred*, could perhaps more adequately be classed as a kind of "dramatic poem," because its chief generic proclivities are lyrical rather than dramatic, its main interest being the expression of a state of mind and not the presentation of a definite action.

Some of the plays of the twentieth-century theater of the absurd and other styles akin to it would be no less interesting to discuss from this point of view. T. S. Eliot's *Murder in the Cathedral,* Dylan Thomas's *Under Milkwood* would also merit some more concentrated attention in generic terms.

What is perhaps of greater importance for our proper understanding of Renaissance poetic drama is to focus on its possible roots in the past. First of all, we should consider the native tradition of medieval religious drama, which had been flowering in England for a couple of centuries almost into Shakespeare's own lifetime. These plays were written in rhymed verse, at times running into fairly sophisticated stanzas, and some of their inset songs and monologues can have a certain emotional urgency. It should, however, be made clear that neither their metrical form, nor the rhyming is used for specifically dramatic or lyrical purposes. These features have a purely formal function of structuring the text and perhaps the mnemonic one of making it easier for the players to memorize. No expressive variety is aimed at. As for the emotional quality of occasional insets and speeches, it is generally piously subdued in cases of grief or joy and drowned in ranting in cases of wrath. The predominant tone is didactic and it is very seldom that we can find in these plays a foretaste of Renaissance lyrical individualism. As Rosemary Woolf observes in her in-depth study of the mysteries, "Imaginative intensity . . . or sublimity of style are not within the compass of the authors of the mystery cycles."[173] For the very nature of the genre, "which required a willing submissiveness to a communal tradition, would anyway have made it unsuitable for a poet of large talent."[174] Similar conclusions could be drawn about the morality plays. Thus, though the legacy of the native dramatic tradition should not be disparaged, it could not have offered Shakespeare or his contemporaries especially valuable tips for their genre experimentation.

The examples of classical antiquity are definitely worth looking at, since the very word Renaissance suggests first of all a revival of interest in its lessons. According to W. R. Johnson, ancient Greece had a kind of lyric drama, created by Euripides. His characters ceased to be "agents of dramatic conflicts" and turned into mere "vessels of lyric meditation." The monologue that expresses a troubled inwardness became central to his plays. Through Seneca, Roman drama carried this tendency a step further: here "lyric impulse, liberated by Euripidean example, overwhelms dramatic form to a degree Euripides never dreamed of." Dialogue disappears almost completely to make room for the victorious monologue.[175]

And, of course, it is Senecan drama above all that the pioneers of Elizabethan and Jacobean tragedy chose to emulate. Was this a fortuitous choice of a model that happened to lead them toward the creation of the generically complex poetic drama without which the English Renaissance is unthinkable? Hardly so. The choice was rather predicated on an ingrained aesthetic disposition, on an artistic need stemming from the very essence of the age. Johnson sees this influence as unfortunate, for in the work of most playwrights of the time it ended up "in the triumph of lyrical melodrama," in a disproportionate spread of the lyrical monologue, in a kind of lyrical mannerism.[176] One could add to these observations that the classical examples, coupled with an ambition to emulate them on the fresh material of a young and still unshackled national literary language, encouraged indulgence in enthusiastic rhetorical exercises, resulting for the most part in long magniloquent orations, which could only petrify the sometimes considerable lyrical impulse behind them. There is little to choose from between Tamburlaine's high astounding terms and Hieronimo's heavy sententiousness even when they mourn their nearest and dearest. Perhaps the only exceptions to the rule can be found in the last scene of Marlowe's *Doctor Faustus* and particularly in the hero's closing soliloquy, without whose precedent it would be difficult to imagine the lyrodramatic eloquence of Shakespeare's mature tragedies.

Shakespeare brought the Renaissance tendency of lyricizing drama to a head, and, as Johnson concludes, he—almost alone—struck that happy balance that saved the dramatic principle from dilution while allowing its lyrical counterpart an unprecedented sway at every compositional level.[177] He departed considerably from both the medieval and the classical precedents. Some facets of his symbiosis, achieved mainly through the mechanism of modulation, have been discerned by commentators of his work, especially at the level of style. James Calderwood, for instance, sees Shakespeare's consistent artistic pursuit as directed toward "finding a dramatic style that mediates between the corruptions of public speech and the lyricism of pure poetry."[178] In his own creative explorations, one of the most influential poets of our age, T. S. Eliot, discovers the lessons of his great predecessor: "I have before my eyes a kind of mirage of the perfection of verse drama, which would be a design of human action and of words, such as to present at once the two aspects of dramatic and of musical order. It seems to me that Shakespeare achieved this at least in certain scenes—even rather early, for there is the balcony scene of *Romeo and Juliet*—and that this was what he was striving toward in his late plays. To go as far in this direction as it is possible to go, without losing that contact with the ordinary everyday world with which drama must come to terms, seems to me the proper aim of dramatic poetry."[179] And it is again Eliot who notices that Shakespeare writes his finest poetry in his most dramatic scenes and that what makes his writing most dramatic is what makes it most poetic.[180]

Commentators have pointed out that "the drama is far less conducive to study from the perspective of the logic of language than is either epic or lyric literature. It offers no opportunity to grasp the laws of creative language. . . . For just that linguistic form which of all mimetic presentational forms the drama has preserved, namely direct discourse, as such offers us no poetological criteria."[181] But the impressive bulk of perspicacious studies in the language of Shakespeare's plays shows that there are striking exceptions to this generally valid rule—exceptions that, at least in this case, can be explained through reference to the fruitful blending of the dramatic and lyrical principles.

The critic who comes closest to the problems of lyric's penetration beneath the surface of style into the architectonic structures of Shakespeare's drama is Rosalie Colie. "In language," she writes, "Shakespeare is as prodigal and as economical [as in plot construction], throwing away lines, speeches, even whole scenes. Whenever we pause over language, we can see the ways in which apparently careless lines and speeches support character, further plot, and stress theme."[182] And it is Colie again who notices Shakespeare's characteristic knack for playing with lyrical and other heterogeneric topoi and their dramatic transformation in his plays so that conventional style turns into original plot and character: "One of the most pleasurable, for me, of Shakespeare's many talents is his 'unmetaphoring' of literary devices, his sinking of the conventions back into what, he somehow persuades us, is 'reality,' his trick of making a verbal convention part of the scene, the action, or the psychology of the play itself."[183] The examples culled by her from *Romeo and Juliet* alone include the love-at-first-sight motif, the aubade song, the *hortus conclusus* theme, etc. Most of these are sonneteering clichés transformed into dramatic elements. There is, obviously, a lot left to be done in this area of research, which extends a good deal further than the method of "unmetaphoring" and is as many-faceted as Shakespeare's creative genius.

In the conclusion of her overview of genre problematics and its exploration by literary theory and criticism published in 1982, Heather Dubrow remarked that the interesting phenomenon of genre interaction as one of the major mechanisms of form development in literature was still unduly neglected.[184] Almost a full decade before her, in an even more detailed survey of the area Paul Hernadi made it clear that, although nonnarrative aspects of narrative fiction had been partly elucidated by a number of twentieth-century studies, nondramatic aspects of drama had not received the critical attention they deserved.[185] The situation has not changed very much since then.

The creation of the remarkable synthetic genre of *poetic drama* in the Renaissance and the full development of its potential in the work of William Shakespeare seems to provide an ideal ground for the exploration of these more general theoretical issues. But even in itself, from a purely historical point of view, it contains a good deal of interest. In the ensuing chapters we will trace the gradual emergence of this synthesis through the phase of generic mixture in the plays of the mid-1590s to that of organic integration at the turn of the century. Lastly, a glance will be thrown at the aftermath of this aesthetic development at the peak of Shakespeare's dramatic career marked by the creation of his most impressive heroic tragedies.

2
Generic Mixture:
Lyrical Incursions into Drama

LOVE'S LABOUR'S LOST

"In perhaps no other play does language so nearly become an autonomous symbolic system whose value lies less in its relevance to reality than in its intrinsic fascination. The referential role of words as pointers to ideas or things is consistently subordinated to their relational role as pointers to other words."[1] This assessment of the distinctive characteristics of *Love's Labour's Lost*, offered by James Calderwood, highlights the close kinship of Shakespeare's Navarre comedy to the lyric mode, which is conditioned exactly by the privileging of the intralinguistic (poetic) over the referential function of language.

The presence of the lyric principle is indeed so pervasive that the play seems to depend on it at every compositional level. Its most conspicuous aspect is, of course, that of the poetic inset, whose examples are numerous and varied. Their greater thematic and formal compactness makes them stick out even in the midst of the lyrically tinted environment in which they appear. As C. L. Barber observes, here "the lords each 'turn sonnet.'"[2] Soon after the arrival of the French Princess and her retinue, the main concern of the sworn academic recluses becomes a kind of a surreptitious contest of amorous poetry writing. This activity comes to a head in 4.3, a truly climactic scene right at the midpoint of the play, which centers on the lyrical texts produced by three of the enamored scholars. However embarrassed by the breach of their oath to shun all society and devote themselves entirely to intense study, these young aristocrats are compelled by their newly awakened loves to put their feelings into words and to pour these words over the world before posting them to their mistresses.

So one by one, in the manner defined by Mandelstam as quintessentially poetic, they run if not "to the shores of desert waves" then "to broad and resonant oaks" and present their verse to a sympathetic universe free of the "suborn'd informers" and wicked mockers that humanity so readily supplies.[3] As it happens, however, there are ears concealed behind every tree in this idyllic retreat, and the poets unwittingly betray their innermost secrets to each other. The close relation this scene bears to John Stuart Mill's famous phrase about lyric being overheard rather than heard is conspicuous.[4]

All three poems read aloud in the woods are in praise of the ladies to whom they are addressed. They imitate recognizable genres of the time. The first one belongs to the King and is written in the form of the typical English (Shakespearean) sonnet, though it is reluctant to stop where it should and expands into a second closing couplet in order to crown its eulogy of the royal beloved with an enthusiastic exclamation. The poem is strongly reminiscent of Donne's "A Valediction: Of Weeping" with its over-ingenious string of imagery exploiting the idea of the lady reflected in the lover's tears. Shakespeare may have come across that striking masterpiece of metaphysical mannerism circulated in manuscript and he seems to be parodying the style in a way that foregrounds its disjunctive artificiality: in the first quatrain the eye-beams of the mistress are sunrays gilding the dewdrops on his cheeks, in the second her face is a silver moon shining in the watery deep, and in the third she rides as a triumphant queen in the tears' transparent coaches. The King's rather clumsy exercise in tackling the fashionable conceit lyric is, admittedly, way below its original, but the inspiration is of the same kind and so is the method—passion seasoned with wit and producing the effect of elitist sophistication.[5]

Longaville has also prepared a love sonnet of the Shakespearean type, no less intellectual than the King's if imaginatively less ingenious. Should we look for a model again, it comes closest to Shakespeare's own sonnets. The avowed topic is the breaking of the scholar's vow. This poet argues that he has sworn to stay away from women, but his mistress is a goddess rather than an ordinary woman and therefore no perjury has been committed. Thus, in the elegantly oblique Petrarchan way, the sonnet has arrived at its actual center of interest, which is once again the exorbitant (and quite conventional) praise of the beloved. And once again, the poet is unable to stop after having completed his argument at the end of the second quatrain, but from the opening line of the third he has to start a new one with a figurative logic of its own: now the mistress is—no less conventionally—addressed as the "fair sun," and as his own vows are no more than breath or vapor exhaled from the low earth of his own self, they will necessarily be drawn and absorbed by this heavenly luminary. In effect, Longaville's sonnet contains two figurative arguments instead of one in defense of the speaker's perjury, culminating in two eulogies of its addressee. Thus she will be offered the worth of two sonnets packed in one. Again, as in the King's offering to his own mistress, the poetic largesse is great—perhaps greater than necessary. The excess of Elizabethan amplification is gently parodied in both cases.

Now it is Dumaine's turn to read his poem. This, for a change, is a string of ten rhymed couplets written not in the staple sonnet measure of the iambic pentameter but in trochaic tetrameter—a lighter, tripping kind of verse, reminiscent of some sections of Spenser's *Shepheardes Calender*. The author defines it as an ode. It belongs to a type of lyric widely practiced in the Elizabethan age, which evolves a pseudoclassical legend featuring a god or a goddess of the pagan pantheon. Most English sonneteers from Sidney on, including Shakespeare, composed pieces of this subgenre. Though the metaphorical logic of the piece is somewhat confused, Dumaine's "ode" breathes the sweet air of spring and youth and, like the sonnets of his brethren, is enveloped in the elegant imagery of the current lyrical vogue. The intertextual gesture here is closer to the pastiche than to the parody.

Berowne, the fourth of the company, who in this scene happens to occupy the privileged position of, as he puts it, "a demi-god" sitting in the sky and watching the spectacle of serial self-revelations, has been the first to break the vow and send his beloved Rosaline a poem that falls into the wrong hands and thus, although undivulged to his fellow academicians, similarly becomes public property. We have already had the opportunity of hearing it read within the pedantic circle of Nathaniel the curate and Holofernes the schoolmaster in the preceding scene (4.2.105–18). This is a perfect English sonnet, whose only eccentricity is the adoption of the six- rather than the usual five-foot iambics for its metric scheme. Such sonnets, though rare, were, of course, not unknown at the time: a notable sample is the introductory one in Sidney's *Astrophil and Stella*. Holofernes calls it a "canzonet" (line 120), which is reminiscent of Petrarch's original generic term for this form. Berowne's exercise is more volatile than those of the others, abounding as it does in shorter syntactic periods, rhetorical questions and exclamations, less concerned about thematic and figurative continuity, intent on what sounds like a more spontaneous expression of emotional urgency. The conventional eulogy of the paragon of beauty is, of course, there.

None of these four lyrics is a true masterpiece, though three of them were included in *The Passionate Pilgrim* in 1599 as examples of contemporary love poetry that could stand on their own. In spite of their parodic orientation, through their variety of familiar stylistic devices (rhyming patterns, lexical repetition, alliteration and assonance, metaphors, similes, mythological allusions, etc.) they radiate from the center of the play an atmosphere of youthful emotionality and aestheticism. This lyric eruption creates a dramatic climax highly appropriate for a comedy of love. It also contributes to the overall characterization of the play's protagonists as a company of young aristocrats stunned by their first encounter with the amorous passion.

We are faced, then, with a group of insets integrated quite successfully in the architectonics of drama. Moreover, whatever their effect might be in the different environment of an anthology of lyrics, here the dramatic element in which they are placed is not only affected by their presence but in its turn reacts to them and modifies their impact on the audience. First of all, their imperfections seem to have been intentionally worked out by their ultimate, actual author to reflect the poetic inexperience of the fictional authors. Further, and perhaps more importantly, these imperfections are dramatically highlighted and exploited: none of the four lyrics is left without a critical comment by its uninvited and unsuspected stage audience after its presentation. Holofernes is quick to notice the irregularity of ictus in the last line of Berowne's sonnet, though he blames this shortcoming on Nathaniel's inept reading. However, he goes on to suggest that the only virtue of the poem in hand is its mechanical adherence to the prosodic pattern required by its genre ("Here are only numbers ratified" [121–22]) and that it lacks the true qualities of the art ("the elegancy, facility and golden cadence of poesy" [122]). And he threatens to prove that the verses are "very unlearned, neither savouring of poetry, wit, nor invention" (156–57). The irony of the situation is that, instead of reaching its beautiful addressee, Berowne's love epistle has been intercepted by a pedant. Consequently, it is not appreciated for its intimate message that is its raison d'être but is scrutinized for its formal defects.

Ironically, this very mishap turns Berowne's text, by Mandelstam's criteria, from a mere love letter into a poem per se. The quintessential lyric poses, as we have seen, as an utterance sent into the void. Its ideal reader is a chance overhearer enchanted by its magic revelation. The presence of a professional literary critic in this miraculous event, however, is destructive, because it draws the eye to the mechanism of the poetic miracle and thus reduces the latter to an illusionist trick. And, when criticism is as disparagingly hairsplitting as it is in this case, the magic of the experience can be completely dispelled. What really takes place on the occasion of the presentation of Berowne's poem is the invasion of the monolithic world of the lyric by its multivocal dramatic environment and the subsequent relativization of the hitherto absolute values it holds at its core. As a host genre, drama has welcomed and utilized the lyric inset in its midst, but in the process of doing so it has abolished the autonomy of that inset, subjecting it to the rules of its own larger economy.

The other three poems do not fare any better, having been intercepted—this time in an oral form—by less pedantic but equally ruthless critics. It is now Berowne who proves the least sympathetic commentator. His remarks are indeed ethical rather than technical, but they are not the less scathing for that. When the King appears before him with his sonnet sheet, Berowne gloats at the prospect of catching him at the same offence he has himself just committed and chuckles at Navarre's role of a lover even before the reading of the poem has started. As Longaville immediately enters the stage, Berowne redirects his mockery to him without delay, and now he has some additional time after the recital to assess the composition as gross exaggeration and "pure idolatry" (4.3.72). Dumaine, is even less fortunate. As in a prelude to his set text he plunges into an endless praise of his paramour, Katherine, Berowne intersperses this enthusiastic paean with caustic remarks. Eventually, the three eavesdroppers leap out of their concealment in order to denounce each other for breaking their oaths, ironically quoting phrases and images from each other's poems. The texts we have heard in the recital are thus—like Berowne's sonnet—relativized by their dramatic context.

Another group of lyrical insets in the play is similarly focused on the topic of love, but the filter now is burlesque or directly satirical rather than idealistic. Don Adriano de Armado's highfalutin prose epistle to Jaquenetta (4.1.61–92), gone astray like Berowne's letter to Rosaline, flourishes a verse appendix in the form of a sixain, which presents the relationship between the wooer and the object of wooing in a way diametrically opposite to the traditional Petrarchan scheme. He pictures himself as the roaring Nemean lion, while his beloved is reduced to a pitiful "*lamb, that standest as his prey*" (88). If she proves submissive enough, he warns her, her life might be spared, but should she dare to strive, she is sure to become "*Food for his rage, repasture for his den*" (92). Armado's ludicrously inflated self-image is thus exposed to ridicule. As if the absurdity of his text is not obvious enough, the Princess is made to comment on it or rather on its author, whom she rightly calls a vane and a weathercock. This poem may be seen as a parody of the typical love lyric of the time or, perhaps, a pastiche of the so called "masculine line" in English amorous verse, best illustrated by the work of poets like Wyatt and Drayton. Its caricature leanings notwithstanding, its compact imagery and complex alliterative schemes make it stylistically no less sophisticated than the bona fide Petrarchan lyrics of the first group.

In terms of alliteration, another inset of the burlesque type far surpasses Armado's. In the next scene (4.2) Holofernes produces a poem (56–61) that must demonstrate his familiarity with and his mastery of all embellishments of versification. The lyric celebrates the Princess's recent hunting exploit. It is, like Armado's piece, a sixain, but the measure is iambic heptameter, ponderous enough to confirm the author's academic credentials. Before reading his composition, which he defines as "an extemporal epitaph on the death of the deer" (49–50), the schoolmaster proclaims proudly that in it he "will something affect the letter, for it argues facility" (54–55). And the letter—as well as the sound it stands for—is indeed so central to the poem that there is very little else of similar importance in it. The first line does not leave a single notional word out of its alliterative scheme based on the consonant p: "The preyful Princess pierced and pricked a pretty pleasing pricket" (line 56). Every strong beat is included in the series. Moreover, five of the seven stressed syllables start with not just the consonant p but a consonantal cluster, pr, which reinforces the phonetic effect and makes the sound recurrence even more conspicuous. As a matter of fact, this expansion of the phonetic echoes is carried even further in "Princess," "pricked," "pretty," and "pricket," where the pr alliteration is coupled with an i assonance.

And, finally, in "pricked" and "pricket" the acoustic effect of the two words becomes nearly identical. This makes us think of their possible semantic relatedness and prepares us for the introduction of yet another technique that will be even more essential to the poem but to which we may return a little later.

The employment of phonetic repetition in the opening line of Holofernes's opus is so markedly overdone and the resulting mechanical rhythm so lifeless, that we are prepared for another caricature of some current poetic conventions, similar to that in Armado's sixain. Alliteration, indeed, was one of the technical preoccupations of the Elizabethan age. Its excessive use could have a definitely cloying effect even in the work of such poets of genius as Spenser, not to speak of Lyly's overly patterned prose. The second line (57), weaving a new alliterative scheme ("Some say a sore") culminates in a pun on the various meanings of the last word. And then Holofernes picks up another letter—L—to play with in the third line, subsequently achieving a many-sided paronomastic effect by accumulating new senses at every step. The closing line of the sixain attempts to carry the intricacy of suggestions a stage further. In the process, the root "sore" (the topic lexeme in the poem) crops up a dozen times in this composition, establishing its continuous presence from the second to the sixth line and sounding like a rhythmical drum beat.

Holofernes's technical tour de force goes too far in its overuse of alliterative cum paronomastic devices. On the one hand, it points back to the pedantic nature of its author, thus characterizing him in an ironic way; on the other, however, it parodies some endemic features of Elizabethan poetry and, by extension, of lyrical poetry in general. The audience reaction evoked by this overly diligent exercise in versification is a mixture of amusement and irritation, admiration and contempt. The onstage commentary is unequivocally positive. Dumbfounded by his friend's feat of poetic mastery, the curate Nathaniel exclaims: "A rare talent!" (62). Constable Dull follows suit with a pun on Nathaniel's last word, a legitimate Elizabethan form of "talon": "If a talent be a claw, look how he claws him with a talent" (63–64). This rather gauche and therefore ambiguous praise of Holofernes's poetic method is perhaps more to the point than the curate's unstinted adulation. The pedant himself is the one most astounded by his own inexplicable genius: "This is a gift that I have—simple, simple; a foolish extravagant spirit, full of forms, figures, shapes, objects, ideas, apprehensions, motions, revolutions.

These are begot in the ventricle of memory, nourished in the womb of *pia mater* and delivered upon the mellowing of occasion. But the gift is good in those in whom it is acute, and I am thankful for it" (65–71). So, through the usual accompaniment of comments, the insert of Holofernes's metric exercise is embedded in the dramatic environment and integrated into the host genre.

One more example can be added to these lyrical burlesques, and that is probably the first verse inset in the play. In 1.2, Armado, who feels a strong need to express his newly kindled amorous flame for the country wench Jaquenetta, urges his page Moth to discuss the blend of white and red in her complexion—a kind of coloration that is pivotal to the Petrarchan praise sonnets. Moth responds with what appears to be another impromptu poem, an eight-line epigram in which iambic tetrameters and trimeters alternate as they frequently do in the traditional ballad (lines 94–101). The cross-rhyme pattern, however, distances the poem from this generic type and so does its rather sophisticated content. The satirical tinge here is sharper than in the other members of the group. The crux of the argument is that a lady's complexion that shows the combination of white and red is a perfect instrument for the concealment of her real nature, for neither fear of blame can make it paler than it is, nor shame for faults can cause her cheeks to blush. The Petrarchan paragon of beauty is thus radically debunked and turned into a figure of suspicious duality. The verse enters the genre territory of the epigram. As Moth is the first to make its tenor clear in a brief comment, this is "A dangerous rhyme, master, against the reason of white and red" (102–3). Armado, however, does not seem to be interested in the moral of his page's poem. He is fully engulfed in his own amorous infatuation, and what he expects of poetry is not the gift of wisdom but rather that of sweet sound ("Sing, boy. My spirit grows heavy in love" [line 116]) and witty wordplay—the familiar melos and opsis principles brought together. Of course, he fails to realize that the stylistic preference of the epigram is for contrast and paradox rather than for euphony and evocative imagery.

Still, the poems of this second group, reflecting and magnifying some fashionable aberrations in contemporary love poetry as they do, continue to stress the play's lyrical leanings. They also offer material for the delineation of personages, more often than not shedding an ironic light on the author of the particular text or on his immediate interlocutor(s). And, finally, they contribute to the creation of the

overall comic atmosphere. Thus, beside their literary-critical function, they evince some inherently dramatic ones.

A third group of insets is comprised of texts further removed from
the essentially lyric concerns and tonal parameters. The earliest of
these is a kind of riddle composed jointly by Armado and Moth as a
kind of recreational punning on "odds":

> The fox, the ape and the humble-bee
> Were still at odds, being but three.
>
> Until the goose came out of door,
> Staying the odds by adding four.

(3.1.92–95)

This is apparently an example of nonsense verse, coloring the
characters involved in its invention and reinforcing the general
mood of purposeless playfulness that is at the heart of the comedy.
The group also contains the set speeches uttered by Moth as the
prologue to the Muscovite masque and then, in the same endless
scene, 5.2, those of Costard as Pompey, Nathaniel as Alexander, Holofernes as the presenter and as Judas Maccabaeus, and, finally, the
one of Armado as Hector—all in the Nine Worthies masque. The
texts amount to a medley of verse forms—blank iambic pentameters,
rhymed heptameter couplets, hexameter quatrains, a sixain of an
uncertain metrical scheme, and so forth. In spite of their heroic vein,
they are rather stilted and unimpressive to start with. The pedantry
of Holofernes and the pomposity of Armando, their most probable
authors, have left an indelible stamp on them. The amateur perform-
ers try their best to complete their roles according to the script, but,
in Holofernes's memorable phrase, they are "put out of countenance"
by the derisive comments of the aristocratic audience, and the entire
recital is sadly botched up. No one escapes this comic catastrophe
unscathed: the actors are put to shame for their inadequacy, but so
are also the unruly spectators for their callous arrogance. The commentary on the inset has finally invaded its subject's territory and
mauled it irredeemably. The dramatic impulse has demonstrated
its prevalence over the lyric. This triumph of the host genre leads us
directly to the resolution of the comedy, which manifests the final

defeat of the lyrical as juvenile affectation silenced by the mature dramatic pressures of life.

But the play does not end before the presentation of what is perhaps its most notable lyric inset, the epilogue of Ver and Hiems (5.2.882–917). An indisputable example of the traditional débat, its place in the whole has in its turn long been the object of critical debate. At first sight, this double song has little to do with what precedes it. However, as has been suggested by more than one insightful commentator, in a distanced, symbolical way it reflects the central issues rooted in the dramatic action and especially the one foregrounded by the comic catastrophe. The first half of the lyric presents the bright world of spring with its meadows bedecked by colorful flowers, enlivened by the gentle melodies of the shepherd's pipe, the birds and the maidens preparing their summer smocks. If this is not an account of what has taken place in the play, it is certainly a reflection of the youthful flamboyance that is at its very heart. On the other hand, the flowers of this poetic spring are "pied" and they "paint" the meadows, perhaps a suggestion of artificiality, of a cover of beauty imposed on the world in order to beguile the senses.[6] We have indeed discerned in the action of the comedy such suspicions undermining the impact of the love poetry. The association of the cuckoo's song with the threats of foul play in marriage, the state toward which the revels of love necessarily tend, sounds an even more jarring note and sours the joyful atmosphere of the whole.

The unthinking optimism of youthful fantasies has indeed been eclipsed by the final abrupt break in the dramatic action, when, to cap the sad disintegration of the last courtly game of the noble company, Mercadé, the messenger from France, appears unexpectedly to announce the death of the Princess's father, thus putting an end to the revels. Vis-à-vis this new development, all the highly aestheticized shows of love are reduced to a flimsy veil thrown over reality, a veil that has now been ripped to reveal the actuality of life. The French ladies must retire to where they came from, and their Navarre wooers are advised to devote themselves to more worthy pursuits, such as monastic seclusion, assistance to the sick, honest work, etc. Only after the successful passing of this test can they hope to be rewarded with requital of love. From the self-imposed study of bookish knowledge, later replaced with the more exciting study of beautiful eyes, as Berowne has put it, the lords are finally directed to a much more substantial and basic kind of study, necessary for the formation of a personality, the study of life in its often tragic dimensions. This is the Princess's last address to the King of Navarre, to which the other three ladies seem to subscribe in a flurry of farewell admonitions to their suitors—

> If frosts and fasts, hard lodging and thin weeds,
> Nip not the gaudy blossoms of your love,
> But that it bear this trial, and last love;
> Then, at the expiration of the year,
> Come challenge me, challenge me by these deserts,
> And, by this virgin palm now kissing thine,
> I will be thine . . .

(795–801)

And so, quite appropriately, instead of the expected summer for which the maidens have been bleaching their smocks in the first half of the closing song, directly after the "gaudy blossoms" of pied spring, in the second half we encounter the "frosts and fasts, hard lodgings and thin weeds" of winter:

> When icicles hang by the wall
>   And Dick the shepherd blows his nail
> And Tom bears logs into the hall
>   And milk comes frozen home in pail,
> When blood is nipped, and ways be foul,
> Then nightly sings the staring owl:
>   "Tu-whit, Tu-whoo!"
> A merry note,
> While greasy Joan doth keel the pot.
>
> When all aloud the wind doth blow
>   And coughing drowns the parson's saw
> And birds sit brooding in the snow
>   And Marian's nose looks red and raw,
> When roasted crabs hiss in the bowl,
> Then nightly sings the staring owl:
>   "Tu-whit, Tu-whoo!"
> A merry note,
> While greasy Joan doth keel the pot.

(900–917)

In his discussion of the epilogue song of *Love's Labour's Lost,* Francis Berry observes that "It is tacked on and, it might be argued, it is detachable and, detached, the winter half, if not both halves, makes a beautiful self-sufficient number in an anthology of lyrics."[7] And indeed it does. This piece of lyrical poetry, allegedly composed for the sake of the final masque by "the two learned men," Holofernes and Nathaniel, has nothing to do with the dry pedantry and rhetorical mannerism we have learnt to associate with them. It cannot have been written by anybody else but Shakespeare himself and it shows his poetic genius at its very best in creating this lively Breughelian scene of bustling country life in the midst of the least congenial season of the year. Note that against the only human presence in the spring half, the maidens bleaching their smocks, here we have at least five much more concrete ones: Dick the shepherd, Tom the logbearer, the preaching parson, greasy Joan struggling with the pots and Marian with her red and raw nose, even if we decide to forget about the anonymous agent who has to help the milk come frozen home in pail and the coughing congregation in the church. These delicate but incisive sketches from life become so important and so sufficient in themselves that all other poetic devices, even the alliteration, which is so consistent in the first half, are effectually disposed of. There is not in this part a single stroke that would smack of the make-believe world of the spring's painted promises of idyllic existence and yet everything carries on the inextinguishable vitality that fills this comedy to the brim and that has sustained the human race in its long and strenuous journey through history. Hard-featured winter is perhaps closer to the realities of existence than lighthearted spring, but in the community of unstinted effort it keeps all hopes alive. And the song of the owl, the bird of wisdom, unlike that of the cuckoo, is merry.

Without this epilogue, as Francis Berry points out, the play would have ended too abruptly or on too sour a note.[8] It is at once a fascinating piece of lyrical poetry and an excellent conclusion of a generically problematized work, helping a gravely rattled comedy regain its balance without relinquishing the added somber dimension of its closing scene. Lyric in its most detached form has once again been drawn into the service of drama and has stood it in good stead.

The form that comes closest to the inset poems and songs in its relative isolation from the *azione parlata* is the monologue. There is no lack of longer utterances in *Love's Labour's Lost*. Of course, not all of them are of equal interest for our particular topic. Some of them are entirely actional—almost indistinguishable from the surrounding dialogue. Such are the Princess's reproach of Boyet for his unnecessary compliments (2.1.13–34), the King's exposition of his point of view about the territorial dispute between Navarre and France (2.1.128–52), Berowne's disclosure of his confrères' hypocrisy after the poetry reading in the woods (4.3.148–71), etc. Others, like Boyet's account of the Navarre conspiracy overheard by him (5.2.89–118), though reflective, are wholly informative and therefore similarly irrelevant to our discussion.

Quite a few of the remaining reflective monologues are commentative but of the essayistic rather than the lyrical variety, being for the most part character sketches or assessments of personages. Such are the King's caricature of Armado (1.1.160–74), the French ladies' portraits of their respective suitors (2.1.40–51, 56–63, 64–76), Moth's prose disquisition on the art of courting (3.1.10–23), the Princess's view of the royal sport of hunting (4.1.21–35), Boyet's conclusion about "the tongues of mocking wenches" (5.2.256–61), Berowne's satirical character of Boyet (5.2.315–34), and the Princess's praise of unpremeditated art (5.2.513–18). Armado's intercepted love letter to Jaquenetta (4.1.61–92) is a burlesque version of its genre. Some of the examples listed above are enveloped in a fairly sophisticated form (e.g. the King's speech in 1.1 would have been a perfect English sonnet if it had not ended in a triplet instead of a couplet, whereas Boyet's in 5.2 is a fine sixain); they are almost invariably written in rhymed verse and exhibit the entire paraphernalia of contemporary lyric: alliteration and assonance, lexical repetition, figures of speech, etc. Formally, therefore, these monologues contribute to the accumulation of melos and opsis elements that "lyricize" the play, and yet we would have to stretch the notion of lyric if we chose to subsume them under this heading.

There remain over a dozen longer utterances that can be discussed as wholly or partly lyrical. The vast majority of these belong to Berowne. The play, however, opens with a monologue of the King (1.1.–23) that is worth glancing at. Its first, long sentence, which takes up seven lines, nearly a third of the whole, has all the marks of a lyric inset. To start with, it addresses itself not to an actual person but to an

2 / generic mixture

abstract notion, fame, animized by its collocation with the verb "live," and then adds to this inchoate allegorical scene another similar figure, that of "cormorant devouring time" (4). The interwoven themes of mortality, fame, time, honor, eternity are a traditionally lyrical preoccupation, especially prominent in Renaissance poetry, and they are treated here in a patently lyrical manner, which comprises not only the intricate figurative language of the piece but also the lexical repetitions (lives–live, grace–disgrace) and the rather dense alliteration. These rhetorical devices raise the emotional temperature of the passage and help to imbue it with a passion, which strives for adequate expression rather than for the achievement of a practical goal. It is in the remaining two thirds of the speech that this goal is concretely defined and the passion is transformed into pathos. Now the agent addressed by the speaker is no longer eternal fame but his immediate interlocutors, the aristocrats Berowne, Dumaine, and Longaville, whom he expressly names and treats as actual human beings, albeit the metaphorical way of speaking is carried on for a while. This part of the monologue is actional rather than reflective, though it contains a short informative section too. The entire speech is sustained in blank verse and closes with a rhymed couplet, an appropriate form for a solemn pronouncement.

Unlike the other two, Berowne responds with a fairly long speech in blank verse again (1.1.33–48). His monologue is rhetorical, resting on systematic repetitions and an emphatic refrain, but it is clearly actional. Yet his two lengthy utterances coming shortly after this and forming a single monologue are of a markedly different kind. The first (1.1.59–69) is structured as a complex stanzaic combination of rhymed elements: a couplet—a quatrain—a couplet—a triplet. At first sight, this speech expresses dramatic intention again: Berowne vows to pervert the tenor of the oath by the extension of the meaning of the word "study" into its figurative uses covering all epicurean pursuits. There is, however, very little planning in all this. Instead, it is a witty game of antitheses and paradoxes, played in a series of finely balanced parallel constructions and punctuated by the insistent repetition of polysemous keywords ("study" and "know") underscored by alliteration and assonance. In effect, the monologue's links to the dramatic action become quite tenuous and its real focus is the expression of a playful mood in an appropriately playful poetic form.

The second part (1.1.72–93) is formally even more complex: a couplet—a quatrain—a couplet—a sonnet. It is not only thoroughly reflective but undeniably lyrical from beginning to end. Before picking up the keywords of the first and adopting them as its own thematic and rhetorical pivot in the sonnet section, it develops an elaborate preamble harping on several recurrent words: vain, pain, truth, eyes-eyesight, and, most importantly, light, which monopolizes the whole of the strikingly aphoristic line 77: "Light seeking light doth light of light beguile." This almost attains the extreme concentration on and exploitation of the semantic possibilities of a single word which Holofernes was found guilty of in his deer poem, but there is no technical pedantry here, rather the ebullience of youth that sets off the unexpected firecrackers of language and watches their effect with amused gusto. The light of the student's eyesight (according to contemporary physiology eyes emitted light to be reflected by the object of contemplation and send its image back to them) is directed to the light of truth (i.e. the only true light coming directly from God), but this effort brings about extinction of the light of eyesight and inability to receive any light from the outside world. Thus the polysemy of a word is exploited to the full in an ingenious game of lexical repetition reinforced by a scheme of dense assonance. Language turns its gaze onto itself, amazed by its own apparently limitless resources.

The sonnet section opens with the already established keyword "study" (line 80), now employed exclusively in its figurative sense, the object of the activity suggested by its being not bookish knowledge but appreciation of beauty. The purpose of such study is to please the eye of the beholder by "fixing it upon a fairer eye" (81), which will dazzle it by emitting a stronger light and then restore its powers by lending this superior radiance. The conceit is intricate, offering the satisfaction of an enthusiastic praise of female beauty coupled with the intellectual challenge of a riddling figure. Moreover, there is the added complication of the common Elizabethan pun on the homophones "eye" and "I," extending the idea of amorous interaction from the gaze to the self. The phonetic overlay is as sparkling as ever without being excessive. With its measured and functionally determined style, this sonnet approaches the average quality of Shakespeare's sequence. A comparison between it and the already discussed inset sonnet composed by Berowne for Rosaline reveals an interesting community of themes and expressive devices, making it clear that there is little difference in this play between the presentation of set poetic texts and supposedly spontaneous monologic utterances, both of them contributing to characterization. Berowne's speech is even commented upon by its onstage audience, just as the inset poems were, though the focus now is less on its form and more on the contents.

At a distance, Armado's prose soliloquy closing the first Act (2.160–77) with its grotesque image of the poet's psychological preparation for his artistic feat can also be seen as an indirect commentary on this and other amorous effusions in the comedy. Here we observe the Don working himself up to his task and gradually bringing his material to a lyrical focus. Of course, all conventional ideas and figures of Petrarchan poetry which Armado touches upon are ironically transformed into their opposites: the beloved turns out to be base rather than exalted, perjury becomes a sign of true love, Cupid is not a god but a devil. In this whirlwind of paradoxes, Armado's dizziness reaches the conclusion that he "is in love. Yea, he loveth" (line 174). And so, like the other would-be poets in the play, the Spaniard rises to his exploit: "Assist me, some extemporal god of rhyme, for I am sure I shall turn sonnet" (175–76).

Curiously, the frenzy of love which Armado strives to express in this speech informs Berowne's next extended soliloquy ("And I, forsooth, in love!" [3.1.169–200]), a probing examination of the deeply disturbed and innerly divided self of the contrite perjurer. It abounds in exclamations of surprise, indignation and sheer fury, combined with rhetorical questions, elliptical or broken sentences, enumerations, climaxes, etc, remotely anticipating Hamlet's agitated speeches. The alliteration is pervasive, but it is especially dense in the monologue's most bitterly satirical part, intent on debunking the figure of Cupid, where it joins hands with syntactic patterns of antithetical parallelism like "Regent of love-rhymes," "sovereign of sighs and groans," "Liege of all loiterers and malcontents," "prince of plackets," "king of codpieces"—a section which, with its formidable emotional drive and its unbridled fantasy producing a welter of grotesque imagery, foreshadows Mercutio's Queen Mab rhapsody in *Romeo and Juliet*. The entire soliloquy is markedly lyrical, and it is only in its close ("Well, I will love, write, sigh, pray, sue, groan./ Some men must love my lady, and some Joan" [199–200]) that Berowne finally "comes to his senses" and returns to a state of mind that could be considered actional, though this is a statement of resignation rather than any practical planning for the future.

The remarkable third scene of act 4, which contains the poetry reading in the woods, opens with another soliloquy of Berowne's

(1–18), this time in prose and bearing a striking resemblance to Armado's preparation to "turn sonnet." The situation is similar, for Berowne enters the stage *"with a paper in his hand"* and begins to read a poem that seems to be still unfinished, but then gives it up and plunges into emotional self-analysis, whose strain is expressed in a continuous grappling with language, proceeding through a medley of puns, classical allusions, lexical repetitions, and alliterations. This buildup of creative impetus is interrupted by the entrance of a fellow poet, the King, at which, as already observed, the young wit turns from a producer of lyric texts into their consumer and commentator.

In the close of the scene (and the act) Berowne, being the cleverest "sophister" of all, is implored to devise a justification for the academicians' collective perjury under the onslaught of love and plunges into his most extensive and concentrated monologic outpouring (4.3.285–339). The speech has been singled out by Coleridge for particular praise as "logic clothed in rhetoric" through which Shakespeare "in his two-fold being of poet and philosopher" conveys "profound truths in the most lively images."[9] The seriousness of this crowning piece—the fifth and last of a long monologic series—is signaled by its departure from the string of rhymed quatrains and the adoption of the grand prosodic instrument of Elizabethan drama, blank verse. Berowne begins with an overtly rhetorical section addressed to his comrades, revealing once again his fiery temperament in the alternation of exclamations and questions denouncing their academic vow (285–97). After the first dozen lines, however, the speaker seems to gradually withdraw into himself and forget his audience. The interpersonal monologue soars into the sphere of soliloquy enthused by the realization of love's superiority to all other pursuits (298–328). Right after this the speaker turns back to his audience and closes the monologue with another heavily rhetorical part (329–39). The orator's skill is amply demonstrated in this section—perhaps excessively so.

But the really impressive section of the monologue, the one that must have caught Coleridge's eye, is certainly that of the central soliloquy (298–328). Its mode is intensely lyrical, emulating the tone of emotional reflection that we witnessed in Berowne's self-probing speech in 3.1, though free of its inner strife and therefore less turbulent and centrifugal. Here the pivotal image is that of the life-giving women's eyes with which the section opens and closes. It is reinforced by a number of auxiliary ones, to which the speaker adds a series of mythological allusions as if to sublimate all traditional knowledge into the incomparable omniscience of love. Its rhythm is lively and vigorous, yet triumphantly unified. Though technically far less ostentatious than its rhetorical frame, this soliloquy in its entirety wields a far greater impact. And its definition of love becomes simultaneously a definition of lyrical poetry, of its empathic unity with the world that is effected not just by the brain but by the whole being with all its faculties.

Berowne's character, in general, fluctuates between the type of exulted lyrical hero, the caricature of this type and its cool-headed critic. A number of commentators starting with Walter Pater have discerned in this character "Shakespeare's raillery at his own poetic manner."[10] In M. C. Bradbrook words, "Berowne, who is both guilty of courtly artifice and critical of it, plays a double game with language throughout; the same double game that the author himself is playing. He runs with the hare and hunts with the hounds."[11] We have seen how close Berowne is allowed to come to Shakespeare's own lyrical style. A character granted the privilege of soliloquizing always creates the impression of being to some extent the author's mouthpiece or alter ego, because the lyrical mode suggests an unmediated expression of the self generating the text. Yet, surprisingly, Berowne's continuous association with the lyric does not give us any particular insight into his individuality. All we get to know about him is his sparkling wit and love of life. The reason for this relative opacity—or thinness—of character is the fact that most of his speeches, as well as those of the other dramatis personae, are concerned not so much with the expression of hidden depths as with the manner of expression. The topic is established beforehand and it does not amount to much more than the sweet pains of love, while the only conflict seems to be the classical one between love and honor and it is soon resolved by a general decision to relax the norms of the latter for the sake of the former. So the main thrust of Berowne's strongly lyrical presence in the comedy can be said to be atmospheric, tonal and aesthetico-critical rather than psychological.

Now we must turn briefly to Berowne's series of shorter monologues preceding his just considered crowning piece in 4.3. This sequence starts with an appeal for general reconciliation in the richly alliterative sixain "Sweet lords, sweet lovers, O, let us embrace!" (210), and continues as a blazon lyric. The King's matter-of-fact intervention (216) is fused smoothly into the general run of the poetic text by Berowne's rhyming his next line with it and proceeding to develop his poetic argument through a couple of quatrains. He maintains, in the conventional Petrarchan mode, that his beloved is like the sun worshiped by the savages of Inde and dazzling all peremptory eyes with its radiance. The second quatrain is completed by the King with an amazed question, actually a commentary on Berowne's enthusiasm: "What zeal, what fury hath inspired thee now?" (225). Then he adds an unrhymed praise of the superior beauty of his own mistress. Berowne steps in again with a vehement refutation in a couple of lines, which rhyme with those of the King, thus securing the third quatrain, and then adds three more to further eulogize his own lady.

Berowne's second monologue (228–42) is structured like a reversed sonnet, starting with a couplet, or rather the second half of a dialogic quatrain, and continuing through three full-fledged quatrains that order the overall argument in the usual well-defined stages. A supernumerary unrhymed line at the end contains the poet's exultant exclamation, the climax of Rosaline's poetic praise: "O, 'tis the sun that maketh all things shine" (242). This prompts the King to challenge Berowne's untoward infatuation, and thus a new, dialogical quatrain is evolved by the banter exchanged between the two.

The third short monologue (244–49) adds a single quatrain to its opening couple of lines hooked by their rhymes onto his interlocutor's cue. In a paradoxical defense of dark-complexioned Rosaline, it argues that only swarthy ladies can be truly beautiful—a conceit that Shakespeare develops more elaborately in his *Sonnets* by way of problematizing conventional Petrarchism. The King intervenes again with an objection. His three-line cue (250–52) is in need of another rhyme to complete the quatrain, which Berowne promptly supplies to promote his own metaphorically-paronomastic argument. This ingenious extolment of his paramour takes up two more quatrains and informs the fourth monologue of the series (254–61). It sets off a flurry of ironical reactions among his fellow academicians, which Berowne tries his best to fend off in a similarly biting manner, contriving meanwhile to go on with the praises. The repartee is mostly based on the witty tackling of poetic imagery from a variety of viewpoints. It runs through a sequence of six more quatrains (262–85), bringing their sum total in the series up to seventeen. Within this frame, the cues are carefully balanced against each other in single or double lines.

The close reading of Berowne's long monologic series and its interpellations by the fellow academicians takes us away from the lyric inset toward other, more pervasive forms of generic interaction in drama. We have noticed the consistent use of the quatrain throughout the passage and the systematic subsuming of all cues under this overall rhyming pattern. The melos principle is thus clearly imposed on the entire text; it is rooted not only in the regularity of rhyme but in the pervasive alliteration too. The opsis counterpart is also present in the numerous puns and images. The employment of rhyme, alliteration, wordplay and figurative language is indeed a characteristic quality of the entire comedy, cutting across the distinction between monologue and dialogue.

Nonmechanical rhyming being primarily a feature of the lyrical generic repertoire and the use of rhyming in *Love's Labour's Lost*'s being so ubiquitous in its rich variety, this formal device would seem to merit separate consideration as a possible factor in the overall lyricization of the play. According to A. H. Moncure-Sime's count, "it contains twice as many rhymed lines as blank verse."[12] There is hardly another Shakespearean play that is so overwhelmingly rhymed. The dialogue, no less than the monologues, is organized in couplets, quatrains, sixains and other stanzaic patterns. The pairs of rhymes frequently bulge into triplets, quadruplets and even larger sets producing a general effect of ebullience, of lyric excitement. In terms of Alastair Fowler's typology, however, the phenomenon of extensive rhyming molding the dramatic text would be more correctly defined as some kind of partial hybridization rather than modulation, for the preferred component of the lyric repertoire introduced into the host genre is not substantive but formal. It is functionally relevant as an important signal of the play's preoccupation with lyric poetry, transpiring in Berowne's crowning speech as well as at many other points in the play.

At times the imposition of stanzaic structure on the flow of dialogue is clearly external—as in most medieval drama—and apparently has little or nothing to do with its substance. Such is, for instance, the case with the series of quatrains enveloping the exchange between the Princess and her retinue after the withdrawal of the "Muscovites" in 5.2.265–85, where rhyming units do not in any way underscore dramatic utterances. A little later, however, the use of much the same device (six quatrains with an intervening couplet) in the repartee between the King and the Princess (339–64) is dramatically quite pertinent: here the quatrains outline the contrapuntal nature of their conversation. The distribution of the units between the two parties is carefully measured, each being allotted a single line first, then a couple of lines splitting the quatrain evenly in two halves, etc. On one occasion only, the Princess monopolizes a full quatrain and turns it into a sixain by adding a couplet to it. The last, sixth quatrain of the sequence is allowed to disintegrate before the return of the couplet structure. In the alternation of stanzaic sections informing most of the dialogue, the Princess is invariably given the closing part, which completes the rhyming pattern and thus imparts a sense of finality to her cues, rendering her position in the debate more salient and victorious. An essentially lyrical formal device, whose contribution to earlier plays has been purely external, is to a great extent naturalized by drama and used for its specific purposes.

We are alerted to this intergeneric function of rhyme very early on in the comedy, when, after Berowne's first monologue remonstrating against the unbearable austerity of the academicians' vow, the other three comment on his speech and provoke him into an ironic response. The four cues are bound together into a stichomythic rhymed quadruplet:

> KING. How well he's read, to reason against reading.
> DUMAINE. Proceeded well, to stop all good proceeding.
> LONGAVILLE. He weeds the corn, and still lets grow the weeding.
> BEROWNE. The spring is near when green geese are a-breeding.
>
> (1.1.94–97)

A section of the dialogue is encapsulated here in a module suggesting a sense of community in the Navarre team. This technique, as we are going to see in the next chapter, will be further developed and perfected to form an important part of the dramatist's artistic arsenal. Here the community is, of course, undermined by the riddling opaqueness of Berowne's closing contribution with its ironic undercurrent. Challenged to explain his cue, the wag responds in his characteristic way:

DUMAINE. How follows that?
BEROWNE.   Fit in his place and time.
DUMAINE. In reason nothing.
BEROWNE.   Something then in rhyme.

(98–99)

The familiar phrase is wittily deconstructed to reassert rhyme as an expression of carefree playfulness independent of the tedious dominance of logic, a kind of carnival liberation of language that is at the heart of lyric utterance. Rhyming has thus become an element of dramatic action, employed in the molding of character and atmosphere.

Much of the ingenious repartee in the further development of the play relies on rhyme to emphasize the festive spirit of communication between personages. Rhyme, punning, and other kinds of wit often go hand in hand, as in the following exchange:

LONGAVILLE. Will you give horns, chaste lady? Do not so.
KATHERINE. Then die a calf before your horns do grow.
LONGAVILLE. One word in private with you ere I die.
KATHERINE. Bleat softly then; the butcher hears you cry.

(5.2.252–55)

This is the kind of language game that is played in the comedy on the slightest occasion. As C. L. Barber points out, each character "keeps jumping the other's words to take them away and make them his own, finding a meaning in them which was not intended," thus opening up and activating their polysemous potential.[13] Such expansion naturally brings one word into contact with another that sounds nearly the same. It gradually blurs the borderline between dictionary items, revealing their real or pretended kinship and freeing language of all discursive constraints. Rhyme in combination with other phonetic echoes further reinforces the effect of persistent paronomasia.

An especially interesting category of rhymed cues is that of incomplete communication, which can be best illustrated by some asides of the Navarre lords overhearing each other during their furtive poetry reading. Berowne is in a privileged position, as he is the first to arrive on the scene and hide, so that he can see and hear all the others while remaining undetected by them to the end. Thus concealed, he can afford to comment on their self-addressed utterances in a series of ironic asides spoken to himself or to the theater audience and connecting to them by rhyme:

> KING. What, Longaville, and reading? Listen, ear!
> BEROWNE. Now, in thy likeness, one more fool appear!
>
> (4.3.41–42)
>
> KING. In love, I hope. Sweet fellowship in shame.
> BEROWNE. One drunkard loves another of the name.
>
> (46–47)
>
> DUMAINE. Once more I'll read the ode that I have writ.
> BEROWNE. Once more I'll mark how love can vary wit.
>
> (96–97)

Here, as in most of the comments made on Dumaine's earlier cues, Berowne seems to rhyme on purpose, capping the other person's utterance and obtaining ironic preeminence over that person for his own and the audience's satisfaction.

There are other cases, however, when there can hardly be any dramatic motivation for the rhyming. Thus, in the poetry-reading scene Dumaine's exclamation "As fair as day" echoes Berowne's "Stoop, I say," after which Longaville sighs "And I had mine!" in unison with Berowne's "but then no sun must shine" (86–89), though neither of the two has been in a position to hear Berowne. So it is not they but Shakespeare who suddenly intrudes over and above the characters to rhyme in such cases. This kind of rhyming, then, is not truly dramatic, for its only function is obviously that of textual integration.

A more intricate use of the technique can be detected in the poetry-recital scene. In the course of his surreptitious comments on Longaville's sonnet, Berowne exclaims: "God amend us, God amend! We are much out o'th'way" (line 73). Longaville in the meantime is trying to contrive how to get his poem over to its addressee, but then he notices Dumaine who comes in with a poem of his own, so his cue is split in two: "By whom shall I send this?—Company? Stay" (74). The rhyme bridging the gap between the asides of the two speakers is dramatically impossible. And it is curious that when Berowne speaks again after Longaville he seems to ignore the latter's contribution (which he could not have heard anyway) and supply his own completion of the current rhymed couplet: "All hid, all hid, an old infant play" (75). Thus, for once, the two alternative principles of rhyming, the quasi-lyrical and the dramatic, seem to operate in combination.

It seems appropriate at this point of our discussion to stress once again that, unlike the earlier examples of English rhymed dramatic texts, Shakespeare's writing, even before the poet's mature period, rarely lapses into a mechanical run of rhyming patterns. With him, rhyme configurations vary and they also alternate with blank verse—sometimes even with prose. Behind this variation and alternation, we feel, there is more often than not a functionally motivated choice of forms. Moreover, as we have seen, at times rhyme can perform specifically dramatic tasks, which makes it difficult to assume that when it does not it is simply automatic. In most cases of dramatically relevant rhyming, of course, it is largely up to the critical interpreter and the theater director to decide who rhymes the dialogue, the character or the playwright, but the very possibility of a dramatic motivation is indicative of Shakespeare's characteristic knack of not just imposing an external generic element onto his plays but going to considerable lengths to ensure its integration and "naturalization" in the dramatic medium.

The last example considered above brings us face to face with the role of triplets and, occasionally, even larger rhyme sets in *Love's Labour's Lost*. It has already been said that such formations are most often due to the overabundance of youthful energy and playfulness, yet we saw how apt the early quadruplet shared by the four Navarre academicians was from a purely dramatic point of view. Quite a few of the "extended couplets" are, in fact, used for the same purpose of focusing a multiple exchange of cues on a single topic, though perhaps in a less impressive way because of the more relaxed scheme of syntactical and lexical parallelism. The best result is achieved when such exchanges revolving around a pun crystallize into stichomythia, as in the following set:

> MARIA. Come, come, you talk greasily, your lips grow foul.
> COSTARD. She's too hard for you at pricks, sir. Challenge her to bowl.
> BOYET . I fear too much rubbing. Good night, my good owl.
>
> (4.1.136–38)

Sometimes one character adds an extra line to the already completed rhymed couplet of another, thus canceling its finality by an external comment:

> BEROWNE. Give me the paper, let me read the same,
>   And to the strictest decrees I'll write my name.
> KING. How well this yielding rescues thee from shame.
>
> (1.1.116–18)

The dramatic effect of establishing a character's superiority through such reopening of closed verse structures in the course of *azione parlata* is inescapable.

But the most interesting type of triplet in the play is probably that of a monologic couplet hooked onto the last line of somebody else's cue. Almost all examples of this kind seem to come from the interventions of the Princess. We have already noticed how she manages to keep for herself the right of the last word in the series of quatrains structuring her dialogue with the King in 5.2. It can be added now that whenever the Princess engages in dialogue, she almost invariably behaves as everybody else's superior: the last word is again reserved for her and she is usually the one to complete authoritatively any rhyme set initiated by the others, a rule only broken when she asks a question that needs to be answered or gives an order that has to be acknowledged. This is perhaps the prerogative of her elevated position, but it is even more likely a sign that in this lyrical comedy she is a projection of the commanding Petrarchan mistress. The King's social standing is no lesser than hers, and yet his manner of communication is much more amenable.

To form a self-contained couplet on a rhyme supplied by someone else's line is to disregard the other character's participation in the dialogue or to appropriate his/ her contribution by virtual retreat from the act of communication. Here is a characteristic instance, in which the King is handed the Princess's official letter and offers to peruse it:

> KING. Madam, I will, if suddenly I may.
> PRINCESS. You will the sooner that I were away,
>   For you'll prove perjured if you make me stay.
>
> (2.1.111–13)

Several more examples of the same configuration can be adduced from the Princess's dealings with the Forester and Boyet in 4.1. To be fair, other characters occasionally act in a similar way. Katherine puts Dumaine in his place by the use of the same device (5.2.811–13), and Rosaline in a state of fury dares even apply it to the Princess (5.2.58–60). Once again, these distributions of rhyme are ambivalent and on occasion can be treated as no more than a part of the wealth of phonetic echoes enhancing the festive atmosphere of the comedy. Their basically lyrical quality retains its salience, but it does not prevent them from functioning as an integral element of drama.

In view of the evidence demonstrated above, it would be hard to deny that *Love's Labour's Lost* is permeated by the lyric repertoire in every section of its text. First of all, it contains a significant number of inset poems and songs. Secondly, quite a few monologues, especially those of Berowne, are either entirely or in large part suffused with the lyrical mode, crystallizing in a variety of generic forms, among which the sonnets loom large, numbering at least half a dozen. There is no lack of other kinds in meters ranging from iambs through trochees to the fairly unusual amphibrach and from tetrameters through the staple pentameter and different hexameters to the septenary. Thirdly, even the dialogue is for the most part molded by the imposition of stanzaic patterns that make it stylistically indistinguishable from the monologues.

A fairly homogeneous, though far from uniform, medium is thus created in the play, lyrically tinged not only by its strong melic character, formed by meter, rhyme and alliteration, but also by its optic counterpart residing in the profusion of poetic imagery and punning. The lyrical saturation of *Love's Labour's Lost* by means of inclusion, modulation and partial hybridization is in fact so intense that it brings the text to the brink of generic instability. Walter Pater was perhaps the first to notice the play's static quality, its concentric composition: "The merely dramatic interest of the piece is slight enough—only just sufficient, indeed, to be the vehicle of its wit and poetry. The scene—a park of the King of Navarre—is unaltered throughout; and the unity of the play is not so much the unity of a drama as that of a series of pictorial groups, in which the same figures reappear, in different combinations, but on the same background. It is as if Shakespeare had intended to bind together, by some inventive conceit, the devices of an ancient tapestry, and give voices to its figures."[14] Many later commentators have corroborated this observation in a variety of ways. Colie points out that "even the play's plot is made up of what might be called linguistic situations and Calderwood notes that "the evolution of action and plot is reduced to a series of verbal events: vows made and broken, games of wit and wordplay, penned speeches, songs, epistolary sonnets, and even 'sentences' pronounced on the scholars by the ladies."[15]

Lyric as a "theoretical kind" and the entire paraphernalia of Renaissance lyrical poetry as a "historical genre" were thoroughly searched by Shakespeare for elements that could be integrated into his comedy of immature love. The consequence is a radical transformation of the nature of drama. On the other hand, however, by entering a different generic medium, the elements of lyric are forced to relinquish their hitherto autonomous status and are subjected to the pressures of the complex host genre. The lyrical forms inserted in the drama or crystallizing in its midst, are not as sacrosanct and untouchable as they would be if contemplated in isolation. An apparently completed sonnet can bulge out into an additional couplet or turn its closing couplet into a triplet, or its whole structure can be reversed, so that it opens with a couplet to be followed by three quatrains. At times a poetic prelude leads to the emergence of a sonnet, thus making the latter a part of a larger form. Such variations dynamize the fixed lyrical genre, transforming it into something still in the making, free to move around and seek its final shape. Often a lyric form grows as an improvisation from the promptings of the dialogue and remains partly attached to the preceding cues by a community of rhymes, images, etc. Or, conversely, its fixedness is unraveled by later cues that, hooked onto it, treat it as part of the ongoing dialogue.

❦   ❦   ❦

There are times, however, when the very essence of lyric is problematized or its raison d'être is questioned by the different logic of drama. Lyric insets, as shown above, are frequently subject to onstage criticism, sometimes rather technical and formal but more often leaning toward ideas and attitudes. The comments are ironic, even satirical, and apt to relativize the impact of the piece. We are not granted the reader's privilege of being left alone with the text to experience its unchallenged suggestive power but are faced with an artifact which is shown to be as imperfect as its creator. By entering the dramatic medium, the lyric relinquishes its exceptional status and descends from the heights of Parnassus into the real world. This demotion is due to its changed function: from the aesthetic projection of "impersonal individuality" expressing in the accents of a specific voice the general human condition and thus conducive to empathy, it shrinks to the reflection of a dramatic character to be observed and judged from aside impartially and critically, even condescendingly. The irony is chiefly leveled at its respective author but, by inference, it debunks Petrarchan love poetry in general, depriving it of its sublimity.

Further, the relativization of lyric is carried out by means of the burlesque. Even the "straightforward" insets of poems composed by the Navarre gang are far from being masterpieces in their genres: they are indeed presented as the dabbling of amateur poetasters in versification and may be seen as parodies of established contemporary types. Another group of metric endeavors, comprising the verse written by Armado and Holofernes, are open spoofs on current poetic practices, such as the anti-Petrarchan "masculine" line and mannerist linguistic ingenuity. Fun is poked more than once at familiar lyric conventions by dramatic juxtaposition of the idealized portrait of the beloved and her actual appearance, exposing poetry's departure from realism, as in the case of Berowne's comments on Dumaine's infatuation with plain Katherine (4.3.80–88). Berowne, of course, has no inkling that his irony will backfire as soon as his wooing of the similarly flawed Rosaline comes out into the open.

An even more radical criticism of lyrical language is that of its self-centered opacity and lack of pragmatic value, i.e. of its being what we know it tends to be by definition, a kind of antidiscourse, or nondiscourse. That the figurative manner of speaking characteristic of lyric is in need of translation into the ordinary language of everyday communication is a point recurrently made in the comedy. The first demand for breaking the code occurs after Berowne's riddling addition to the rhyming game of the Navarre academicians in the wake of his sonnet-monologue, "The spring is near when green geese are a-breeding" (1.1.97). The speaker is compelled to concede that the image is nonsensical and introduced only for the rhyme. The problem is brought forward again, and even more clearly, when, having read his allegorical ode about Cupid's infatuation with a spring flower, Dumaine expresses his concern that the conceit may not be understood by Katherine, for whom it has been designed, so the poem will need an interpretative accompaniment (4.3.118–19). Further in the same scene, when the King and Berowne summon the frustrated scholars to a different kind of venture, that of courtly love, Longaville fails to see what concrete actions their conventional war metaphor can refer to:

> KING. Saint Cupid, then! And, soldiers, to the field!
> BEROWNE. Advance your standards and upon them, lords!
>   Pell-mell, down with them! But be first advised
>   In conflict that you get the sun of them.
> LONGAVILLE. Now to plain dealing. Lay these glozes by.
>   Shall we resolve to woo these girls of France?
>
> (340–45)

And somewhat later still the Princess is similarly nonplussed by Boyet's couching his defense strategy against the Navarre warriors in lyrical language that can offer no clue to the kind of concrete action to be taken:

> PRINCESS. Will they return?
> BOYET.   They will, they will, God knows;
>   And leap for joy, though they are lame with blows.
>   Therefore change favours and, when they repair,
>   Blow like sweet roses in this summer air.
> PRINCESS. How "blow"? How "blow"? Speak to be understood.
>
> (5.2.290–94)

Boyet, however, is so much carried away by his ability to embroider beautiful imagery and ingenious wordplay for their own sakes that he continues in the same vein:

> Fair ladies masked are roses in their bud;
> Dismasked, their damask sweet commixture shown,
> Are angels vailing clouds, or roses blown.
>
> (295–97)

He seems to be advising the ladies to unmask for their next encounter with the Navarre wooers, but, in the manner of speaking he has adopted, the word "dismasked" is more intent on its intralinguistic phonetic connection with its immediate neighbor in the line, "damask," than on its basic referential meaning. Thus the whole message is destabilized. The Princess is exasperated:

Avaunt, perplexity! What shall we do
If they return in their own shape to woo?

(298–99)

The moral of these recurrent clashes is clear. By creating a self-contained, however aesthetically captivating, paralanguage, love lyric, like all artistic obfuscations of direct communication, seems to defeat its purpose as a means of wooing and winning its addressee. Its focus on language and, consequently, on the speaker and shaper of its own sophisticated expression rather than on its avowed object encloses its message within itself and cuts it off from the world of action. This reduces love lyric to a childish game revolving around a vacuous center.

The French ladies in *Love's Labour's Lost,* unlike their Navarre wooers, come from the world of grown-ups and may be momentarily amused by the lyric gambols of the young men but will not take them seriously and, therefore, cannot be won by the poetry they have unwittingly inspired. In the closing scene the Princess expresses this difference of attitude in her usual no-nonsense manner. The academicians' love letters are rated by her "At courtship, pleasant jest and courtesy,/ As bombast and as lining to the time," and can only be treated "In their own fashion, like a merriment" (5.2.774–78). The stupendous collapse of the Muscovite masque brings the brightest of the lords back to his senses—in a famous monologue Berowne renounces all forms of amorous affectation in which he has participated and, above all, that of conventional lyric poetry:

O, never will I trust to speeches penned,
    Nor to the motion of a schoolboy's tongue,
Nor never come in visor to my friend,
    Nor woo in rhyme like a blind harper's song.

(5.2.402–5)

Berowne harbors no doubt that his greatest fault has been his infatuation with the pretentious courtly language of the Petrarchan vogue:

Taffeta phrases, silken terms precise,
    Three-piled hyperboles, spruce affectation,
Figures pedantical: these summer flies
    Have blown me full of maggot ostentation.

(406–9)

Thus he works himself up to yet another oath after the miscarriage of the previous two:

> Henceforth my wooing mind shall be expressed
>   In russet yeas and honest kersey noes.

(412–13)

And without wasting any more time, this penitent lover proceeds to court his mistress in what he thinks is an unaffected and honest fashion, suggesting that she is not one of those alabaster-skinned ladies of the conventional lyric blazon, addressing her bluntly as "wench" and declaring right away: "My love to thee is sound, *sans* crack or flaw" (415).

Ironically, Berowne's recantation of the sonnet vices is replete with them. His monologue is as oversaturated with similes, metaphors, lexical repetitions, alliteration and other rhetorical devices as were his earlier speeches. The very elements of the language he disowns are defined in the same figurative language as items of fashionable clothing ("taffeta phrases," "silken terms"), while those that he promises to embrace from now on are similarly enveloped in—admittedly coarser—kinds of cloth ("russet" and "kersey"). And the climactic section of this monologue, designed to deal a death blow to feigning sonneteering, is structured as a bona fide Shakespearean sonnet, displaying its thematic and figurative unity as well as the carefully graded argument, neatly adjusted to the rhyming pattern. Finally, in his closing line, Berowne, who has just vowed to exchange the pompous taffeta phrases of courtly language for the russet and kersey simplicity of common speech, resorts to the pretentious bookish preposition "sans," which provokes at once Rosaline's censure, "Sans '*sans*', I pray you" (416), and compels her wooer to admit that the old sickness is still with him and that it may take some time yet to cure it.[16]

The same goes, of course, for the other three scholars-turned-lovers. As it becomes evident toward the end of the play, their case, in fact, is even worse. The King proves so insensitive to the abrupt change of situation caused by Marcadé's message that he continues to coax the Princess into continuing the love game in much the same Petrarchan terms. The language of his oration, opening characteristically with the seesaw line "The extreme parts of time extremely forms" (5.2.734–45), is as affected as the public speeches of such conceited characters in Shakespeare's later dramas as, for instance, Claudius in *Hamlet*. The Princess once again requires translation of what she has heard, this time not for stylistic reasons alone: "I understand you not. My griefs are double" (746).

And now Berowne, to his credit, volunteers to act as the interpreter, a role that he feels he is up to, since he has learnt that "Honest plain words best pierce the ear of grief" (747). It is, of course, precisely the use of plain words that continues to elude him, for the old metaphorical posturing has not been fully overcome. And although his "interpreting" steers clear of the King's moribund clichés, it weaves its complex rhetorical web with strands of imagery familiar from his earlier speeches. Berowne seems to have relinquished the niceties of rhyming and ascended to the lofty seriousness of blank verse, but his infatuation with figurative language and its rhetorical accompaniments on the levels of syntax, lexis, and phonetics is unabated. One feels though that it would be a pity if this propensity was ever completely lost. For then indeed the pall of Marcadé's shadow would fall over the splendor of the world, extinguishing its chiefest glory. We have already heard the words of Mercury and they are indeed unpleasantly harsh after the songs of Apollo. The flowers of spring may be "pied" and the birds' songs may be delusive, but without them it would be too hard to bear the realities of winter. The pleasantries of lyric poetry may appear insubstantial when placed in the context of mature life, yet after the somber close of the play they continue to linger in our minds as the happy memory of youth. The lyric impulse has been chastened by drama, almost expelled from it at the end, but not before enlivening it through and through from within.

ROMEO AND JULIET

The "persistently lyrical tone" of *Romeo and Juliet* is a critical commonplace.[17] Nicholas Brooke has even declared this play "a dramatic exploration of the world of the love sonnet."[18] The very prologue with which it opens is, rather unexpectedly, a regular sonnet. In this introductory piece the staple lyrical genre of the age is employed for a totally uncharacteristic purpose, the summary account of the dramatic plot, which is a narrative, epic task. Arthur Brooke's poem *Romeus and Juliet*, probably the major source for Shakespeare's tragedy, is prefixed with a sonnet too, and the function of that preamble is exactly to provide an outline of the story. Though Shakespeare must have borrowed the device from Brooke, his introductory sonnet takes a more abstracted, bird's eye view of the plot, of thematic rather than fictional orientation. Unlike Brooke's Petrarchan type, this one is English, or Shakespearean, providing the perfect form for an argument developed in ideationally distinctive stages. The first quatrain tells us about the fresh eruption of the old enmity between the two noble houses in Verona; the second adds the story of the "star-cross'd lovers," whose death finally resolves this conflict; the third explains that the play will show "The fearful passage of their death-mark'd love/ And the continuance of their parents' rage"; and the closing couplet appeals to the audience for patience and trust in the actors' good intentions. The matter is not exactly lyrical, but its thematic organization and figurative language make the discrepancy between form and content less conspicuous.

The question remains: why did Shakespeare—and, indeed, Brooke before him—choose to encumber the sonnet with the most uncongenial task of sketching out a fictional work? According to Brian Gibbons, the dramatist's purpose in this choice was that of "attuning the audience to the play's verbal music and, subliminally, to its sonnet-like symmetries and intensities of feeling and design."[19] The sonnet tradition as the stronghold of lyric in the Elizabethan age can be discovered behind every aspect of the conception, composition, and textual realization of *Romeo and Juliet*. Its author was apparently conscious of this close connection and decided to signal it by supplying a prologue-sonnet not only before the first act of the play but before the second too.[20]

However foregrounded by the prologues, the sonnet as a fixed form does not crop up in the text of this play as often as it does in *Love's Labour's Lost*. But it makes one striking—and even less conventional—appearance toward the end of act 1, when Romeo and Juliet first meet and fall in love with each other (5.92–105). The episode is enveloped in another English sonnet. Romeo takes the lead in the dialogue and urges Juliet to yield to his entreaties for a kiss. She is as modest as behooves a maid but is far from refusing. In the event, Romeo manages to snatch not just one but two kisses and an assurance that his feelings are requited. The entire dialogue is carried on in an oblique, metaphorical language, which presents the lover's approach to his beloved as a pilgrimage to a shrine. The poetic imagery organized around this conceit is homogeneous and compact. It is wittily worked out step by step in the exchange of cues between the two, and they prove equal in the game. The sonnet form ensures a fairly balanced participation in the dialogue, Romeo starting with a full quatrain and Juliet responding with another one, after which each of them speaks a single line and Romeo concludes the third quatrain only to let Juliet share the closing couplet with him so that the completed form can be sealed with the kiss. The technique first experimented with in the Navarre academicians' playfully rhymed stichomythic quadruplet in *Love's Labour's Lost* has now been considerably developed to produce a much more sophisticated dialogic module.

The text is as richly lyrical as that of any Elizabethan sonnet. Its metaphorical compactness is reinforced by a web of lexical repetitions, alliterations and assonances enhancing its sonority. Such a poem may be a little unusual in the context of the Petrarchan tradition, not so much because of its dialogical form—precedents of this kind can be found—but because of the unison of the two voices amalgamating into that perfect "dialogue-of-one" that only Donne knew how to suggest in his happiest paeans of idealized love. At this important point of the action the two lovers seem to raise around themselves the immutable structure of the sonnet as a privileged lyrical space, which must isolate and save their love from the surrounding public world of violent hatred. And the audience cannot but view with joy and relief the protective bubble that envelopes them, for it has just witnessed Tybalt's uncontrollable rage directed against their union. Though spun out of dreamy words, stuff as flimsy as gossamer, this edifice has been credited by poets, including Shakespeare himself, to be more sturdy than "rocks impregnable" and "gates of steel" and to encase in itself the glory of love "even to the edge of doom."[21]

It is worth noting that the protagonists' withdrawal into the lyrical dimension does not for a moment stop or hinder the dramatic action. Indeed, it is there that the inception of the tragedy takes place. Thus drama and lyric merge to perfection. The dialogic action is not retarded but only heightened as a result. Yet, the dynamic medium reimposes its supremacy and opens anew the form of the sonnet as soon as it is completed. Unable to stop at the first kiss, Romeo adds an extra line, continuing the metaphorical logic of the piece beyond its boundary: "Thus from my lips, by thine, my sin is purg'd" (106). Juliet is similarly tempted to carry on the lyrical dialogue in the same terms: "Then have my lips the sin that they have took" (107). And so they go on to inscribe the second kiss within a full-fledged supernumerary quatrain (106–9) compromising the untouchable definitiveness of the genre. The quatrains—and the kisses—would most probably have multiplied if Juliet's Nurse had not intervened to put an end to the amorous conversation and take her charge away from the lyrical back to the dramatic world.[22]

While recognizable poetic constructions were similarly deprived of their finality by additional improvisations in *Love's Labour's Lost,* the impression they created was one of boisterous youthfulness. Now there is something symbolically ominous in the destabilization of an aesthetic triumph, prompted by the weakness of human nature. The insecurity of lyrical forms in the dramatic medium is used to generate important dramatic meanings: the lyrical edifice which we erect to protect us from an inimical public world may be good enough in itself, but our nature can seldom measure up to its ideal perfection. We may be able to "build in sonnets pretty roomes" for ourselves, as Donne maintains, but will we have the perseverance to stay within their boundaries?

Much of this effect of the fusion of lyrical and dramatic strains through the ordering of the inception dialogue into a sonnet and its subsequent subversion will, unfortunately, be lost on the modern audiences, for it is unlikely that they will recognize the sonnet form on hearing it. Shakespeare's contemporaries, however, were so much exposed to the variety of lyrical genres performed in public that they could hardly have missed the subtle suggestions of the versification.

Act 2 closes with another fourteen-liner shared between Romeo and Juliet (6.24–37), though this time it is unrhymed except for the closing couplet and is different in other important ways. We are now at the midpoint of the play, and its plot has reached a new high-water mark, the clandestine marriage of the protagonists. The passage is again shared between the two in almost equal portions, again slightly tipped to Romeo's side, his part consisting of the first six lines and Juliet's of the next five. The contributions of the lovers are more compact than before, approaching the form and tone of monologue. However, just as in the inception sonnet, they are unified by a set of common images, this time revolving around the love-wealth conceit. While the texture of the imagery is now less thick and intricate, the phonetic layer, replete with alliteration, is as supple as in that sonnet, and the lyrical enthusiasm of the two merging speeches is indisputable. But the lovers are not allowed to complete their quasi-sonnet by themselves, for their lyrical isolation is invaded by a third voice, very much unlike theirs, that of the practically minded Friar Laurence, who interrupts their cooing and urges them to immediate action:

Come, come with me and we will make short work,
For, by your leaves, you shall not stay alone
Till holy church incorporate two in one.

(35–37)

Whereas, on the previous occasion, the Nurse had intervened only after the completion of the sonnet and its excrescence, the Friar intrudes in the midst of it. The lovers can no longer "stay alone" in the exclusive space that they have created for themselves. Albeit through the benevolent presence of the friar, the public world that they have tried to shut out makes its inevitable inroad into their private existence. The dramatic environment punctures the lyrical bubble with its actional urgency and deprives it of its autonomy. The lyrical form has relaxed by shedding its rhyming pattern and has admitted into its exclusive space a third voice, which is allowed not only to replace the lyric locution of the quasi-sonnet with dramatic speech but also to provide the closing couplet sustained in its characteristic accents. The love sonnet, constructed as the dialogue-of-one, the linguistically monolithic world of lyrical poetry, has been penetrated and subverted by the disruptive heteroglossia of its dramatic environment.[23]

Our next step takes us to the last, fifth scene of act 3, opening with another crucial episode in the plot of the tragedy, that of the protagonists' wedding night, executed in a way similarly reminiscent of the first-encounter sonnet (1–36). The lovers are alone again as they were in the shared sonnet. The scene, commonly referred to as the Aubade, is a dramatization of that traditional lyrical genre. The protagonists are discovered in Juliet's bedroom at the break of day. Romeo, who has been sentenced after the murder of Tybalt not to set foot in Verona on pain of death, knows that it is time for him to depart; Juliet is unwilling to let him go, but she soon realizes that his life is in grave danger and urges him to leave. This synopsis makes the episode sound altogether actional, and deep down it is as intensely dramatic as any other scene. But its language is amply lyrical. The entire dialogue of the newlyweds is organized around a system of imagery involving the polar oppositions of day and night, light and dark, and above all, their living symbols, the lark and the nightingale. The insistent repetition of these keywords, coupled with a host of sound echoes, creates the unmistakably lyrical tone of the episode and imposes on it a concentric form uncharacteristic of the fictional genres. The parity of the two participants is again ensured, as each of them is given three cues, though this time Juliet has twenty lines to speak as against Romeo's sixteen. Not only is the text again unrhymed apart from its two closing couplets, but it is also far too long for a sonnet, extending to as many as thirty-six lines. Generic inclusion/hybridization has obviously fully receded to make room for the much looser procedure of modulation.

This time no uncongenial external voice is allowed to interfere with the dialogue-of-one as long as it lasts. But the unity of the lovers within their lyrical encasement has become untenable, and they are compelled to yield to the dramatic pressures of outside reality. Romeo has not quite departed when Juliet's Nurse enters "hastily" to warn the bride of her mother's approach (37–40). The bridegroom cannot linger any more: the public world has reasserted itself and the tumultuous drive of drama has swept through the lyrical refuge of the protagonists.

The fourth example of a duologue isolated from the verbal action of the drama and forming a concentric lagoon detached from its kinetic flow comes in the opening scene of act 4, when Juliet visits Friar Laurence's cell to seek help against her father's matchmaking and runs into the latter's favorite suitor, who has come to arrange their impossible marriage. The poor girl cannot reveal before this stranger the truth of her position and resorts to cryptic paronomasia. Paris's every cue evinces from her an answer that tries not to destroy his assurance while retaining the possibility of a second, more truthful meaning at another level of her speech, thus emitting simultaneously two opposite messages, one to the count and another to herself, the Friar and all of us, who are in the know. The act of withdrawing from the realm of interpersonal communication in order to retain the true meaning primarily to herself is patently lyrical, and by practicing it in such tragic earnest Juliet anticipates the characteristic manner of Hamlet.

This episode is almost a parody of the first-encounter sonnet and even more so of Romeo and Juliet 's lyrical dialogue on the eve of their secret wedding (2.6). The parallel is striking, to the point of the friar intervening again just as he had done before. The new dialogue is almost equally enveloped in lexical repetition, harping chiefly on two keywords: "love" and "face" this time, but also weaving the repetition of "wife," "confess," "tears" and a host of sound echoes into a verbal texture that smacks of the lyrical. At the same time, it is almost the opposite of what the lyric stands for. Now we are witnessing anything but a "dialogue-of-one" in which "both meant, both spake the same." For one of the participants, the center of meaning to which her cues gravitate in reality is not that to which the other's cues tend. It is, in fact, shared not with her immediate interlocutor but rather with those who are allowed to overhear the conversation. And, interestingly, the duality of reference, on which figurative speech is by definition based, produces not poetic images but puns. The inner-orientated lyrical impulse operates in a markedly ironic context.

A different kind of parallel to the pre-wedding dialogue-of-one forms something like an epilogue in the last fifteen lines of the play (5.3.295–309). The lyrical protagonists of this love tragedy are dead now and, ironically enough, their bellicose fathers come together cheek by jowl to repeat the amorous dance of their children's first encounter. Just as Romeo and Juliet had touched each other's hands worshipfully to mark the beginning of their inseparable union, so Montague and Capulet now leave their swords aside and shake hands over the dead bodies of the lovers to put an end to the age-old destructive conflict of the two families. The gesture of peace and love has passed from the young generation to the old and has finally replaced the gestures of war and violence. At last the two enemies both mean and speak the same, just as once their children had done. Of course, the lyrical temperature of this dialogue is considerably lower than that of the lovers' shared sonnet, but it is there. The polysemy of "give" and "rich" provides the links between the speeches of the two nobles, allowing them to merge into a single voice almost in the way their children's speeches had done. And their dialogue ends with the metaphor of "sacrifices," returning to the language of religious solemnity that had enveloped the lyrical exchange of the young and provided the building material for their hermitage.

The public world of vigorous dramatic action, comprised of an endless series of thrusts and counterthrusts, has come to a point of thoughtful rest, the immobile stance of lyric. Far from being punctured by the onslaught of death, for one beautiful moment in the wake of the tragic catastrophe, the lyric bubble has expanded to embrace the entire public world. Even the Prince of Verona, its highest representative, enters this privileged space by concluding the exchange between Montague and Capulet, very much in the way Friar

Laurence had done earlier. The Prince's contribution is, unsurprisingly, rhetorical, opening up the finale of the play to the public space once again—even this last lyrical lagoon is not left untouched by the ongoing rush of drama. Incidentally, the actional drive pierces it through from beginning to end, just as it did the earlier ones. Only, this time the drive is toward a final close, the reconciliation, the building of the monument, the administering of justice—a cycle coming to a tired end, conducive to contemplation rather than any further action.

Formally, this passage too is certainly not as neatly accomplished as the first-encounter sonnet. But, in its conspicuously unsteady, mangled way, it staggers painfully toward the unreachable height of that precedent. Capulet opens the exchange with the following cue:

> O brother Montague, give me thy hand.
> This is my daughter's jointure, for no more
> Can I demand.
>
> (295–97)

The first line is rhymed unexpectedly with the third, which comes to a precipitated, emotionally charged halt after its second foot. Montague cancels this sudden closure by completing the truncated pentameter and restoring the tonal balance of the utterance. Now he rearranges the stanzaic pattern by coupling the third line not with the first but with the second by means of an epistrophe ("But I can give thee more") instead of a rhyme, thus suggesting an absolute identity of meaning and speech between the two parties of the colloquy. The opening lines of the passage are, then, either three regular pentameters, comprised of an unrhymed one and a shared epiphoric couplet, or four cross-rhymed iambics of various lengths. In either case the prosodic irregularity undermines the drive toward formal unification. What ensues is a couple of unrhymed, though assonantally conjoined lines followed by two rhymed couplets, one spoken by each interlocutor as his final statement. And at this point the Prince adds his metrically impeccable sixain. The web of alliterations and assonances is perhaps not as thick as in the lyrically more intense passages, but there is the necessary modicum of such patterns, however subdued. One can hardly expect a tragedy to end with an upbeat epilogue. It conveys the feeling of defeat as well as enlightenment not only in its tone but in the hesitancy of its formal organization too.

To sum up, there is an obvious recurrence of isolated lyrically molded dialogues at the crucial moments of *Romeo and Juliet,* which not only in each separate case introduce intensely inward withdrawals from the hectic rush of events but also, in their totality, create a concentric structure over and above the linearly organized plot. In the midst of dramatic action such modules open up the dimension of psychological and philosophical depth without slowing down that action. It can in fact be argued that by bringing together the monologic and the dialogic principle they achieve a fusion of the lyric and the dramatic, enhancing the energy of the plot by illuminating its hidden meaningfulness.

The patterns of recurrence in *Romeo and Juliet* go far beyond the dialogue modules of the type discussed above to form a complex system of compositional and stylistic structures of the concentric kind, characteristic of thematic genres. Superimposed on the linear, kinetic structure of dramatic plot, they combine it with that of lyrical stasis.

One of these patterns is the frequent narrative replay of already completed episodes of dramatic action, which problematizes the plot's linearity. Benvolio is the main instrument of this doubling technique. In the first scene of the play he is called upon to explain to the vexed Prince why and how the servants of the two aristocratic houses flew into their ugly brawl disturbing the peace of Verona.[24] And, together with the local dignitaries, we in the audience are compelled to hear from him a summary of what has just happened in front of our eyes (1.1.104–13). When, a little later in the same scene, Romeo makes his first appearance, he asks Benvolio to tell him all about it and another repetition of the story is narrowly averted as the protagonist remembers that he has already heard enough about it.[25]

Moreover, in the first scene of act 3, Benvolio is obliged again to give the Prince an account of a much more serious fight, the series of duels between the offspring of Verona's nobility which have left two dead bodies—of Mercutio and Tybalt—lying in the city square and have opened the floodgates of the lovers' tragedy.[26] His speech at this point (154–77) is long and detailed, and once again its narrative summary brings us back to something we have just seen played out. Friar Laurence is even more profuse when, at the very end of the play, he has to report to the Prince about all the unfortunate turns of events that have littered the stage with corpses. His peroration (5.3.228–68) does shed some additional light on the cause-and-effect links between events, but in its totality it is a narrative repetition of previously represented action.

Another method of doubling plot elements is that of "rhyming" scenes or episodes, e.g. the initial servants' brawl as a prefigurement of the climactic aristocratic duels, or Juliet's two prewedding meetings in Friar Laurence's cell, first with Romeo at the end of act 2 and then with Paris at the beginning of act 4. Examples can be multiplied with such twinned events as Capulet's preparations for the two feasts, the one at which Juliet is destined to meet her true love and the other, meant to celebrate her marriage to Paris. Many commentators have noticed the associative mise-en-scène links between the crucial scenes of the tragedy: the lovers' first encounter at the feast, the balcony scene, the wedding-night scene and the catastrophe in the charnel house, especially between the last two, which reflect each other even in visual terms. Such echoes tend to transform imperceptibly kinetic structures into concentric ones.

The recurrence of symbolical gestures at crucial points of the action reinforces the same tendency. The part of joined hands in the lovers' shared-sonnet episode and in the reconciliation epilogue of the tragedy has already been discussed. It is no less pertinent that this love story starts with a ritualized exchange of kisses between the protagonists and ends with another one, though this second time the kisses cannot be shared. The Nurse's garrulous reminiscences about Juliet's childhood fall and her husband's bawdy joke: "Thou wilt fall backward when thou hast more wit" (1.3.42), readily accepted by the infant, seem to foreshadow both the wedding-night scene and what it eventually leads to, the heroine's mock deathbed turned real.

The last example brings us directly to dramatic ligatures transcending the compartmentalization of time and thus leading toward a kind of lyric "timelessness." These are not so often related to memories of the past as to premonitions of the future. Romeo opens the series on his way to the Capulets' feast and his first encounter with Juliet:

> ... my mind misgives
> Some consequence yet hanging in the stars
> Shall bitterly begin his fearful date
> With this night's revels, and expire the term

Of a despised life, clos'd in my breast,
By some vile forfeit of untimely death.

(1.4.106–11)

In the ensuing balcony scene, Juliet confesses that although she
rejoices in Romeo's presence she has "no joy of this contract tonight:/
It is too rash, too unadvis'd, too sudden" (2.2.117–18). And in their
parting after the wedding night she has a prophetic vision of how it
will all end, which stems from the very mise-en-scène of the episode.
In the dusk of the hateful dawn the bride peers from her high balcony at the departing bridegroom merging into the shadows of the
garden that had once been their locus amoenus, and her lover appears to her "As one dead in the bottom of a tomb" (3.5.56). Romeo
shares her premonition by reciprocating with a somber vision of her
paleness. Little do they know that their next meeting will be in a
tomb indeed and there will be very little blood in their cheeks.

The last act opens with a soliloquy in which Romeo shares with
us the prophetic dream he has seen during the night preceding the
catastrophe:

I dreamt my lady came and found me dead—
Strange dream that gives a dead man leave to think!—
And breath'd such life with kisses in my lips
That I reviv'd and was an emperor.

(5.1.6–9)

Is the protagonist deluded in embracing this vision as the promise of
a happy reunion, or is love indeed unsusceptible to death? However
that might be, Romeo is allowed to experience in summary fashion
what is still in store for him. And so are we, through his mediation.
The crucial event of the plot is preceded—as so often in the Elizabethan theater—by a kind of introductory masque—albeit in a related
dream—presenting its matter in a nutshell. The resulting form is
concentric rather than linear—a circle within a circle.

The circularity of plot construction is reinforced by some stylistic
devices of a similar kind. Sets of recurrent images impose their revolving pattern throughout the drama. Many of these are associated
with Juliet. When the heroine hears about her lover's banishment she
falls into a fit of despair and concludes the last of a series of passionate monologues with the following couplet:

Come, cords, come, Nurse, I'll to my wedding bed,
And death, not Romeo, take my maidenhead.

(3.2.136–37)

In a much more elaborated form, this image of death as a substitute bridegroom crops up once again in Capulet's wailing speech after Juliet's insensate body has been discovered in her chamber. He addresses Paris with these words:

O son, the night before thy wedding day
Hath Death lain with thy wife. There she lies,
Flower as she was, deflowered by him.
Death is my son-in-law, Death is my heir.
My daughter he hath wedded. I will die,
And leave him all: life, living, all is Death's.

(4.5.35–40)

And the same figure emerges for the third time in Romeo's dying soliloquy in the charnel house, when he exclaims:

Ah, dear Juliet,
Why art thou yet so fair? Shall I believe
That unsubstantial Death is amorous,
And that the lean abhorred monster keeps
Thee here in dark to be his paramour?

(5.3.101–5)

Another strain, interwoven with the death-paramour one, is that of the flowers, linking together Juliet and Paris. It is first used as a praise for the latter in a dialogue between Lady Capulet and the Nurse (1.3.77–78). Next, Juliet lying on her mock deathbed is likened to a flower by her devastated father (4.5.29, 37). And, lastly, the association of both characters with flowers is reasserted as we see Paris bedecking Juliet's prostrate body with the words: "Sweet flower, with flowers thy bridal bed I strew" (5.3.12). The image of the body-bark is first introduced by Capulet again in the bewailing scene in reference to his daughter (3.5.133–37). And then, at his last breath in the charnel house Romeo sees himself in much the same visual terms (5.3.116–18). The figure of the lightning appears three times at central moments: once in the balcony scene, to express Juliet's fear of the sudden eruption of their love (2.2.118–20); then in Benvolio's account of the fatal duels (3.1.174); and lastly, as an exhilarated foretaste of death in Romeo's final soliloquy (5.3.88–91).[27] Thus the lightning conceit strikes right through the heart of the love story, fusing joy into fear and death into life and highlighting the experience which makes these tragic oxymora possible.

One last pivotal example must be added to the list of recurrent figures that could be extended ad infinitum. This is the association of the lovers with birds, first introduced in the balcony scene as Juliet tries to prolong the happy tryst calling back her departing wooer:

> Hist! Romeo, hist! O for a falconer's voice
> To lure this tassel-gentle back again.
>
> (2.2.158–59)

Romeo replies along the same figurative lines: "My nyas" (line 167), after which Juliet plunges into a reverie in which she sees herself in the role of the falconer giving his bird only such modicum of freedom as can ensure his recovery with a "silken thread" and Romeo gladly agrees: "I would I were thy bird" (2.2.182). Three scenes later the Nurse refers to Juliet's own chamber as a bird's nest into which her secret bridegroom must be assisted to climb (2.5.75). And another five scenes later, on the eve of the clandestine wedding night in the same chamber, Lady Capulet elaborates on the same metaphor when she says to Paris: "Tonight she's mew'd up to her heaviness" (3.4.11). The association of the lovers with birds acquires a new striking dimension a minute later, as the symbolical presence of the lark and the nightingale in the Aubade seems to shape their fortunes.

A stylistic device related to lyrical repetition and so close to recurrent imagery as to be sometimes indistinguishable from it is the recurrence of key words, punctuating the entire play or large parts of it and foregrounding its central preoccupations. These lexical items—abstract and concrete nouns—acquire the status of symbols by virtue of their insistent repetition and form an intricate network of pointers to the drama's meaning. *Romeo and Juliet* abounds in keywords. Two of these—*love* and *death* together with their cognates—are clearly pervasive. They highlight the perennial "poemly" theme at the core of the Verona play. There is, however, a host of others, such as *day* and *night*, *light* and *dark*, *morning/ morn/ morrow*, *stars*, *blood*, *peace*, *kiss*, *tears*, *heart*, *hands*, *lips* and, notably, *banishment* in the second half of the drama, whose incidence is very high.

Repetitions on every structural level of the play—some more noticeable, others less extensive and dispersed but equally pervasive—reinforce the work's dianoic, thematic aspect. Their overall effect is the imposition of a concentric movement over the generically fundamental linear one and the subsequent problematization of dramatic time, which is so pivotal to the genre.

The "persistently lyrical tone" of *Romeo and Juliet* resides also in the formation, juxtaposition and operation of its characters and, above all, of the protagonists. As usual, they are not the ones who appear first on the stage. Only when the dust settles after the servants' noisy skirmish—and the groundlings' attention is diverted from their own probably no less noisy affairs—the time is ripe for the introduction of the central figures. Romeo's close association with the lyric mode is made clear as soon as we first hear his name. He is introduced to us in absentia, so that before we see the young hero we already know what to look for in him. Benvolio, the customary nuntius, obliges Lady Montague with a report about her son in the elegantly poetic manner of the Renaissance, picturing Romeo as the stereotypical melancholy lover wandering alone under the shade of the sycamore grove and shunning all company (1.1.116–22). Incidentally, Benvolio admits that he is himself suffering from the same amorous sickness and can well understand his cousin's condition (124–28). Romeo's father confirms his nephew's impressions as he adds further telling detail to this conventional portrait in the familiar style of Petrarchan sonneteering, blending the inner weather (tears and sighs) of the amorous persona with the elements, harping on the suggestive homophony of "sun" and "son," and drawing in allusions to classical mythology (129–40).

After this preparation, Romeo makes his first entrance on the stage. In Benvolio's sympathetic company he bewails his own lot as the victim of unrequited love. Yet, having made the conventional aphoristic expostulation—"Alas that love whose view is muffled still,/ Should without eyes see pathways to his will" (1.1.169–70),—he unexpectedly turns around to say in a totally different tone: "Where shall we dine?" (171). It is as if a mask has been shed for a minute. We hear a revealing aside from an absolutely normal flesh-and-blood lad, who may find it amusing to play the role of the melancholy lover, but nonetheless has to think about his stomach from time to time. At such moments, in spite of his self-isolation, he would not detest the company of other lusty fellows.[28]

Is the Petrarchan pose just that then—no more than a pose? The glimpse of that other Romeo is too brief to tell. And he returns to his assumed role with might and main to pour forth a cascade of oxymora of the kind so often met with in the sonnet sequences of the time:

> Why then, O brawling love, O loving hate,
> O anything of nothing first create!
> O heavy lightness, serious vanity,
> Misshapen chaos of well-seeming forms!
> Feather of lead, bright smoke, cold fire, sick health,
> Still-waking sleep, that is not what it is!
> This love feel I, that feel no love in this.
>
> (1.1.174–80)

The basis on which this whimsical construction is erected—the traces of the recent servants' brawl—has so little to do with it that one cannot but be puzzled by the nothingness at the heart of this torrent of mismatched words.[29] Romeo seems to be conscious of its absurdity, as he stops suddenly with the question: "Dost thou not laugh?" (181). But Benvolio, being, as we know, in a similar plight, is brought to tears rather than guffaws by what he feels is the voicing of his cousin's "good heart's oppression" (182). The meeting of the two lovers augments their melancholy to a point at which Romeo's poetic frenzy runs uncontrolled to produce another eruption of such figures molded on familiar conceits but mixing them in an impossible cocktail:

> Love is a smoke made with the fume of sighs;
> Being purg'd, a fire sparkling in lovers' eyes;
> Being vex'd, a sea nourish'd with lovers' tears;
> What is it else? A madness most discreet,
> A choking gall, and a preserving sweet.
>
> (188–92)

And, once again, a momentary sanity peeps out of this verbal madness when the protagonist turns round to warn his cosufferer:

Tut, I have lost myself, I am not here.
This is not Romeo, he's some other where.

(195–96)

The overall impression Romeo produces in the early parts of the play is of a young man who has donned the role of the languishing inamorato as constructed by the *fin amour* tradition and whose real normal self can only occasionally be discerned behind this mask. The role is linguistically substantiated with the resources of contemporary lyrical poetry.

At his cousin's request, the hero ventures to describe his beloved as the conventional Petrarchan mistress—beautiful, chaste and unattainable. Gradually, his speech becomes more and more excited, flowing from blank verse into rhyming couplets. Now Benvolio offers him a cure from the pains of love that Dante in *Vita Nuova* and Sidney in *Astrophel and Stella* have tried out with little success: he suggests that Romeo should turn to other beauties, who might make him forget his ruthless mistress. Though the advice is rejected offhand, Benvolio keeps returning to it through the next scenes and, ironically, it proves the wonder drug that does the trick. This dramatic development can be interpreted as undermining the lyrical overlay, but, as we will soon see, it only disrupts a compromised hackneyed type of lyricism in order to replace it with "the real thing."

Juliet's first appearance falls to scene 3, where we get a more striking picture of her in her infancy as presented by the Nurse's wordy reminiscences than from her actual dramatic presence. This presence is minimal and only speaks of a placid young girl whose life is stage-managed by her elders. There is not the slightest infusion of lyric here. The heroine seems to inhabit a purely dramatic world, in which the present moment is no more than the neck of a sandglass through which the future flows freely into the past.

At the climactic moment of the lovers' first encounter in the whirlpool of the feast, the young Montague is so stunned by Juliet's beauty as not only to forget his past infatuation, but also to rise from poetic imitation to genuine inspiration. The genre he employs for self-expression is, as before, that of epideictic lyric poetry. But the conventional courtly compliment, based on the association of the mistress with precious stones and metals and the luminaries of the sky, has been so naturally rooted in the scene, with its sparkling nocturnal festival, and so imaginatively transmuted into an individual vision that it cannot fail to stamp itself on our minds as the palpable objective correlate of what it feels like to fall in love at first sight:

> O, she doth teach the torches to burn bright.
> It seems she hangs upon the cheek of night
> As a rich jewel in an Ethiop's ear—
> Beauty too rich for use, for earth too dear.
>
> (1.5.43–46)

These enthusiastic lines effectively marry the tropic opsis to the melos of the rhymes, the balanced alliteration and assonance (teach-torches, burn-bright, seems-cheek, jewel-beauty-use) and the repetition of "rich." Nothing is mechanical and imitative. And everything is rooted in the current setting. Wolfgang Clemen generalizes about the special effect of figurative expression in *Romeo and Juliet:* "Shakespeare does not simply abandon the language of conceit or the use of artificial and highly elaborated imagery. The change lies rather in the different impression these passages make on us. For they strike us as being more natural, more spontaneous. And this is due to their being more closely adapted to the situation and the moment."[30]

Romeo's ten-line speech has the unmistakable sound of a self-addressed lyrical soliloquy, although it is apparently overheard by Tybalt, for he exclaims directly after its completion: "This by his voice should be a Montague" (53). Not only does this striking poetic outburst signal the inception of the drama, but it also marks Romeo's sudden transformation from an adolescent aping the courtly lover into a grown-up who can let his own heart speak without unnecessary promptings. The lyrically modulated dramatic text is used subtly to mold both plot and character development. And, of course, it sheds its inimitable light on the setting, from which it has sprung up.

Calderwood ingeniously links the Verona play with *Love's Labour's Lost,* pointing out that "Romeo comes to Juliet not merely from the streets of Verona and the house of Montague but from the shallows of Petrarchan love dotage as well, since he begins this play as Berowne ended his, an unrequited wooer of 'Rosaline' (who is appropriately no more than a 'name' in *Romeo and Juliet*)."[31] But, surely, Berowne at the end of his play is, to some extent at least, a reformed mature person, for he has, notwithstanding some later lapses, disowned all "Taffeta phrases, silken terms precise,/ Three-piled hyperboles, spruce affectation,/ Figures pedantical," etc., and Romeo, when we first meet him, is still very much under the spell of these "summer flies." But he grows out of the habit much sooner than Berowne had done, for the moment of truth for him comes not at the end of the action but at its beginning.

It is true though that "like Berowne, who prematurely thought himself cured of the Petrarchan style, Romeo still has 'a trick/ Of the old rage.'"[32] On his initiative, even the first-encounter sonnet—the crowning part of the inception—is couched in the clichés of amorous worship. There is something comical in the hero's tackling of the convention "like to a bold sharp sophister."[33] Quite like the love-novice of Marlowe's *Hero and Leander*, to which Shakespeare's tragedy owes so much, he tries on Juliet argument after needless argument, "wherewith she yielded, that was won before." But by entering this superfluous role, he reveals once again his true nature as a young lad "with love unacquainted," trying to cope as best he can with the exigencies of an entirely new experience.

What takes us by surprise is that the hitherto docile Juliet proves Romeo's equal, if not his better, in this delightful contest of wit "full of conceits and quibbles."[34] Yet her speech remains largely untouched by the conventional courtly discourse. As soon as Romeo is gone and his identity is revealed to her, she bursts into a string of oxymora, which, however, are very different from his:

My only love sprung from my only hate.
Too early seen unknown, and known too late.
Prodigious birth of love it is to me
That I must love a loathed enemy.

(1.5.137–40)

There is not the slightest trace of imitativeness and pretension in this lyrical explosion, in which the rhetorical forms do not precede the speaker's agitation but crystallize as they issue from it. Whereas Romeo's paradoxical figures derive from a literary rhetorical tradition, Juliet's spring from the dramatic action itself—the line is drawn between conventional and genuine lyrical expressions.

The next crucial episode, the balcony scene, as noted above, was singled out by T. S. Eliot as a particularly impressive achievement in bringing together the two orders of organization in poetic drama, the dramatic and the melic, in the early phase of Shakespeare's career.[35] It opens with nearly fifty lines of soliloquies uttered in alternation by the two protagonists. Juliet speaks from her balcony and can be clearly seen and heard by Romeo, hidden in the shadows of the garden below until he chooses to come out in the open and start a real dialogue. The series begins with Romeo's long speech spun out of Petrarchan compliments: Juliet is the bright sun, the moon's maid and, finally, an angel. On this canvas the lover embroiders a few fairly original conceits, which give his utterance a measure of individuality, enhancing its lyrical verve. He first notices the light issuing from Juliet's window and metaphorically identifies it with the dawn. Juliet must therefore rise to lighten the world. Thus the mistress-sun cliché is granted new life as, derived from the scene, it is felt to be inseparable from its setting and its action. The method is sustained in the next lines, as Romeo observes that Juliet's gaze is directed to the night sky, and "Two of the fairest stars in all the heaven,/ Having some business, do entreat her eyes/ To twinkle in their spheres till they return" (2.2.15–17). The ingenious continuation of the conceit is related to the Petrarchan superiority tropes, but the hero's skills in the style of courtly preciosity are no longer imitative or negligible. And lastly, Juliet, still in her nightgown as a "creatura bella bianco vestita," appears high above her wooer's head as nothing less than a "bright angel."[36] His own position in the lower sublunary world is that of the ecstatic mortal graced with a mystical vision, who falls back in a trance to gaze on the "winged messenger of heaven" with "white-upturned wondering eyes" (28–29).

Romeo's entire speech (2–32) is undeniably lyrical. His figurative material is drawn from the Petrarchan stock-in-trade, but his artistic method is a mixture of two very different individualizing tendencies: one, toward fanciful weaving of familiar images into intricate precious conceits, and another, toward the rooting of these images in the visual reality of the dramatic scene, so that they can receive nourishment from it and grow in unexpectedly evocative ways.[37] Juliet's voice in her ensuing soliloquy of comparable length (33–49) is no less lyrical, but it is markedly different from his. To start with, her topic is not conventional: instead of elaborating on one of the established themes of courtly love poetry, she straightaway addresses the problem that this particular love affair faces, namely, its context of accumulated social prejudice. So, instead of playing with poetic clichés, she grapples with actuality. From this emotional engagement, it turns out, there can be born a lyrical force that needs no borrowed poetic robes. Her theme is Romeo's name (his socially defined personality) as the chief obstacle for their relationship. There is, she feels, a substantial reality beneath the insubstantial veil of names and words. Out of this topic Juliet weaves highly intellectual poetry bodied forth in striking images, some of which have become catchphrases of universal symbolism, substantiating Sidney's claim that "the poet is indeed the right popular philosopher":[38]

> That which we call a rose
> By any other word would smell as sweet . . .
>
> (43–44)

The lyrical force of both longer soliloquies in this initial phase of the scene resides not just in their opsis, but also, to a no lesser degree, in the melos constituted by the ring of their multiple questions, exclamations, apostrophes, climaxes, repetitions of keywords and phonetic resonances. The resulting tone is that of a spontaneous utterance delivered under the impact of immediate emotional experience, and although both speeches are thematically focused, the evolving dramatic action affects their flow so strongly that they do not strike us as a total withdrawal from it.

The second part of the scene (starting at line 49), which is nearly three times as long as the first, is interactive, made up of actual dialogue. The voices of the lovers are now even more sharply contrasted, as Juliet's mind is intent on the starkly practical problems she has already broached and will not be deflected from their urgency into any lyrical abstraction, while Romeo continues to wander in the nebulous regions of Petrarchism. Now Juliet is aware of her lover's presence and is eager to find out how and why he has got into the garden, considering how high its wall is, and how dangerous it is for him to be there. Romeo's answer belongs to an entirely different kind of discourse, or perhaps nondiscourse:

> With love's light wings did I o'erperch these walls,
> For stony limits cannot hold love out,
> And what love can do, that dares love attempt:
> Therefore thy kinsmen are no stop to me.
>
> (66–69)

The emphatic repetition of "love" and the dense alliterative patterning (with-wings-walls, love-light-limits) form a subtle, though unoriginal, lyrical vein. Juliet is truly concerned about her lover's safety—and

Tybalt's threats at the feast show that she is not inventing hazards: "If they do see thee, they will murder thee" (line 70). Romeo's reply now is even wider of the mark:

> Alack, there lies more peril in thine eye
> Than twenty of their swords. Look thou but sweet,
> And I am proof against their enmity.
>
> (71–73)

The implacable eyes of sonnet mistresses are supposedly capable of killing poor sonnet lovers, but is there the slightest trace of this poetic construct in Juliet's person? As referred to her, the cliché is absurd. Nonetheless, Romeo adheres to the same jargon throughout. The lover's attachment to the Petrarchan form of lyricism reflects on his character in a mildly ironic way, revealing his youthful inexperience of the kind Marlowe finds in his Leander and Shakespeare in the Navarre academicians. Juliet's behavior is worlds apart from that of the coy sonnet lady. Her refusal to tune herself in to Romeo's sonnet discourse, indicative of her greater realism, shows her concern for his safety. But one thing her speech cannot be called is prosaic. It can indeed soar high up in regions of genuine lyrical expression, combining the exciting emergence of fresh tropes with the infectious rhythms of heartfelt enthusiasm and the rich phonetic echoes of rhymes, alliterations, assonances and anaphoras as, for instance, in the following lines:

> My bounty is as boundless as the sea,
> My love as deep: the more I give to thee
> The more I have, for both are infinite.
>
> (133–35)

But then she switches back to the starkly actional matter of their marriage arrangements, only to fly once again into the lyrical vision, in which she is the falconer and her lover the captive bird. Romeo, on his part, makes his exit with four rhymed couplets (186–93), similarly switching from the lyrical to the dramatic mode as a transition to the next scene, in which he visits Friar Laurence to plan the wedding.

The protagonist relates his love story to the friar in the recognizable accents of poetic jargon. The gist of his speech is the conventional representation of the lovers as enemies waging an allegorical war (though in this case there is a literal dimension to the figure).

The "holy father" is nonplussed by his visitor's figurative locution:

> Be plain, good son, and homely in thy drift;
> Riddling confession finds but riddling shrift.

(2.3.51–52)

This is the kind of request for a dramatically relevant translation of lyrical metaphoricity, repeatedly encountered in our analysis of *Love's Labour's Lost*.[39] Romeo is quick to provide the gloss:

> Then plainly know my heart's dear love is set
> On the fair daughter of rich Capulet.
> As mine on hers, so hers is set on mine,
> And all combin'd save what thou must combine
> By holy marriage.

(53–57)

The adroitness with which Romeo changes his style reminds us once again that he has donned the Petrarchan cloak for fashion's sake rather than out of inner compulsion. In spite of the regenerating experience of requited love, the trick of the old Navarre rage is still with him.

In the beginning of 2.4, Mercutio returns after his first appearance in 1.4, when he had engaged Romeo in a punning match, apparently a customary pastime of the two friends. Though at that point the abject lover continued to harp on his sad plight of the dejected inamorato, under the Petrarchan affectation we could glimpse the agile mind of a zesty young man, which had not at all been "sicklied o'er with the pale cast of thought." In that exhilarating contest of wit between the two friends, Romeo struck us as much more authentic than in his usual emulation of a poetic vogue. Now Mercutio challenges him again by presenting him ironically as the archetypal lover and draws him into another punning bout. Romeo quickly forgets his lyrical role and rises to the occasion, making Mercutio exclaim with delight: "Now art thou sociable, now art thou Romeo; now art thou what thou art, by art as well as by nature" (2.4.89–90).

This is, of course, no more than another momentary resumption of the young man's old self. When the Nurse appears as Juliet's messenger, Romeo resumes at once his quasi-lyrical parlance:

> Within this hour my man shall be with thee,
> And bring thee cords made like a tackled stair,

Which to the high topgallant of my joy
Must be my convoy in the secret night.

(184–87)

Although his speech is basically actional, it transforms the mundane count of time into an image of timeless bliss by fusing the separate compartments of actual experience into an integral imaginative space impervious to change and decay. The material cords, obtained for the practical purpose of scaling Juliet's balcony, are transmuted into a dreamy miraculous apparatus of happiness. Drama is imperceptibly sublimated into lyric.

Scene 5 takes us back to the heroine with a soliloquy expressing her wish to speed up time until the Nurse's return (1–17). Although it keeps grappling with the passage of time and is intent on the niceties of dramatic action, this speech, with its strong emotional commitment showing in its excited rhythm, is undeniably lyrical. Juliet does not shun overused figures like Venus and Cupid, but instead of serving the common purpose of elegant decoration, they now give vent to her anxious impatience. As the Nurse's sluggishness is the particular cause of the speaker's distress at the moment, the closing, much less ethereal image of the soliloquy is focused on this topic:

Had she affections and warm youthful blood
She would be as swift in motion as a ball:
My words would bandy her to my sweet love,
And his to me.

(12–15)

This Donnean tennis conceit is as original as can be. The *b* alliteration, punctuating the passage (blood-ball-bandy), bounces through it like a ball indeed. The final return "to me" quickens the movement and completes it with the suddenness of a line ending on its second foot.

Act 2 is wound up with the lyrical dialogue of the protagonists in Friar Laurence's cell. After the highly dramatic opening of act 3, with the fatal duels in the city square and Romeo's subsequent banishment, the action recedes into Juliet's private space. The second scene is taken up by a series of her intensely passionate lyrical soliloquies. In a famous long speech she once again expresses her wish to speed up time and thus shorten the interval of her lover's absence before the wedding night:

> Gallop apace, you fiery-footed steeds,
> toward Phoebus' lodging . . .
>
> (3.2.1–2)

This initial apostrophe, with its reversal of a clearly recognizable Mar-
lovian/Ovidian line, sets the tone of the soliloquy, which is punctuated by five more apostrophes to the eagerly anticipated night and
to Romeo, giving it an extremely agitated sound.[40] The imperatives
denoting vigorous action (gallop, leap, come-come-come, give, take)
coupled with adverbs of urgency (apace, immediately) contribute to
its conjuring power. The speech is also studded with poetic images
of increasing freshness and beauty: from the opening mythological
allusion through a personification of night to an enthusiastic eulogy of Romeo, in which Juliet seems to respond to a memorable
figure marking his first impression of her at the fatal feast ("So shows
a snowy dove trooping with crows/ As yonder lady o'er her fellows
shows" (1.5.47–48). She sees him in the terms of the same contrast
between white and black, light and dark, day and night, so central to
the visual symbolism of the play:

> Come night, come Romeo, come thou day in night,
> For thou wilt lie upon the wings of night
> Whiter than new snow upon a raven's back.
>
> (3.2.17–19)

If we set the two bird similes side by side, Juliet's one will probably
surpass Romeo's in its organicity and originality. But this is just the
beginning—her really impressive lyrical feat comes in the next few
lines:

> Come gentle night, come loving black-browed night,
> Give me my Romeo; and when I shall die
> Take him and cut him out in little stars,
> And he will make the face of heaven so fine
> That all the world will be in love with night,
> And pay no worship to the garish sun.
>
> (20–25)

Now she has risen to that height of poetic inspiration and aesthetic
accomplishment that her lover attained earlier with the vision of the
"rich jewel in an Ethiop's ear." But very soon Juliet's imagery takes one

final turn, as she leaves the courtly tradition behind and plunges into another, much more authentically experiential element, reminiscent of the minute observations of country life in Hiems's closing song at the end of *Love's Labour's Lost*:

> . . . So tedious is this day
> As is the night before some festival
> To an impatient child that hath new robes
> And may not wear them.
>
> (28–31)

This rings so true, especially if we remember that she herself is still almost a child.[41] The descent from the exquisite realm of precious poetry to psychological realism can produce a mildly bathetic effect. What follows directly after it, however, is a much sharper drop at the interface of lyric and drama. After so many excited apostrophes— "come night," "come Romeo"—Juliet exclaims: "O, here comes my Nurse." (31)

The confused and confusing report of the fatal duel delivered by this messenger throws Juliet into a turmoil of emotions—grief, fear, anger, love, repentance—that find expression in a string of shorter but no less passionate soliloquies. She departs from the dialogue with the Nurse into a torrent of poetic imagery, apostrophes, troubled questions and exclamations. Unable to reconcile in her heart the love she feels for Romeo and the astonished indignation at the murder of her cousin, Juliet bursts into a new storm of oxymora:

> O serpent heart hid with a flowering face.
> Did ever dragon keep so fair a cave?
> Beautiful tyrant, fiend angelical,
> Dove-feather'd raven, wolvish-ravening lamb!
> Despised substance of divinest show!
> Just opposite of what thou justly seem'st
> A damned saint, an honourable villain!
>
> (73–79)

There is nothing derivative in these contraries: unlike Romeo's earlier series, they spring up from a dramatically substantiated experience whose authenticity is unquestionable and their lyrical impact is strong.[42]

The heroine's last soliloquies revolve around the newly introduced keyword "banished"/ "banishment" and concentrate on the amazing power words can wield in people's lives. In a richly lyrical, thematically concentric way, this speech deals not with the self-reflexive way in which language accumulates power in a lyrical utterance but with its perlocutionary, action-generating potential in dramatic reality. The shattering force of this revelation brings Juliet to an impressive poetic conclusion:

> There is no end, no limit, measure, bound,
> In that word's death. No words can that woe sound.

(125–26)

Since the balcony scene, through the process of tragic personal experience, the heroine has matured to the realization that it would be naïve to ask: "What's in a name?" The world of fixed names and tyrannous words is the space of public affairs that encompasses the private one of the lovers and that cannot be shrugged off with a mere lyrical gesture—for this is the world of drama. Words in it can be as substantial as material reality and capable of controlling it.

Juliet's serial soliloquies, which fill 3.2, anticipated from afar by some elements in Berowne's speeches, achieve a new kind of self-probing lyrical concentration, revealing a kind of inner drama as a reflection and a counterpart of the outer one. Far from hindering the action, these withdrawals into the recesses of the individual soul seem to further what is happening and enhance its momentum. The lyric, in spite of its static character, forms an integral part of its kinetic dramatic environment, as the latter permeates it from within and dynamizes it. This symbiosis will come to a head in *Hamlet*, with the establishment of the inimitably Shakespearean lyrodramatic soliloquy.

The next scene (3.3) is similarly full of Romeo's soliloquies. Again the keywords are "banished" and "banishment," coupled with "death" and "love." The tone is as intensely lyrical as that of Juliet's series, though the imagery is somewhat paler. It is noticeable, however, that the Petrarchan diction has been relinquished, and the hero's most striking conceit belongs to the class of those "mundane" observations verging on the prosaic that we first found in Hiems's song:

> . . . Heaven is here
> Where Juliet lives, and every cat and dog
> And little mouse, every unworthy thing,
> Live here in heaven and may look on her,

But Romeo may not. More validity,
More honourable state, more courtship lives
In carrion flies than Romeo. They may seize
On the white wonder of dear Juliet's hand
And steal immortal blessing from her lips,
Who, even in pure and vestal modesty
Still blush, as thinking their own kisses sin.
But Romeo may not, he is banished.
Flies may do this, but I from this must fly.
They are free men but I am banished.

                                                    (3.3.29–42)

This is a compact thematic piece, informed by genuine emotion and carefully structured in a repetitive pattern including an effective refrain. The only element that might be considered a vestige of the courtly poetic tradition, which Romeo emulated earlier in the play, is the bit about the blushing vestal lips of the beloved. And the speech ends with two overtly epigrammatic lines containing a pun on flies-fly and an ironical reversal of status, in which the flies usurp the speaker's position as a free citizen.

The wedding-night scene momentarily reunites the two solo voices of the protagonists in a harmonized duet. From this crucial point on almost until the end of the tragedy, they utter chiefly actional monologues related to the exigencies of the plot. There are, however, a few interesting exceptions. In her dialogue with Friar Laurence in 4.1, when the mock-death stratagem is conceived, Juliet makes an impassioned speech that retires into the recognizable domains of lyricism without breaking altogether away from the act of communication: "O, bid me leap, rather than marry Paris" (77–88). The breathless rhythm of this proleptic vision of being buried alive is rooted in a number of parallel constructions, starting with verbs in the imperative. The accumulation of morbid images is truly compelling. An even closer conjunction of the lyrical and the dramatic is effected at the point when Romeo arrives at the Capulets' tomb and endeavors to pry it open in order to join his bride in a final reunion:

Thou detestable maw, thou womb of death
Gorg'd with the dearest morsel of the earth,
Thus I enforce thy rotten jaws to open,
And in despite I'll cram thee with more food.

                                                    (5.3.45–48)

Actions and words go hand in hand here, the direct address to the tomb being as much a poetic apostrophe in the realm of imagination.[43] Romeo's attention is at once focused on Juliet in the charnel house, and he eulogizes her beauty as the source of light, just as he had done when he first set eyes on her in act 1. But his lyricism is very different now—there is no trace of the earlier courtly preciosity, no rich jewels, no suns and stars. Instead, Romeo employs the simplest possible image of a luminary that is not far removed from the circumstances in which he finds himself: the tomb is metaphorically turned into a lantern lit by Juliet's beauty.

The closing section of Romeo's last soliloquy once again fully integrates dramatic action and lyrical reflection as the speaker embraces and kisses his beloved and then drinks up the poison. There is little lyrical space left for Juliet when she wakes up only to find out that everything has gone astray and to kill herself in the interval between two intrusions. But there is enough time for a final image, with which she lyricizes the dramatic action while promoting it in the already established manner:

> Yea, noise? Then I'll be brief. O happy dagger.
> This is thy sheath. There rust, and let me die.
> *She stabs herself and falls.*
>
> (5. 3. 168–69)

Some generalizations can be made at this point. We have traced through the play an evolution in the two protagonists' way of expressing themselves. Romeo, who first appears in the borrowed linguistic terms of the Petrarchan poetic convention, attains a striking measure of originality when he falls in love for real and, under the pressure of authentic emotional experience, gradually disencumbers himself from his imitative rhetorical habits. Occasionally from the very beginning, in the relevant social context, we are allowed a glimpse of his youthful intelligence and nimble wit, which enliven his character and make the final blossoming of his individuality credible. Juliet's first appearance is rather unpromising in its blandness, but on experiencing the magic of love, she exhibits a powerful imagination closely associated with the realities of life. The quickness of her mind does not leave her behind Romeo at any point of repartee calling for linguistic ingenuity. Her more authentic bent seems to help cure her lover of his earlier affectations and enable him to find his real self.

Both characters become capable of combining resolute action with poetic vision. In the ever closer dramatic interaction between the protagonists, then, a complex but well-defined movement is clearly discernible: away from imitative to genuine and from conventional to individual lyrical expression, away from courtly/idealistic to down-to-earth aesthetics and, finally, away from a divorce between drama and lyric to their interaction.

Though at first Romeo and Juliet isolate themselves in an enclosed private space of lyrical reflection, they soon learn that their bubble is compelled again and again to admit the surrounding world of action. Yet, far from yielding to it, their poetic vision is infused into the action, thus bringing together the two generic principles. So, by modulating the drama at its very roots, the lovers endeavor to modify the public world.

As has already been noted, Romeo's father and Benvolio speak in a lyrical manner when they introduce the hero prior to his appearance on the stage. After the midpoint of the play, occasional lyrical outbursts from a variety of characters become more frequent. Two of these belong to Friar Laurence: his address to Romeo when the young man comes to him devastated after the fatal duel (3.3.1–3) and his attempt to contrive with Juliet her avoidance of a second marriage through the mock-death ruse (4.1.89–120). Old Capulet makes several contributions: first, in 3.5.126–38, expressing his sympathy for what he interprets as his daughter's grief for Tybalt's untimely death and elaborating on the body-bark allegory; second, in 4.5.28–29, constructing, on the discovery of her insensate body, the death-frost-on-flower figure followed by the death-bridegroom conceit in 35–40; and, third, in the charnel house (5.3.202–4), bringing forth yet another image, which, incidentally, she has used herself, that of the dagger "mis-sheathed in my daughter's bosom." In the latter two cases Capulet's poetic speeches have a sequel: a series of dirges in Juliet's chamber (4.5.41–64) from Paris, the mother and the Nurse, wound up by him again, plus a couple of figurative lines added by Lady Capulet at the tomb (5.3.205–6). Paris's contribution when he strews flowers over the Juliet-flower has already been discussed. And, finally, even the Prince descends from the lofty impersonality of his public stance to some brief spurts of lyricism before the lovers' dead bodies in 5.3.215–19 and 304–5. Interestingly, none of these speeches appears to suggest the existence of an important poetic aspect in the character of its speaker, though they all add to the strong lyrical coloring of the protagonists, for they are inspired by the lovers' romance.

Thus, the lyrical transformation of the play's public world by the forceful integration of the two lovers in it is at best only superficial. It does not impede in any significant way the dramatic impetus precipitating the ultimate destruction of the young. The epilogue with the vows of the heads of the two families in the charnel house, as already pointed out, can be considered as an echo of the first-encounter shared sonnet. Yet, on closer inspection it reveals a very different, publicly-rhetorical, nonlyrical character, resulting, inter alia, in much paler figurative language. The sense of relief that this tailpiece is meant to convey after the grim tragic catastrophe is consequently rather feeble.

In the perspective of our topic, two strongly idiosyncratic personages certainly merit more attention than most of the others: Mercutio and Juliet's Nurse. We have glanced at the former as a lover of wordplay. But what is his relation to the tragedy's lyricism? Does this strain permeate his character in greater depth than it does the others? Mercutio's most impressive textual moment is probably the Queen Mab aria (1.4.53–95) preceding the protagonists' first encounter. Rosalie Colie remarks that the speech deals with something irrelevant to the plot's action, yet proclaims it "fundamental to the theme of brilliant youthfulness and to the sociological setting of these glittering, imaginative, under-employed young men." She then goes on to say that it also draws our attention to another closely related interest of the play, that of "the wastefulness of foolish feud."[44] For it offers us a glimpse of Mercutio's rich imagination, and against this background his subsequent death acquires the dimensions of a tragic loss.

Francis Berry views the monologue as an inset arresting the hasty dramatic action and creating a hiatus in the play.[45] In it the actual flow of time is suspended, and we are immersed in the continuing present of all men's and women's dreams. The speech may at first sight appear quite irrelevant or even unnecessary. Yet Berry discerns in it several important functions. First of all, it provides a vital hinterland to the play—"remove it, and the picture consists purely of a foreground; limit *Romeo and Juliet* to its foreground and the play is limited—it becomes a period play, a late medieval Veronese tale, a perfected action, time-expired, local and dated, unrepeatable, a kind of *Aucassin and*

Nicolette" (10). So, Mercutio's monologue provides a larger meaning-fulness to what takes place in the dramatic action. Second, the relation between foreground and background is not unidirectional: "Mab is the cause of dreams, and dreams are the cause of the foreground action" (ibid.). Third, in principle at least, a voluntary inset can help "the audience's understanding of the character who narrates it" (76), and we certainly get to know Mercutio better after hearing his aria.

Structurally, then, the utterance is both detached from the action and interrelated with it. Stylistically, it is both satirical and self-revelatory, as Brian Gibbons suggests:

> The Queen Mab speech is a burlesque show, debunking a motley assembly of folk-tale figures, contemporary urban caricatures and jest-book types, proverbial rural superstitions, old wives' tales and ancient myth. It proceeds at an ever-increasing pace which makes dream-like changes and inconsistencies of scale seem absurdly abrupt, and fearful distortions only ridiculous. It consciously exhibits its own process of free association of ideas and words as further evidence of the crudely mechanical causes of fantasy, its spiritual nullity. Mercutio offers to caricature the working of the imagination, yet his speech displays his own real imaginative creativity, assembling under the pressure of excitement a fascinating rival to the objective everyday world. There is wit and vitality in his improvisation which belies the reductive argument.[46]

What we have here, then, is a medley of different generic features mostly gravitating toward the epigram or the verse satire but enveloped in a poetic vision of evocative power and spoken in an undeniable state of trance. While listening to such a speech, Drayton's praise of Marlowe's artistic abandon comes to mind:

> For that fine madness still he did retain
> Which rightly should possess a poet's brain.[47]

Mercutio's poetic disposition is indeed Marlovian rather than Petrarchan: it "attains its effects by something not unlike caricature."[48] And, like Marlowe's, Mercutio's propensities as a commentator of love are Ovidian, i.e. erotic, bawdy, subversive rather than platonically idealistic. But, like his again, they are not the less lyrical for that.

In our minds, Mercutio, as we have noted, is chiefly associated with wordplay. His punning can often be no more than a lighthearted pastime, but it can also rise to the profound earnestness of lyric, becoming its most organic form, as when Mercutio quips in an emotionally committed way on the word "grave," replying, on the threshold of death, to Romeo's soothing words about the size of his wound: "No, 'tis not so deep as a well, nor so wide as a church door, but 'tis enough, 'twill serve. Ask for me tomorrow and you shall find me a grave man." (3.1.97–99)

The Nurse is the other character concerned with the problem of locution. Her two missions as a messenger end in similarly incoherent reports that make sense to the speaker but not to Juliet, who is exasperated by their insusceptibility to interpretation. In the first case, when the woman returns from her meeting with Romeo, bringing news about the marriage arrangements (2.5), what we witness is in fact a teasing postponement of important and eagerly awaited information rather than a specifically linguistic problem. The second case, however, is entirely based on the ambiguity of the message. Here (3.2) the Nurse brings Juliet the rope that should help Romeo to climb up into her chamber on their wedding night. This task has been accomplished, but the Nurse's words throw the young bride into despair for the wrong reason. The two women have just been speaking about Romeo, when the old crone bursts into a wailing fit:

> Ah, weraday, he's dead, he's dead, he's dead!
> We are undone, lady, we are undone.
> Alack the day, he's gone, he's kill'd, he's dead.
>
> (37–39)

Of course, Juliet can only interpret these words as referring to her bridegroom and is crushed, though the person in question, we know, is Tybalt. The Nurse continues to express her grief and horror at what has happened in a series of emotional effusions deprived of any logical framework. The clarification, "Tybalt is gone and Romeo banished./ Romeo that kill'd him, he is banished," with which she should have begun, comes in the wake of this long and confused emotional exchange (69–70).

Some features of the Nurse's dialogue relate it to the lyric, and others do not. Her speech is, undeniably, "from the heart," and its impetus finds expression in characteristic stylistic devices: apostrophes, repetitions, parallel constructions, alliteration, etc. As happens in lyrical poetry, the utterances are logically discontinuous, fitful. They are generated by an extreme immersion into the self of the speaker, whose back is turned on the audience. This attitude privileges the expressive over the referential function of language and creates a kind of anti-discourse. What the speech lacks is a sufficient thematic organization and aesthetic compactness, or the necessary activation of the poetic function. As a result, the centrifugal force takes over and dissipates its energy. This kind of talk is the grotesque reverse of lyric.

The Nurse's first appearance on the stage in 1.3 leaves no doubt that she is a garrulous person given to endless repetitions of banal old stories and pieces of folk wisdom. Her logorrhoea cannot be checked by the joint efforts of the whole family of her masters. Later in the play we have more than one occasion to confirm this initial impression of her character. In spite of his condescending attitude to the Nurse, Mercutio is of much the same disposition. His Queen Mab speech sounds like a torrent of words and pictures of the mind that can continue to pour on and on. Note how the interlocutors of these two characters react to their compulsive speechifying in a markedly similar way:

LADY CAPULET. Enough of this. I pray thee, hold thy peace.
                                                        (1.3.49)

JULIET. And stint thou too, I pray thee, Nurse, say I.
                                                        (1.3.58)

ROMEO.   Peace, peace, Mercutio, peace.
      Thou talk'st of nothing.
                                                        (1.4.95–96)

Somewhat later, after the first unpromising meeting of the two chat-terers, Romeo will thus define his friend to the indignant woman: "A gentleman, Nurse, that loves to hear himself talk, and will speak more in a minute than he will stand to in a month" (2.4.144–46).

What brings both Mercutio and the Nurse close to the type of the lyrical persona is their infatuation with the possibility of express-ing themselves publicly, without paying too much attention to the benefit of the audience, and their reliance on the uses of language. What distances them from the lyrical type, on the other hand, is their diffuse, unfocused manner of speaking, the blatant lack of interest in the concentrated rendition of a single emotional experience, the insufficient probing into the hidden power of words. These defects are more characteristic of the Nurse than of Mercutio, for his imagination, as we have seen, can be quite rich and original, while hers seems to be nonexistent. Yet a certain vacuity does show from time to time at the very heart of his wordiness, and it puzzles and worries both his friends and himself.

It should not be concluded, however, that these two characters, whose importance for the play is second only to that of the protagonists, are introduced for no other reason but to provide, through the almost total liberation of language they stand for, a foil for the lyrical mode enveloping the latter. Their speeches, as many commentators of *Romeo and Juliet* have pointed out, create a good deal of the atmosphere of the play. It is this very linguistic abandon that forms the element from which the protagonists' revolt against the oppression of tradition can lift its beautiful lyrical head. The lyric soars high above this element but it cannot disown it completely.

Language and its uses are as central a concern in this play as they are in *Love's Labour's Lost*. We have already discussed the protagonists' questioning of the validity of names, their discovery about the unrelatedness of words to the ontological substances they are supposed to denote. A number of stylistic devices further probe into this preoccupation. Wordplay is, of course, among the chiefest. According to M. M. Mahood's research, "*Romeo and Juliet* is one of Shakespeare's most punning plays; even a really conservative count yields a hundred and seventy-five quibbles. [Shakespeare] knew what he was about in his wordplay, which is as functional here as in any of his later tragedies. It holds together the play's imagery in a rich pattern and gives an outlet to the tumultuous feelings of the central characters. By its proleptic second and third meanings it serves to sharpen the play's dramatic irony."[49] Some of these effects have been dealt with already. Their lyrical character is irrefutable.

Punning, however, is not invariably associated with lyric; as a matter of fact, at times it may be seen as diametrically opposed to it. Thus, in the matches of wit between Mercutio and Romeo there is not the slightest attempt at withdrawing into the depths of the self. These belong to a kind of sport resembling the quick alternation of action and counteraction in fencing or tennis. All that matters in them is the agility of mind expressed in the prolixity of unexpected verbal associations. Such games can be played in a friendly, sportsmanlike manner, in an atmosphere of mutual appreciation and admiration of skilful thrusts, as they are between the two friends; but they can also be viciously aggressive and nasty as in the servants' brawl in 1.1.1–60 or in Mercutio's mockery of the Nurse in 2.4.101–41. The force that propels such exchanges is not the centripetal one, characteristic of lyric's engagement with an emotionally charged theme, but wildly centrifugal, striving to spread out as far afield as possible along a chain of arbitrary verbal associations, without any concern for a common theme. And yet, all punning sprees—like the lyric incursions— help both in the creation of atmosphere and in character building. The effect of punning can be less gentle and thoughtful than that of lyric, less conducive to self-surrendering empathy, but often more vigorous and lively, challenging and stimulating. In this particular play it helps to explode the languid affectations of the conventionalized lyric and clear the way to a more genuine self-expression.

And then, all of a sudden, heated by an overwhelming passion, quibbling is miraculously transformed into the highest form of lyric expressiveness. Robert Evans draws our attention to this almost imperceptible transition: "Romeo's role begins with a word game in which he tries to score points against Benvolio, and later Mercutio, and virtually everything Romeo says up to the ball at the Capulets is part of the game. Even when he meets Juliet, they are playing word games, though not of course the same ones."[50] Not the same ones indeed! We are almost taken aback by the revelation that both the verbal scuffle between Romeo and his pals and the ensuing first encounter sonnet shared between him and Juliet could be treated under the same stylistic rubric.

One particular kind of paronomasia is worth discussing separately. The first to try it out is Romeo when, approached by Capulet's illiterate servant carrying the list of feast invitees with the question—"I pray, sir, can you read?"—he replies in his usual Petrarchan manner—"Ay, mine own fortune in my misery" (1.2.57–58). This answer—a foretaste of Hamlet's characteristic manner—is obviously quite beside the line of meaningful discourse as far as the servant is concerned, for Romeo has switched from the literal to a figurative meaning of the verb "read," and the actual addressee of his answer is none other but himself, the self-pitying lover. Such is the typical stance of the lyrical persona, producing antidiscourse by declining to speak to the audience. Juliet resorts to similar quibbling when, devastated by the news of the duel, she is promised by her unsuspecting mother that

Romeo will be tracked down in his exile and poisoned in revenge for Tybalt's murder. "Indeed," she agrees, "I never shall be satisfied/ With Romeo, till I behold him—dead—/ Is my poor heart so for a kinsman vex'd" (3.5.93–95). She manages to make the syntax equivocate for her: "I never shall be satisfied with Romeo, till I behold him" is her true meaning, but it has to be retained for her own satisfaction only; so she is obliged to reverse it completely by adding after a pause the fatal word "dead"; but then, as if afraid of its proleptic power, after another short pause she detaches it from the preceding sentence and makes it open a new, less ominous one—a connection that Lady Capulet is allowed to overlook. Thus Juliet's communication vacillates between two addressees, her mother and herself, sending at once two diametrically opposite messages and keeping the true meaning undivulged. In the next scene, as we know, she resorts to a similar double-talk again with Paris in Friar Laurence's cell. This method will become quite central to Shakespeare's later drama, in which lyric and irony are closely intertwined.

Other, more formal, features from the generic repertoire of lyric poetry, such as rhyming, are less prominent in *Romeo and Juliet* than in *Love's Labour's Lost*. This can be partly explained by the reduced number of unintegrated insets, but, much more importantly, by the fact that the dialogue is no longer patterned into stanzaic figures. Still, the old uses of rhyme recur, though more rarely. The difference is that now they are always dramatically functional. Formal language is usually marked by rhyming. Personages like the Prince or Friar Laurence tend to speak in rhyme, and so does the chief upholder of the feud tradition, Tybalt. At the feast in 1.5, when Capulet tries to assuage his anger at Romeo's intrusion by a well-balanced speech in blank verse, Tybalt insists on rhyming and, moreover, counters his uncle's prudent advice by hooking his own cue onto that of the older man. The effect of this trick, as we have seen in *Love's Labour's Lost,* is to claim the prerogative of the final statement, and it is perhaps this audacity as much as the impudence of his statement, "I'll not endure him," that makes the host explode: "He shall be endur'd./ What, goodman boy! I say he shall! Go to,/ Am I the master here or you? Go to" (75–77).

Another familiar use of rhyming is when it couples the ironic commentary of an eavesdropper to someone else's overheard cue.

Berowne was the master of this device in the earlier play; his successor, Romeo, practices it at least once, when, hiding from his friends
on the way to Juliet's garden, he hears Benvolio say—"Go then, for
'tis in vain/ To seek him here that means not to be found" (2.1.41–
42)—and as soon as they are gone he comes forward completing the
dramatically split couplet with the aphorism: "He jests at scars that
never felt a wound" (2.2.1), thus straddling the divide between two
scenes as well as between two separate discourses.

A preference for rhyming can on occasion show a playful mood
in a character as in the dramatic lead-up to the Queen Mab monologue, when Mercutio tries to involve Romeo in his game by insistently supplying rhymes to their dialogue but fails to trigger a similar
response (1.4.44–53). Characters in *Romeo and Juliet* are at least as
good at the game of impromptu versifying as are their predecessors
in *Love's Labour's Lost*. At the end of the first-encounter episode, after
learning who she has just fallen in love with, Juliet improvises the
already discussed "My only love sprung from my only hate" four-line
epigram (1.5.137–40).[51] When the Nurse exclaims—"What's this?
What's this?"—her answer is—"A rhyme I learn'd even now/ Of one
I danc'd withal" (141–42). So, this turns out to be the composition
of a character, not of the author. One wonders after this if the shared
sonnet itself was not meant to be received as an extempore creation
of the lovers, a perfect lyrical poem composed collectively on the spur
of the moment, a dramatic fact rather than just an element of form
imposed on the dialogue.

Some other uses of the rhyme appear to be quite novel. They are
to be found at the interface of verse and prose in azione parlata.
Thus, when the Nurse comes in to interrupt most prosaically the
aubade conclusion of the wedding-night episode, Juliet, as if unwilling to let the magic moment go, continues to attach rhymes to her
and Romeo's cues (3.5.40–43). A little earlier, when Romeo hears
about Mercutio's death, he declares:

> This day's black fate on mo days doth depend:
> This but begins the woe others must end.

> (3.1.121–22)

The aphoristic finality of rhymed couplets is frequently used to conclude an important speech or scene in Renaissance drama, and
Romeo's contribution is no exception to the rule. However, it has
added interest in the context of the entire crucial scene, whose

connotations Nicholas Brooke reveals in the following eloquent passage:

> It is not quite clear that Mercutio's last lines should be printed as verse: the imprint of metre within them is very faint, and they are far more obviously a continuation of his prose utterance. What is clear is that Romeo's lines have an undisturbed rhythm that is far more closely related to the verse in which he proceeds after Mercutio's exit. And this smooth obliviousness, the feebleness of "I thought all for the best," is shocking in its obtuseness. It is "not his fault" Mercutio died, yet he stands terribly reproved; reproved by prose. That is to say, the fanciful world of poetic romance which is fulfilled by a poetic death is reproved by a prosaic one; as poetry is apt to be reproved by life.[52]

A little too harsh though he may be in his censure of Romeo, Brooke makes a valuable observation about the play's use of the opposition of verse and prose to suggest the contrast between two apparently incompatible worlds, those of lyric and of drama, especially as he proceeds to a more general statement: "The whole play is challenged and redirected by this scene. The genre in which it is conceived is set sharply against a sense of actuality as Mercutio dies the way men do die—accidentally, irrelevantly, ridiculously, in a word, prosaically."[53]

The contrast between poetic verse and prosaic prose continues to emerge within the verse part of the text too, as shown above. The movement of *Romeo and Juliet*—like that of *Love's Labour's Lost* is from fanciful idealism to sober realism, yet to a realism that is capable of embracing a wider vision. The conquest of drama over lyric is coupled with the former's thorough lyricization—not by imposition, as in the earlier comedy, but by permeation from within, mainly through the construction of characters. On the surface of text, this process is marked by a gradual reduction of rhyme and its replacement by the freer and less explicitly lyrical prosodic form of blank verse.[54] Lyric has started seeping into the deeper layers of the play and is no longer so conspicuous on the surface.

RICHARD II

In a letter to the young John Gielgud commenting on the performing style of a production of *Richard II* in which he took part, Harley Granville-Barker insists that the verse organization of the text should not be blurred, for "It is a lyrical play."[55] Since Walter Pater's likening of its tonal unity to that of "a lyrical ballad, a lyric, a song, a single strain of music," this distinctive quality of Shakespeare's historical drama has become a commonplace.[56] Stanley Wells even grants it an exclusive status: "*Richard II* is the most purely lyrical of Shakespeare's histories—perhaps of all his plays—and the role of King Richard is the most lyrical among the tragic heroes."[57]

What is striking about this play on the formal level of text structuring is that it is entirely written in verse and that 19 percent of the sum total of its lines are rhymed, producing a few quatrains and sixains plus a large number of couplets. However, although Charles R. Forker maintains that rhyming in *Richard II* is most often dramatically functional, my impression is that its importance is lesser than in the previous two plays.[58] W. B. Piper has argued that in the episode of the clash between Mowbray and Bolingbroke in the King's presence in 1.1 the resistance of the two barons to the sovereign's control is reflected in the breakdown of the closed-couplet balance that the latter has endeavored to impose on the dialogue. Whereas Mowbray seems eventually to submit to Richard's mode of utterance, Piper contends, Bolingbroke continues to oppose it by enjambing his couplets in an energetic individualistic manner. But then Richard apparently recaptures the situation "by his reassertion of closed-couplet utterance after a brief lapse into blank verse." This demonstration of authority, according to the commentator, is hollow, and thus "Shakespeare's handling of the couplet throughout this passage . . . underscores the inadequacy of Richard as a king and the fragility of his rule."[59] I find Piper's interpretation a little forced. For one thing, Richard's couplets at the end of the episode are no less enjambed than Bolingbroke's, and, then, couplets in this scene, as well as everywhere in the play, are so frequently intermixed with blank verse within the same speech that it becomes very difficult to see them as an instrument of political order. John Baxter's elaboration on Piper's theory is even more extreme and less convincing, as he concludes that in 1.1 "Shakespeare is clearly using the couplet to work out an adjustment between the temper or tone of individual characters and the theme of political stability and order."[60]

While there does not seem to be any need or warrant for endowing the rhymed couplet with such fargoing ideological significances, neither should its occasional dramatic employments be overlooked. In several scenes we can detect techniques of the kind already tried out in Shakespeare's dramatic career. Thus, in 4.1.182–222, Richard insists most of the time on speaking in couplets, not so much in order to preserve political stability, I feel, as to indulge in poeticizing his dilemmas on the brink of abdication. And as Bolingbroke attempts to break his endless monologue by impatient single-line reminders about the business at hand, Richard loses no time in weakening the other's cues by making them part of his ongoing couplet series through involving them in the rhyming pattern. The jarring last one ("Are you contented to resign the crown?") is simply ignored and left dangling as almost impertinent. In the King's parting with the Queen (5.1.81–102), the unbroken rhymed couplets are initially shared between the two in stichomythic alternation, and their later longer cues are persistently linked with each other by the unbreakable bonds of rhyme until the very end of the dialogue, when the inevitable separation of the royal couple is emblematized by the separation of their final couplets. An interesting case is presented by the episode of Bolingbroke's reception of the flustered York family in 5.3.45–145. As soon as the Duchess enters the new king's presence, anxious to prevent her husband from denouncing their son, she starts rhyming on each of the others' cues, as if afraid to let their utterances acquire an impetus of their own and bring about irreparable destruction. And, finally, at the very end of the play (5.6.30–52), Bolingbroke is intent on muting Exton's unwelcome reminders of his heinous crime of the regicide by capping each of his cues with a rhymed line of his own, thus merging them in the flow of his solemn oration, sustained in unbroken heroic couplets.

These instances show that in *Richard II* Shakespeare continues to use the rhyme for dramatic purposes in ways familiar from his earlier plays. There is little reason to suspect that the couplet passages were borrowed from an older and more primitive drama, as some have suggested.[61] On the other hand, we can hardly speak of any important new development in the use of rhyme here. The author's interest in the suggestive possibilities of this feature of lyrical form has markedly waned. And, apart from the few instances of functional use quoted above, rhyming has generally become less noticeable, its chief contribution reduced to bolstering the overall symmetrical neatness of the composition and the dominant rhetorical tone of the speeches. Only infrequently, as will be shown, does rhyming signal the presence of lyric in *Richard II*. The case of more integral phonetic devices, such as alliteration and assonance, is, admittedly, rather different.

On deeper substantive levels of the text too, if we leaf through the first half of the play, we can find very little to support the claim of *Richard II*'s exceptional lyricism. That early section is almost entirely given to action, and if there is any reflective element here it is only occasional and does not belong to the protagonist. A sprinkling of poetic images can indeed be detected in the speeches of many characters, but the tenor of these speeches is chiefly actional or rhetorical, and the sparse intrusion of the opsis principle cannot change their essentially dramatic character. A case in point is Richard's intermittent medical conceit in his threatening oration in 1.1.153–57 ("Wrath-kindled gentlemen, be ruled by me").

The play's first sustained poetic image appears in the passionate monologue of the Duchess of Gloucester in 1.2, as she tries to incense John of Gaunt to seek revenge for her husband's murder. This extended figure is an interesting twinning of two parallel vehicles representing King Edward's seven sons as "seven vials of his sacred blood,/ Or seven fair branches springing from one root" (12–13). So deliberately neat and symmetrically balanced is the structure of the double simile that, in spite of the Duchess's undeniable agitation, it anchors the entire speech in the genre of rhetorical persuasion and does not for a moment suggest lyrical withdrawal into the inner recesses of the speaker's self. Pathos is what fills her oration to the brim.

Another noticeable outburst of emotionally charged figurative expression occurs in Mowbray's reaction to Richard's sentence of eternal banishment pronounced on him in the next scene. The speech is worth quoting in full:

> And now my tongue's use is to me no more
> Than an unstringed viol or a harp,
> Or like a cunning instrument cased up—
> Or, being open, put into his hands
> That knows no touch to tune the harmony.
> Within my mouth you have engaoled my tongue,
> Doubly portcullised with my teeth and lips,
> And dull unfeeling barren Ignorance
> Is made my gaoler to attend on me.
>
> (1. 3. 161–69)

This time two fairly elaborate consecutive images centered on the speaker's tongue as their tenor—the incapacitated musical instrument and the incarcerated prisoner—follow each other in quick succession. Both figures are quite original and, however rhetorical, evince the intense lyrical tone of a complaint not unlike those in some Old English elegies.

A few more examples could be adduced. A particularly intriguing one is supplied by Sir John Bushy in his attempt to console the apprehensive Queen in 2.2.14–27. His is actually a mixed conceit, comparing her tears to "perspectives" multiplying and augmenting the image of grief. Here the word "perspectives" is made to refer to: (1) the glass cut into a number of facets each producing a different reflection of the object observed; (2) the mannerist painting in which certain forms can be discerned only if looked at from a particular angle; (3) a magic crystal through which one could peer into the distance or the future. By compounding these disparate meanings of the word, Bushy seems to reinforce the Queen's misgivings while attempting to allay them. His—in more senses than one—optical exercise is in its own way a tour de force along the lines of metaphysical imagery, yet its mode is rhetorical rather than lyrical.

This accumulation in the opening section of the play of such carefully constructed and fairly intelligible, though unusually complicated and condensed, images—on the borderline between public oratory and lyrical withdrawal—sets the right tone for its protagonist's characteristic appearances in its advanced stages, as well as for the full development of the work as a distinctive example of Renaissance poetic drama.

Scene 4 of act 2 is very short and given wholly to a dialogue between the Earl of Salisbury and a Welsh Captain in a military camp in Wales expecting the King's return from his campaign in Ireland and sharing their fears about his fate. This is, in fact, a prologue to Richard's ensuing tragedy, and its locution is intensely lyrical. First the Captain offers a list of omens: the untimely withering of the bay leaves, the frightful meteors, the bloody moon, the confusion of social order—a cosmic turmoil that will accompany all unnatural events in Shakespeare's later tragedies. These references in themselves build up into a symbol of disaster. Then Salisbury mounts on them a heap of similes and metaphors issuing from his troubled imagination and prophesying the fall of his sovereign (18–24). The personal tone of his speech, the apostrophe to the absent King with the insistent repetition of the pronoun "thy," the parallel constructions strengthened by the anaphora, the passage to rhymed verse, the multiple alliterations—all these, coupled with the apocalyptic imagery, create the

tone and atmosphere of a lyrical utterance, though the banality of
the overall picture diminishes its individuality and spontaneity and
relates it to the clichés of didactic oratory.

Without any doubt, the most memorable passages in these early
sections of the play are associated with Gaunt's appearances, rising
to a majestic stance in 2.1. Not for nothing does the play open with
the name of this formidable aristocrat, uttered by the protagonist
himself. For a fairly long time, however, the old man is no more than
a make-peace between the monarch and his own rebellious son, as
well as a reluctant listener to the Duchess of Gloucester's seditious
incitation. These attitudes muffle his voice and compel us to wait for
the emergence of its truly characteristic accents. The pronouncement
of the harsh sentence of Bolingbroke's banishment is what triggers
his first outburst of poetic imagery encased in the finality of rhymed
couplets:

> My oil-dried lamp and time-bewasted light
> Shall be extinct with age and endless night.
> My inch of taper will be burnt and done,
> And blindfold Death not let me see my son.
> . . . .
> Thou canst help Time to furrow me with age,
> But stop no wrinkle in his pilgrimage;
> Thy word is current with him for my death,
> But dead, thy kingdom cannot buy my breath.
>
> (1.3.221–32)

This is still the distant rumbling of an approaching storm of passion, but the strong personal engagement is hard to miss. The impact
of the imagery is enhanced by the sturdiness of the meter, the determination of the end-stopped lines, the purposefulness of the syntactic
parallelism, the rhyming and the alliteration. So far it is all dialogue.
Gaunt has been speaking to Richard, and now he turns to his son to
advise him how to make the best of a bad bargain. His tone remains
the same. This lengthy speech of admonition culminates in a cluster
of figures amounting to an imaginative transformation of unpleasant
reality. Bolingbroke is advised to exchange his clear-sighted, matter-
of-fact attitude to the surrounding world with a dreamy, make-believe
vision that can ensure him peace of mind at the price of relinquishing all chances of mending his fortune through decisive action. What
Gaunt offers is, in fact, the substitution of the lyrical for the dramatic

stance, something that, as we will later see, is against Bolingbroke's nature and therefore utterly unacceptable to him.

The opening of act 2, however, brings the long-deferred thunder. The reconciliatory notes are erased from Gaunt's speech, and he seems to come into his own with the proclamation: "Methinks I am a prophet new inspired" (2.1.31). Although he is still in the midst of other people, the old man now soars to the heights of prophetic revelation that is not addressed to anybody in particular, not even to everybody who cares to listen, but that *has* to be articulated, because his soul needs to be delivered of the weight of what has long oppressed it. This is the necessary condition for the birth of lyric.

The prologue to the great monologue (2.1.5–16) is an essayistic rhymed piece about the impact of dying men's pronouncements on the living. Having completed his logical disquisition on the topic, Gaunt can now proceed to his last testament. This is a thirty-eight-line blank-verse speech, which contains some of Shakespeare's most forceful poetry. It opens with a series of adages (34–39) denouncing King Richard's rash reign, punctuated by vehement lexical and phonetic iteration, and then plunges into a eulogy of England as a nonpareil in order to end rather unexpectedly and anticlimactically with the observation that the realm has been leased out piecemeal by its king. This second section (40–60) of the monologue, comprising twenty-one lines, is a single periodic sentence, accumulating tremendous emotive power in the process of its gradual rise to supreme heights of idealism, only to drop suddenly into a realization of the factual situation and return from enthusiasm to ire. The emotional range is formidable, and the utterance is rhetorically as pregnant as the best passages of Shakespeare's dramatic poetry. The cascade of evocative imagery—at times hybridized in surprising ways by the compelling onward drive of the utterance—is underscored by the insistent rhythmic recurrence of the deictic "this," creating a sense of immediacy and urgency.[62] In addition, the oratorical effect is enhanced by an emphatic repetition of key words and an abundance of alliterative clusters. This central section of Gaunt's speech straddles the divide between rhetoric and lyric. It is amply persuasive and consciously endeavors to be so, yet it is propelled by a genuine passion, which seeks its clearest and most infectious expression. The third, and last, section is considerably shorter (61–68). It builds on the already formulated contrast between England's natural greatness and its deplorable diminution by a careless overlord, growing into a concise two-stage paradoxical scheme of a zeugma followed by a kind of chiasmus, in both cases ascending from the literal to the figurative plane and masterfully fusing the two. The rational impulse seems to have taken over and disciplined the emotion without extinguishing it. And then comes the antithetically balanced closing couple of lines, which, in spite of its epigrammatic neatness, gives vent to a sigh of desperation:

> Ah, would the scandal vanish with my life,
> How happy then were my ensuing death!
>
> (67–68)

The spontaneity of the lyric probes again and again through the premeditated medium of the rhetorical and marks this overtly public speech as born of a deep personal commitment.

On arriving with his retinue, Richard straightaway turns to his flustered uncle: "What comfort, man? How is't with aged Gaunt?" (72). The nobleman's reply is a monologue playing on the meaning of his name (73–83). The word "gaunt" occurs seven times in its eleven lines. A number of related key words, such as "old," "fast," "watch," "lean," "grave," and their derivatives also recur to provide the logical and emotional skeleton of the paronomastic utterance. Lexical iteration is coupled with insistent alliteration. The ensuing hostile dialogue between Richard and Gaunt passes through three more puns—on "name," "dying men–living men," and "ill." Gaunt manages to weave all these meanings into his main concern, thus making the punning game centripetal and closely related to a lyrical immersion in the hidden suggestive powers of language. His last contribution along these lines consists of two long monologues (93–115 and 124–38), containing extended conceits and skillfully structured by methodical lexical and phonetic repetition. Yet their relentless drumming on the second-person pronouns—thou, thee, thy—sounds like pointing an accusing finger at the hateful opponent. In the final analysis, what predominates throughout the entire exchange is not so much a thoughtful probing into words as a battle of words, a bout of rhetorical thrusts.

This becomes apparent by contrast when, in the next act, Richard, having heard of Bolingbroke's rebellion, returns from the war in Ireland to utter his first great monologue (3.2.4–26). It is, in fact, a soliloquy, in spite of the fairly crowded stage. The King expresses his emotional attachment to his country, so the speech can be meaning-fully compared to Gaunt's earlier oration. The difference is striking. To start with, while Gaunt speaks of England in the third person, as almost an object of essayistic cogitation, Richard addresses it directly as a human being. In contrast to his uncle's rhetorical admiration of the previous act, he projects an intimate relation that is soon concret-ized as that of "a long-parted mother with her child"(8). The initial address—"Dear earth, I do salute thee with my hand" (6)—sets the overall tone. Here, in a nutshell, we have it all: the mystical link be-tween the two, implied by the phrase "Dear earth," the prominence of the speaker's ego declared by the confident imposition of the pro-noun "I" right after the apostrophe, the highlighting of the king's anointed body through the placing of "my hand" in the cadence, and, finally, the close interweaving of first- and second-person pro-nouns that is going to pervade the whole, suggesting the inseparable unity of sovereign and country. Another significant difference be-tween Gaunt's and Richard's treatments of England is that while the former imagines it as, above all, a sum of artifacts symbolizing power and authority, the latter evokes its vital potential, calling upon it to raise against his enemy the natural forces of "spiders that suck up thy venom," "heavy-gaited toads," "stinging nettles" and lurking adders. It is a conjuring oration, seeking to mobilize the teeming life of the land for a decisive clash with the adversary.

The speech's strong impact is achieved by the urgency of the apostrophe, the string of emphatic monosyllabic actional verbs in the imperative mood and the accumulation of images reminiscent of the Old Testament. The melic component is less prominent: no lexical repetition, no rhymes, sparse alliteration. The speaker's rhe-torical skills are not on show. Instead, we are made conscious of his communion with his country, his total immersion in the emotional experience he is undergoing, and his obliviousness of any immediate audience. Only at the very end does Richard seem to wake up to the reality of his environment and try to ward off any possible derision for this "senseless conjuration." And even now, when addressing his actual interlocutors and not a poetically construed personification, he restates his belief in the existence and efficacy of the magic pow-ers he has been evoking (24–26). Thus the King carries the poetic vision of his lyrical dream over into the world of dramatic action, obliterating the boundary between the two spheres of experience.[63] Such transgression cannot but doom his further progress, for action requires clarity of sight and can only be baffled by the dreaminess of contemplation.

One final observation remains to be made about Richard's first quasi-soliloquy. It is about what John Gielgud has called "his constant egotism and self-posturing" and many other commentators have referred to as his "theatricality."[64] The protagonist of this play seems to observe carefully every gesture he makes, as well as every expression of his own face. The initial focus on his hand saluting his country recurs a little later in the context of a more elaborately sentimental self-representation:

> As a long-parted mother with her child
> Plays fondly with her tears and smiles in meeting,
> So weeping, smiling, greet I thee, my earth,
> And do thee favours with my royal hands...
>
> (8–11)

The histrionics of this stance, however, does not detract from the genuine vehemence of the feeling expressed in the speech. Theatricality only helps the speaker to lick this feeling into a communicable shape. Ritual reveals its latent poetic symbolism. The lyric impetus of the speech is undeniable and, though somewhat cheapened by ostentation, it is never reduced to a mere scholastic exercise, as was the case in Holofernes's exemplary versification.

If we set Richard's plea to his homeland side by side with Gaunt's earlier praise of England's glory, we cannot fail to notice how much more personal—to the point of absolute egotism indeed—Richard's monologue is. It has none of Gaunt's public pathos. And if it is impossible to decide whose passion is more powerful, the lyrical withdrawal from the actual world is definitely more strongly felt in Richard's words than in those of his uncle.[65] This withdrawal is emphasized impressively by his waking up to the presence of an onstage audience and turning from the lyrical apostrophe to a dramatic address, when Richard is still unable to shake off his engagement with the imaginary world he has constructed.

Alarmed by the King's departure from the exigencies of the political scene, the Bishop of Carlisle tries gently to alert him to reality and to remind him of the need for practical action. But Richard's response is another long monologue (36–62), which, though this time it does not retire from the immediate communicational act and remains fully rhetorical, continues to claim that the crisis will resolve itself in the metaphysical context of the sovereign's divine right. The larger part of the speech (36–53) is taken up by an epic simile, first introducing an elaborate vehicle and then offering the tenor in a manner resembling that in some of Spenser's *Amoretti* sonnets. What is presented in the vehicle section is the spurious power of criminals: they can appear quite frightful while on the rampage in the dark of the night, but are reduced to pitiful creatures as soon as the sun rises again and reveals their faces. Then follows the tenor section:

> So, when this thief, this traitor, Bolingbroke,
> Who all this while hath revelled in the night
> Whilst we were wand'ring with the Antipodes,
> Shall see us rising in our throne, the east,
> His treasons will sit blushing in his face,
> Not able to endure the sight of day,
> But self-affrighted tremble at his sin.
>
> (47–53)

This part of the monologue is a compact thematic unit, instinct with considerable pathos. Its symmetrical structure, the evocative imagery and the emphatic alliteration build up to a powerful climax. But it is largely a public oration with some lyrical overtones provoked by the speaker's heartfelt indignation. The remaining nine lines contain a succession of scattered images, amplifying the idea of the divine nature of royal power and its consequent invulnerability. Richard has returned to the public appearance, so typical of him in the first half of the play, yet the wealth of evocative poetic imagery marks off his speech as belonging to the later phase.

In the ensuing dialogue with Salisbury and Aumerle, the King continues to develop imaginatively the same idea of close identification with his country to the point of absorbing it in his personality and even in his physical being. Here is how he responds to a remark about his sudden paleness at the news of his troops' desertion:

> But now the blood of twenty thousand men
> Did triumph in my face, and they are fled;
> And till so much blood thither come again,
> Have I not reason to look pale and dead?
>
> (3.2.76–79)

This strongly emotional rhetorical question is structured as a quatrain to which a rhymed couplet is then appended to complete the cue formally as a sixain. Its lyrical quality is rooted in the excitedly spontaneous and yet thematically focused expression of a state of mind. When next Richard is reminded of his position, he skyrockets from the depths of dejection to the heights of confidence and resolution. His positive feelings, however, are again divorced from the practicalities of the situation at hand and enclosed in an inner reality. The cue opens with a lyrical self-apostrophe:

> Awake, thou coward Majesty, thou sleepest!
> Is not the King's name twenty thousand names?
> Arm, arm, my name! A puny subject strikes
> At thy great glory.

(84–87)

"What's in a name?" Juliet had asked. Her journey into lyricism took her from social surfaces to the essence of being, though later this progress became direly complicated. Richard's stance is less radical: as Lear will do later, he tends to essentialize the surface. Oddly enough, such an attitude is also capable of producing lyricism, as long as it is genuinely internal, unmotivated by practical considerations. But it inevitably returns to expedience in the last analysis. In this case, the King concludes his speech on a purely actional note: "I know my uncle York/ Hath power enough to serve our turn" (89–90)—a hope that proves delusive and will again take the protagonist from the dramatic back to the lyric, which is destined to become gradually his only true element, his asylum from the troubles of the actual world.

The decisive blow that jettisons Richard from the world of action into that of contemplation comes, interestingly, from a richly figurative speech delivered by a nuntius figure, Sir Stephen Scroop, describing the surge of Bolingbroke's formidable rebellion (3.2.104–20). This description is so vivid as to be, despite its fundamental impersonality, markedly lyrical. After a brief statement of purpose, the monologue falls into two well-defined sections. The first, shorter one (106–11) is an epic simile, which likens the uprising to a storm making the rivers flood the land. Within the vehicle are interwoven additional figurative strands, enriching its sensuous potential and reinforcing its evocative capacity: the rivers are *silver*, they *drown* their shores, and the whole picture is humanized by a telescoped simile: "As if the world were all dissolv'd in tears." The tenor is similarly interspersed with figurative touches:

> So high above his limits *swells the rage*
> Of Boligbroke, covering your *fearful* land
> With *hard bright steel and hearts harder than steel.*

A metaphor followed by a couple of metonyms and a simile (all highlighted by my added italics) work in conjunction with the syntactic parallelism, lexical repetition and alliteration in the closing line to seal up the cumulative poetic effect of the first section. The second, longer section (112–20), which decodes the tenor of the last image, grows into a climactic enumeration, representing the universality of the rebellion in lively glimpses of human types and enthused by the vigor of the common drive. The emotional momentum of this verbal picture is inescapable and its radical is a combination of the familiar melos and opsis principles lying at the basis of all lyrical utterances. Richard acknowledges the poetic impetus of Scroop's speech in his immediate comment: "Too well, too well, thou tell'st a tale so ill" (121). And then, having heard about the death of his loyal followers, he refuses to accept all further information from the world of dramatic reality, in order to plunge into another long self-absorbed monologue (144–77), fully focused on the "poemly theme" of death: "Let's talk of graves, of worms and epitaphs" (145). Notwithstanding the speaker's overt address to his interlocutors, repeated in the opening lines of each of its three sections, the speech evinces his retreat from interactive communication into the inner space of soliloquizing. Its introductory section (144–54) generates a number of scattered images, all leaning toward the central theme. Writing with tears in the dust, telling sad stories—a world of memories, dreams and fantasies, a life of contemplation and purposeless self-expression—must replace the hateful necessity of action. The topic Richard chooses for this meditation is "the death of kings," and thus he enters the central, climactic section of his monologue (155–70), built around one of the play's most striking emblematic images:

> . . . within the hollow crown
> That rounds the mortal temples of a king
> Keeps Death his court . . .

(160–62)

The closing, third section (171–77) foreshadows Lear's tragic real-ization that his hand "smells of mortality" and that kingship does not reside in the natural body of the prince. This illumination is rendered in the simplest possible way, but in its lexical concreteness and in its terse syntax it bears the unmistakable accents of lyrical self-expression:

> I live with bread like you, feel want,
> Taste grief, need friends. Subjected thus,
> How can you say to me, I am a king?

The thematic compactness of the monologue, informed as it is by a strong emotion bringing forth one memorable image after another, points forward to Hamlet's famous soliloquies. What makes it differ-ent from them is its relative immobility, the somewhat static quality of Richard's mind, its tendency to dwell on a topic with a concentra-tion that subjects the initial emotion to the ordering supremacy of reasoning, and thus at times brings the lyrical utterance to the brink of the essayistic. This self-contemplation often breeds sentimentalism. There is nothing in Richard's meditations that could suggest the rest-less interplay of emotion and thought characteristic of Hamlet's solilo-quies. Here the two elements are still in sufficient balance to create a self-contained thematic lagoon in the midst of the dramatic flow.

Carlisle's next intervention (178–85) tries once again to admon-ish the King that what he must do is act rather than succumb to daydreaming. As if to throw Richard's lyrical utterance into relief, Carlisle speaks in an extremely formal rhetorical manner, overload-ing his locution with lexical and phonetic repetitions (additionally highlighted in my quotation):

> **My** lord, wise **m**en ne'er sit and <u>**wail**</u> their **woes**,
> But **presently** **prev**ent the **ways** to <u>**wail**</u>.
> To <u>fear</u> the <u>foe</u>, since <u>fear</u> oppresseth <u>strength</u>,
> Gives in <u>your</u> weakness <u>strength</u> unto <u>your</u> <u>foe</u>,
> And so <u>your</u> folies <u>fight</u> against <u>yourself</u>.
> <u>Fear</u> and be slain—no worse can come to <u>fight</u>;
> And <u>fight</u> and <u>die</u> is <u>death</u> destroying **<u>Death,</u>**
> While <u>fearing</u> <u>dy</u>ing pays **<u>Death</u>** servile br<u>**eath**</u>.

This speech is charged with pathos to the bursting point, but as right after it Richard is apprised of York's apostasy, the bishop's advice falls on deaf ears. Here, at the midpoint of the play, the protagonist turns his course from external action to passive inwardness. Despite this change, he continues to pose as the sovereign, who can only be compared to universal symbols of power and magnificence. Earlier on he saw himself as the sun, whose rising in the east exposes the thieves of the night and reduces them to trembling naked sinners. In the next scene, on Bolingbroke's first rebellious approach to his stronghold, the sun-image returns in its association with the hero. This time it reflects the way in which his adversary sees him, some-what ironically, as Richard stands up on the castle's walls:

> See, see, King Richard doth himself appear,
> As doth the blushing discontented sun
> From out the fiery portal of the east,
> When he perceives the envious clouds are bent
> To dim his glory and to stain the track
> Of his bright passage to the Occident.

> (3.3.62–67)

It is as if Richard's poetic imagination throws its reflection on the others, and they see him in his own figurative terms, however criti-cally. York adds to Boligbroke's sun simile another, similarly supernal one:

> Yet looks he like a king. Behold, his eye,
> As bright as is the eagle's, lightens forth
> Controlling majesty. Alack, alack for woe
> That any harm should stain so fair a show!

> (68–71)

The last word of this wail is very apposite: the King's majesty, his customary public posture, is now no more than a show, yet a show to which he continues to cling, notwithstanding the already expressed realization of his common humanity. Even his genuinely lyrical ex-cursions are not free from this posturing. As we have seen, Richard has the rare ability to watch himself as if from aside and stage his appearance theatrically, even when he is obviously in the grip of a potent emotion.

Later in the same episode, enraged by Northumberland's disre-spectful attitude, the King produces an eruption of imagery, which seems to derive from his earlier poetic vision of the land and the sky pouring biblical vengeance on the miscreant to uphold the divine right of the anointed sovereign (85–90). The lyrical impetus in this interpersonal communication is not a whit feebler than that in its soliloquy-like precedent. Then, after a short actional exchange with Aumerle, the protagonist lapses into a series of self-absorbed monologues shared with this cousin of his, the person who now is closest to him, less as a comrade-in-arms than as a confidant. The first of these extensive speeches (133–41) expresses Richard's reluctance to accept the humiliating diminution of his stature. It is comprised of a number of exclamations, an apostrophe to God and another one to his own heart, ending with a bitter play on the verb *beat*. The lyrical mode is pervasive, foreshadowing at a distance Hamlet's self-searching.

On hearing of Bolingbroke's offensive arrogance, Richard utters a second, longer and more impressive speech (143–75), starting with the unanswerable questions: "What must the King do now? Must he submit?" However, instead of weighing the pros and cons of the dilemma, the protagonist takes resignation as a foregone conclusion and plunges into the fantasy of an exchange of all signs of sovereignty for the humble symbols of monastic retirement from political life. This section of the monologue is structured as a series of parallel anaphorical lines, each constituting an antithesis—an arrangement similar to that of sonnet 66:

> I'll give my jewels for a set of beads,
> My gorgeous palace for a hermitage,
> My gay apparel for an almsman's gown,
> My figured goblets for a dish of wood,
> My sceptre for a palmer's walking staff,
> My subjects for a pair of carved saints,
> And my large kingdom for a little grave . . .

> (147–53)

The extreme prominence of the first-person possessive pronoun both highlights the hero's characteristic egotism and strengthens the lyrical self-absorption of the speech. While the opsis is richly furnished with the concrete emblems of the two contrasted kinds of life, the melos relies on the prosodic cum syntactic parallelism and the phonetic effects of the anaphora and the alliteration.

As soon as Richard mentions the word *grave*, moreover, in relation to his own impending death, he is mesmerized by this compelling image and cannot resist the temptation to explore its inexhaustible "poemly" potentials, bringing into play more parts of the king's dual body:

> . . . A little, little grave, an obscure grave;
> Or I'll be buried in the king's highway,
> Some way of common trade where subjects' feet
> May hourly trample on their sovereign's head;
> For on my heart they tread now whilst I live,
> And, buried once, why not upon my head?
>
> (154–59)

It is amusing to watch how again and again Richard's imagination tends to free itself from the initial emotion and continue to harp on the vision that was generated by that emotion for its own sake, thus leaving the original lyrical impulse behind and veering ever more decisively toward sentimental essayism. In the process, the genuine feeling is diluted into something that looks very much like an aesthetic game. This game, however, as we are going to see, may at times rekindle the feeling and, anyway, it is never completely detached from its initial impulse.

In the midst of all that seemingly withdrawn fantasizing, Richard is apt every now and then to wake up to the presence of an onstage audience witnessing his musings and to resume contact with it. The above-considered first section of the monologue is wound up with a direct address to his sympathetic interlocutor: "Aumerle, thou weep'st, my tender-hearted cousin!" (160). But this new turn of the dramatic action prompts the compulsive monologizer to make another excursion into the realm of sentimental fantasy, this time featuring two actors instead of one on the inner stage of the mind:

> We'll make foul weather with despised tears;
> Our sighs and they shall lodge the summer corn
> And make a dearth in this revolting land.
> Or shall we play the wantons with our woes
> And make some pretty match with shedding tears,
> As thus, to drop them still upon one place
> Till they have fretted us a pair of graves
> Within the earth; and, therein laid, there lies
> Two kinsmen digged their graves with weeping eyes?
>
> (161–69)

The image of graves has thus reemerged to crown the imaginary scene. And once again, the speaker wakes up to the immediate context of his utterance by commenting on its total dissociation from that context and the possible alienating effect it may have on its audience: "Well, well, I see/ I talk but idly, and you laugh at me" (170–71). He is thus brought down to earth and devotes the closing section of the monologue to actional matters, addressing himself directly to Northumberland. Even here, however, we are made aware of the lyrical strain in his speech by the meaningful ambiguity of the pun and the (additionally highlighted) alliteration-cum-assonance-cum-internal-rhyme of his bitterly ironical question:

> Will his majesty
> *Give* <u>Richard</u> leave to *live* till <u>Richard</u> die?
>
> (173–74)

Northumberland's announcement that Bolingbroke is waiting for the King to come down to the base court of the castle prompts Richard to pick up the words *come down* and *base court* as emblematic of his own situation and to start playing on them in an incantatory manner:

> Down, down I come, like glist'ring Phaëton,
> Wanting the manage of unruly jades.
> In the base court? Base court where kings grow base
> To come at traitors' calls and do them grace.
> In the base court? Come down? Down court, down king!
> For night-owls shriek where mounting larks should sing.
>
> (178–83)

The polysemy of these words, their suggestive power, their emotional charge, the monosyllabic concentration of energy in their throbbing repetition, reinforced by the plosive consonants with which they open, are all deftly brought into play together with the classical mythological allusion and the metaphorical proverb framing this speech to secure a strongly lyrical effect. The transition to rhymed verse and the growing alliterative overlay add to it. Needless to say, Richard again manages to contemplate himself from aside as he begins his descent from the heights of royal authority to a new baseness of common existence. He notices keenly the symbolical significance of every move he takes, turning it into poetry that is addressed above all to himself and only then to anyone who cares to listen and is capable of appreciating the implications of what is going on. To people of mater-of-fact mentality like Northumberland, such lyrical withdrawals from the dramatic exigencies of the moment verge on lunacy, and his diagnosis is unequivocal:

> Sorrow and grief of heart
> Makes him speak fondly like a frantic man.
>
> (184–85)

Finding himself face to face with his challenger, who has ceremonially knelt before the sovereign he has come to dethrone, Richard addresses him by continuing to harp on the word *base*, coupling it with its near antonym *up*, and weaving around both of them a synonymic web of antitheses, suggestive of his and his adversary's contrasted courses (highlighted in the quotation):

> Fair cousin, you de**base** your princely knee
> To make the **base** earth proud with kissing it.
> Me rather had my heart might feel your love
> Than my unpleased eye see your courtesy.
> **Up** cousin, **up**. Your heart is **up**, I know,
> [*Raises Bolingbroke*]
> Thus **high** at least, [*Indicates crown.*]
>   although your knee be **low**.
>
> (190–95)

The persistent lexical and phonetic repetition culminating in the closing rhyme, as well as the pervasive, though fairly unobtrusive, metaphors and metonyms give this speech a distinctively rhetorical flavor. But its general impact is more contemplative than persuasive, an impression that is probably due to its central self-referential and emotionally charged section.

The abdication scene is, of course, climactic. On his way into Westminster Hall Richard utters a complaint, comparing himself to the betrayed Christ. This speech (4.1.163–77) has the characteristic tone of a soliloquy, though the speaker is not alone on the stage. The King acknowledges to himself his psychological unpreparedness for the radical change he is heading for. What follows is a series of monologues accompanying the dramatic action of resignation, spoken in the presence of Bolingbroke and a crowd of barons and officers, yet addressed primarily to the speaker in his attempt to come to terms with the stupendous event.

The first of these monologues is again a product of Richard's need to lyricize the dramatic action and reveal its manifold significance. Factual reality is imaginatively transformed into a much greater experience. At this point the protagonist creates one of the most original images in the play, focusing with emblematic force on its central developments, the crown/well simile enveloping this crucial episode and its major actors in an aura of vast repercussions:

> [*to York*] Give me the crown. [*Takes crown.*]
> [*To Bolingbroke*]
> Here, cousin, seize the crown. Here, cousin,
> On this side my hand, and on that side thine.
> Now is this golden crown like a deep well
> That owes two buckets, filling one another,
> The emptier ever dancing in the air,
> The other down, unseen and full of water.
> That bucket down and full of tears am I,
> Drinking my griefs whilst you mount up on high.
>
> (4.1.181–89)

The poetic theme of the two contrasted courses of the antagonists— down and up—is thus pursued and made to produce new striking imagery. Crucial physical dramatic activity is once again—as in the important scenes of *Romeo and Juliet*—accompanied and enhanced by a lyrical verbalization.

Bolingbroke is nonplussed: "I thought you had been willing to resign" (190). A man of practical action, he is unable to understand Richard's purposeless peregrinations in the regions of the soul. The latter's reply (in the form of zeugma) is characteristically metaphorical: yes, he is ready to resign his crown but not his griefs (191–93). So the exchange between the two proceeds on parallel levels, which do not intersect at any point—the prosaic and the poetic. Bolingbroke observes: "Part of your cares you give me with your crown" (194), to which Richard responds:

> Your cares set up do not pluck my cares down.
> My care is loss of care, by old care done;

> Your care is gain of care, by new care won.
> The cares I give, I have, though given away;
> They 'tend the crown, yet still with me they stay.

> (195–99)

It is amusing to see how closely this lyrical argument resembles the conventional Platonic conceit of the mystical exchange-retention of hearts in love, so often employed in Elizabethan sonnets, including Shakespeare's. The insistent play on the keyword (*care/s*) and the syntactic parallelism are also reminiscent of the inherent features of the age's dominant lyrical genre.

The King's next monologue (4.1.201–22), triggered by Bolingbroke's impatient action-prompting question, "Are you contented to resign the crown?" (200), begins with an evocative pun on the homonyms *ay/ I*, reflecting the paradoxical situation in which the speaker finds himself and forming a theatrical prologue to the ritual act: "Now mark me how I will undo myself" (203). As he hands over his regalia item by item, Richard poeticizes every gesture, passing imperceptibly from the visible to the invisible, from the outer to the inner:

> I give this heavy weight from off my head,
>   [*Gives crown to Bolingbroke.*]
> And this unwieldy sceptre from my hand,
>   [*Takes up scepter and gives it to Bolingbroke.*]
> The pride of kingly sway from out my heart . . .

> (204–6)

By going through these necessary symbolic motions, he divests his natural body from the accretions that have so far made it identical with the body politic. The doubling of stage business with its lyrical verbalization is again pervasive. The succeeding passage continues to cultivate the antithetical opposition between the king's two bodies, informing each line, though the order is now reversed, the body natural taking precedence:

> With mine own tears I wash away my balm,
> With mine own hands I give away my crown,
> With mine own tongue deny my sacred state,
> With mine own breath release all duteous oaths.

> (207–10)

Here the parallelism, closely resembling that in 3.3.147–53, is even more salient. The speaker's resolution seems to have grown stronger. And so the monologue continues, gradually becoming less self-absorbed and "self-posturing," in spite of the fact that the first-person pronouns chime on until the very end. For awhile Richard appears to have left behind the lyrical mode in order to negotiate more propitious terms for his abdication, but he cannot get out of his skin and renews his pathetic self-identification with Christ—now at the next stage of his passion, the encounter with Pilate (239–42). The ensuing couple of monologues (244–52, 254–67) vacillate between the outer and the inner addressee, the first one dealing with the theme of treason without and within, literal and figurative, and the second centering on the loss of identity, which results from loss of status. Striking images appear in both speeches, especially in the second with its Marlovian exclamation (echoing Faustus's last soliloquy again):

> O, that I were a mockery king of snow,
> Standing before the sun of Bolingbroke,
> To melt myself away in water-drops!
>
> (260–62)

At the very end of this monologue Richard asks for a mirror to resolve his identity problem, and then plunges into one of his most famous speeches (273–91), evincing the speaker's ingrained habit of expressing his inner self while observing his outer one most closely. It starts with a metaphor refuting Northumberland's reminder that the commons should be pacified by Richard's acquaintance with his formal indictment. By a single gesture he replaces the importance of public reality with that of the private. What follows is a lyrical apostrophe to the looking-glass and a galloping series of rhetorical questions, focusing on the idea of his face and again bearing strong resemblance to some of the greatest poetic speeches in *Doctor Faustus*. The emotional charge is powerful and the thematic concentration unflagging, as the speech harps endlessly on the keyword *face*. This is a true lyrical outburst, yet its dramatic pertinence, its close engagement with the hero's predicament is quite obvious.

The blending of the lyrical with the dramatic is effected by connecting the former with a stage prop, which is an indelible part of the latter. What is more, toward the end of the monologue this stage prop undergoes a visible change as an element of stage business. After expressing his dissatisfaction with the brittleness of glory and the royal face that is supposed to materialize it, Richard decides to prove this conviction by dashing the mirror on the floor and concluding:

> For there it is, cracked in an hundred shivers.
> Mark, silent King, the moral of this sport,
> How soon my sorrow hath destroyed my face.
>
> (289–91)

This technique of manipulating a dynamic image in a way allowing the poet to develop and expand its changing connotations is typical of Donne's ingenious early poetry and can be amply illustrated from such peaces as "The Flea," "A Valediction: Of My Name, in the Window," "A Jet Ring Sent" and other examples of the emblem-in-motion technique.[66] Though such dynamism in lyrical poetry can be called dramatic, what we are witnessing here is another example of the lyrical doubling of dramatic action.

The next turn in the dialogue reveals once again Richard's truly poetic interest in the latent suggestiveness of lexis. As Bolingbroke makes light of his opponent's feelings by retorting: "The shadow of your sorrow hath destroyed/ The shadow of your face" (292–93), the King, in spite of his grief, is struck by the potential of this word to express the essence of his state of mind. He recognizes (as Hamlet will do later) the inability of the outer to convey fully what is within—a typical poetic concern—and formulates it in a thoughtful, yet emotionally contagious way:

> Say that again!
> The shadow of my sorrow? Ha, let's see.
> 'Tis very true, my grief lies all within,
> And these external manner of laments
> Are merely shadows to the unseen grief
> That swells with silence in the tortured soul.
> There lies the substance...
>
> (293–99)

From this point on the protagonist seems to grow more keenly aware of the unbridgeable gap that divides his consciousness from that of his antagonist and switches from the confessional to the ironically distancing, yet no less lyrical, mode of speaking as his staple manner for the rest of the dialogue, again anticipating Hamlet's characteristic stance—and even the theme of the Prince's first monologue, "Seems, madam? Nay, it is."[67]

The last act opens with a parting duologue of the royal couple (the whole of 5.1), as Richard is being escorted to the Tower, later replaced by Pomfret Castle. The Queen initiates the exchange with a lyrical apostrophe to her husband in which she projects him figuratively as "Richard's tomb,/ And not King Richard" and a "beauteous inn" in which "hard-favour'd grief" is lodged. The King responds in a similar vein, preaching resignation, to which Isabel remonstrates, pointing out that he should not accept his end meekly but should rage against his enemies as a dying lion would do, for, being a sovereign, he is himself "a lion and the king of beasts." And once again Richard is struck by the phrase he has just heard and starts exploring its ability to express more meanings than one:

> A king of beasts, indeed! If aught but beasts,
> I had been still a happy king of men.
>
> (5.1.35–36)

As he goes on to implore his wife to go to France and bemoan his death there, he imagines her seated by the fire amid "good old folks" exchanging with them tales "Of woeful ages long ago betid." By that time Richard himself will have turned into no more than "the lamentable tale of me," a reality transmuted into fiction. This idea makes him fantasize a sentimental picture (strongly reminiscent of a famous Ronsard sonnet), tinged with pathetic fallacy, which emerges from the spinning out of an elaborate conceit:[68]

> For why the senseless brands will sympathize
> The heavy accent of thy moving tongue
> And in compassion weep the fire out;
> And some will mourn in ashes, some coal-black,
> For the deposing of a rightful king.
>
> (46–50)

Unsurprisingly, imagination again takes precedence with Richard over the exigencies of the day, the lyrical transcendence of the present moment replacing the urgency of dramatic action. The aesthetic reconstruction of an experience is more important for him than the necessity to cope with it in actual life.

The final section of the parting dialogue (81–102), sustained in rhymed couplets, seems to be modeled on *Romeo and Juliet* 's shared sonnet.[69] It starts with an exchange of sighs and groans and culminates in the exchange of kisses:

> RICHARD. . . . One kiss shall stop our mouths, and dumbly part;
>   Thus give I mine, and thus take I thy heart.
>   [*They kiss.*]
> QUEEN. Give me mine own again; 'twere no good part
>   To take on me to keep and kill thy heart.
>   [*They kiss again.*]
>   So now I have mine own again, be gone,
>   That I may strive to kill it with a groan.
> RICHARD. We make woe wanton with this fond delay.
>   Once more, adieu. The rest let Sorrow say.   *Exeunt.*]
>
>   (95–102)

Though perhaps not so metaphorically rich and prosodically intricate as the Verona lovers' precedent, this new dialogue-of-one is as closely knit. It should be noted that the almost identical exchange of two kisses here is associated with the Platonic/ Petrarchan exchange-retention-of-hearts-in-love conceit. And once again, the lyrical verbalization of current action is employed to enlarge the significance of the stage business.

The protagonist is absent from the next three scenes, but this absence soon proves to have been the lion's crouch before the leap. The catastrophe scene (5.5), which centers fully on the King, is his true apogee. He is all alone in his prison until a groom of the royal stable arrives for a brief conversation, to be followed by a warder bringing in his (apparently poisoned) meal and then by the assassins under Exton's command. During the first half of the scene, Richard is, for once, unencumbered by the presence of others. The crowded political world is left far behind or, rather, beyond the walls of Pomfret Castle. The dream that later will be harbored by Lear, of making the prison his fortress against the vanity of social existence, has momentarily come true for Richard. And, paradoxically, it turns out that in his cell the deposed monarch is freer to indulge in the essential values of his private self. His longest speech ever (5.5.1–66), considered

by some critics to be his only true soliloquy, begins in a characteristically contemplative manner:[70]

> I have been studying how I may compare
> This prison where I live unto the world . . .

This opening resembles closely the first lines of some Elizabethan
sonnets, like Spenser's *Amoretti* 9 ("Long-while I sought to what I might
compare/ Those powerful eies") or even Shakespeare's own sonnet
18 ("Shall I compare thee to a summer's day?"). G. Wilson Knight remarks that Richard's "state is now exactly analogous to the creative
consciousness which gives birth to poetry. The first lines which he
here speaks outline a Shakespearean aesthetic psychology and are
interesting as a poet's commentary on the creative act..."[71] No mater
how forcefully Peter Ure and other critics after him have contended
that there is nothing inherently poetic in Richard II as a personality, and that any poetic quality that may be detected in his manner
of speaking stems not from an inherent lyrical predisposition of the
character but directly from his author, this moment alone can refute
their arguments and show that Shakespeare's intention was to endow
the protagonist with a distinctive artistic bent.[72]

In a finally attained solitude, Richard paradoxically yearns for
the multitudinous bustle of actual existence that he is now forti-
fied against. And this multiplicity is soon readily reproduced in the
thoughts that populate the individual mind:

> My brain I'll prove the female to my soul,
> My soul the father, and these two beget
> A generation of still-breeding thoughts;
> And these same thoughts people this little world...
>
>   (6–9)

A moment later the speaker realizes that the habitat of the mind is
not more peaceful and idyllic than that of the world from which it has
chosen to enclose itself, for the mental world recreates the external
one by trying to make sense of its puzzling and oppressive imperfections. The dramatic reality has inundated the lyrical enclosure—not
yet from without as in *Romeo and Juliet* but from within, in a way that
is even less resistible. In desperation, Richard enlarges upon the human condition:

> . . . But whate'er I be,
> Nor I nor any man that but man is,
> With nothing shall be pleased till he be eased
> With being nothing.
>
> (38–41)

Thus the poemly theme of the impossible balance between life and death has been resumed once again in an aphoristic statement playing deftly on the chiasmic repetition of the keywords *man* and *nothing* as well as on the internal seesaw rhyme of "shall be pleased till he be eased."

The gist of the ensuing second part of the soliloquy is prompted by the sound reaching the prisoner's ears from afar:

> Music do I hear?
> Ha, ha, keep time! How sour sweet music is
> When time is broke and no proportion kept!
>
> (41–43)

In a new guise, the poemly theme reemerges again, for time is the sure way from life to death and also the borderline between the two. In constructing the poetic image of time with its larger existential and metaphysical significances, Richard plays paronomastically on both meanings of the word as related to musical rhythm and as referring to the fourth dimension of our existence. Gradually the latter takes over, and the speaker realizes that he is no more than a time machine, an instrument measuring the passage of time. This metaphor is strikingly original. In a way similar to Donne's poetic manner, it is turned into an elaborate conceit:

> For now hath Time made me his numb'ring clock.
> My thoughts are minutes, and with sighs they jar
> Their watches on unto mine eyes, the outward watch,
> Whereto my finger, like a dial's point,
> Is pointing still, in cleansing them from tears.
>
> (50–54)

One cannot help noticing how Richard adheres to his habit of observing carefully his every gesture, endowing it with emblematic significance. And although he is for once all alone on the stage, the hero continues to be so acutely conscious of acting a role that in the

next line he addresses an imaginary audience of one in order to expand the image further for that person's sake as well as for his own.
Or is this address but a self-reflexive apostrophe? Here is the relevant
passage:

> Now, sir, the sound that tells what hour it is
> Are clamorous groans which strike upon my heart,
> Which is the bell. So sighs, and tears, and groans
> Show minutes, times, and hours. But my time
> Runs posting on in Bolingbroke's proud joy,
> While I stand fooling here, his jack o'the clock.
>
> (55–60)

The soliloquy ends on a note of uncertainty as to whether the
music is welcome to the speaker or not. It is associated in his mind
with his need for love in "this all-hating world." The lyrical tone is
now maintained not by the optical power of imagery but by the melic
effect of lexical and phonetic iteration: *music, more, mad, men, love.*

This—the protagonist's last sustained dramatic speech—is among
the greatest Shakespeare had written by then. Wolfgang Clemen might
have been thinking first of Richard II when he wrote: "We feel that
characters such as Shakespeare creates them, endowing them with a
peculiar kind of poetic speech and self-expression, must soliloquize
at certain moments of tension, heightened awareness of inner conflict. And we feel, too, that poetic drama, such as Shakespeare shapes
it—with its rhythmic sequence of movement and halting suspense, of
outer and inner drama—must give space to the monologue."[73]

Richard is probably Shakespeare's first hero who is allowed to take
center stage and express himself through solo speeches so persistently. He is also the first of an impressive line of tragic characters
endowed with "unusual imagination and the poetic gift."[74] And so,
the expressive quality of his speeches is heightened to an unprecedented extent, enhancing the lyricism inherent in contemplative
soliloquies by definition.

Albeit the King has no further chances to withdraw from dramatic
urgencies for so long, what follows is sustained at a similar level of
lyrical vision and locution. The Groom's arrival has two dramatic
functions: one, to prove to Richard that not everybody hates him and,
two, to supply him with another theme for contemplation and self-
analysis. The Groom brings the news that on the day of his corona-

tion Bolingbroke rode on the King's favorite horse. Richard is stung by this intimation, which gives rise to a new emotional monologue:

> That jade hath eat bread from my royal hand;
> This hand hath made him proud with clapping him.
>
> (85–86)

The royal hand is made prominent again. The protagonist's consciousness of the importance of his anointed body—and, above all, of his hand as the symbol of majesty—has not changed since the inception of the dramatic action, no matter how much change has occurred in his status and life. But a moment later Richard wakes up to the reality of his transformation and utilizes the idea of the seized horse as the vehicle for a self-exploratory simile. The lyrical quality of this monologue—or quasi-soliloquy (90–94)—is inescapable. It manifests the typical combination of feeling and thought in an integral thematic whole, pivoted around a poetic image and energized by a medley of questions, exclamations, word repetitions and patterns of alliteration.

The final act of the King's ultimate destruction comes with the entrance of the murderers. For once, Richard is not in a contemplative position but in a vigorously active one. He grapples with his attackers and manages to turn their own weapons against them. Yet, even in the midst of the skirmish his speech continues to be poetically supple and evocative:

> How, now! What means Death in this rude assault?
> Villain, thy own hand yields thy death's instrument.
>   [*Seizes a Servant's weapon and kills him with it.*]
> Go thou, and fill another room in hell!
>   [*Kills another Servant.*]
>
> (105–7)

Thus, just as in the last scenes of *Romeo and Juliet*, the meaning of the dramatic action is enhanced by the lyrical perspective adopted by its executor. And his royal exclusiveness is upheld to the bitter end to generate imagery, as "the king's blood" stains "the king's own land."

It is worth noting that at this last moment the protagonist's being splits, and in the same breath as he sends his assassins tumbling down into the "never-quenching fire" and sees his own "gross flesh" descending into the earth he calls upon his spiritual part to rise victoriously: "Mount, mount, my soul! Thy seat is up on high" (111). With this heroically mustered force, in his last battle Richard reverses his emblematical downward course to gain a final ascendance over fate, a fact that Exton acknowledges in a confused comment on the outcome of his own treacherous deed.

This final spurt of energetic action notwithstanding, Richard's intimate and unflagging association with the lyrical mode from the midpoint of the play, when he senses that the tide of events is turning against him and gives up the idea of resistance, characterizes him as a contemplative rather than active personality. The change from his previous guise as an authoritative and imposing political figure, not averse to court intrigue, conspiracy and even assassination, is rather abrupt and splits his character into two irreconcilable halves. Very little in the early parts of the play implies the existence of a reflective, keenly sensitive nature in this overbearing prince.[75] The only barely perceptible hint may be discerned in York's critical remark about the King's objectionable attachment to the "lascivious metres" of poetry and, generally, to the "fashions in proud Italy" (2.1.19, 21). But the protagonist's radical transfiguration could be exploited to an advantage in the theatre for the sake of highlighting the contrast between a heroic façade and a contemplative private self, a contrast that is further underlined by Richard's being set against an adversary fully given to action and representing his antipodal opposite, Henry Bolingbroke.

The hero and his antagonist should be seen in their revealing conjunction. First of all, let us try to define Richard as he appears in the second half of the play. The protagonist has the irrefutable proclivities of a *poet*, intent on studying and expressing adequately his inner self to the extent of complete dissociation from practical action. As Edmund Chambers notes, "He becomes an interested spectator of his own ruin, dressing it out with illuminating phrases and exquisite images"—and, it could be added, perhaps slightly overdoing this.[76] For Richard's poetry is not at all the sole property of the author. It exists, first of all, to characterize him as a person. However expressive, it is for the most part theatrical, showy, over-aestheticized—above all, it lacks spontaneity and as such can hardly be identified with Shakespeare's poetic manner. In his famous late soliloquy Richard, as we saw, sets himself the task of comparing his prison to the world and, after finding this almost impossible to accomplish, admits: "I cannot do it. Yet I'll hammer't out" (5.5.5). Once he sets his mind on a poetic theme, he must see it through one way or another by evolving elaborate similes and metaphors. This is his idiosyncrasy and not just a linguistic register. In a sense, he is a poet sui generis, just as Berowne and Romeo are poets—and just like them he is in love with words to the point of besottedness. The dramatist not only studies him empathically from within but also observes him ironically from without.

In Bolingbroke, on the other hand, there is not the slightest touch of the poet. His aversion to any movement of the inner self that has no practical goal in sight is made quite clear very early on in the play, at the point when he rejects outright his father's advice to alleviate his banishment by transforming it imaginatively into something that it can never be, a pleasure trip. Hard reality for this man is all that exists, and it is irreplaceable by any kind of fancy. His unacceptance of the solace that can be found in an inner space of immaterial essences sets him in sharp contrast with his royal cousin.[77] Unlike Richard, Bolingbroke speaks little and acts an awful lot throughout the play. Also, even when he does speak, as M. M. Mahood observes, "his words, unlike those of Richard, are no sooner said than done."[78] Language for the contender has one chief function, the referential one, while for the King the expressive and poetic functions are foremost. It is small wonder, then, that these two can hardly ever converse with one another meaningfully. We have witnessed how impatient Bolingbroke can grow at Richard's habitual withdrawal into what appears to be a flimsy make-believe world of words at a time when concrete action should be taken. The two are almost opposite poles, Richard being quintessentially the lyrical persona and Bolingbroke the dramatic, the existence of the former always tending to soar above the plot, whereas that of the latter is unthinkable in isolation from the action's implacable mechanism. In Edmund Chambers's formula, "the antithesis between Richard and Bolingbroke goes much further than politics; it rests upon one of the ultimate distinctions amongst mankind, that of the practical and artistic temperaments, the men of deeds and the men of dreams and fancies."[79]

If at this point we return to the Todorov/ Novalis parallel table of "heroes" and "poets" in literature, we will see that the two characters we have been considering provide a perfect illustration for its two

contrasted categories.[80] Their names could in fact be uncondition-
ally substituted for the general rubrics. The *Hero*, the man of action,
the essentially dramatic persona is, of course, victorious in the world
of drama, for that is his own element. In it the *Poet*, the contemplative type, the lyrical persona is defeated by definition. The contrast
between the two adversaries is most vividly presented in York's report
about their passage through the streets of London after the transfer
of power in Westminster Hall. Their pictures are juxtaposed in two
consecutive monologues of almost equal length to highlight the difference even more strongly (5.2.7–21 and 23–36). The outcome of
this juxtaposition is a foregone conclusion. But is Bolingbroke's victory absolute? Has he won the ultimate battle and is his triumphal
return to London what finally and unequivocally seals up the end
of his progress? The populace of the great city may meet him en-
thusiastically, as it is thrilled by the dramatic change at the heights
of political power. But we observe this triumph from afar, through
the account of an eyewitness. What is immediately before us is the
emotional reaction to the related scene of the two people whom we
see on the stage. First, there is the hint at the victor's "politic" popu-
lism in York's narration, followed by the Duchess's heartfelt commiseration for the victim as expressed in her exclamation: "Alack, poor
Richard! Where rode he the whilst?" (22). And then, there is the
half-concealed sympathy for him at the end of York's account of the
ex-king's humiliation.

The exigencies of politics—and those of dramatic action—are irrefutable. And yet, our sympathies as readers and spectators cannot
help going to the loser rather than to the winner in the clash of incompatible personalities. This is not so much due to the tendency of
human nature to pity the downtrodden, even though they may have
mainly themselves to blame for their hard lot, as to the very opposition between the two characters, which has tipped the balance of
forces in favor of the dramatic one. His lyrical counterpart has proved
less capable of winning the battle on the stage, but he has made a better headway into our hearts, and has managed to do that not because
he is necessarily the better person of the two, but because, unlike the
other, through his lyrical self-expression he has allowed us to know
him more intimately as an actual, vulnerable human being and to
empathize with him.[81] This may be said to be the ultimate triumph
of lyric in drama—reaching out beyond the stage world to the larger
one, which encompasses it, and accomplishing its conquest there.

A group of more peripheral and not so overtly contemplative monologues, which do not belong to the protagonist and are largely narrative or essayistic, may also betray some signs of lyrical modulation.
Among these are, first of all, the so called nuntius reports. The type
has been considered in the preceding chapter on the example of
Montague's and Benvolio's accounts of Romeo's strange behavior as
a romantic lover. It was noted that, in spite of their epic orientation,
such speeches have a markedly lyrical tone. Such a conclusion is even
more warranted with a view to the nuntius interventions in *Richard
II*, more particularly Scroop's description of the rebellion in 3.2 or
York's just discussed relation of the Londoners' reception of the deposed king and the usurper after the transfer of power in 5.2. We
need not dwell on them again. Suffice it to reiterate our impression
of both speakers' strong emotional involvement and the sensuous
vividness of their presentation, compelling the hearers to share the
related experience as if it were happening at the moment of telling.
These are, no doubt, the features of lyrical locution, modulating the
epic insets and imparting to them the power of unreserved empathy
characteristic of this literary kind.

A couple of other speeches, which are thematically oriented but
have been defined as hortatory rather than lyrical, can also be considered here: (1) the Duchess of Gloucester's long monologue inciting
John of Gaunt to avenge her late husband's death on his murderers
including the King (1.2.9–36) and (2) the Gardener's essays in political philosophy in 3.4 (between 29 and 66). Some lyrical propensity
can be detected at times in both, above all in the suggestive potential
of their poetic imagery, which, in spite of its rhetorical character,
contains unpremeditated freshness, reflecting back on the speakers
and betraying a genuine involvement on their part. In the Duchess's
speech such moments occur in the dual conceit of King Edward's
seven sons, seen simultaneously as "seven vials of his sacred blood"
and "seven fair branches springing from one root," and also in the
abrupt transition from the somewhat artificial neatness of this aesthetic construction to an impassioned appeal for Gaunt to put things
right. As for the Gardener, the case is curiously similar, for he also
passes suddenly from a well thought-out parable of the garden as the
type of the political state to what sounds like a spontaneous reaction
to the current turmoil in the country. A discharge of explosive energy

at these interfaces between the essayistic constructions and the give-and-take of dramatic action generates lyrical explosions illuminating and enlivening the respective scenes.

Lyrical overtones were identified in Gaunt's great patriotic oration and in other strongly rhetorical speeches in this play. All in all, the lyrical mode spreads over the whole of it almost as widely as it does in *Romeo and Juliet,* coloring the text in its unmistakable way. And yet, the case of *Richard II* is different, for the lyrically tinged passages here are the monologues rather than the dialogue. It may be due to the fact that this is a largely monologic play, and genuine dialogue is impossible in its setup. Bolingbroke and his henchmen are the only dramatis personae who are outright excluded from the lyrical sphere and are thus doomed to isolation. The entire play moves away from them tonally and leaves them on the barren shallows of purely dramatic discourse confined to practical goals and deprived of larger visions. Such is their ultimate punishment.

The lyric mode that the protagonist gradually cultivates is not the one to which Juliet belongs and to which Berowne and Romeo aspire in their half-attained maturity. Richard is genuinely self-probing, yet never oblivious of the effect he can have on the others. Not for a moment does the central speaker of this play turn his back on the audience fully in the way defined by Northrop Frye.[82] That is why his speech remains structured in a rather obtrusively rhetorical manner. Those of the others, as we have witnessed, are even more awkwardly poised between the two kinds of discourse, the persuasive and the self-expressive, often partaking of both.

While it is true that the lyrical quality of *Richard II* is, first of all, to be sought in the elocution of its many and varied monologues, lyricism is also generated by some recurrent structural elements over and above individual characters, forming elaborate concentric patterns in the play's composition and superimposing a thematic organization over its fictional one—a technique similar to that already observed in *Romeo and Juliet* but more pervasive. Such elements frequently pivot on the protagonist again, since the whole is almost entirely centered on him—even Bolingbroke is no more than the reverse of the medal bearing the distinctive impression of King Richard's face. And yet they are not confined to him alone.

At important points in the construction of the plot there recurs a strongly dramatic type of episode, that of the clash between two powerful aristocrats in the presence of the sovereign, imposing on him the need to make a public decision. Such an episode first takes place in Windsor Castle, in the opening scene of the play (1.1), as Mowbray and Bolingbroke challenge each other in front of Richard and compel him to set in motion the line of action that is eventually going to bring him down from the throne and destroy him physically. An almost identical conflict flares up before Bolingbroke in Westminster Hall between Bagot and Aumerle on the eve of Richard's formal abdication, giving the new sovereign an opportunity to assert his authority by assuming the position of the supreme arbiter (4.1).[83]

Another interesting—clearly thematic—scheme that pervades the entire play and structures the relation between Richard and Bolingbroke in a clear and meaningful way is what could be defined as the descent/ascent mechanism. This emblematic figure moulds not only the plot but also the stylistic layer and, more specifically, the poetic imagery. It is first introduced in 3.3, when Richard is forced to climb down from the walls of Flint Castle to the base court to meet his formidable adversary and utters his bitterly punning monologue "Down, down I come, like glist'ring Phaeton" (178–83). Significantly, right after this speech, which turns his physical descent into a metaphorical mortification, he finds himself standing in front of the ceremoniously kneeling contender and exhorts him to rise with the words: "Up, cousin, up" (194). The contrast between the king's downward and his cousin's upward movement is underlined by the juxtaposition of the two keywords—*down* in the first speech and *up* in the second.

In the next scene, the philosophical Gardener takes the idea of this contrast a step further toward an emblematically focused shape, when he reveals to the distressed Queen the factual truth of the political situation in the country:

> King Richard he is in the mighty hold
> Of Bolingbroke. Their fortunes both are weighed:
> In your lord's scale is nothing but himself
> And some few vanities that make him light;
> But in the balance of great Bolingbroke,
> Besides himself, are all the English peers,
> And with that odds he weighs King Richard down.

(3.4.83–89)

Yet another touch is added by York in 4.1, when, having finally changed sides, the old man advises his upcoming nephew to replace the down-going one, though the encouragement is rather superfluous: "Ascend his throne, descending now from him" (112).

The true crystallization of the emblem, however, is reached some-what later in this scene, in Richard's abdication monologue, when, while proffering his crown to Bolingbroke and yet continuing to cling to it, he compares it to "a deep well/ That owes two buckets, filling one another,/ The emptier ever dancing in the air,/ The other down, unseen and full of water," and then does not fail to make the tenor of his parable unmistakable: "That bucket down and full of tears am I,/ Drinking my griefs whilst you mount up on high" (184–89). One can-not help noticing that Richard's well metaphor is a transformation of the Gardener's scales one, both stemming from the same underly-ing idea of the descent/ascent power mechanism. The difference be-tween the two images is also telling: the Gardener's almost scientific rationality is counterpoised by the King's visualization and emotional apprehension of the imagined scene ("The emptier ever dancing in the air,/ The other down, unseen and full of water"). The poet has supplanted the essayist. Richard also has the added advantage of the visible stage prop, the crown held symbolically on either side by each of the two antagonists, drawing the attention of the audience to its materiality and its figurative potential. Dramatic and lyric are thus firmly interlocked.

The King's metaphorical self-reduction to "an ass,/ Spurred, galled and tired by jauncing Bolingbroke" in his conversation with the Groom (5.5.93–94), projecting the idea of reversal in passion-ate terms, could be considered part of the same thematic pattern. For a more general precedent, one might even go back to Richard's bemoaning his fate in front of Aumerle and imagining his utter hu-miliation in being buried in the highway, so that his subjects "May hourly trample on their sovereign's head" (3.3.157). The pattern is pervasive and multifaceted. And yet, as we have already noticed, this abominable reversal of what appears to be the right order of things in the political world is corrected at the last moment by a single heroic gesture, which replaces the physical perspective with the metaphysi-cal or, could we say, the dramatic with the lyrical. The villainous regi-cides are sent where they belong by rights, to eternal damnation in the bottomless pit, whereas the soul of the martyred prince rises to its glorious seat on high.

If the descent/ascent pattern is indisputably the most fundamental thematic construction in *Richard II*, a considerable number of less extensive but similarly suggestive ones orbit around it. The hollow crown conceit is an especially striking recurrent image. It makes its debut in Gaunt's castigation of the insouciant king: "A thousand flatterers sit within thy crown,/ Whose compass is no bigger than thy head;/ And yet, incaged in so small a verge,/ The waste is no whit lesser than thy land" (2.1.100–103). In one of his first introspective monologues Richard elaborates on the same conceit in an even more morose and certainly more copious vein: "within the hollow crown/ That rounds the mortal temples of a king/ Keeps Death his court, *etc.*"(3.2.160–61). And finally, the crown-well scene (4. 1) does crown this thematic structure as it does the other, more central and more extensive one, thus bringing both strands to a common knot.

A number of other recurrent conceits acquire similar salience. Gaunt's great patriotic monologue in 2.1 ushers into the play the metaphor of England as "This other Eden, demi-paradise" (42), a hortus conclusus surrounded by "the silver sea,/ Which serves it in the office of a wall/ Or as a moat defensive to a house" (46–48). A servant of the Gardener in 3.4 returns to the same idea when he refers to England as "our sea-walled garden, the whole land" (43). And a little later the Queen, on hearing from the Gardener about her husband's political crash, addresses him in a way that stresses the same biblical association by referring to Adam, Eve, the serpent, and the fall of "cursed man" (72–80).

In an attempt to allay the Queen's fears about these dire developments, in 2.2, Bushy argues that in her troubled imagination she sees "shapes of grief more than himself to wail,/ Which, looked on as it is, is nought but shadows/ Of what it is not" (22–24). This, as we saw earlier, is part of a larger elaborate conceit based on *perspectives* and their strange reflection/ representation of real objects. In 4.1, Richard's disquisition on the implications of a royal face reflected in the mirror he holds in his hands, and of its fragmentation after the mirror is shattered, is followed by Bolingbroke's disparaging comment that the King's theatrical gesture of despondency is no more than the shadow of his sorrow (292–93).

As he summons his native country to crush his enemies for him in 3.2, Richard constructs his own image as that of the "long-parted mother with her child," who "Plays fondly with her tears and smiles" (8–9), and concludes: "So, weeping, smiling, greet I thee, my earth"

(10). The tears-and-smiles image recurs impressively in York's relation of the Londoners' reception of Richard after his abdication (5.2), as the deposed king does his best to contain his emotional turmoil shaking off the dust thrown on his head from the windows:

> His face still combating with tears and smiles,
> The badges of his grief and patience. . .
>
> (32–33)

A whole network of related conceits, all having to do with the idea of blood and its dramatic repercussions, can be traced through the play. In 2.1, Richard reacts angrily against Gaunt's public indictment of his reign. He is infuriated by the audacity of the old man, who has dared "Make pale our cheek, chasing the royal blood/ With fury from his native residence" (118–19). When he returns to the same image in 3.2, it is, ironically, a reflection of Gaunt's warnings, now come true as a massive desertion of the sovereign's forces. To Aumerle's question, "Comfort, my liege. Why looks your grace so pale?" (75), Richard, as we saw earlier, replies dejectedly that the blood of twenty thousand soldiers has glowed in his face until recently, but has withdrawn with their fatal desertion (76–79). The transformation of the image is quite striking: first of all, the protagonist's paleness is no longer indicative of wrathful pride but of the stunned realization of absolute disaster, and then, the king's person is no longer a natural body but a body politic, containing the entire state in himself. And yet, the metaphor is recognizably the same and its recurrence is apparently meant to knit the two episodes together, revealing their underlying relatedness.

Another strain of the blood theme has to do with the massacre of civil war. Bloodshed is associated metaphorically with agriculture and growth in general. King Richard's challenger starts the series when he thunders in front of his followers at Flint Castle that if his banishment is not repealed:

> . . . I'll use the advantage of my power
> And lay the summer's dust with showers of blood
> Rained from the wounds of slaughtered Englishmen—
> The which how far off from the mind of Bolingbroke
> It is such crimson tempest should bedrench
> The fresh green lap of fair King Richard's land
> My stooping duty tenderly shall show.
>
> (3.3.42–48)

In his threatening speech later in the same scene, the King himself responds to the rebels in similar terms, as he prophesies that the dire consequences of their heinous act will "bedew/ Her [England's] pastor's grass with faithful English blood" (99–100). Somewhat later, Carlisle warns the traitors that, if they dare crown their leader, "The blood of English shall manure the ground" (4.1.138). This ominous image resounds throughout the latter parts of the play and crops up even in Bolingbroke's closing speech, in which he regrets "That blood should sprinkle me to make me grow" (5.6.46), thus giving a final ironic twist to his earlier threats.

Bolingbroke is consistently associated with Pilate and the idea of hypocritically, though ineffectually, washing one's hands of the blood of a martyr. The first instance of this figure can be detected in his own monologue indicting the two barons who remain loyal to King Richard, Bushy and Greene, and ordering their execution, but taking good care not to besmirch himself:

> . . . yet to wash your blood
> From off my hands, here in the view of men
> I will unfold some causes of your deaths . . .
>
> (3.1.5–7)

In the abdication scene, Richard certifies explicitly this damning association for the whole gang of his adversaries, warning them against deluding themselves that their crime can go unpunished:

> Though some of you, with Pilate, wash your hands,
> Showing an outward pity, yet you Pilates
> Have here delivered me to my sour cross,
> And water cannot wash away your sin.
>
> (4.1.239–42)

And at the very end, Bolingbroke (as Henry IV) returns to the same image. Having committed the unforgivable crime of regicide and usurpation, he resolves to cleanse himself by going on a pious pilgrimage "to the Holy Land/ To wash this blood off from my guilty hand" (5.6.49–50). Thus the antagonist is branded by a methodical identification with the mythological recreant.

In his penetrative study "Symphonic Imagery in *Richard II*," R. D. Altick traces an impressive number of figurative units recurring in the play and creating a network of suggestive relations. He lists and illustrates such images as earth, land, ground, garden and gardening; king-sun, balm, crown, jewels; tears, weeping; tongue, mouth, speech, word; snake, venom; illness, injury, wound; marks on parchment, books, writing; sour, sweet; womb, generation, nurse, midwife, heir, etc.[84] Charles R. Forker further elaborates on these patterns by examining their relation to the central preoccupations of the play.[85] True, Caroline Spurgeon and Wolfgang Clemen and a host of other scholars have discovered such structures in many of Shakespeare's plays, and we did observe some in *Romeo and Juliet,* but their density in *Richard II* is indeed remarkable.[86] It testifies to the persistent imposition of the concentric (thematic, lyrical) principle over the kinetic (fictional, dramatic) one to a point at which the two become intimately interrelated and inseparable.

With *Romeo and Juliet* and *Richard II,* by the mid 1590s, Shakespeare had succeeded to outgrow the largely self-contained local inscription of the lyric in drama through insets and rhymed patterning of certain passages, as demonstrated in *Love's Labour's Lost,* and reached a stage of fuller interpenetration of the two kinds. While the methods and effects familiar from the earlier play can still be discerned, they have now evolved into a more organic lyrical molding of the entire text through a pervasive modulation, replacing the previously dominant inclusion and formal hybridization mechanisms, as well as through the suffusing of some dramatis personae in the lyrical mode, resulting in their meaningful opposition to the others. The lyricized characters have already acquired a privileged status, but another step in the amalgamation of genres must be taken before they could establish a complete preeminence over their play and irradiate their lyricism through it all from within. Our task in the next chapter will be to examine this subsequent development.

3

Generic Integration:
Lyrical Presence in Drama

In the case of *As You Like It* we can hardly speak of an imposition of concentric structures over a basic kinetic one. Here the principle of concentricity is more obviously present than anywhere else in Shakespeare's drama. But what other principle is there in the play for it to be imposed on? The fact is that this comedy has no plot that amounts to more than a mere frame for its contents. A dramatic inception certainly takes place in the first act, and it boils down to the banishment of Rosalind from the Duke's castle and the expulsion of Orlando from his father's estate shortly after the two have fallen in love with each other. The lovers soon meet in the Forest of Arden, but nothing very important happens until a wedding is arranged for them and their companions in the last act. In the absence of any noticeable kinetic structure, then, the concentric one of the thematic, nonfictional kinds is the only alternative, unless the material is to be left in some sort of haphazard accumulation. But since there are no prominent plot elements that such a structure could organize, it concerns itself with the characters.

As a result, we get four pairs of lovers who have established their temporary residence in the forest and whose sentimental affairs are shown to us in alternation, until they all come to their simultaneous consummation in the final round of marriages. The relation between the four couples is one of juxtaposition, revealing similarity or contrast, and a minimum of interaction. Thus the pattern that imposes some meaningful order on their appearances is static rather than dynamic. In a brief outline of this pattern, it could be said that the gist of the central Rosalind-Orlando component is a test of the young man's tenacity as a lover in the face of all displeasures and disappointments that the experience of love can bring. The case of the Phoebe-Silvius one is almost identical, though the mistress's tyranny here is very real, whereas with Rosalind it is only playful. The Celia-Oliver relationship is a pale reflection of the Rosalind-Orlando romance as an example of love-at-first-sight, though Celia and Oliver function merely to tie loose ends up. And, finally, there is the Audrey-Touchstone component, which can be seen as a grotesque transposition of the Phoebe-Silvius affair. Taking the latter to its absurd extreme, the Audrey-Touchstone burlesque subjects the whole experience of being in love to a cynical scrutiny, while the Rosalind-Orlando story, on the contrary, pours on it a romantic glow, saved from sentimentality by its sparks of mild irony.

Admittedly, the different pairs interact to some extent: Phoebe falls in love with Rosalind in the latter's disguise as the shepherd Ganymede, which for awhile complicates the action, as far as there is one; Oliver meets Celia only after he has been rescued from grave trouble in the woods by his brother Orlando and has been asked by him to take a message to Rosalind; and lastly, Audrey turns out to have had a country suitor, William, whom Touchstone feels obliged to scare away. But all these hardly amount to more than occasional links between the parallel presentations of fairly isolated planes of dramatic material. Only Phoebe's infatuation with Ganimede could be seen as more than accidental.

Since there is very little physical action to support the play with any notable change of circumstances, it is replaced almost entirely by azione parlata and other forms of dramatic speech. A survey of these may tell us something about the way the comedy works. The lyrical element is not very visible on the surface, but it is very much at the heart of the whole and will make itself known only in the midst of a larger thematic medium.

A sizable group of repartee passages spread over the comedy seem to be tonally closer to the essay than to the lyric, though they are not completely deprived of lyricism. This series starts as early as 1.2, when the heroine, on her first appearance, gets drawn into a kind of philosophical debate with no other apparent purpose than to amuse her and make her forget her grievances. It is a match of witty observations and comments on the abstract theme "Fortune versus Nature," which may have some relevance to Rosalind's condition but does not affect the action in any noticeable way.[1] And, at no point does it appear to sound a serious note of personal concern. Although sustained in prose, the whole conversation is stylistically very intricate, emulating the fashions of courtly expression with its penchant for euphuistic syntactical balance, lexical repetition and euphony.

Somewhat later Jaques tries to involve Orlando in a very similar debate. Whereas the first one had started with Celia's words "Let us sit and mock the good housewife Fortune from her wheel" (1.2.31–32), the invitation now is extended to Orlando in the following manner: "Will you sit down with me, and we two will rail against our mistress the world and all our misery?" (3.2.269–71), but it does not meet with positive response.

Before that, however, Touchstone, has confronted simple Corin in a country versus court dispute (11–82), that is thematically quite relevant, it would seem, to the experience of the exiles forced to live among nature, yet, once again, without any direct impact on dramatic action. The jester's argumentative prose is a parody of Renaissance essayism. He defends both sides of the proposed dichotomy, shifting his position relativistically from one pole to the other, whereas the shepherd's "philosophy" is banal, verging on silly tautology, such as "the more one sickens the worse at ease he is" or "a great cause of the night is lack of the sun" (3.2.22–27). Corin's later arguments about the different manners at court and in the country make some sense from a narrowly practical point of view, but Touchstone refutes them in his usual sophistic fashion and tells his opponent off roundly, calling him shallow and raw. The jester's witty manipulation of all arguments is quite amusing and constitutes the chief attraction of the passage. His victory is not to a small degree due to his knack for using language in the highly patterned way of Elizabethan precious prose.

Toward the end of the comedy a similar exchange takes place between Touchstone and William, a country fellow even more simple-minded than Corin, who has hoped to win Audrey for himself and must therefore be chastened by his sophisticated rival. The man of court monopolizes the "dialogue" and pours on the country bump-kin absolute nonsense, presented as logical arguments. He ends up by chasing the lad away with an angry eruption of pretentious high-

style language with running translation into a more common vocabulary provided for the latter's sake. The result of this exercise is
superfluous verbosity, consisting of clusters of synonyms like those
of Don Armado in *Love's Labour's Lost.* Touchstone manages to win
a purely linguistic victory over his inadequate opponent and keep
Audrey to himself.

A number of shorter witty dialogues between Rosalind and Celia
ensue after their initial debate. The two cousins do not miss an occasion to elaborate a discussion of one kind or another. If such verbal
games have little to do with the dramatic structure, they perhaps contribute to illuminating the young ladies' characters and their high
spirits. Here is a typical example:

> ROSALIND . . . . O, how full of briers is this working-day world!
> CELIA. They are but burs, cousin, thrown upon thee in holiday
>   foolery. If we walk not in the trodden paths our very petticoats
>   will catch them.
> ROSALIND. I could shake them off my coat; these burs are in my
>   heart.
> CELIA. Hem them away.
> ROSALIND. I would try, if I could cry "hem" and have him.
> CELIA. Come, come, wrestle with thy affections.
> ROSALIND. O, they take the part of a better wrestler than myself.
>
> (1.3.11–22)

The ambiguous use of *burs,* derived by association from the mention
of *briers* and then employed in two concurrent figurative meanings, is
characteristic. And so are the insistent alliteration: *working-day world,
but burs, we walk—will, paths—petticoats, could—coat,* rising to the internal rhyme *try-cry,* the pun *hem—hem—him,* and the root repetition
in *wrestle—wrestler,* underlying the play on the figurative and literal
meanings of the word, which finally points to the object of Rosalind's
affection. The dialogue's main function is to show through its essayistic mold Rosalind's agility of mind as springing from her agitated
emotions, the necessary basis of lyric. This is as close as we get to the
lyric mode in the debate passages of the play—the approximation is
at best tangential.

The "treatises" presented in extended monologues are even more
typically essayistic than the debates. And, like the debates, they can

at times approach the lyrical in their details. The first striking example of this kind of argumentative speech on a well-defined topic is Jaques's famous seven-age disquisition (2.7.140–67). It is a catalog of the phases of human life from infancy to senility, succinctly presented through sets of characteristic traits. In one or two cases though the glimpses become so poignantly vivid as to remind one of the brief sketches of country life in the winter section of the closing song in *Love's Labour's Lost*. The following lines provide a good illustration:

> Then the whining schoolboy, with his satchel
> And shining morning face, creeping like snail
> Unwillingly to school . . .
>
> (146–48)

This picture is so true to life, so intensely atmospheric and so incisively etched that the whole is suffused in the unquestionable empathy of the teller (or, more probably, of the poet who has written this speech for him). The lyrical moment is difficult to miss.

A somewhat similar example of the full-fledged treatise is presented by Rosalind's typology of psychological time, as it trots hard with the young maid between the marriage contract and the church ceremony, ambles "With a priest that lacks Latin, and a rich man that hath not the gout," gallops with a thief on his way to the gallows, and stands still with lawyers between court terms (3.2.299–322). The difference between the respective tones of Jaques's and Rosalind's discussions lies in that the first leans toward the pole of opsis in its reliance on the verbal caricature of each type, while the second opts for the melos principle and, adopting a more abstract approach, relies on syntactical parallelism and alliteration to convey the necessary sense of flow. It should also be pointed out that Rosalind's monologue is punctuated by Orlando's brief questions, a device that helps to break it into short sections and thus gives it a more lively rhythm.

The third speech of this kind belongs to Touchstone (5.4.68–81, 89–101). It deals with the catalog of courtly quarrels. The classes of the so called "causes" are again seven, as were the stages in Jaques's periodization of man's life. Touchstone's tract is as technical and dry as possible, without any lyrical admixture. It is an obvious parody of the fashionable courtesy books on dueling and other skills characteristic of Elizabethan life, mainly of Italian origin.[2]

A few other solo utterances, albeit less extensive, come close to the above-considered type. One of these is Rosalind's formulation of

love as a mental disease (3.2.384–88), another is Touchstone's definition of poetry (3.3.17–19), and yet another presents his disquisition
on horns (3.3.44–58). For a final taste, we must return to Rosalind:
4.1 contains a series of humorous essays about love and marriage,
spoken by her extempore in a playful conversation with Orlando
(86–99, 136–46, and 150–64). Needless to say, all these longer or
shorter "treatises" are part of the ongoing game of love's testing.
They focus attention on the central theme of the comedy and generate the atmosphere of lighthearted fun, which it chiefly aims to in-
still in its audience. Their effect on dramatic action is close to nil.

Further afield, some monologues in this play are just as focused on
a definite topic as the treatises, and approach it in a similarly logical
or pseudo-logical way, but they deal with a more subjective concern.
Such, for instance, is Jaques's ardent apology for satire and satirists
(2.7.70–87), a speech much more impassioned than the ones we
have considered, for the speaker is defending himself against unwar-
ranted accusations. It is all in the first person singular and is replete
with rhetorical questions. Soon in the same scene we come upon a
no less agitated monologue uttered by Orlando and addressed to
Duke Senior and his retinue as they prepare for their woodland feast
(107–20). Another instance of the type belongs to Rosalind, who
relates to Orlando the obviously invented story of how once upon a
time she succeeded in curing a besotted lover of his miserable condition (3.2.390–406). This monologue is likewise in the first person
singular and, in spite of its narrative mode, it is rhetorically as tightly
patterned as the others, abounding as it does in balanced phrases
and both lexical and phonetic forms of repetition. The speech is in
fact an essayistic sketch of the fickle mistress, who can drive even the
most infatuated lover up the wall. Such sketches of psychological or
social types were quite popular in Shakespeare's time and went by the
generic name of "characters."

There are in *As You Like It* quite a few compact *character* texts,
which would merit a quick glance as members of the multifaceted
class of essayistic writings. In 2.7, Jaques opens the series with a portrait of the Fool as the most outspoken castigator of people's weak-
nesses (36-61).[3] Later in the play, he presents a Burtonesque essay
on melancholy and his own variety of this modish malaise (4.1.10
–18). Both *characters* are developed from a strongly personal angle,
yet they move toward a degree of generalization mandatory for the
genre.

Rosalind also contributes two pieces of the same type: one, in 3.2 (359–67), depicting the conventional lover, and another, in 4.1 (19–34), poking fun at the fashionable traveler. Her usual tripping rhythms are recognizable in both, as she resorts again and again to enumerations and syntactic parallelism. Her irony is much more subtle and delicate than Jaques's irritated satirical thrusts. In 5.4 (43–47), Touchstone offers a short sketch of the courtier, using himself as the model. Parallel constructions create the energetic but fairly playful tone in many of these critical essays. Their intonations bring Touchstone and Rosalind closer together and distance them from the more pensive, languid rhythms of Jaques's speeches.

Given the likely origins of the essay in the adage, the fact that *As You Like It* is so full of adages is noteworthy. Touchstone is a fountain of such compact formulae of traditional wisdom, which amounts to this character's favorite mode, parody. His memorable pronouncements are more often than not structured in the neatest possible way, anticipating Oscar Wilde's sparkling aphorisms: "as all is mortal in nature, so is all nature in love mortal in folly" (2.4.51–52), "honesty coupled to beauty is to have honey a sauce to sugar" (3.3.27–28), "to cast away honesty upon a foul slut were to put good meat into an unclean dish" (3.3.32–33), etc. Other characters produce similar gnomic pieces, but Rosalind is the one who comes closest to Touchstone's brilliance, for she is very much a compulsive jester herself: "to have seen much and to have nothing is to have rich eyes and poor hands" (4.1.21–22) and "Men have died from time to time and worms have eaten them, but not for love" (4.1.97–99).

Often couched in images and balanced syntactical constructions, such unexpected observations about life's paradoxes approach the tone of lyric. That is more often the case with Rosalind's than with Touchstone's sayings, her advantage over the jester residing in the superior rhetorical pointedness of her style but also, at a deeper level, in her emotional commitment sublimated in memorable phrases, which soar high above his impersonal charades.

Thematic insets of various essayistic kinds, including the "poetic" one or veering toward it, are obviously abundant in *As You Like It*.[4] But so are the narrative (or epic) ones. Since there is hardly any action to be presented on stage, offstage action is often reported in monologues of the nuntius-speech type. They distance us from the immediate rush of the drama and contribute to the overall static character of this play, creating the necessary conditions for the emergence and spread of the lyrical mode. There is probably a greater number of nuntii here than anywhere else in Shakespeare. I have counted nine. Most of them, though not all, are peripheral personages, as is to be expected, and in two of the cases message-bringing is their only function in the play.

Charles the professional wrestler (or "the general challenger") is first in line. He appears at 1.1.91 to break to Oliver de Boys the news, of which the latter must be well aware, that "the old Duke is banished by his younger brother the new Duke" and is now living in the Forest of Arden, where there are "many merry men with him," but his daughter Rosalind has been given permission to remain at court. The real purpose of this announcement is obviously to let the theater audience overhear a piece of necessary background information. Another nuntius, in 1. 2, is Monsieur Le Beau "with his mouth full of news" (91), concerning the progress of Charles's wrestling match and advice for Rosalind and Celia to watch its next round. When Orlando defeats Charles, to everybody's surprise and Duke Frederick's displeasure, Le Beau appears as nuntius again to inform the young man about the ill will the potentate bears him and to enlighten him on the identity of Rosalind and her impending banishment, after which he vanishes from the play without further notice.

As soon as we are ushered into the Forest of Arden in the beginning of act 2, another nuntius pops up. This personage is as short-lived as Le Beau and is not even supplied with a name. Identified as *1 Lord*, his only task is to apprise Duke Senior of Jaques's commiseration with a wounded stag and his satirical expatiations. In 2.3, old Adam brings Orlando word about his brother's plotting against the latter's life and implores him to leave his home right away (16–28). A little later, in 2.7, Jaques alerts the banished Duke to Touchstone's unexpected appearance in the forest and reproduces for him their conversation (12–43).

The reports we hear in the next three acts have mostly to do with the lovers and their stories. They are entrusted to more central characters. First, in 3.2,120–243, Celia tries to tell Rosalind about how she found Orlando in the woods, but her cousin is so agitated that it is impossible to stop her from interrupting and confusing the poor nuntia. Then, in 4.3.74, Oliver approaches the heroine with a report about her lover and his chivalric exploits. The narration stretches from line 97 to 155 and is twice interrupted by short dialogues to render it more stageworthy. A shorter account is given by Rosalind to Orlando in 5.2.28–40 about Oliver and Celia's miraculous falling in love at first sight.

Toward the end of the play, in 5.4, someone makes his first entrance on the stage with the surprising announcement "I am the second son of old Sir Rowland" (150), i.e. Orlando and Oliver's third brother, of whose existence we have barely heard in the opening lines, and it turns out that he has materialized only to tell Duke Senior—and, of course, all of us eavesdroppers in the theater—that the usurper has reformed and that he restores all power and property to his brother and the "many merry men with him."

Compared with the striking narratives of the fewer nuntii in *Richard II*, these reports are considerably drier, lacking in the empathy of a Scroop or a York, which approximates their speeches to the lyrical. Neither Le Beau's gory relation of the wrestling match, nor Oliver's story of adventures characteristic of exotic romances can measure up to those earlier speeches as far as their emotional impact is concerned. Even Rosalind's account of her cousin's amorous encounter with Orlando's brother is less intent on recreating the experience, though its rhetorical structure is tighter and more lively than those of the others. The lyric is absent from these monologues with the possible exception of some moments in the First Lord's rendition of the stag's wake, whose implied irony, however, is too strong to allow any true sympathy.

To sum up, in *As You Like It* Shakespeare seems to shun the overtly lyrical oration. Here lyricism, as we are going to witness, is allotted a different domicile. Even so, the unusual accumulation of essayistic and narrative (report) speeches, replacing the dramatic action and underscoring the concentric structure of the play, creates a sense of pervasive stasis, congenial to the lyric. Though the lyrical element in these pieces is minimal, by opening an ample space for the expression of personal reactions to characters and events they form the right textual environment for its emergence.

After the violent clashes of act 1 and the enforced departure of the protagonists from the world of political and financial rivalry and despotism, at the opening of act 2 we are ushered into a totally different reality, which is going to accommodate almost uninterruptedly all further matter until the very end of the play and is lyrically-contemplative rather than dramatically-dynamic. In fact, we are imaginatively introduced to this locus long before we first see it, when Charles describes it in his compact but glowing terms: "They say he [Duke Senior] is already in the Forest of Arden and a many merry men with him, and there they live like the old Robin Hood of England. They say many young gentlemen flock to him every day and fleet the time carelessly as they did in the golden world" (1.1.109–13). The tone of this message is balladic, lyrical: They say . . . They say . . . The slow fluent rhythm and the lulling effect of the repetition of longer syntactic periods help us to immerse ourselves in this dreamy alternative space familiar from the legends of the past, a projection of the mythological golden world mentioned by Charles, which man once inhabited and to which he yearns to return.

The golden age nostalgia, Thomas Rosenmeyer points out, "makes its triumphant entry into the Renaissance pastoral," and this is done mainly "in the form of pastoral drama, as in Tasso's *Aminta*, and Daniel's 'A Pastoral.'"[5] One might add Shakespeare's *As You Like It*, which obviously belongs to the same genre. For it too introduces its audience into what Rosenmeyer calls "Theocritus' *otium*," that state of "vacation, freedom, escape from pressing business, particularly a business with overtones of death" (67), in which a person may be lucky to sojourn. And to pick up another important feature of the otium condition, as Rosenmeyer outlines it, this is "the vital experience of a moment which it is known will be brief, but which is so fully entertained that the future and the past are largely shut out" (86). The generic kinship of the pastoral and the lyric is striking.[6] It is rooted in their common focus on the present moment, though the tendency of lyric, as noted earlier, is inclusive rather than exclusive, endeavoring to merge all time in the present and raise the latter to the status of timelessness.[7]

Time, the perennial concern of lyric poetry, the core of the "poemly theme," turns out to be the recurrent topic of *As You Like It*, this unusual play with a predominantly thematic, nonfictional generic orientation, that brings us so close to the lyric.[8] As it is also a Renaissance work concerned with the pastoral nostalgia for the golden age, it would be relevant to refer this interest to the specificity of the period, succinctly formulated by R. Quinones and discussed in my introductory chapter, viz. the concurrence of its discovery of time and the resuscitation of the golden age myth.[9] One is tempted to add that the flowering of the lyric in the Renaissance and the unprecedented growth of interest in time, in spite of their seeming opposition, are perhaps aspects of the same development.

But, to return to our text, the theme is first broached by Touchstone and that, of course, is done in his burlesque manner. When he brings to the exiled lords the story about his unexpected meeting with the fool in the forest, Jaques tells them how this person took out "a dial from his poke, / And looking on it with lack-lustre eye" began to philosophize in a banal way about the ineluctable passage of *time* (2.7.20–28). Touchstone's timepiece is no more than a childish toy in his new surroundings. The mechanical dissection of time into hours and minutes, imposed at the dawn of the modern age by the new hurried world of always pressing business, sounds absurd in the space of pastoral otium.[10] When, next, Orlando bumps into the carousing retinue of Duke Senior, he defines them at once as a company of fellows "That in this desert inaccessible, / Under the shade of melancholy boughs, / Lose and neglect the creeping hours of time" (111–13).

The apprehension of existential time that governs the life of man, though the word is barely mentioned, forms the framework of Jaques's seven-age monologue. The first long dialogue between Rosalind and Orlando in 3.2 is an important contribution to the topic. Rosalind starts her game with the ludicrous question "I pray you, what is't o'clock?" (291), to which Orlando quite reasonably responds: "You should ask me what time o'day. There's no clock in the forest" (292–93). Indeed, there is no time-measuring instrument in the Forest of Arden, if we do not count the one smuggled in by the court jester and rendered absolutely useless in this new context. Time can be sensed here only as part of nature, the diurnal cycle, perhaps the seasonal one, and the ages of human life. But it has no task-oriented reality, no mathematical existence, and therefore the clock is discarded offhand.

At this point, however, Rosalind posits another way of calibrating the passage of time, rooted in the central human experience for romantic comedy, that is, love. It seems to be as fastidious as the mechanical one, if not more so: "Then there is no true lover in the forest, else sighing every minute and groaning every hour would detect the lazy foot of time as well as a clock" (294–96). Later on the heroine will develop the same idea while accusing Orlando of not keeping time in their trysts and thus showing that he is not a true lover: "He that will divide a minute into a thousand parts, and break but a part of the thousand part of a minute in the affairs of love, it may be said of him that Cupid hath clapped him o'th'shoulder, but I'll warrant him heart-whole" (4.1.40–44). This internalization of time is an important aspect of *As You Like It*. Rosalind dilates on the relativity of life's temporal dimension in her memorable speech opening with the topical sentence, "Time travels in divers paces with divers persons" (3.2.299–322). Understood as an exclusively psychological phenomenon, time, she seems to suggest, can vary widely from person to person, depending on the social condition, the emotional state and the frame of mind of a particular individual. This notion of time deprives it of its objectively regularizing function and absorbs it in the lyrical attitude.

Duke Senior's monologue opening act 2 (1.1–17) transfers us from the court and the castle to the enticing Forest of Arden, the place where people can still live "like the old Robin Hood of England." This is a speech addressed to the lords of his retinue but, in equal measure it seems, to himself. The monologue starts with rhetorical questions praising the life of the exiles as "more sweet/ Than that of painted pomp" and the woods as "More free from peril than the envious court." The weather here can be inclement—the Duke refers to "the icy fang/ And churlish chiding of the winter's wind," but its harshness is preferable to the flattery of courtiers, behind which there always lurks dangerous double-dealing. Far away from the bourn of hypocrisy one can come to know oneself. And so the triumphant conclusion comes naturally:

> Sweet are the uses of adversity,
> Which, like the toad, ugly and venomous,
> Wears yet a precious jewel in his head;
> And this our life, exempt from public haunt,
> Finds tongues in trees, books in the running brooks,
> Sermons in stones, and good in everything.
>
> (12–17)

Though this is a public oration, there is hardly a more lyrically colored argumentative speech in the entire play. As a matter of fact, the comedy does not contain any actual soliloquies. As Agnes Latham remarks, "Private meditations and complaints have little part in *As You Like It,* where very few speakers lack a hearer."[11] Yet lyrical identification between subject and object can radiate sometimes even from public utterances like this. The rhetorical quality of the Duke's introductory monologue is sterling. The speech is free of superfluity, the syntax is balanced without being rigid, the imagery is atmospheric, the alliteration is semantically justified, and the closing lines with their skilful combination of all these merits turn into the emblem of Arden. Amiens, who is privileged to be the chief addressee of the oration, rightly compliments his master on his accomplishment:

> Happy is your grace
> That can translate the stubbornness of fortune
> Into so quiet and so sweet a style.
>
> (18–20)

Thus the lyrical character of the pastoral locus as an alternative reality is stamped on the audience's minds from the very beginning of the Arden section by a speech in the appropriate register. Not so long after that, in the opening of 2.5, we hear the first of a series of songs, confirming in a lighter vein the Duke's view of what this forest stands for. It is Amiens's "Under the greenwood tree" ditty—at bottom an invitation to all those who would like to make their lives consonant with nature to join the happy exiles. The song endorses the Duke's conviction that this kind of life, in spite of its hardships, is preferable to life at court, for in it one can find "no enemy/ But winter and rough weather" (6–7). The second stanza amplifies the same general idea, stressing the exiles' repudiation of ambition and willingness to carry the burden of self-sufficient existence. The tripping iambic trimeter, the jingling couplets and the refrain that takes up half of the stanza emanate a lighthearted mood. There is almost nothing personal in this example of communal lyricism, typical of most popular songs of any age.

A delightful appendix to Amiens's composition is produced by Jaques, who adds another stanza, written to the same tune and adopting the established scheme, but providing a diametrically opposite attitude, satiric rather than lyrical (44–50). In it the melancholy malcontent brands as asinine stupidity and stubbornness any preference for primitive life in nature over the "wealth and ease" of civilization. This is an acid parody of Amiens's lyricism, relativizing its point of view and exposing its one-sidedness but also making it obvious that skepticism deprives one of joy. Interestingly, after the clash of the two opposites on the arena of the song, Jaques plans to retire and get some sleep or "rail against all the first-born of Egypt" (53–54), while Amiens is eager to join the jolly company of his peers around the table, for the "banquet is prepared" (55–56). It is the caustic satirist and not the lyricist who shuns his fellow humans. The kind of lyricism dominant in this play, as will continue to transpire, is unexpectedly gregarious rather than solitary, almost a contradiction in terms, a paradox worth examining further.

At the end of the second act, Amiens sings yet another song, devoted to much the same theme as his previous one: "Blow, blow, thou winter wind" (2.7.175–94). Its refrain harps on the pessimistic conclusion that "Most friendship is feigning, most loving mere folly." This generalization, of course, extends the range of criticism far beyond court manners and seems to concur with Jaques's satirical negativism, verging on Timonian misanthropy. Consequently, the closing exclamation, "This life is most jolly," especially as it rhymes with the least heartening line, is somewhat fatuous. The meter is the same as in the earlier song and the refrain is as extended, but the rhyming is more intricate now. Since the merriment of the first song has soured, the proximity of the two insets, their prosodic similarity, and the fact that they are sung by the same character invite us to see them as a debate of twin poems and warn us not to take the promises of Arden too naively. Thus the interrelated lyrical insets continue to shape the significances of the dramatic space.

"There are more songs in *As You Like It*," Latham notes, "than in any other play by Shakespeare."[12] And, indeed, they are plenty. Even Touchstone intones a couple of verses to chase Sir Oliver Martext away at the end of 3.3 (88–97), and in 4.2 Jaques and some members of Duke Senior's retinue sing a mocking lay about the infamous killer of the deer (10–19). Hymen too is given a short song to perform in the closing scene of the play (5.4.139–44). Yet, the really important musical inset that balances Amiens's songs in act 2 is the charming "It was the lover and his lass" in 5.3.16–39, whose sprightly tune (probably by Morley) has been luckily preserved. But even if it had been lost, like the musical scores for most of the other songs in Shakespeare's dramas, the text would have been enough to suggest the song's lyric vivacity. The ditty is sung by two pages introduced for the purpose— young lads not as respectable as Lord Amiens. Their piece is not about "winter and rough weather" but about the joys of "spring-time, the only pretty ring-time,/ When birds do sing." The sweet season of the lovers has come to replace "the icy fang/ And churlish chiding of the winter's wind." Ver has now proved stronger than Hiems, and under its aegis the play is ready for its happy Hymenal denouement. It is curious that some critics have been led astray by Touchstone, siding with his adverse remarks on this lighthearted song. "Truly, young gentlemen," the jester opines, "though there was no great matter in the ditty, yet the note was very untunable" (40–42). It is impossible to judge how qualified cynical Touchstone is to evaluate amorous music but, surely, to expect "great matter" of a "ditty" is quite absurd. The song has all the necessary qualities—light catchy rhythm, unobtrusive suggestive imagery of vegetation and the vigor of life, nonsensical refrain words enhancing the phonetic orchestration of the verse, and so on. It is an important atmospheric piece, as pivotal for our prehension of the comedy's overall message as the dual epilogue in *Love's Labour's Lost*. And, like Amiens's early songs—perhaps even more so—it is an impersonal, communal kind of lyric.

Agnes Latham lists many intriguing similarities between *Love's Labour's Lost* and *As You Like It*, but three of these loom large: the formal patterning of several courting couples, the "plot" consisting of conversation rather than action, and "the young men's lyrics" or the exercises in amorous lyrical poetry recited on the stage.[13] The first two we have already dwelt upon and it is time to pay some attention to the third. In this play we can isolate a group of lyrical insets, similar to the songs but, unlike them, individual rather than communal. Naturally, these texts bear the stamp of trans-personal expressive traditions, such as the Petrarchan line of amorous poetry, but that is another matter.

While the would-be poets in *Love's Labour's Lost* are quite a few and each of them is eager to divulge his poetry orally—to the resonant oaks if not to fellow humans—in *As You Like It* there is just one such character, Orlando.[14] He is as deeply and helplessly in love as his Navarran predecessors, and he, like them, does not know of a better way of dealing with the situation than to pour his feelings out in verse. But no one ever hears him read his poems aloud—others will do that for him in good time. His manner of publication is uncommunicative. Though all his works that eventually come to our notice are addressed to the same person, the author never tries to make them reach her, since he is not aware of her whereabouts, so the address is simply a lyrical apostrophe, an appeal to someone absent from the space of communication. This is how we first see the poet engaged in the broadcast of his poetry:

> Hang there, my verse, in witness of my love.
> And thou, thrice-crowned queen of night, survey
> With thy chaste eye, from thy pale sphere above,
> Thy huntress' name that my full life doth sway.
> O Rosalind, these trees shall be my books,
> And in their barks my thoughts I'll character,
> That every eye which in this forest looks
> Shall see thy virtue witnessed everywhere.
> Run, run, Orlando, carve on every tree
> The fair, the chaste and unexpressive she!
>
> (3.2.1–10)

Orlando shares his lyrical effusions with the woods just as the Navarre academicians had done, but his method is not that of oral presentation and comes closer to the new culture of the printed book. For awhile the author's identity remains mysterious—like that of the authors of many anonymous early modern poems. Our immediate concern, however, is not the technology of the texts' distribution but the generic character of the above-quoted monologue, introducing this section of the play. This is clearly a lyrical praise of an idealized mistress, complete with four excited apostrophes, a cluster of poetic imagery echoing the close of Duke Senior's oration in 2.1, internal assonantal echoes and even a rhyming scheme related to the English sonnet, that of the disain.

Orlando's first poem (3.2.85–92), dedicated to Rosalind and discovered by her later in the same scene, is disappointing. As it chances to fall into the addressee's hands, she reads it aloud in total dismay. This is a pathetic attempt at composing conventional amorous verse by a very inexperienced versifier. We recognize the hackneyed association of the beloved with "both the'India's of spice and Myne" and the usual superiority figure. But everything is miserably watered down, the single rhyme is repeated ad nauseam and the meter is irredeemably lame. Michael Morgan remarks that Orlando's poetry is "just about as accomplished as Peter Quince's playwriting."[15] Touchstone seems to be of the same opinion as he offers his prompt commentary, "I'll rhyme you so eight years together, dinners and suppers and sleeping-hours excepted. It is the right butter-women's rank to market" (93–95), and then adds his parody of Orlando's couplets, reducing their idealistic hyperboles to bawdy innuendos, which turn the beloved from a worshiped goddess into a female animal in heat (98–109). The parodic method of appending to a poetic text more rhymed units is the same as Jaques's vis-à-vis Amiens's song. Here, however, we have two-tier hypertextuality. First, Orlando's own poem, as designed by the ironic author, is a spoof on Elizabethan Petrarchism (though the butt of the irony is not so much its affectation as the amateur poet's clumsiness), and second, this attempt at romantic versifying is mimicked derisively by an inveterate cynic. The final effect is a relativization of the lyric, depriving it of its absolute impact, an effect contrived more than once in *Love's Labour's Lost*.

Another, more ambitiously composed poem in a similar vein arrives on the heels of the first. This one has been found by Celia and will be read aloud by her in front of Rosalind and company (3.2.122–51). The piece consists of seven quatrains and a closing couplet—a hugely overgrown English sonnet. Like Orlando's previous effort, it is sustained in trochaic tetrameter, at times rather shaky. The author announces his intention to make the whole forest speak about his love through the poems he posts upon the trees. Then he proclaims the topics of his lyrics. One of them is the brevity of life—the staple poemly theme. Another is the disloyalty of friendship—an elegiac concern aired by the poetasters in *Love's Labour's Lost* and in Amiens's second song. But the main purpose of the lover will, of course, be to eulogize his lady, for she is "The quintessence of every sprite" that has ever graced the earth with its presence. God has charged Nature to epitomize in her the perfection of all illustrious women of old: "Helen's cheek but not her heart," "Cleopatra's majesty," "Atalanta's better part" and "Sad Lucretia's modesty." She has been devised "by heavenly synod" to combine in one body the best features "Of many faces, eyes, and hearts." There are in this conceit recognizable jocular allusions to the Elizabethan sonnet tradition and to Shakespeare's own *Sonnets* with their extreme interest in the epitome of Nature's treasures.[16] Orlando is a poor match for Shakespeare as a lyrical poet, but the author's self-pastiche is inescapable.

The addressee of this eulogy lets fly at it without the slightest delay: "O most gentle pulpiter, what tedious homily of love have you wearied your parishioners withal, and never cried: 'Have patience, good people!" (152–54). This first reaction has mostly to do with the unusual length of the pseudo-sonnet and its monotony. A few lines later Rosalind returns to it at Celia's provocation to take it apart on more precise technical grounds, remarking—very much as Holofernes had done vis-à-vis Berowne's intercepted sonnet—that some of the verses just heard "had in them more feet than the verses would bear," and that "the feet were lame, and could not bear themselves without the verse, and therefore stood lamely in the verse" (161–67).[17] Luckily for poor Orlando, Touchstone has meanwhile been sent away, or he would not have missed the occasion to find more faults with the lover's poetic venture.

We need not be so harsh. Neither of the lad's two poems is a masterpiece, and yet, just like the clumsy attempts of the lords in *Love's Labour's Lost*, Orlando's efforts enhance the humorously romantic atmosphere of the comedy by injecting into it the spirit of lyricism. The ironic distance that the playwright obliges us to keep from his character does not in the least hamper our appreciation of this character's genuine affection. Love is conducive to poetry, and poetry without love is unthinkable, but poetry is not reducible to love. Shakespeare makes no bones about this, and he lets us share his amusement at the incessant and inevitable attempts of lovers to obliterate the border between the two.

One more amorous poem crops up later in the play (4.3.40–63), though it is an epistle sent expressly to its addressee and thus, by definition, not a pure lyrical piece. Its author is a woman, the shepherdess Phoebe, writing to someone who she has mistaken for a man, Rosalind in her Ganymede disguise. The addressee is the one who reads the letter aloud and sprinkles over it bits of scornful commentary, willfully turning its message from complimentary into disparaging. Phoebe poses as the Petrarchan amorous suppliant to the extent of declaring that the failure of her beloved to requite her love would mean that she must die. The standard gender relation is reversed. The text is of indifferent aesthetic quality. Its rhetorical apparatus is minimal and weak, the measure is the trochaic tetrameter that marks off most amateur poetry in Shakespearean comedies and is rather unsteady, tending to slip into the more usual iambics. So, although the text is genuinely emotional, and its lyrical tone is indisputable, its artistic ineptness and the ironical situation in which it is forced to function (i.e. the mistaken addressee) relativize it and give it a comic rather than a romantic sound.

Exceptions notwithstanding, it would be hard to deny that most of the love declarations, in whatever kind of language and verse they are couched, are lyrical insets by rights and thus contribute to the overall tonal character of this poetic drama. And yet, one cannot help feeling that the strongest lyrical infusion comes into the play from a source that, on the face of it, has very little to do with lyrical poetry proper. This is the heroine herself, whose preference for prose as a prosodic medium, and also as a down-to-earth way of looking at things, does not prevent her from becoming the most ample generator of lyricism. The images Rosalind brings forth effortlessly are many, and most of them are fresh and striking. Her interest in the potentials of words also makes her a capable wielder of paronomasia in repartee. Even a professional pun-monger like Touchstone has to bow to her, however reluctantly, as in the following exchange about Orlando's rhymed couplets harping on the name of his sweetheart:

> TOUCHSTONE. This is the very false gallop of verses. Why do you
>   infect yourself with them?
> ROSALIND. Peace, you dull fool, I found them on a tree.
> TOUCHSTONE. Truly, the tree yields bad fruit.
> ROSALIND. I'll graft it with you, and then I shall graft it with a med-
>   lar. Then it will be the earliest fruit i'th'country, for you'll be rot-
>   ten ere you be half ripe, and that's the right virtue of the medlar.
> TOUCHSTONE. You have said.—But whether wisely or no, let the
>   forest judge.
>
> (3.2.110–19)

There is no hard and fast line between verse and prose in this comedy. If anything, the hierarchy between them is reversed. "When verse is spoken in *As You Like It*," Agnes Latham observes, "it is often no more than a rapid rhythmic *façon de parler*. The prose tends to be more vigorous, more highly stylized and more obviously artificial. It has point, gaiety, imagination, formal patterns and rounded cadences. Examples proliferate, especially where Rosalind is the speaker."[18] And, let us make this absolutely clear, her prose, however stylized, is not euphuistic.

Rosalind comes truly into her own when she becomes a denizen of the Forest of Arden. She exudes an irresistible lyrical charm in those scenes of acts 3 and 4 which are devoted to her love game with

Orlando. Direct lyrical utterances here are very rare, and there is not a single metric line. Still, the lyrical mode permeates everything in a way that is hard to analyze, because it is seldom on the surface. When, in 3.2, Celia hints to Rosalind about Orlando's presence in the forest, Rosalind appears to change her color and express an overpowering impatience to know the truth: "One inch of delay more is a South Sea of discovery. I prithee tell me who is it quickly and speak apace." And then again: "Nay, but the devil take mocking! Speak sad brow and true maid" (191–93, 207–8). As soon as Celia confirms her suspicion about the identity of the newcomer, Rosalind bursts into emotional queries that cannot wait for an answer. Her participation in the dialogue is not communicative; it is an unedited expression of her inner condition rather than a conversational gesture. She does not allow herself a single declaration of love, yet the state of being hopelessly enamored is rendered forcefully. The manner is both lyrical in its total emotional commitment and dramatic in that it gives us as spectators the opportunity to watch the speaker with the ironic sympathy of superior onlookers.

Further, Rosalind continues to interrupt her cousin's report in the same agitated manner, preventing her from producing a coherent and sufficiently informative narrative with a series of exclamations, all to do with her appreciation of Orlando, most of them in figurative language. And after that comes her treatise on the relativity of time and its dependence on personal condition and state of mind. There is in this avalanche of impressions something of the compulsive outpouring of fancy in Mercutio's Queen Mab speech, although, as already noted, Rosalind's monologue leans more toward the melos than the opsis pole of poetry, and it is certainly more logical than dreamy. Yet, her compulsion can still be felt for talking in order to both reveal and conceal the pent-up turmoil of an awakened passion, as in her previous speech. This compulsion is also conspicuous in the overwhelming loquacity of the heroine's essay on love's madness and its cure (3.2.384–406) as well as in the agitated tone of a number of her shorter monologues in later episodes. A similar dialogue occurs between Rosalind and Celia in 3.4 (starting at line 1), in which the former is on the verge of crying, since she is not sure how to make sense of her heart's condition and what to think of her lover. Here Celia wisely plays the role of a mere echo to her cousin's contradictory cues, for she knows well that it would be absurd to argue with someone so desperately enamored.

The last part of this series comes in 4.1, where Rosalind tries to inculcate into her remiss sweetheart the point that one cannot afford to "Break an hour's promise in love (40)." This speech has a lyrical vehemence, as do several others after it, the sequence culminating in Rosalind's conjuration before the lovers' parting: "By my troth, and in good earnest, and so God mend me, and by all pretty oaths that are not dangerous, if you break one jot of your promise or come one minute behind your hour, I will think you the most pathetical break-promise and the most hollow lover and the most unworthy of her you call Rosalind that may be chosen out of the gross band of the unfaithful. Therefore beware my censure and keep your promise" (176–84). As in most of the heroine's speeches, we can hear in this one too the unmistakable music of her voice, born of an emotional urgency and structured in a climax of parallel phrases to be resolved in a well-measured cadence. The lyrical impulse is the drive that gives the words their power. Rosalind's prose is in no way inferior to verse as a conveyer of this impulse.

When the two girls are left alone, Orlando's beloved immediately sheds her Ganymede mask and explodes into a rare confession, thoroughly permeated by the lyrical mode that at last gives free vent to her pent-up emotions: "O coz, coz, coz, my pretty little coz, that thou didst know how many fathom deep I am in love! But it cannot be sounded—my affection hath an unknown bottom, like the Bay of Portugal. . . . That same wicked bastard of Venus that was begot of thought, conceived of spleen and born of madness, that blind rascally boy that abuses everyone's eyes because his own are out, let him be judge how deep I am in love. I'll tell thee, Aliena, I cannot be out of the sight of Orlando. I'll go find a shadow and sigh till he come"(193–205). What she yearns for is the lover's sylvan retreat into private meditation. And the poet's! For one who is not in love, there must be a more sensible way of spending the time between the sessions of communication with others. Celia can still do it—for a while longer: "And I'll sleep" (206).

Rosalind's is undoubtedly a crucial lyrical presence in *As You Like It*, though she never attempts to express her inner self directly, and she often seems to poke fun at the very notion of love, as if trying to get the better of her passion. What she mocks, though, is chiefly the conventional posturing in love. There is no established language for a genuine personal experience of the amorous condition, and she is reluctant to borrow—like others—the shibboleths of poetic convention. The Rosalind-Orlando opposition of types of lyrical speakers, as tending to natural personal expression versus being attached to convention, repeats at a distance the similar Rosaline-Berowne and Juliet-Romeo oppositions. This time, though, there is no sign of the male partner evolving toward the more mature rhetorical state of the female one.

Rosalind never utters a soliloquy, writes a poem, or sings a song. It is only in conversation with the others that she betrays her emotional state by the way she expresses herself. And we get to know her not in the way we get to know King Richard II, through a series of self-analyses, but by listening to the revealing slips of her tongue—overhearing! Seldom does the lyrical mode that radiates from her words crystallize into a hardened lyrical form, a generic inset. It is dissolved in the dialogue. But her animated part in all dialogue is invariably central, and that is due to her quick mind, her lively temperament and, last but not least, to her inherent pervasive lyricism.

It could be argued that with Rosalind, for the first time in Shakespeare's drama, lyric ceases to strive toward hardening in recognizable poetic insets and takes the opposite course, toward dispersion in the predominantly prose organization of the azione parlata, thus infiltrating and conquering the very citadel of drama from within. Lyric in Rosalind penetrates the defences of the host genre disguised as nonlyric, as irony—and who more expert in the art of disguise than the impersonator of Ganimede? The turn of the tide, of course, has already been noticed in the gradual relaxation of the formal parameters of the lyrical module in *Romeo and Juliet*, but now the new direction has gained unprecedented centrality and momentum. In the process, lyric seems to have doffed the externals of its generic repertoire and withdrawn into its least palpable essentiality, that of the poetic stance and attitude.

An interesting foil for the obliqueness of lyrical expression in Rosalind is provided in the play by Phoebe's attempt to come to terms with the novel sensation of being in love, expressed in her long monologue in 3.5.110–36. The shepherdess cannot help mouthing what she feels has got into her. At the same time, however, she tries to resist this new feeling or, rather, hide and twist it before others, particularly before Silvius, whom she has just mocked and tyrannized for precisely the same infirmity. The result is an incessant wavering between admission and denial, which moulds the monologue in a pattern of syntactic oppositions marked by such connectives as *but, yet, though, nor.* At times Phoebe's speech comes pretty close to Rosalind's earlier utterances about her infatuation with Orlando, thus turning into something like a parodic echo. Compare the following examples that succeed one another with little interval:

> ROSALIND. His very hair is of the dissembling colour.
> CELIA. Something browner than Judas's. Marry, his kisses are
>   Judas's own children.
> ROSALIND. I'faith, his hair is a good colour.
> CELIA. An excellent colour—your chestnut was ever the only
>   colour.
> ROSALIND. And his kissing is as full of sanctity as the touch of
>   holy bread.
>
> (3.4.6–13)

> PHOEBE. Think not I love him though I ask for him.
>   'Tis but a peevish boy—yet he talks well.
>   But what care I for words? Yet words do well
>   When he that speaks them pleases those that hear.
>   It is a pretty youth—not very pretty –
>   But sure he's proud, and yet his pride becomes him.
>   . . . .
>   He is not very tall, yet for his years he's tall;
>   His leg is but so-so, and yet 'tis well.
>
> (3.5.110–20)

Shakespeare seems to have learned this comic presentation of the vacillations occasioned by the unexpected onslaught of love from Marlowe's *Dido*. The comic effect in Phoebe's case is, of course, stronger than in Rosalind's, for the oscillation here is longer and more mechanical. Perhaps no less important, Phoebe's ambivalence is willful too, while Rosalind speaks with the spontaneous reaction of a soul subjected to the impact of an unfamiliar experience. In the end, Rosalind's prose cues contain a lyrical charge which Phoebe's verse monologue lacks, apart from a few occasional sparks. It could be concluded that the paralleling of the two similar and yet different cases of young women who have unexpectedly fallen in love has the effect of drawing us into an empathic relation with Rosalind and placing us at an ironical distance from Phoebe. The contrast is due to the presence of the lyrical mode in the former's speech and behavior and to the purely dramatic, external representation of the latter's stirred emotions.

We will return to Rosalind as the bearer of the lyrical principle in the play in order to study the changes in the realization of this principle in her later appearances, but before that we should pay some attention to another important lyrical agent, with whom the heroine will eventually join forces, the simple shepherd Silvius. Because his love for Phoebe is as ineradicable as it is inexplicable, and because he occasionally resorts to the conventions of courtly love poetry, Silvius has been generally reduced by criticism to a mere joke, a caricature of the Petrarchan sonneteer in pastoral garb or, rather, in country russet.[19] Undeniably, there is some of this in him, as we can see in a speech steeped in the emblematic imagery of Elizabethan lyrical poetry:

> Sweet Phoebe, do not scorn me, do not, Phoebe.
> Say that you love me not, but say not so
> In bitterness. The common executioner,
> Whose heart th'accustomed sight of death makes hard,
> Falls not the axe upon the humbled neck
> But first begs pardon. Will you sterner be
> Than he that dies and lives by bloody drops?
>
> $\qquad\qquad\qquad\qquad\qquad\qquad\qquad$ (3.5.1–7)

There is more originality in this treatment of the mistress-murderess conceit than in that of Orlando, and his tone is more natural, less stilted, thanks to the insistent enjambments. Still, the lad is largely a spoof of the Petrarchan lover prostrate at the feet of his unrelenting beloved. For this unmanly meekness, Rosalind despises him and rails at him furiously in 4.3. However, it would be wrong to approach Silvius with the traditional critical prejudice. He may tend to turn into a laughing stock at times—but who is the lover that is immune to such misfortunes? And though he may every now and then imitate the conventions of the fashionable love poems that the theater audience was familiar with, few of his brethren have managed to do without such props. However superior we feel in relation to him, his first, unannounced appearance in 2.4 is quite striking. As a spokesman of the passion that all true lovers know only too well, he is quite eloquent, and his voice is clear and free of unnecessary borrowings. It all starts with an exclamation heaved from the depth of his soul:

"O Corin, that thou knewst how I do love her!" (20) in order to rise into an unadulterated paean:[20]

> If thou rememb'rest not the slightest folly
> That ever love did make thee run into,
> Thou hast not loved.
> Or if thou hast not sat as I do now,
> Wearing thy hearer in thy mistress' praise,
> Thou hast not loved.
> Or if thou hast not broke from company
> Abruptly as my passion now makes me,
> Thou hast not loved.
> O Phoebe, Phoebe, Phoebe!
>
> (31–40)

These blank-verse tercets with their simple yet imposing diction, the powerful refrain "Thou hast not lov'd" (rhythmically reminiscent of Tamburlaine's magnificent dirge for Zenocrate), and the closing triple apostrophe amount to a most effective lyrical outburst, miraculously crystallized into a perfect form. Setting them side by side with Romeo's early Petrarchan affectation shows a world of difference between lyrical imitation and true lyric. Rosalind is the first to appreciate the compelling drive of Silvius's confession:

> Alas, poor shepherd, searching of thy wound,
> I have by hard adventure found mine out.
>
> (41–42)

There is not a trace of mockery here. A young woman who is frequently ready to make fun of the slightest trace of pretence is obviously taken by the shepherd's performance. Does she not perhaps sense in it something that she cherishes—together with her creator—above all in the expression of feeling, the "simple truth miscalled simplicity"? Rosalind's comment illuminates the empathic effect that lyric poetry obtains on its "audience," the exciting discovery of a profound identity of all individual experiences, which is the radical of this genre. The unmistakable sound of Silvius's poetic utterance has unlocked the lyrical potential in its hearer—but in only that hearer who has had it latent in her heart. For Touchstone is also present on stage, and his response to Silvius's romantic uplift is the grotesque debasement of love, so central to the fool's role (43–52). This, no doubt, is an ironic shaft shot at Silvius's earlier statement that a man in love is known by his follies, his "many actions most ridiculous," which he himself is not ashamed to confess his own. But it does not parody the shepherd's lyrical outburst, leaving it largely unharmed by the relativizing strokes of ironical echoes. Even the bathos of Celia's ensuing reminder of the physiological framework within which all our spiritual flights must be eventually placed ("I pray you, one of you question yon man/ If he for gold will give us any food./ I faint almost to death" [60–62]) cannot cancel the vehemence of the shepherd's speech, though it does put things in perspective, a balance Shakespeare's drama always takes care to strike. The invulnerability of Silvius's lyricism reveals the special place allotted to this character in the design of *As You Like It*.

Before he next enters the stage, the enamored shepherd and his inamorata are supplied with a prologue for their stage audience—the heroine and her cousin—spoken by Corin:

> If you will see a pageant truly played
> Between the pale complexion of true love
> And the red glow of scorn and proud disdain,
> Go hence a little, and I shall conduct you,
> If you will mark it.
>
> (3.4.48–52)

This identification of Silvius as the paragon of "true love" joins Rosalind's fixation on his story and her eagerness to continue her close observation of its progress as important signals for the audience. Of course, the affair gets ludicrously complicated, and the heroine is enmeshed in it by Phoebe's uninvited love. Amid this absurd entanglement Phoebe provokes Silvius to another lyrical definition of love like the one triggered earlier by Corin. She asks the inspired shepherd to tell Ganymede "what 'tis to love," for she has found her own gifts of persuasion inadequate, and she has to resort to the assistance of the by now established poet of this passion. Without much ado, Silvius once again rises to the occasion with his natural lightness of touch, refreshing simplicity and infectious expression:

> It is to be all made of sighs and tears,
> And so am I for Phoebe.
> . . . .
> It is to be all made of faith and service,

And so am I for Phoebe.
. . . .
It is to be all made of fantasy,
All made of passion, and all made of wishes,
All adoration, duty and observance,
All humbleness, all patience and impatience,
All purity, all trial, all obedience,
And so am I for Phoebe.

$$(5.2.80–95)$$

The third stanza, erupting out of all proportion, yet sustaining the metrical flow, is admirably effective.

A rhetorical miracle occurs at this point, which will eventually bring the whole actionless drama to its logical conclusion. All lovers present on the scene join in by repeating Silvius's refrain, only substituting the names of their respective counterparts for Phoebe's name after each stanza. Thus the solo recital is turned into a litany of voices, or a collective lyric happening:

PHOEBE. And I for Ganymede.
ORLANDO. And I for Rosalind.
ROSALIND. And I for no woman.

From these incantatory repetitions a concentric pattern is evolved, reasserting the underlying identity of all individual experiences in love. Silvius becomes the spokesman for all, the shaman of the amorous condition, and the others are drawn into the meaningful ritual of the refrain returning with slight variations after every one of his poetic statements. The language of lyric can work these wonders. We remember that Shakespeare has tried it in the closing couplet of sonnet 74, in which body, soul and poetry become one through the recurrence of the same or similar words, capable of referring to all these entities by identical linguistic signs (demonstrative pronouns) and thus confirming their essential identity.[21]

In *Roots of Lyric*, Andrew Welsh outlines some aspects of traditional charm rituals that seem to underlie the Arden collective lyric: "Communal participation also creates the regular refrain: the main verses are sung by a leader, but all the dancers sing the refrain. . . . Speech rhythm gives way to chant rhythm, yielding a special chant language characterised by strong patterns of repetition in sound, word, and verse-line."[22] The leader's role is chiefly concerned with the setting of the theme and tone of the communal event. This is precisely what Silvius does. As he eventually steps down from his central position in the magic exercise, it appears to be carried on by its own momentum:

> PHOEBE. [*to Rosalind*] If this be so, why blame you me to love you?
> SILVIUS. [*To Phoebe*] If this be so, why blame you me to love you?
> ORLANDO. If this be so, why blame you me to love you?
>
> (99–101)

At this turn the common identity of the individual contributions becomes complete and thoughtlessly automatic. The words are reiterated without discernible reference to the reality of the situation. Such is certainly the case of Orlando, whose mistress is supposedly absent. Rosalind is puzzled: "Who do you speak to, 'Why blame you me to love you?'" (102–3), though in this very act she is herself drawn into the incantatory repetition of the question. Orlando, as if still dazed by the magic of the ritual, responds in the same five-foot iambic measure, with an internal homophone rhyme to boot: "To her that is not here nor doth not hear" (104). This is getting out of hand and becoming eerie in its separation from dramatic action. Rosalind must put an end to it, and she switches promptly to her trustworthy prose: "Pray you no more of this, 'tis like the howling of Irish wolves against the moon" (105–6).

Now the heroine takes over the shaman's role to structure the denouement in the same way as the "dialogue" has been structured, by actually taking advantage of its centripetal inertia. For, as she has already told Orlando, she is a trained sorceress. Her ensuing speech, radiating toward each of the participants in the ritual, is the first step toward the transformation of the whirling *azione parlata* into action proper. The recurrent pattern of the concentric form, with its respective personal variations, evolves through three consecutive stages from declaration to command:

> *(1)* [*to Silvius*] I will help you if I can. [*to Phoebe*] I would love you if I could . . .
> *(2)* [*to Phoebe*] I will marry you, if ever I marry woman, and I'll be married tomorrow. [*to Orlando*] I will satisfy you, if ever I satisfied man, and you shall be married tomorrow. [*to Silvius*] I will

content you, if what pleases you contents you, and you shall be
married tomorrow.
(3) [*to Orlando*] As you love Rosalind, meet. [*to Silvius*] As you love
Phoebe, meet.—And as I love no woman, I'll meet.

(106–15)

The participants respond in an identical manner, following Silvius'
lead, as usual:

SILVIUS. I'll not fail, if I live.
PHOEBE.   Nor I.
ORLANDO.   Nor I. *Exeunt.*

(117)

The next step will include Duke Senior and engage everybody in the
common scheme by a formal oath. Verse is the appropriate medium
for this solemn act:

ROSALIND. Patience once more whiles our compact is urged.
    [*to Duke Senior*] You say if I bring in your Rosalind
    You will bestow her on Orlando here?
DUKE SENIOR. That would I, had I kingdoms to give with her.
ROSALIND [*to Orlando*]. And you say you will have her when I
    bring her?
ORLANDO. That would I, were I of all kingdoms king.
ROSALIND [*to Phoebe*]. You say you'll marry me if I be willing?
PHOEBE. That will I, should I die the hour after.
ROSALIND. But if you do refuse to marry me
    You'll give yourself to this most faithful shepherd?
PHOEBE. So is the bargain.
ROSALIND [*To Silvius*]. You say that you'll have Phoebe if she will?
SILVIUS. Though to have her and death were both one thing.

(5.4.5–17)

Rosalind adheres consistently to the formulaic iteration of "magic"
phrases, yet she never lapses into thoughtless automatism but weaves
with great care the web of concrete dramatic action that she has designed by means of lyrical locution. The parallel answers are similarly
formulaic.

And the heroine completes the oath-taking ritual by another monologue of radial addresses sustained in the same shamanic iterative
language:

I have promised to make all this matter even.
Keep you your word, O Duke, to give your daughter,
You yours, Orlando, to receive his daughter.
Keep your word, Phoebe, that you'll marry me,
Or else, refusing me, to wed this shepherd.
Keep your word, Silvius, that you'll marry her
If she refuse me; and from hence I go
To make these doubts all even.

(18–25)

In the anagnorisis scene, when Hymen appears and her true personality is finally revealed, she initiates the last bit of the amorous litany with everybody else's willing cooperation:

ROSALIND [*to Duke Senior*]. To you I give myself, for I am yours.
    [*to Orlando*] To you I give myself, for I am yours.
DUKE SENIOR. If there be truth in sight, you are my daughter.
ORLANDO. If there be truth in sight, you are my Rosalind.
PHOEBE. If sight and shape be true,
    Why then, my love adieu.
ROSALIND. I'll have no father, if you be not he.
    I'll have no husband, if you be not he.
    Nor ne'er wed woman, if you be not she.

(114–22)

This incantatory dialogue sounds so cryptic by making a number of different references with its minimalistic use of nearly identical chunks of language that Hymen, as the new leader of the game, feels obliged to step in and unravel the mystery. Then, without delay, the god of marriage solemnizes the weddings of all four couples in their own linguistic mode (129–34). One final bout of this concentric-language rite remains to be completed by Jaques's benison (184–90). The Duke has already announced the dances for the "brides and bridegrooms all" (176–77), and the rounds of words quite naturally transform into similarly patterned physical movements.

In the whirls of the incantatory ritual encompassing the last acts of the comedy, lyric has won the upper hand and has succeeded in shaping the dramatic action in its own way. It has managed to do so by ceasing to seek an isolated space for itself and by permeating the drama in its entirety, replacing its kinetic organization with a concentric one.

In *As You Like It* Shakespeare returns to the theme of the conventional lyric and its hackneyed ways of expressing the passion of love, a theme that he has tackled in *Love's Labour's Lost* and *Romeo and Juliet*. However, his critique of Petrarchan artificiality is no longer so disparaging. If we leave aside Touchstone's variant of the amorous malaise, which is a grotesque, convex-mirror reflection of romantic love, there are three other personages worth dwelling upon in relation to this topic: Orlando, Silvius, and Phoebe. Orlando is, quite obviously, a humorous portrait of the Elizabethan sonneteer, yet it is equally clear that the joke is not leveled at the entire lyrical movement but rather at the lover turned poet under the impact of his feelings and producing amateurish verse of indifferent quality. Much of the familiar paraphernalia of the tradition crops up in his poems, as well as in his conversations with Ganymede/ Rosalind, becoming an easy target for the latter's irony. It is important to note, however, that, unlike Berowne and Romeo, Orlando does not feel obliged to shed his traditionalism and evolve into a mature person who can express his feelings in a more genuine way. He does not, at any point, grow conscious of the unoriginality of his expression, as his predecessors were forced to do, and Rosalind, who is so keenly sensitive to the ways of language, seems to accept him gladly for what he is the way he is. His sin is venial, its radical being not imitative affectation but inexperience.

Orlando's rather extensive dialogue with Jaques in 3.2 is interesting to consider. The two of them are antipodal in their attitude to life and love. One is the type of the romantic lover with a lyrical bent, and the other is the nihilistic satirist. From the very start, they do not appear to like each other very much. Jaques asks Orlando to "mar no more trees with writing love-songs in their barks" (and we know from his earlier elegy on the wounded stag that his ecological concerns are serious), to which the poet replies with a request that the satirist should no longer mar his verses "with reading them ill-favouredly" (252–55).

Orlando does not change his romantic manner of speaking for the sake of his skeptical interlocutor. When Jaques enquires how tall his beloved is, his answer is, characteristically: "Just as high as my heart" (262). The other pays him a tongue-in-cheek compliment, "You are full of pretty answers" (263), and continues to suggest that the lover draws his style of speaking from the clichés of ring engravings. At this point Orlando unexpectedly returns, in the same metaphoric vein, to the ironical bite with a no less ingenious reference to Jaques's own triteness. His opponent is impressed with the lover's nimble wit and suggests that the two of them could become a good satirical duet, an invitation which Orlando rejects offhand, for his disposition is not to find faults with anybody but himself. Romeo's "split personality" is not his. To Jaques's conclusion that his worst fault is to be in love, Orlando replies confidently: "'Tis a fault I will not change for your best virtue" (275–76). The two part company in a significantly ceremonious way, which turns their separation into something more than a personal event and gives it the sound of finality:

> JAQUES. I'll tarry no longer with you. Farewell, good Signior Love.
>   [*Exit Jaques.*]
> ORLANDO. I am glad of your departure. Adieu, good Monsieur
>   Melancholy.
>
> (283–86)

Whatever his shortcomings indeed might be, Orlando as the champion of true love manages to hold his own against the blight of Jaques's skepticism. His conduct in this single combat of words is indeed exemplary, almost heroic. The language of love, albeit not terribly original—and this comedy, as we have noted, teaches us that deep down all love stories are identical—is a good language if it is employed to express the truth of one's inner self.

Even Rosalind, who cannot tolerate any artificiality, and who, as Rosalie Colie points out, "makes fun of Orlando's assumed courtly poses, such as the role of pastoral lover," is not exempt from occasional recourse to the courtly treasure trove of expressive hyperboles, as in her half-jocular, half-serious reaction to the news of Orlando's approach in the garb of a hunter: "O ominous, he comes to kill my heart" (3.2.239).[23] This exclamation can indeed be interpreted as humorous, though the underlying seriousness in the heroine's speech is indisputable. In *As You Like It* courtly conventions are, no doubt, poked fun at just as they were in earlier plays, yet they are no longer mocked in the same superior manner as before.

The case of Silvius and Phoebe is even more indicative of this shift of attitude to the tradition. Theirs is a love affair that unmetaphors the standard Petrarchan scheme of the moaning lover and the disdainful mistress. Silvius's absolute humility, his readiness to content himself with the least favor dropped in his way have already been considered. Phoebe, on her part, treats Silvius like dirt. She even goes as far as employing him as her postman and making him take her amorous message to another person, Ganymede. Then she offers to use him as her speech writer and spokesman. Silvius puts up with all the humiliation because his love, however misdirected, is strong. We seem to be invited both to chuckle at the befuddled lover's absurdities and to appreciate his complete dedication to the promptings of his heart. When Silvius becomes the supreme lyrical eulogist of love, accepted by all lovers as their instrument of self-expression, his stature can no longer be questioned or undermined by his comic self-effacement.

Phoebe, on the other hand, is not only the proud and cruel *she* of the sonnet tradition, but also the reversed image of the Petrarchan paragon of beauty and chastity, a simple shepherdess not of the refined pastoral type but of the crude country mould emerging from the Corin-Touchstone "philosophical" debate. Her features, nevertheless, seem to be derived from those of Berowne's beloved Rosaline and from the Dark Lady of the *Sonnets*. Rosalind refers to her "inky brows," her "black silk hair," her "bugle eyeballs," her "cheek of cream" and, somewhat later, to her "leathern hand."[24] She advises Phoebe not to be too choosy about her lovers. And again, this debunking does not amount to a total satirical destruction of the Petrarchan cult of love, for there are in the play two other women in love, Rosalind and Celia, who cannot be equated with Phoebe. The comedy certainly caricatures the construct of the sonnet mistress, but the ideal is not undermined. Having deconstructed to the end the fashionable lyrical language of love, in the Arden play Shakespeare seems finally to make his peace with it, as he recognizes the universal truth buried under its extravagances.

An overview of the workings of the lyric in *As You Like It* reveals important new developments in its author's generic experimentation. When, after the happy ending of this love comedy, largely due to her manipulation of its diverse strands, Rosalind turns directly to the offstage audience, she starts her farewell speech with the following words: "It is not the fashion to see the lady the epilogue; but it is no more unhandsome than to see the lord the prologue." Thus she takes us back to the beginning of the play, which was opened with a similarly long informative monologue for the sake of the audience (although technically addressed to another character) and, indeed, spoken by the "lord," Orlando. In this way the outermost circle of the concentrically conceived drama is completed. Within it there is the smaller, inscribed circle of the action itself: the falling in love of the lord and the lady compounded with their banishment from the usurped court, at one end, and their marriage and preparation for a triumphal return to the restored court, at the other. Still further in, one can find the innermost inscribed circle—or is that the motionless center itself?—of the pastoral locus called the Forest of Arden, the place of exile for all concerned but also the sphere of being where love reigns supreme and the dreams of happiness materialize without fail.

On the verge of their passage from the land of wrangling to this blessed bourn of peace and affection, at the close of act 1, Celia tells Rosalind:

> Now go we in content
> To liberty and not to banishment.
>
> (1.3.134–35)

This is the realization of Gaunt's advice not taken by Bolingbroke. The two young women decide to transform their banishment into a delightful liberation from tyranny. The Forest of Arden, to which they—like all other fugitives from oppression—choose to retire, is a locus amoenus created by the imagination, theirs or that of their author. It is a pastoral make-believe world, which may at times reveal its disturbing closeness to the crudities of actual country life, but is generally blissful. As Orlando is the first to point out, there are no clocks in the woods—apart from perhaps the odd absurd timepiece smuggled in by an escapee from the world left behind. Time here, like everything else for that matter, can only be an inner reality, for the books of this sphere of being are in the running brooks, and its sermons are in the stones. There is no pressing business of any kind. It is the realm of otium, in which all human beings can shed the alien accretions of life within the body politic and dive into their actual selves in order to become truly human and whole. This is, then, par

excellence the lyrical space. And lyric is bound to become its preferred language.

Lyric is easily detectable even from a cursory look at the text of
the play. It makes itself palpably present in a number of inset poems
and songs, which have become the hallmark of *As You Like It*. These
intrusions, however, as we have seen, function in an environment
conditioned by a variety of other thematic inserts belonging to the
essayistic type: debates, treatises, character sketches, adages, etc.
The dianoic element in the comedy is so bulky and ubiquitous that
it largely replaces the fictional, as reflective talk replaces dramatic
action.

An ingredient that is particularly salient in this mixture of thematic genres is that of satire. Of course, the last years of the sixteenth
century, when the play was written, were exceptionally drawn to satirical literature. The year 1599, in fact, is remembered for the formal
suppression of satirical publications and their public burning. It was
probably because of this act that satirists tried to find a new outlet
for their compositions in the theater. Jaques and Touchstone, two
characters indispensable for Shakespeare's play but nonexistent in
its source, Lodge's *Rosalynde*, have been introduced for this specific
purpose. Like Mercutio in *Romeo and Juliet*, they make an important
contribution to the thematic and atmospheric contents of the drama,
yet, unlike him, have no relation to the development of its action.
This, naturally, could be explained by the lack or, at least, the unim-
portance of plot in *As You Like It*.

For Heather Dubrow, Elizabethan pastoral and satire are opposed
to each other as genre and counter-genre.[25] However, as Thomas
Rosenmeyer points out, pastoral "obtains some of its effects by playing the country against the city, and exploiting the tension between
them. To emphasize pastoral or rural happiness by placing the *locus
amoenus* against a foil of court luxury or city misery is a technique that
has appealed to many."[26] The contrast is revealing, and it is through
this contrast that the acidity of satire finds its way into the sweetness
of idyllic otium.

But despite the spread of satirical and other thematic genres of
all sorts through the body of the play, lyric, even if left without an
autonomous space of its own among their dizzying variety, manages
to secure an unchallenged centrality for itself. And it does so again
through the creation of a concentric structure, viz. the innermost
circle that informs the middle of the play, its Arden component. This

section opens and advances toward the core of the drama through a number of insets: Duke Senior's introductory monologue in 2.1, Amiens's songs, Orlando's tree poems, etc. Such relatively isolated examples of generic inclusion, only partly integrated into the host genre through their dramatic relativization by a sparkling wake of commentaries and parodies, are familiar from the earlier plays.

In the latter scenes of the Arden section, however, the playwright introduces an entirely new, hitherto unattempted kind of lyrical molding of the dramatic text. This is the ritualistic quasi-litany dialogue, first developed around Silvius's lyrical adulation of love but soon adopted by Rosalind and turned into an instrument of molding the concluding dramatic action in the characteristically lyrical concentric manner. Susanne Langer is perhaps right in saying in the course of her discussion of folk lyrical poetry that "No one has ever known a crowd to invent a song, although successive members may elaborate one, adding stanzas or proposing parodies, once its poetic theme, rhyme scheme, and tune have been proposed (the meter is usually dictated by the tune). The idea comes from one person; and a serious song, such as a 'spiritual,' is usually presented in a complete form, however simple."[27] We have indeed witnessed in this comedy cases of elaborating on a lyrical piece by the addition of parodic stanzas. Yet, in these later scenes the lyric is generated by a simultaneous collective effort—very similar to the one Andrew Welsh describes on the material of shamanic practices. Here Rosalind, with Silvius's help, manages to fuse the individualities of several dramatis personae into a single lyrical persona, a single lyrical voice expressing the essential oneness of all love experience. For, lyric in principle, as we know, always tends to rise to generalized impersonality from the midst of its inherent subjectivism.[28] And by transforming this lyrical unification into a unitary dramatic action, the heroine succeeds in summarily bringing the romantic comedy to its necessary conclusion with the collective ceremony of multiple marriages.

Collective lyric is almost a contradiction in terms, an oxymoron. Yet, as John Erskine points out, it can occur in such exceptional cases "when the community is thoroughly united and fired by a universal enthusiasm."[29] This is exactly what we observe in the scenes in question—a choric unity of a number of individual voices expressing the same theme in an identical way. The technique may be seen as a development and expansion of dialogue modules from the earlier plays, culminating in the shared sonnet of *Romeo and Juliet*. Through the creation of a universally meaningful language, capable of bringing together all individual experiences and strivings, it manages to organize the whole of drama by lyrical means.

It should be nonetheless conceded that the ritualistic collective lyrics lack the inimitable spontaneity of the individual poetic voice. They are formulaic by definition and the absolute symmetry of form that is so vital for their functioning deprives them of the ability to express the delicate nuances of emotion and attitude. Such is the price that has to be paid for the universality of their message. Ironically, it is exactly this rigidity of their conception that makes them as uncharacteristic of their directress as the courtly solo compositions of the kind represented by Orlando's love poems. The public nature of these litanies compels them to strive toward a formality comparable to, though of a different nature from, that of Richard II's lyrical oratories. But Rosalind's heart—like Juliet's—prompts her to break through all public conventions to a genuine expression of the truth that is hidden within.

Now we can finally push off from the circumference of the innermost circle of the play's structure with its individual or communal single-voice lyrical insets, on the one hand, and its collective, polyphonic modulations of dialogue, on the other, and arrive at the very center of this amazingly concentric work to find its primum mobile in the inimitable presence of the heroine. A presence intensely lyrical, though formally sustained in prose. For it is a kind of prose that, as A. Latham notes, modulates easily into verse and is frequently more closely patterned than verse without being pretentious.[30] In Latham's words again, "Rosalind's high spirits jet like a fountain" (xx). It is this lively temperament, perked up by the still unaccommodated passion of love, that pours itself forth into delightfully fresh images, witty wordplay, adages, jokes, parables and invented stories, but above all, into the excited tripping rhythms of syntactical parallelisms, enumerations and climaxes of all kinds. Such overflowing linguistic energy suggests the still unformed expression of a strong inner compulsion and we cannot help being conscious of it. So powerful and uncontainable is the compulsion that it must erupt on the slightest occasion and recreate the entire world in its own likeness.

Moreover, it seems to affect the other denizens of the Forest of Arden, often molding their way of speaking in a similar springy rhythm in monologues and dialogue alike. The heroine's lyrical presence is thus diffused throughout the play to form its general atmosphere and its entire world in the way that we learn to associate above all with her. The Forest of Arden is after all an inner territory of her mind, of her poetic imagination, and she has all the prerogatives to shape it the way she wishes. Even its scenic reality in the Elizabethan theater is a thing of the imagination created by the lyrical power of language, not by any stage props or sets. As Arden is, then, not a truly dramatic but a personally lyrical space, Rosalind as its poetic shaping spirit meets with little resistance from the other characters when she places them in the roles she has allotted each of them.

Shakespeare's youthful heroine, who is too reticent or too unprepared to put her feelings into a carefully articulated thematic utterance, is generously willing to share the impulse of her heart with all humanity and become the inspired lyrical demiurge, the harbinger of universal happiness. Her lyrical presence seldom finds a complete isolated expression. It is inimical to the method of generic inclusion, but its modal spread throughout the comedy is so pervasive that it transforms the drama from its innermost center into something approaching the theoretically impossible centaur-like generic hybrid, not of lyrical drama but of a more organic blend that could be called *lyrodrama*.

HAMLET

It would not be an exaggeration to say that Shakespeare's quintessential lyrodrama is the tragedy of the Prince of Denmark, which was created most probably within a year of the Forest of Arden comedy. Shaftesbury was the first to remark that *Hamlet* has "but one character."[31] The play has been defined as "a prolonged description of a single consciousness."[32] In what is known to be the longest dramatic text of the canon we are faced with a protagonist's role of unparalleled length. According to Harold Bloom's calculation, the Prince is given three eighths of the total number of lines "and is almost always the center of concern, even when he is offstage."[33] This centrality of an individual presence brings us, of course, into the realm of the lyric. As George T. Wright points out: "In their 'pure' forms the lyric presents one speaker, the drama more than one. We call lyrical, therefore, those dramas in which one character (with his point of view) so predominates that his confrontations of other characters seem falsified: the meetings with other personae are merely opportunities for their spiritual domination by the hero."[34] Harold Bloom offers other comments that suggest the lyricism of Hamlet's role and the play it belongs to: "Shakespeare's investment in *Hamlet* is more personal and more potentially illuminating than is his attachment to any of his other plays, including even *The Tempest*."[35] "Hamlet potentially is a great poet-dramatist, like his creator" (88). Hamlet's "power over language is so enormous" (109–10). Hamlet is "an archetype of the artist" (137). "Unlike Oedipus or Lear, Hamlet never seems victimized by dramatic irony. What perspectives can we turn upon Hamlet other than those he himself has revealed to us?" (144).

Here, indeed, to a greater extent than in any other play, we seem to hear the poet through his hero. Kenneth Burke defines *Hamlet* as an unusually confessional drama, which "makes statements not merely because of their function in the play, but because Shakespeare *as a man* had to say them."[36] In this sense, Hamlet is more akin to the speaker of *The Sonnets* than to other dramatic characters. Gradually, he monopolizes the point of view on all matters tackled in the tragedy, teaching us to trust him only and to see the world through his eyes, as if he alone is in possession of the ultimate truth. This is, of course, the way the lyrical voice usually imposes its unqualified dominance over us so fully that our identity is subsumed under his. Hazlitt was perhaps the first to proclaim the Prince's lyrical sway over his audience: "It is *we* who are Hamlet."[37] And Coleridge was no less aware that we all have "a smack of Hamlet" in us.[38] It is, arguably, the lyrical propensity of the Romantics, born of their extreme individualism, that can explain their unprecedented attachment to this hero.

Further, we should consider Hamlet's proverbial preference for contemplation, lyric's basic mode. Burke notes that in this play "Shakespeare nearly dissolved the identity of drama, removing it from the realm of action to a realm of pre-action that would amount to no action."[39] And he makes it clear that "Drama is dissolved by the turn from dramatic *act* to lyric *state*."[40] Northrop Frye concurs: "*Hamlet* is best approached as a tragedy of *Angst* or of melancholy as a state in itself, rather than purely as an Aristotelian imitation of an action."[41] *Hamlet*, in other words, is more easily classed with the thematic rather than the fictional genres. And its thematic cast is, beyond all doubt, the poemly one, as it demonstrates the full set of Crane's "reduction terms": life and death, good and evil, love and hate, harmony and strife, order and disorder, eternity and time, reality and appearance, truth and falsity, emotion and reason, complexity and simplicity, nature and art.[42]

The thematic (predominantly lyrical) nature of *Hamlet* is made most apparent by the profusion of insets in it. Francis Berry, who has carried out the most thorough study of such elements in Shakespeare's drama, ranks it highest in the canon for its abundance and variety of generic inclusion.[43] This is most frequently found in the speeches of the protagonist, whom Harold Jenkins calls "the greatest of all soliloquizers."[44] Hamlet's soliloquies—all seven of them—are deservedly famous. They offer the most natural point of entry into our analysis of the dianoic features of the play. It would be interesting to find out to what extent these features are specifically lyrical and how they interconnect with elements of other kinds.

The very first of the soliloquies, "O that this too too sallied flesh would melt . . ." (1.2.129–59) rings a new note in Shakespeare's dramatic art, which ushers in his mature period. It starts with an emotional exclamation, reminiscent of Faustus's desperate last wish to escape eternal punishment by melting into the mists of the night. At the height of this poetic outburst, Shakespeare seems to find a foothold in the example offered by Marlowe, who had, a decade earlier, discovered in the Doctor's parting speech the rudiments of the lyrodramatic soliloquy.

In its entirety, this first long speech of the hero is from the heart—unpremeditated, disjunctive, repetitive, abounding in sudden interruptions, switchbacks, parentheses, questions and exclamations, which break through the logical argument and disrupt it with the vehemence of an inner tempest. Wolfgang Clemen maintains that what it offers "is not a train of thought nor a consistent process of feeling but a turmoil of emotion, recollection and violent accusation."[45] I would beg to differ: the feeling is turbulent yet pretty consistent throughout, and the train of thought is not as desultory as it would appear at first sight. It is curious that the long, nearly shipwrecked sentences in the middle somehow manage to steer their course in spite of the rough emotional seas they have to cross. The shorter first section of the soliloquy (129–37) is purely lyrical in its uncompromising intent to express a troubled state of mind without any explanation of its causes. The longer second section (137–57) is more complex, as the speaker grapples with the disorderly emotions aroused by his mother's puzzling and unforgivable betrayal of his father's memory.

Although the speech withdraws from the immediate action and is obviously of the reflective (commentative) type, it considers closely the dramatic situation at hand and its repercussions. It is not absolutely detached from the plot and would make little sense if considered in isolation from the play.

This second section proceeds in an apparently antidiscursive way, entering into the subject of its central concern in a disorganized, nonrhetorical manner that generates fresh poetic images, characteristic of the lyrical (nonoratorical) mode. Yet, there is something that makes us hesitate whether such instances of dramatic speech could be defined as lyrical, and that is exactly the impression they create of an emotional state that has not found its stable aesthetic form, its equilibrium of feeling and thought, but is still struggling toward an adequate expression. Could we surmise that what we witness are lyrical pieces in the making? Clemen sees them as recessions from the outer into some "inner drama."[46] The question arises: is inner drama a dramatic or a lyrical genre? Is it a dramatization of the lyrical stance or the opening up of a new dramatic dimension by lyrical means? There are poems of this kind (e.g. John Donne's "metaphysical lyrics" or Robert Browning's "dramatic monologues"), usually dubbed "dramatic" because of their inherent dynamism. Yet their essentially lyrical organization cannot be questioned. What I have been trying to say is that soliloquies of the kind of "O that this too too sallied flesh would melt" can hardly be considered as cases of generic inclusion (i.e. lyrical insets in the midst of drama). Rather, they are examples of modulation resulting in a kind of hybridization that could be defined as modal—an organic fusion of the substantive parts of the generic repertoires of both literary kinds.

The close of Hamlet's first soliloquy is somewhat abrupt. Its enormous emotional energy has been exhausted, or the entry of Horatio, Marcellus, and Barnardo makes it impossible for the protagonist to go on delving into his hurt feelings—in either case some sort of a rational conclusion has to be drawn from this passionate outburst. So the hero sums it up: "It is not, nor it cannot come to good" (158), and waking up to the necessity of having to keep his counsel in the midst of the others, he switches to something like a resolution: "But break, my heart, for I must hold my tongue" (159). We leave the lyrodramatic fusion behind, passing through the essayistic inset of the penultimate line and exiting with the actional orientation of the closing one. The whole soliloquy then may be seen as compounded of four sections of varying lengths: (1) lyrical inset (129–37); (2) lyro-dramatic hybrid (137–57); (3) essayistic inset (158); (4) actional (dramatic) aside (159).

The second soliloquy (1.5.92–112) comes in the wake of Hamlet's tête-à-tête with his father's ghost and evinces the speaker's state of mind, as it is gravely shaken by the revelation just received. The soliloquy might almost be taken as actional because of its marked orientation to the future and its resolute tone. Yet at a closer look it reveals its total lack of planning. The energy of the speech is wholly internal and its target is within the speaker, not in any relation between him and the outer world. We are faced with an outburst of confused feelings, starting with a cluster of exclamations, questions and apostrophes: "O all you host of heaven, O earth—what else?—/ And shall I couple hell? O fie! Hold, hold, my heart,/ And you, my sinews, grow not instant old/ But bear me stiffly up" (92–95). If there is a thematic center in this tumult, it is the idea of memory, which punctuates the entire passage with the refrain-like repetition of "Remember thee" and the recurrence of words like "tables," "records," "book," "brain," and "memory." The discontinuity of the utterance points to its inwardness again, but its engagement with the action of the play is unflagging. Both the lyrical inwardness and the dramatic pertinence come into a knot in the heaping apostrophes: "O most pernicious woman,/ O villain, villain, smiling damned villain" (105–6). The lyrodramatic hybrid has emerged again in a different guise, that of the quasi-actional monologue.

Hamlet's third soliloquy (2.2.484–540), which is almost twice as long as either of the previous two, is a combination of many generic strains—from the oratorical through the dramatic to the almost solipsistically lyrical and back again. It also contains some shreds of epic relation. And, finally, in spite of its tumultuous emotionality and apparently impromptu character, the underlying logical structure of the entire speech is even firmer than that of the previous one. The dramatist seems to have discovered some kind of a middle ground between the lyric and the essayistic mode, complicating the generic character of the text even further and drawing into it the potentials of all literary kinds.

The speech is very important in the construction of the tragedy, as it closes not only the second act but the whole initial phase of the Prince's uncertainty and hesitation with his decision to test the truth of the Ghost's intimation by staging a play and thus determine once and for all the course of action. In other words, this is the point at which the protagonist finally turns into the motor of the plot—the play's *hero*.

The speaker's withdrawal into the inner space is signaled—more for the audience than for him—with the statement: "Now I am alone" (484). The first line of the soliloquy proper—just like that of the previous one—marks the release of what sounds like an unbearably pent-up emotion, this time of self-disgust: "O, what a rogue and peasant slave am I!" (485). Further the speech continues in the same agitated manner through a series of questions and exclamations. The picture that emerges is that of the itinerant actor and his passionate performance, which Hamlet has just observed together with us. We hear the Prince's heated reaction to this impression as he sees in his imagination how the player would have acted if he had had to deal with a real problem like his own. So the first thematic section of the soliloquy (486–501), the one issuing directly from the dramatic action in the preceding episode, is completed.

The second section (501–22), opening with the short emphatic line "Yet I," seems to return to the beginning of the speech to pick up its main concern with the character of the speaker, for which the actor is no more than a foil. And Hamlet bursts once again into a storm of self-recrimination and abuse. He is so flustered that his behavior smacks of the hallucinatory: in his heated imagination he becomes the object of humiliating attacks and degradations. This brings back the memory of his task as revenger and, with it, his hatred and scorn for Claudius, expressed in a spurt of damning epithets. But his mental gaze returns to himself and the scorn is poured lavishly on his own head. The section ends with the breathless exclamations of revulsion that almost defy sensible language: "Fie upon't, foh!"

A completely new note—"About, my brains!"—opens the third section (522–40). The hero returns to the topic of playacting, which was the focus of the first section, though now his main concern is to draw a lesson from the magic of empathy that the theater can work and plan a performance bound to clear all lingering doubts about the untimely death of his father. This last movement ends with the new, aphoristically expressed, assurance:

> The play's the thing
> Wherein I'll catch the conscience of the King.

All three sections are of almost equal length, each comprising some twenty lines. The first one is intensely lyrical in its expression, yet it is firmly rooted in a concrete dramatic episode and keeps referring back to it. The second departs from this concrete event and sinks even deeper into the lyrical recesses of the self, but its referential function is no less active, though this time it is geared not to a single episode but to the entire plot of the tragedy. Both the first and the second sections reveal the hectic rhythms of inner drama and could therefore be termed lyrodramatic. The third, drawing its purposeful energy from their passion, is avowedly actional. After reflecting on the theatrical performance just observed and specifically on one of its roles, the speaker compares his situation and behavior to those of the actor in order to condemn his own inadequacy and finally forges a plan of initiatives that would overcome this weakness and that would, significantly, employ the stratagem of a theatrical performance. Thus the circle action-inaction-action is completed. In rhetorical terms, this movement takes its cue from the dramatic plot in order to withdraw gradually into the intense lyricism of inner drama and then reemerge with a new impulse for action furthering the development of the plot. The lyric mode is integrated into the play in order to serve the generically defined purposes of the drama without relinquishing its own buoyant prominence. The result is another complex lyrodramatic hybrid.

It is also interesting that the entire soliloquy, in spite of its undeniable central inwardness, is framed between the short opening signal mentioned above and a fairly extended close, both half-addressed to the audience in the old theatrical fashion. And it undeniably arises from a concrete plot event in order to lead to another. Thus the poetic flight, however emancipated from the drama, is closely interwoven with it.

The fourth soliloquy, the "To be, or not to be" meditation (3.1.55–87), is the hardest to consider, since it has become the hallmark of Shakespeare's dramatic poetry and, through long overuse, is so clichéd as to preclude any attempt at unprejudiced analysis. Wolfgang Clemen observes that "here a man only thinks and though the thought is transformed into unforgettable images it does not anywhere link up with the inner or outward action."[47] What we have, then, is a thematic inset of the essayistic kind. Ralph Berry's view is not very different, though it does make some important qualifications to Clemen's: "The crucial sampling of Hamlet's powers as intellectual is the 'To be or not to be' soliloquy. It is unreasonable to treat it as a philosophical disquisition—it is an associative meditation, the mind reviewing a diorama of concepts and images. But it is fair to point out that it suggests, in outline, a logical structure. . . . Hamlet begins with the reasoning, and then—more subtly—ends with what looks like a conclusion but is in fact the unacknowledged premise of the meditation."[48] Berry's is, in effect, an attempt to reformulate what Nicholas Brooke has already suggested in his *Shakespeare's Early Tragedies*, regarding the soliloquy as an "imaginative exploration; reasonable and intelligent certainly, but not philosophy."[49]

Let me round off this small excerpt from a vast critical debate on the generic features of Hamlet's (and Shakespeare's) most famous dramatic speech with Rosalie Colie's helpful contribution: "But the terms of his soliloquy on life and death, on living and dying, on action and retirement, are not such as to indicate his studious temperament only, though they surely do that; they are Hamlet's casuistic maneuver to objectify and distance, for a while at least, an overwhelming and immediate life-problem."[50] "To objectify and distance . . . an overwhelming and immediate life-problem"—this is precisely a function of lyric poetry, its therapeutic effect for the poet. And the oppositions of "life and death," "living and dying," "action and retirement," etc., Crane's "reduction terms," are part and parcel of the "poemly theme."

What is, then, the generic disposition of "To be or not to be"? Its logical structure is even more categorical than that of the preceding soliloquy. However, as some of the above-quoted commentators point out, this structure has been consciously imposed on an emotional inquiry into the insoluble problems of being that rocks it from underneath and betrays its profound uncertainty. Significantly, the speech opens with the central dilemma of existence, and its introductory, topic line ends on the word that defines its overall interrogatory tone: "To be, or not to be—that is the question" (55), Some of the fairly long central sentences of the soliloquy are insistently introduced by interrogatives: "Whether 'tis nobler" (56), "For who would bear" (69), "Who would fardels bear" (75). The spirit of this utterance is no less questioning and unsettled than that of the earlier ones.

The whole is very far from a carefully thought-out oration aimed at persuading an audience to accept a particular philosophical view or attitude. Its neat argumentative form is belied by sudden breaks, stumbles, uncertainties and illuminations, encoded in pauses, ellipses, exclamations, repetitions: "to die: to sleep—/ No more" (59–60), "to die: to sleep—/ To sleep, perchance to dream—ay, there's the rub" (63–64), "—there's the respect" (67), Tumbling enumerations, piled-up emotional epithets and nouns work in the same direction. And the logical progression is certainly subordinated to the expression of some deep-rooted preoccupations that clamor not for development but for rhetorical amplification—the concentric form takes precedence over kinetic progression. The crux of the matter, the answer to the question why a weary existence is allowed to drag on, is stated twice in two synonymous, though outwardly different, metaphors: (1) "For in that sleep of death what dreams may come/ When we have shuffled off this mortal coil/ Must give us pause" (65–67); (2) "But that the dread of something after death/ (The undiscovered country from whose bourn/ No traveller returns) puzzles the will/ And makes us rather bear those ills we have/ Than fly to others that we know not of" (77–81).

And, last but not least, let us acknowledge the multiple manifestations of the opsis and melos principles: the overwhelming abundance of fresh illuminating images, the energetic spurts of alliteration and assonance amounting at times to internal rhyming ("With a bare bodkin. Who would fardels bear" [75], "But that the dread of something after death" [77]), and the overall complex musical harmony of the utterance, that compelling rhythm that gives us no respite from its first to its last syllable. Under the guise of a rational argumentative essay we are offered yet another example of the lyrodramatic hybrid, whose purely lyrical variant appears as number 66 among Shakespeare's sonnets.

Unlike the preceding soliloquies, "To be, or not to be" does not take off from any concrete dramatic event or situation.[51] Hamlet enters the stage with its first words on his tongue and, as soon as another character appears, breaks off his speech abruptly with the self-addressed injunction: "Soft you now,/ The fair Ophelia!" (87–88). By then, of course, the rather circular argument of his meditation has been completed. This is one of the very few dramatic speeches in Shakespeare—another obvious one being Jaques's "All the world's a stage" in *As You Like It*—that are easily excerpted and anthologized on a par with autonomous thematic works such as poems or essays. The reasons are more than one: its lack of immediate rootedness in any particular action of the play, its immersion in the mind and heart of the speaker or its flight into regions of uninhibited generalization.

And, finally, it is all of a piece, undivided into sections, focused on a single theme and sustained in a single mood.

Turning to the fifth, short soliloquy, "'Tis now the very witching time of night" (3.2.378–89), one is struck by its different tone. It could be classed as actional, for with it Hamlet prepares for the crucial encounter in the closet scene. However, an apostrophe to his heart, the all too frequent references to his soul, and a welter of poetic images starting at its first line suffuse the whole with the lyrical mode, thus forming a different kind of lyrodramatic hybrid—somewhat akin to the second soliloquy.

Hamlet's sixth solo utterance, the one spoken over the praying King in 3.3.73–96, starts with "now" again and grapples with the reality of the present moment. Unlike the earlier ones, it does not stop the flow of dramatic time, but immerses itself in it, suggesting a certain dynamism of attitude, posture and gesture on the part of the speaker: "Up sword [etc.]" (88). However, even if the speech is actional in that it determines the hero's conduct at the moment of delivery, as well as in the immediate future, it is also self-searching, for Hamlet considers critically his duty as revenger. The flurry of rhetorical questions, the lexical repetition and the alliteration, together with the richly figurative language, signal its lyrical orientation and define it as another example of the same crossbreed type.

Thus we arrive at the last, seventh soliloquy, "How all occasions do inform against me" (4.4.31–65), which is as extended as the longest members of the series and returns to their focus on inner drama. Just as in the second one the Prince compared himself with the passionate actor to his own disadvantage, now he uses Fortinbras as an uncomplimentary foil. The underlying problem again boils down to the hero's proverbial procrastinations and his ultimate failure to spring to resolute action. Like that earlier speech, this soliloquy emerges from a concrete dramatic episode, the march of the Norwegian army across Denmark on its campaign against Poland, which the protagonist happens to witness. And, in a similar manner, the experience prompts intense self-questioning. This time, however, it is less turbulent than before, and the utterance is consequently more ratiocinative. The emotion erupts in a couple of exclamations, confined to the opening and the closing lines, and a couple of self-probing questions.

The whole speech may be divided into two sections: the first one (31–45) deals with the hero's personal problem in apparent detachment from the immediate occasion, while the second (45–65) comes back to that occasion. Self-accusation can be heard in both parts, though it is not as vehement as in "O what a rogue and peasant slave am I." At times this soliloquy has the passionate yet restrained tone of "To be, or not to be." It is a good example of the already established blend of the thematic and fictional—or, more specifically, of the lyrical-essayistic and the dramatic—kinds. The verbal externalization of inner drama is thus allowed to rise to philosophical generalization, which nonetheless does not completely sever its links with the plot. The lyrodramatic hybrid is again in place.

We may conclude that most of Hamlet's solo speeches are closely connected with preceding dramatic events and that, in the final analysis, they consider the need for more or less concrete actions to follow. I find it difficult to accept Ann Thompson and Neil Taylor's conclusion that the soliloquies are "movable or even detachable."[52] The fact that they tend to appear in different places in the different early editions of the play can hardly serve to prove such a point. Most of the soliloquies are in fact quite well integrated into the plot structure. Internally too, they tend toward close integration. Logical discontinuity appears to be given free rein, but it is never allowed to undermine the overall thematic organization of the piece, which at times approximates the neat argumentative development of the essay, without fully succumbing to it. This complex thematic hybrid is further combined with the encompassing fictional (dramatic) element, transforming the outer drama into an inner one and obliterating the boundary between the two through the alternation of differently oriented sections merging into each other. On the stylistic level the merger results in lyrical expressiveness charged with continuous dramatic dynamism.

Hamlet's monologues, spoken in the midst of other characters as part of conversation, are often indistinguishable in quality from his soliloquies and possess a similar combination of generic features. The first of these speeches is "'Seems,' madam—nay, it is, I know not 'seems'" (1.2.76–86), uttered in response to Gertrude's inability to understand the grief of his bereavement. Tonally this thematic piece, with its precise, rounded-off logical argument, is close to the essay; but its chief interest is in the ultimate inexpressibility of emotion, a constant preoccupation of lyric poetry. Also, in spite of its firm rational structure, the monologue betrays its emotive cause in the vehement climax of a long central sentence, accentuated by the recurrent *nor* conjunctions.

A little later, while explaining to Horatio the tradition of excessive drinking at the Danish court, Hamlet, as is his wont, suddenly flies from this immediate topic into a cogitation about the single flaw in a person's nature, capable of destroying his otherwise sturdy and balanced constitution (1.4.13–38). This monologue illustrates the protagonist's characteristic way of blending the impartiality of thoughtful observation and analysis with the empathy of lyricism. On the face of it, the argument is absolutely rational. But on closer inspection it reveals its logical circularity, similar to that of "To be, or not to be," and the predominance of "amplification" over analytical progression. Hamlet projects his reflections in an avalanche of striking images that tumble over one another with compulsive energy: the "vicious mole of nature" (24), the shattered "pales and forts of reason" (28), the habit that "o'erleavens/ The form of plausive manners" (29–30), "the stamp of one defect" (31), "Nature's livery," "Fortune's star" (32), "as pure as grace" (33), and finally the "dram of eale" (36). Though this is not the antidiscourse of solipsistic self-address, it tends toward dreamy expression. The metaphorical series is discontinuous—like so many scattered explosions. The main sentence, comprising the first fourteen lines, follows the meanderings of a thought still unformed as a definitive public statement, halted by parenthetical insertions and returning to earlier points. This speech is not as direct an expression of inner drama as some of the soliloquies, but it is similarly motivated by a deep immersion in the hidden workings of the speaker's soul.

The lyric energy of poetic imagery is even stronger in a striking prose monologue in 2.2.259–76, which starts as an answer to Rosencrantz and Guildenstern's hard-wrenched confession of their spying for the King, in order to become a Picoesque disquisition on the universe and man's place in it. The speech opens and closes with direct verbal gestures aimed at the Prince's interlocutors. But its bulk is as detached from the act of communication as a soliloquy might be. Everything is thematically organized around a central evaluative opposition, stretched between the poles of admiration and contempt. In the first half of the monologue, dealing with the world (261–69), this opposition is expressed by the sharp contrast of epithets of praise

("goodly," "excellent," "brave," "majestical," "golden") and of denun-
ciation ("sterile," "foul," "pestilent"). The image of the earth shifts
unexpectedly from an impressive "frame" to a meager "promontory";
the "canopy" of the air, the firmament, resembling a palatial roof
"fretted with golden fire." is abruptly reduced to a "congregation of
vapours." The second half, devoted to the nature of man (269–76),
is structured as a series of exclamations (What . . . how . . . how . . .),
again piling up appreciative epithets ("noble," "infinite," "express,"
"admirable") and similes ("like an angel," "like a god") to form a
final paradoxical climax: "the beauty of the world; the paragon of
animals. And yet to me what is this quintessence of dust?" Thus the
whole appraisal of being is ultimately referred to a subjective state
of mind, with which the monologue had in fact opened. Within this
circular frame, the tone and the compelling figurative language of
the prose oration ensure its powerful lyrical quality and effect a lib-
erating retreat from the urgencies of azione parlata.

     In an exchange with Horatio in 3.2, Hamlet withdraws again from
dramatic action to consider "timeless issues" in an intensely lyrical
yet essayistically concentrated way, expressing strong personal feelings. The topic of this monologue (52–83) is in fact introduced in
the hero's preceding cue, when he says: "Horatio, thou art e'en as just
a man/ As e'er my conversation coped withal" (50–51). Its first half
(52–70) is devoted to the praise of the type of person that is "not a
pipe for Fortune's finger." This encomium is enthusiastic, energetic
and imaginative, ending with a breathless exclamation:

> Give me that man
> That is not passion's slave and I will wear him
> In my heart's core—ay, in my heart of heart—
> As I do thee.
>
> (67–70)

At this point, however, Hamlet, as one who is unused to and always
suspicious of sentimentality, cuts short his surprisingly voluble and direct interpersonal lyrical outburst with the self-censure: "Something
too much of this" (70), and switches to the second, actional part of
the monologue (71-83), instructing his friend how to assist him in
carrying out the test of the mousetrap play.

     The overall picture is completed by two series of shorter speeches,
delivered by the hero in the midst of dialogue and momentarily ac-

quiring monologic status. The first series occurs in the closet scene (3.4). As it is impossible to consider its every component, a brief survey must suffice. The following bit is not even syntactically autonomous, as it constitutes a reply to the Queen's puzzled question after Hamlet's enraged verbal attack, "What have I done":

> Such an act
> That blurs the grace and blush of modesty,
> Calls virtue hypocrite, takes off the rose
> From the fair forehead of an innocent love
> And sets a blister there, makes marriage vows
> As false as dicers' oaths—O, such a deed
> As from the body of contraction plucks
> The very soul, and sweet religion makes
> A rhapsody of words. Heaven's face does glow
> O'er this solidity and compound mass
> With heated visage, as against the doom,
> Is thought-sick at the act.
>
> (3.4.38–49)

This is no more than an emotional reaction to Gertrude's dishonesty in an eruption of images systematized by their focus on parts of the body, anchoring all abstractions of the spirit in the sensual sphere of experience. Its lyrical impetus is enhanced by the exclamatory tone and the insistent emphatic alliteration: blurs-blush, fair-forehead, makes-marriage, soul-sweet. The rounding off of the entire utterance by the return at the very end to its first notional word, "act," is also a manifestation of the concentric principle.

As the Queen is unable to grasp her son's lyrically heightened meaning, he plunges into a longer, more passionate monologue (51–86) that does not for a moment withdraw from the dramatic action, and even centers on some stage-props, but nonetheless soars into the sublimity of poetry: "Look here upon this picture, and on this." The speech is torn apart by questions, exclamations and apostrophes, intermixed with direct appeals to the Prince's immediate interlocutor. It is replete with metaphors, mythological allusions, lexical repetition (harping on "eyes," "judgment," "sense"), alliteration and assonance. All in all, we are faced with a monologue that is part and parcel of the azione parlata and, therefore, of the dramatic action itself, yet is made lyrical by its speaker's commitment to his topic and the compelling linguistic expression of this commitment.

Another series of monologues unfolds in the graveyard scene (5.1). Though these are mostly in prose, they are no less concentrated and poetically eloquent than the verse ones. Hamlet's tone is bitterly ironic, even satirical. But the theme is the poemly one of life and death. The series takes off from a detail of dramatic action—the Prince picks up a skull just dug up from the earth and starts his meditation by using it as a material prop, the traditional memento mori, the death's head: "That skull had a tongue in it" (71). Technically, this is not a solo-speech but a dialogue with Horatio, who, however, is as usual no more than a sparring partner in the hero's intellectual exercise, always expressing agreement with his inferences and generalizations. Hamlet's thrusts are imaginative and witty. And even though the overall stylistics of his observations is satirical, it is softened by an underlying lyrical sadness. This "dialogue-of-one" goes on for 40 lines up to line 110. Once again, it does not fill a timeless lacuna in the dramatic action, but is concurrent with that action, drawing its material from the continuing work of the gravedigger. The lyric accompanies and expands the dramatic instead of replacing it.

When Hamlet is faced with Yorick's skull, he withdraws into a speech of emotional reminiscences and observations, addressed to the long-dead jester, and thus apostrophically-lyrical, though combined with epigrammatic irony and satire (174–84). This new prose monologue, dwelling on the familiar poemly topic of mutability, is in fact a soliloquy, since it withdraws from the dialogue with the living into private meditation. Directly after this the Prince turns to Horatio, expanding his poetic essay on the same topic by a playful fantasy about the progress of Alexander the Great from a world conqueror to a loam of earth, used to seal a beer barrel (185–205). The last few lines switch to rhymed couplets, substituting Caesar for Alexander and developing the same motif of death's degrading transformation of earthly importance into nothingness, an example of the De Casibus genre in its lyrically essayistic variant.

The epigrammatic mode is pervasive in a few shorter incisive speeches delivered by Hamlet on the eve of the final catastrophe in 5.2. They deal with the deserved fate of Rosencrantz and Guildenstern as the tyrant's willing tools (57–61), the character of Osric as the type of the sycophantic courtier (167–73), and finally, the ultimate resolution of the hero to yield to the course of events in his famous gnomic utterance: "We defy augury. There is special providence in the fall of a sparrow. If it be, 'tis not to come. If it be not to come, it will be now. If it be not now, yet it will come. The readiness is all, since no man of aught he leaves knows what is't to leave betimes. Let be (197–202). There can hardly be a more radical withdrawal from direct action into the recesses of contemplation and a more decisive departure from the fictional toward the thematic. But this monologue could equally be considered as actional. Without spelling out the course of the hero's further moves, it establishes their underlying principle and thus prepares the completion of the plot.

All in all, Hamlet's monologues are almost impossible to divide from his soliloquies, as the hero is capable of retiring into his inner self even among a throng of people. On the other hand, like the soliloquies, the monologues combine fictional and thematic strands in an inextricable blend, simultaneously bridging the gap between the thematic genres of the lyric and the essay. Also, perhaps to a larger extent than the soliloquies, they retain their close connection to the ongoing verbal interaction, thus reciprocally helping to lyricize their dialogical environment.

While Hamlet is, beyond doubt, the chief monologist in the play, nearly monopolizing the privilege of expressing oneself in soliloquies and thus involving the audience in a strong empathic relationship of the lyrical kind, other characters are not completely denied this opportunity. In an emotional soliloquy directly after the nunnery episode, Ophelia bemoans what she sees as a ruination of Hamlet's intellect: "O, what a noble mind is here o'erthrown!" (3.1.149–60). With its frequent exclamations, its climax of parallel constructions, its gentle metaphors and similes, its emphatic repetitions, its alliterative patterns and its melodiousness, this speech has an inescapable lyrical impact. Yet, while withdrawing from the dramatic action, it does not sever its links with it, and would lose much of its meaning and effect if extracted from the play and considered in isolation. The same could be said, with even greater certainty, about Laertes's passionate speeches on discovering his sister's loss of sanity, e.g. "O heat, dry up my brains" (4.5.153–59), and then, at her open grave, e.g. "O, treble woe/ Fall ten times treble on that cursed head" (5.1.235–43). These are lyrical outbursts in the middle of action, incapable of extricating themselves from, yet soaring above, it. Notwithstanding their emotional power, they are examples of lyrical modulation of the dramatic text rather than an organic merger of the two kinds in which neither of them would take precedence.

If there is in this play another compulsive monologist besides the hero, this is unquestionably his chief antagonist. Claudius's habitual manner, however, in sharp contrast to Hamlet's, tends toward public pathos rather than lyrical inwardness. He opens the second scene with a grand oration to the court, running through the first nearly forty lines (1.2.1–39). The first two sentences, rather long and unnecessarily convoluted, set the tone of the whole. The syntactical pretentiousness of the King's speech is coupled with the systematic use of pluralis majestatis in frequent self-reference and with a pompous diction relying mostly on abstract nouns, such as "death," "memory," "grief," "woe," "discretion," "nature," "sorrow," "remembrance," etc. (all these examples coming from the first sentence), and resorting to formal verbs like "befitted," "contracted," and high astounding adjectives like "wisest," "imperial," "auspicious".[53] The monologue is not deprived of poetic imagery, but the figures are heavy-handed and rigidly emblematic rather than imaginatively evocative. Thus, according to the speaker, his entire kingdom ought "To be contracted in one brow of woe" in mourning for the deceased king, though within him discretion has "fought with nature," so that he has decided to marry his late brother's wife "with a defeated joy," "With an auspicious and a dropping eye," "In equal scale weighing delight and dole." His antithetically structured oxymoronic line, "With mirth in funeral and with dirge in marriage," must have made him particularly proud of his oratorical talents. Language for Claudius seems to have above all a rhetorical function, it must impress the voiceless listeners as a magnificent façade. What is behind it is of lesser importance, for, unlike his nephew, he has not "that within which passes show."

One more aspect of this monologue that distances it from the lyric is its orderly logical structure, resembling the method of cataloging or itemization of topics. First of all, Claudius considers the fact that he has replaced his deceased brother both on the throne and in his family (1–16). Then, with the words "Now follows," the speaker introduces the second, unrelated issue of young Fortinbras's annoying insistence that the Norwegian lands lost by his father be restituted to him after the death of their conqueror (17–25). This section is wound up with another unequivocal signal, "So much for him," at which point the King turns to his solution of the problem with the words: "Now for ourself, and for this time of meeting,/ Thus much the business is," proceeding from the informational to the actional part of the oration (26–39) in order to end it with specific commands. At this juncture he addresses first Laertes and then his "cousin and son" in much the same fashion, as if encouraging some—perhaps merely phatic—response. There is not—neither can there be—the slightest amount of spontaneity in such public acts of one-way communication. Structurally, this is a manner of speaking absolutely alien to Hamlet. It is closer to that of Touchstone and Jaques in their technical postures.[54]

The King's later pronouncements are delivered in a more intimate circle of interlocutors, and yet they too adhere to the conventionality of public oratory. A case in point is his monologue in 4.5, attempting to gauge the situation at his court after the discovery of Ophelia's madness: "O, this is the poison of deep grief!" (75–96). It is curious how Claudius proceeds in the same cataloging way as in his first speech from the throne in 1.2. Although the utterance starts with an emotional exclamation and breaks off after the beginning of its second sentence to heave another sigh, "O Gertrude, Gertrude," it is as ordered a logical dissection of the matter at hand as they come. The King introduces the items of his analysis one by one like a meticulous bookkeeper (all in the impersonal passive voice): "first, her father slain" (79), "Next, your son gone" (80), "the people muddied" (81), "and we have done but greenly/ In hugger-mugger to inter him" (83–84), "Last, and as much containing as all these,/ Her brother is in secret come from France" (87–88). Having completed this inventory of the sequence of events endangering his own security, Claudius can once again give vent to his emotion, not without some figurative panache:

> O my dear Gertrude, this,
> Like to a murdering-piece in many places
> Gives me superfluous death.
>
> (94–96)

The military imagery provides a frame for Claudius's entire speech from its opening lines on. A medley of complementary figures punctuates the body of the monologue. It cannot be denied that this character has a penchant for metaphorical language, though his tropes are for the most part predictable and unimpressive, decorative rather than revealing. If they at times have a lyrical tinge, that is rather thin and remains on the surface. Similar conclusions could be made about another couple of short monologues spoken by the King in conversation with Laertes. "O, for two special reasons" (4.7.10–25) catalogs the considerations that have prevented him from punishing Hamlet for the murder of Polonius. The latter half of this symmetrically constructed speech is so overburdened with heterogeneous images that it produces a cloying and disorientating effect. A mechanical series of alliterative pairs of words in its middle confirms the impression of contrived rhetoric. The less interesting second monologue, describing the French fencer (59–74) is sustained in a similar style.

Laertes's and Polonius's long-drawn didactic speeches of guidance and instruction in 1.3 belong to the same class of oratorical exercise. Albeit spoken within the family, they adopt the hierarchical attitude of descent from a higher rank of authority to a lower one of submission in each particular case. The firm logical structure, coupled with the compulsory attribute of fairly indifferent poetic imagery and other rhetorical devices like repetition, alliteration and syntactical parallelism, together with the high incidence of prominently positioned verbs in the imperative mood mark them off as persuasive oratory. One could conclude that Shakespeare's strategy in this play is again, as in *Richard II*, to contrast the Poet and the Hero types, the private and the public man, thus placing the protagonist in the privileged focus of the audience's attention.

Claudius, however, should not be totally submerged in the fairly grey group of uninspiring speakers. On the strength of at least two solo utterances in the central act of the play he rises to the salient position of Hamlet's worthy adversary. These are not part of his usual public performances but self-addressed—an aside and a soliloquy. The former is prompted by a metaphor coined by Polonius:

'Tis too much proved that with devotion's visage
And pious action we do sugar o'er
The devil himself.

(3.1.46–48)

For once, the smiling villain is stung to the quick by this generalization and turns to himself with a no less figurative revelation:

O, 'tis too true.
[*aside*] How smart a lash that speech doth give my conscience!
The harlot's cheek beautied with plastering art

Is not more ugly to the thing that helps it
Than is my deed to my most painted word.
O heavy burden!

                                                                        (48–53)

At this juncture Claudius's "close pent-up guilts" finally do "rive
[their] concealing continents" and make themselves known to his
awakened moral sense. The resulting poetic image centered on the
idea of the beautified harlot is both striking and profoundly appropriate as a reference to the speaker's own condition. And, although
the earlier fleeting metaphor of the lash is seemingly disparate, at a
deeper level of association both figures come together, since the lash
was the conventional instrument of punishment for exposed prosti-
tutes. This unexplicitated organicity in the use of tropes pointing to
a preoccupation with things difficult to express is a sure touch of lyricism. The method will achieve its true preeminence in Shakespeare's
later tragedies.

    If the King's spontaneous aside could be regarded as an arresting
lyrical inset, his soliloquy "O, my offence is rank" (3.3.36–72) is his
real and only chance to rise to the height of his spiritual potential,
attaining momentarily the stature of a tragic hero. This, if anything
in the play, is a verbalization of inner drama, in some ways no less
impressive than Hamlet's. In a desperate attempt to cleanse his soul
of the terrible crime he has committed, the King becomes aware of
his fatal dilemma of both striving to repent in the act of praying and
being reluctant to let go of the gains his damnable deed has rewarded
him with. Perhaps to an even greater extent than Hamlet's first soliloquy, this speech echoes the tossing and turning of Doctor Faustus's
unforgettable final aria:

>   Whereto serves mercy
> But to confront the visage of offence?
> And what's in prayer but this twofold force
> —To be forestalled ere we come to fall
> Or pardoned, being down? Then I'll look up:
> My fault is past. But O, what form of prayer
> Can serve my turn . . .
>   What then? What rests?
> Try what repentance can—what can it not?—
> Yet what can it, when one cannot repent?

                                                              (46–52, 64–66)

Claudius is certainly more rational and less impulsive than Faustus, more thematic and less dramatic than his predecessor. Yet his speech is full of the anxiety of disturbed questions. The frequent enjambments make it almost as emotional as the Doctor's. Some of its images are as palpable and suggestive as anything that will issue from Shakespeare's pen for the soliloquies of his magnificent tragic heroes a few years later. The following examples can illustrate the point:

> What if this cursed hand
> Were thicker than itself with brother's blood?
> Is there not rain enough in the sweet heavens
> To wash it white as snow?
>
> (43–46)

> In the corrupted currents of this world
> Offence's gilded hand may shove by justice,
> And oft 'tis seen the wicked prize itself
> Buys out the law . . .
>
> (57–60)

> Bow, stubborn knees, and heart with strings of steel
> Be soft as sinews of the new-born babe.
>
> (70–71)

In these forcefully compact tropes, complete with emphatic alliteration, we already catch the unmistakable accents of the future Macbeth and Lear. The final series of apostrophic exclamations provide the right kind of close for a thoroughly impressive speech. The Prince's actional soliloquy following directly after seems to have been purposely made so subdued lest it should rob the King's utterance of its lyrical power by relativizing it.

Still, Hamlet's soliloquies, especially the early ones, have in them more combustive energy than does Claudius's isolated outburst. Apart from occasional spurts of impatience, this speech is more deliberative than impulsive. Ralph Berry draws the following revealing comparison with the hero's most famous soliloquy, whose emotional argument he sees as circular: "The complement to Hamlet here is, as so often, Claudius. We have only one opportunity to observe his mind at close quarters, but he uses it to think hard—and accurately—about the issues. 'May one be pardoned and retain the offence?' (3.3.56) is a brutally precise way of defining the problem."[55] Not only is Claudius more capable than Hamlet of clearly formulating the central topic of his speech, but he approaches it in a more concentrated logical fashion, developing an argumentative succession of well-formed syntactical periods. His mind manages to impose its control over the mutiny of emotions to such an extent as to almost stifle them. But not quite. The suppressed emotions find a way out in many of the already considered features of his speech and, most of all, in the disturbed questions shifting the direction of the argument every so often, as well as in the final cluster of turbulent exclamations. For a brief moment Claudius, alone among the dramatis personae of the play, mesmerizes our attention with a passionate soliloquy of a forcefulness comparable to that of the Prince's usual utterances. And, just like Hamlet's great speeches, his tormented outburst grapples vigorously with the exigencies of the action while at the same time soaring above them, thus attaining a comparable lyrodramatic status.

So far we have left out one conspicuous monologue, that of the Ghost divulging the details of his murder (1.5.42–91). This is the longest single speech in the play, and it is representative of a group comprised of the nuntius announcements. It falls into three well defined sections, the first (42–57) markedly lyrical, dealing with the adulterous marriage of the speaker's widow and his brother, and the third (81–91) actional, calling upon Hamlet to take revenge on the foul murderer. The central, and by far the longest, second section (58–80), being an informative narration of how the murder happened, is delivered in a richly figurative style.

This oration is preceded by a series of much shorter speeches of the same informative tenor, those of the royal sentinels giving Horatio an account of the Ghost's earlier visitations, and then Horatio's own summary of the recent history of Danish wars with Norway and their aftermath, but above all, his breaking the news to the Prince and describing to him the apparition and its impact on the observers (1.2.195–211). The cluster of monologues, culminating in the Ghost's own harangue, ushers into the play an important strain of narrative insets, worth tracing as a separate element. These are the familiar nuntius interventions, which, though of a different quality, are as numerous in *Hamlet* as in *As You Like It*. Their usual capability of provoking audience empathy through the narrators' strong emotional engagement with their stories is more often exploited here, bringing them closer to the lyric.

Besides the Ghost's tale, at least seven more nuntius monologues punctuate the play from beginning to end. Among them are Ophelia's report to her father about Hamlet's distracted appearance in her closet (2.1.74–97), Gertrude's account to Claudius of Polonius's murder and her son's confused behavior (4.1.7–12, 24–27), a Gentleman's information about Ophelia's madness (4.5.4–13), a Messenger's news of Laertes's tumultuous rebellion (4.5.98–108), Hamlet's letter outlining the story of his eventful sea voyage to England (4.6.13–28), and his later oral account filling Horatio in on the details (5.2.4–61). But the most distinguished member of this group is probably Gertrude's relation of Ophelia's death by drowning (4.7.164–81). It has the delicate charm of balladic poetry and is suffused in purest lyricism, dissolving the image of the innocent girl in the peaceful translucent watery medium and fusing it into the languid vegetation around it to enhance with this offering the beauty of the environment.

Finally, one narrative is left untold, though commissioned by the protagonist with his last breath. This is Horatio's promised report about everything that we have already seen presented on the stage or have been briefed about. It would have been interesting to hear it all complete with his comments, but one fears that such a synopsis might not have been more exciting than Friar Lawrence's summary of Romeo and Juliet's story. For Fortinbras, for whose ears it is chiefly meant, a dry account of this kind would probably be just the thing, but not for us in the audience, not right now.

What is the reason for this abundance of narrative insets in *Hamlet*? Is it perhaps a sign of the relegation of a good part of the tragedy's dramatic action to the offstage space to provide enough room for the predominantly static, thematic presence of the hero? Be this as it may, as already pointed out, through these epico-lyrical insertions a number of crucial episodes are imaginatively enhanced instead of being acted out. Sometimes these texts are preparatory to the unfolding of dramatic events, as the case is with the news about Ophelia's madness, preceding her appearance on the stage; and sometimes, on the contrary, they double an already acted-out event by offering a colorful close-range impression of it, as when Horatio informs Hamlet about his dead father's appearance. Bearing all this in mind, we could hardly consider these monologues as primarily performing an informational function. Theirs is chiefly a tonal contribution to the play. The operative mechanism is the familiar one of lyrical modulation, but it is superimposed on that of epic inclusion.

One final—and most straightforward—kind of typically lyrical inset remains to be dealt with, and that is the rime/ song genre. Hamlet is once again the chief source of such insertions. The first example of his dabbling in versification is the quatrain he has sent to Ophelia:

> Doubt thou the stars are fire,
> Doubt that the sun doth move,
> Doubt truth to be a liar,
> But never doubt I love.

> (2.2.114–17)

We can perhaps sense here a pastiche of Donne's "metaphysical" love songs ("Goe and catche a falling starre" etc.). The author's self-critical note attached to his poem could be accepted as either written in earnest, or as Socratically ironic: *O dear Ophelia, I am ill at these numbers. I have not art to reckon my groans*" (118–19). But even if this is true, Hamlet is not meant to be an original poet. Expressing himself in verse is for him a kind of game—and not an absorbing one either, as it seems to be for the Navarre academicians or for Orlando. Even so, the tenor of this first inset rime is clearly lyrical. His ensuing verse exercises (in 3.2) pertain to the caustic epigrammatic genre. They spring out of the hero's triumphant yet painful confirmation of the veracity of the Ghost's intimation through the mousetrap theatrical stratagem, and they all satirize the King: "Why let the stricken deer go weep" (263–66), "For thou dost know, O Damon dear" (273–76), and "For if the King like not the comedy" (285–86).

In the next act, Ophelia takes over from Hamlet as chief rime-monger with the simple country ballads she sings in the two episodes of her madness: "Tomorrow is Saint Valentine's Day" (4.5.48–55, 58–66), "They bore him bare-faced on the bier . . . " (160–61), "For bonny sweet Robin is all my joy" (179), "And will 'a not come again?" (182–91). Ophelia's songs are definitely lyrical and expressive of her personal troubles, though rising above them in the regions of poetic typification. They dwell on the problems of love and death, deception and bereavement, pain and grief. Dramatic action is suspended for the duration of their performance, and for the while all other characters turn into a mute audience, watching and listening to the poor maid in consternation and commiseration.

The poemly theme of love and mutability leading to death is also dominant in the ditties of another lyrically epigrammatic songster, the Gravedigger in 5.1: "In youth when I did love, did love" (57–60, 67–70) and "A pickaxe and a spade, a spade . . . " (89–92). Hamlet himself contributes to this last round of rimes with the similarly dismal epigrammatic coda of his De Casibus meditation on "Imperious Caesar" spoken over Yorick's skull (202–5).

The playful, ironic, and often satirical character of the inset rimes in *Hamlet* does not preclude their lyrical quality. Of course, their tone is usually that of the communal rather than the individual expression—a common bent of the song genre—yet the emotional preoccupations of the rimers or their audience are time and again voiced in these unassuming pieces of poetry. Their main contribution is to the building of character and atmosphere, but also, frequently, to the effective and memorable formulation of central thematic concerns of the play. Interestingly, these seemingly casual insets punctuate some of the tragedy's most important scenes. It is as if at moments of greatest dramatic tension the normal textual fabric of drama breaks and the lyric contained in its inner recesses shows on the surface.

The poetic insets in this tragedy are indeed many and varied, but there are other, more novel and intriguing forms of generic interaction, to which we should turn now—these are to be found in the *azione parlata*. What makes Hamlet the chief bearer of the thematic and, above all, the lyrical mode in the play is not only his being its unrivalled soliloquizer, but perhaps to an equal if not greater extent, his distinctive manner of participating in dialogue. The tone is set with the very first words the Prince utters as he appears on stage. The King has just made his long formal oration from the throne, and both Laertes and Polonius have responded in the same wordy, thoroughly predictable court language, whose main concern is not so much to offer information or express inner predispositions as to confirm the established hierarchical structures of society. However, as soon as Claudius turns to the protagonist with the words "But now, my cousin Hamlet, and my son—" (1.2.64), obviously plunging into yet another display of oratorical expertise, his addressee interrupts him with an objection amounting to a refusal to enter the political game: "A little more than kin, and less than kind" (65).

So far all speeches in the scene have been entirely actional, for their chief purpose is to formulate or negotiate future events. This cue is different: unconcerned with any concrete action, it focuses on the problematic relationship between the two parties involved in the communication. The issue now becomes debatable—not axiomatic, as everything coming from the King is a priori deemed to be. Moreover, Hamlet's reaction is enigmatic, since the differentiation of meaning between the two almost synonymous—and almost homophonic—words "kin" and "kind" is not self-evident. Thus his interlocutor is deprived of immediate response.

Some commentators assume that this is an aside rather than a disrespectful interruption. I prefer to view it as the latter, for it represents the hero's idiosyncratic way of participating in conversation, of which there are many later instances. But the cue seems nevertheless to be self-addressed, nondiscursive. M. M. Mahood observes: "After so much ceremonious speech-making, Hamlet's first words have outrageous force, for he begins as he is to continue, a man talking to himself."[56] Such a person has to be either a lunatic or a poet. Hamlet appears to be both. But while his madness is uncertain, his lyrical way of using language to mainly clarify things to himself, rather than to persuade others, is undeniable.

Claudius's next intervention is tritely metaphorical: "How is it that the clouds still hang on you?" (66). Since dead metaphors are tropes reduced to monosigns, this question presupposes a straightforward literal answer. Hamlet, however, is interested in the figurative core of the phrase, which he chooses to resuscitate. And his attitude is once again that of disagreement: "Not so much, my lord, I am too much in the sun" (67).[57] The metaphorical logic prompted by Claudius's cliché has been extended. This choice shows Hamlet's keen sensitivity to the rich semantic potential of words, which characterizes poetic locution. His cue is indeed amply lyrical, for it is tantalizingly suggestive rather than informative.

The Prince's language is, from the very beginning, so fully liberated from discursive constraints that every word "sparkles with infinite freedom" and activates all its denotative and connotative meanings. This necessarily generates ambiguity, paronomasia, antidiscourse. Mahood notes that "he wraps inside a compliment about the King's favor the statement that he is insulted to be called Claudius's son;

whereas Claudius takes the reply to mean that Hamlet considers himself dispossessed, out of house and home."[58] Given that he offers no
verbal reaction, it is difficult to know precisely how Claudius takes
the reply, but the last sense is probably part of the speaker's cryptic
message, for it voices a central preoccupation of his. What Mahood
takes to be Hamlet's intended meaning is itself ambiguous and can
be paraphrased in a variety of ways: "I am too much in the King's
shining presence—far more so than I'd like to be," "I am too much
of a son—for I have had a father and I don't need another one," "I am
too loyal and loving a son to accept a new father," etc. Could we not
also surmise that here Hamlet hints for the first time at his reluctance
to go on living (remaining in the sun) in a world that has lost its attraction for him? Much of this rich ambiguity springs from a play on
the homophones *sun* and *son* that is so common in Elizabethan and
Shakespearean texts. The preference of Q2 for the spelling "sonne"
is indicative.[59] According to Mahood's count, *Hamlet* "has more quibbles than any other of Shakespeare's tragedies."[60] Witty wordplay, as
we have seen, is intimately related to lyric. It breeds the antidiscourse
of suggestive ambiguity, so vital for this literary kind.

There is yet another salient aspect of Hamlet's first cues that relates them to the lyric, and that is their incisive brevity, especially
as they emerge in the midst of a fairly vacuous formal verbosity. We
are riveted to these laconic equivocal remarks, because we sense
their condensed meaningfulness and its importance transcending
the concreteness of dramatic action. So, when next Gertrude tries
to persuade her son that he should not be unnecessarily depressed
by his father's death, for it is common that "all that lives must die"
(1.2.72), and Hamlet picks up the word she has just used to reply: "Ay,
madam, it is common" (74), we hear in this an ironical bifurcation
of sense again: *ordinary*, as the Queen has meant the word to signify,
but also *coarse, vulgar*, as a hinted comment on her attitude. From the
very beginning we learn to listen to what Hamlet has to say atten-
tively, expecting every smallest bit of his language to "radiate toward
a thousand uncertain and possible relations."[61]

Of course, punning as we have noted above, is not an automatic
generator of lyric, and Shakespeare hastens to make this qualification
in the ensuing scene by introducing a very different use of verbal wit,
close to the cataloging method of Claudius's monologues.[62] This time
the speaker is Polonius. Somewhat like Hamlet, he snatches a word
from the preceding cue of his interlocutor to run the whole gamut

of its possible meanings. The interlocutor in this case is Ophelia, who confides to her father that the Prince has "of late made many tenders/ Of his affection to me" (1.3.98–99). Infuriated, the father proceeds directly to admonish his dangerously naïve daughter:

> Marry, I will teach you; think yourself a baby
> That you have ta'en these tenders for true pay
> Which are not sterling. Tender yourself more dearly
> Or—not to crack the wind of the poor phrase,
> Wronging it thus—you'll tender me a fool.
>
> (1.3.104–8)

Ironically, the old man has already cracked the wind of the poor phrase by first playing on the two meanings of *tender*—the one used by Ophelia, "offer of love," and the one he considers more appropriate in the case, "formal presentation of money in payment,"—and then proceeding to elaborate on this second sense and its nuances. Such exhaustive and unidirectional exploitation of a word deprives the pun of intriguing suggestiveness and renders it pedantically tedious, at best a phraseological exercise. But now that Polonius has got into the punning mood, he finds it difficult to extricate himself from it and continues to quibble until the end of the conversation. This kind of mechanical paronomasia is the opposite of Hamlet's: far from being self-addressed, inquisitive, probing, lyrical, it is outward-bound, oratorical.

Unsurprisingly, Polonius becomes the permanent butt of the Prince's gibes. Hamlet withdraws abruptly from actual communication as soon as he meets his rhetorical antipode a little later in 2.2. To Polonius's question "Do you know me, my lord?" he offers a seemingly distracted answer: "Excellent well, you are a fishmonger" (171). Commentators, however, have long learned—as Polonius himself will soon do—to discover an underlying logic beneath Hamlet's apparently wild talk. Here is an editorial footnote: "[*a fishmonger*] In its ordinary sense ridiculously inappropriate for Polonius. But in another aspect a *fishmonger* is seen as one whose daughter had a more than ordinary propensity to breed."[63] Disjunctive though it might sound, Hamlet's part in the dialogue is far from unfocused. Its first thematic section opens with the identification of his interlocutor as the proverbial fishmonger and closes with the injunction that he should take care not to let his daughter get pregnant, a possibility that Polonius, as we have already heard, dreads. Within this metaphorical framework, Hamlet has managed to refer to "kissing carrion" and to philosophize about conception. His figurative manner allows him to shift quickly from one image to another, totally different and therefore seemingly unrelated, while his attention to a central topic remains steady. This is a good illustration of the typical lyric combination of rhetorical discontinuity with thematic fixedness.

The second section of the dialogue switches to a new topic, introduced by Polonius's question, "What do you read, my lord?" (188). Hamlet's answer—"Words, words, words,"—though it suggests the speaker's dissatisfaction with trite uses of language, is starkly uncooperative within the particular discursive frame, since the other's interest is obviously in what the words mean. The question is then reformulated: "What is the matter, my lord?" (190), but the Prince pretends to misunderstand again: "Between who?" Thus "the matter" is liberated from all discursive constraints and allowed to wander. Polonius continues persistently to ram the conversation back into the narrow channel of ordinary communication: "I mean the matter that you read, my lord" (192). At this point Hamlet plunges into an ironical-satirical disquisition on old age and decay, seemingly an answer to the query, but in fact an oblique sarcastic comment on the courtier's person.

While Polonius's wont—exhibited in his earlier conversations— was to cursorily catalog the meanings of a word or a phrase in a lexicographical fashion, Hamlet's is to sound their referential potential and to bridge yawning semantic gaps, thus opening up unexpected visions latent in language. This type of wordplay lies at the roots of lyric. It constitutes the antidiscourse that puts the others in the position of overhearing a basically self-addressed utterance and attempting—not always successfully—to intuit its underlying logic and reconstruct the implied message.

If Hamlet appears for most of this exchange to be mocking the old man under the guise of an incoherent madman's talk—that is, to be evasively satirical rather than inwardly lyrical,—in its closing third section, sustained in much the same paronomastic style of speaking, he fully withdraws into his own overwhelming personal concern:

POLONIUS. Will you walk out of the air, my lord?
HAMLET. Into my grave.

(203–4)

Polonius recognizes the unexpected relevance of this shift of the phrase's meaning: "How pregnant sometimes his replies are—a happiness that often madness hits on, which reason and sanity could not so prosperously be delivered of" (205–8). As usual, he has a theory about what he sees and, burying his head in its narrowness, misses the broader dimension of the truth, though he is ever so close to it. The lyric mode, he could have said, is so pregnant of revelation—a happiness that often poetry hits upon, which the apparent rationality of "actional" existence cannot so effectively produce.

The closure of this uneasy dialogue is sustained in the same vein, as Hamlet continues harping on his obsessive theme ("not to be"), using every new occasion to return to it by transcending the literal sense and opening up the wider figurative perspective of words and phrases—for his own intellectual benefit:

POLONIUS. My lord, I will take my leave of you.
HAMLET. You cannot take from me anything that I will not more
    willingly part withal—except my life, except my life, except my life.
                                                                    (209–12)

The ironist, disguising his contempt as court etiquette, has imperceptibly turned lyricist in order to speak thoughtfully and feelingly of himself to himself.

When, next, Rosencrantz and Guildenstern enter the stage, they at first seem almost antipodal to Polonius. Hamlet greets them excitedly as "My excellent good friends" (2.2.219), and for a while the dialogue trips along merrily. But it does not take the Prince long to size up his interlocutors' new position and, having sniffed out their mission, to switch back to the double-edged language employed in his dealings with Claudius and Polonius. Guildenstern is the first to unwarily set the new tone of the conversation when he answers the question "good lads, how do ye both" in a paradoxically figurative manner: "Happy, in that we are not ever happy./ On Fortune's cap we are not the very button" (223–24). Hamlet's attention is at once fixed onto this emergent image and the wider possibilities it offers him to dig into the truth of the situation. He follows faithfully the logic of the metaphor by interjecting: "Nor the soles of her shoe?" (225), to surmise: "Then you live about her waist, or in the middle of her favours?" (227–28); and when Guildenstern makes a clumsy attempt to extricate himself from the backfiring anatomical figure by switching to another, military one—"Faith, her privates we" (229)—Hamlet pulls him back to it by a paronomastic association to conclude triumphantly: "In the secret parts of Fortune? O, most true—she is a strumpet. What news?" (230–31). His aggressive sarcasm flows imperceptibly into personal grievance, turning dramatic exchange into lyrical self-expression.

Soon after that, as the Prince's allusion to his bad dreams is ascribed by the other two to ambition, that "shadow of a dream," he toys briefly with the trope to expose its shallowness but also to once again remind himself of his being deprived of his birthright, thus continuing an undercurrent of associative thought.[64] A couple of cues later his mind seems to still dwell on the same idea, as he returns to the image of the beggars with reference to himself.[65] And right after that we hear him question his old pals' loyalty in an ambiguously figurative way, at once followed by an unexpectedly literal challenge: "Were you not sent for?" (240). From this point on, the conversation is absolutely straightforward, unbefuddled by tropes, puns and other forms of withdrawal from cooperative communication. Doubt has been resolved into prosaic unambiguous clarity, which cancels the lyric.

The ensuing reappearance of Polonius as the fatuous bearer of stale news provides Hamlet with a new opportunity to make a fool of the old busybody. He comes close to calling him an ass (332) and then discomfits him with the enigmatic allusion to Jephthah and his daughter (339–48), which sounds like an extension of the earlier fishmonger trope. A metaphorical logic already applied to the topic is faithfully, though unobtrusively, sustained. During the mousetrap episode (3.2), Hamlet indulges in a wide variety of oblique talk, which he has by now customized to suit each of his spurned interlocutors. The King comes in for chastisement first. To his question, "How fares our cousin Hamlet?" (88), he gets an answer very much like the ones of their first stage encounter in 1.2: "Excellent, i'faith! Of the chameleon's dish—I eat the air, promise-crammed. You cannot feed capons so" (89–91). Once again a keyword from Claudius's cue ("fare") is wrenched from its discursive frame to send the conversation off on another trajectory, the figurative way of speaking being substituted for the literal one, so that language can be liberated and made suggestive in an elusive, disconcertingly indefinite fashion. The general drift of this utterance is fairly obvious in spite of its indirection: the Prince alludes again to his annoyance at being left out in the cold by his uncle's seizure of power. Its "capon" element contains an additional oblique reference to the royal designs on his life.

When the uncle pleads innocent of what he seems to be accused of ("I have nothing with this answer, Hamlet. These words are not mine" (92–93), the nephew responds in a double-edged way: "No, nor mine now" (94). In his commentary Jenkins reminds us of the proverb: "A man's words are his own no longer than he keep them unspoken."[66] But what does Hamlet imply? Does he regret having let out the truth of a grievance that he had better kept secret? Or does he perhaps, half-apologetically, suggest that what he has spoken does not convey his real feelings? Such language leaves its referential frame uncertain, fluid, and draws the hearers' attention back to the speaker's state of mind, which can only be tentatively surmised.

After a few jokes cracked in similarly cryptic language at the expense of Polonius and then of Ophelia, Hamlet runs again into Rosencrantz and Guildenstern, whose double-dealing is now clear to him. He puns disrespectfully about the King's distemper, drowning the actional dialogue in figurative equivocation. Finally, Guildenstern feels obliged to expostulate: "Good my lord, put your discourse into some frame and start not so wildly from my affair" (300–301). Hamlet tries to explain his willful uncooperativeness by referring to his supposed insanity, an excuse that he will later use again after his altercation with Laertes. Yet the audience cannot help sensing that his linguistic tactics is that of ambiguity laden with sarcasm. Primarily leveled at Claudius, this sarcasm ricochets toward his emissaries too. The hero's keen sensitivity to lexical connotations makes him focus on Guildenstern's choice of the words "affair" and "business" in reference to the task his ex-friends have been enjoined on by the King and define their relation as "trade," resorting for the first time to pluralis majestatis to preclude any further possibility of informal intercourse (324–25).

Thus we reach the last phase of Hamlet's dialogue with Rosencrantz and Guildenstern, the striking recorder episode, of which the celebrated Kozintsev/Smoktunovsky film makes so much so well. The Prince has already got from the actors one of these instruments when he asks Guildenstern a point-blank though metaphorically phrased question: "To withdraw with you, why do you go about to recover the wind of me, as if you would drive me into a toil?" (337–39). The addressee is so confused that he seeks refuge in the meaningless, euphuistically elegant courtly language, carried to an extreme hollowness in the earlier speeches of Polonius, for which the old man was reprimanded by the Queen: "O my lord, if my duty be too bold, my love is too unmannerly" (340–41). The contrast between the two ways of speaking could not be sharper. Hamlet's immediate comment is quite appropriate: "I do not well understand that" (342), and, without further ado, he proceeds to offer Guildenstern a flute, asking him to play on it. The latter's reluctance to do so and his excuse that he does not know how to do it give the hero an opportunity to utter one of his most lyrical short monologues: "Why, look you now how unworthy a thing you make of me: you would play upon me! You would seem to know my stops, you would pluck out the heart of my mystery, you would sound me from my lowest note to my compass. And there is much music, excellent voice, in this little organ. Yet cannot you make it speak. 'Sblood! Do you think I am easier to be played on than a pipe? Call me what instrument you will, though you can fret me you cannot play upon me" (355–63). This speech expresses forcefully Hamlet's hurt feelings, the pain inflicted on him by the gross betrayal of friendship and trust he has been subjected to. It does so by concentrating on a stage prop and turning it into a memorable poetic image. Thus the utterance continues to be firmly attached to the dramatic action in two obvious ways: (1) by being rooted in its immediate physical context, and (2) by being markedly interpersonal. And yet its lyrical preoccupation with the inner problem of dignity is what gives it its barely controlled vehemence.

When Polonius enters as a superfluous messenger once again, Hamlet responds to his "news" in a manner so unrelated to it as to suggest raving: "Do you see yonder cloud that's almost in shape of a camel?" (367–68). One wonders if at a deeper level this is not a gibe at the old man's slowness, both physical and mental. We remember that on other occasions the Prince has already compared him to an ass and a calf. Why he replaces so quickly the camel with a weasel and then with a whale—making the other accept each shift uncritically— and whether there is an encrypted caricature of the old meddler in this series of imagined shapes may be anybody's guess. Hamlet retains the central meaning of his utterance to himself, thus magnifying its semantic and emotive impact ad infinitum. In the final analysis, he always ends up conversing with himself, often puzzling people who seem to be closer to him and putting everybody else on their guard.

The Prince of Denmark is far from being the only Shakespearean character that can inconvenience others by his superior command of punning and does not mind doing that. M. M. Mahood has pointed out that Richard III "takes a solitary pleasure in his wordplay at Clarence's expense," and Buckingham tries to imitate him in his dialogue with the doomed Hastings, though he falls far behind his master in this intellectual game.[67] Is Hamlet different from Richard Crookback? Apparently not, for in his dealing with Polonius, Rosencrantz and Guildenstern, Claudius, Ophelia, and even his mother in the closet scene his quibbling can be acerbic to the point of cruelty. Yet, unlike Richard, he never couples his wit with secret designs against the lives of its butts, although, inadvertently or otherwise, quite a few of them do die at his hands. One thing is clear: Hamlet does not gloat at the deaths he is responsible for, even if he may continue to gibe at some of his victims, such as Polonius and the tandem of his devious schoolmates, after the fact. What is even more important, while his wordplay is frequently practiced at the expense of others, most of the time it ends up being self-addressed, thoughtful, probing into the essential truths concealed behind appearances, and thus suffused in intense lyricism.

Having said that, we must nonetheless concede, as we have done earlier, that quibbling, however penetrating, by and large remains a form of jesting, a sign of youthful lack of mature seriousness. Could not some such observation be made of most lyrical poetry too? *Love's Labour's Lost* seemed to suggest as much. It has been noticed in Shakespearean criticism that after his enforced sea voyage to England Hamlet returns home a different person—no longer doubtful and hesitant, resigned to the mysterious workings of fate and ready to act at the ripeness of time. In the last Act, it might be added, he seems to have lost his knack for wordplay replacing it with a new earnestness and directness in interpersonal relations, perhaps with the obvious exception of his dealing with Osric. More precisely, the change in the hero's behavior occurs after his encounter with the gravediggers in 5.1. Here, for the first time, he is faced with a mirror image of his paronomastic vagaries, as the two clowns indulge in a word game that is devoid of substance and apt to obfuscate communication to an annoying degree. Now that the tables have been turned on him, the Prince does not appreciate the manner any more and distances himself from it.

The quibbling session in the graveyard starts before Hamlet and Horatio enter the scene. The diggers first play on the idea of suicide and justice, then on that of social inequity, and finally, on the glories of their own profession, ingeniously claiming Adam for its originator. When, having immersed himself in the half-playful half-morbid contemplation of death's absolute power of annihilation, the protagonist turns to the more astute of the two clowns to ask him whose grave he is digging, the answer is unexpectedly uncooperative: "Mine, sir" (112). His immediate reaction is to respond with a pun: "I think it be thine, indeed, for thou liest in't" (114). The gravedigger takes up the pun at once and turns it against its maker: "You lie out on't, sir, and therefore 'tis not yours. For my part I do not lie in't, yet it is mine" (115–16). Now Hamlet is compelled to drop all paronomastic duality and start using the word *lie* in a discursive framework delimiting its meaning, so that actual communication can be established. However, the gravedigger is not easily wrested out of his equivocating spree and continues to build up confusion about the person for whom the grave has been dug, now to do with the gender of the deceased. Hamlet is exasperated and indignant as he turns to his faithful companion for sympathy: "How absolute the knave is! We must speak by the card or equivocation will undo us. By the Lord, Horatio, these three years I have took note of it, the age is grown so picked that the toe of the peasant comes so near the heel of the courtier he galls his kibe" (129–33). The Prince is no longer what he used to be. The high-minded philosopher in him has been reduced to a supercilious aristocrat, concerned about the preservation of the customary social order. But he is also chastened by this encounter with his grotesque alter ego, and, like Berowne in *Love's Labour's Lost*, he is by and large purged of his linguistic mannerism. The question remains: is Hamlet thus purged of his lyric self too? Is this the point at which the *poet* in him turns *hero*—inactive, yet prepared to act at the decisive moment—for whom "The readiness is all" (5.2.200)?

The pervasiveness of the lyric principle in *Hamlet* finds its most palpable stylistic materialization in the unprecedented saturation of the entire text in fresh and evocative poetic imagery, which transcends quotidian reality and connects our little lives with a surrounding universe of hidden significance. Most of this imagery radiates from the protagonist. From his first cues ("A little more than kin, and less than kind" [1.2.65], "I am too much in the sun" [1.2.67]) onward he hardly ever speaks in a literal or abstract way. His soliloquies are as figurative as few poems are; and even his briefest contributions to dialogue are pointedly metaphorical. To the Ghost's subterranean injunctions that his associates should take an oath of secrecy after his appearance to them in 1.5, Hamlet replies: "Well said, old mole" (161). When Polonius complains in 2.2 that the player's monologue is too long, his reaction is: "It shall to the barber's with your beard" (437). When, conversely, Ophelia remarks in 3.2 that the prologue of the mousetrap play is very brief, Hamlet snaps: "As woman's love" (147). And a little later, after the opening speeches of the player king and queen about remarrying in widowhood, he exclaims: "That's wormwood" (175).

Some of Hamlet's most striking images are prompted by other characters' cues or by the setting of the scene and they crackle unexpectedly in the middle of a conversation, suddenly raising small talk to philosophical heights or immersing it in unfathomable psychological depths. We need only recall two of the many instances, which have been discussed above: the discussion of Fortune's anatomy with the symbolical place of Rosencrantz and Guildenstern in it (2.2) and the pairing off of the Prince and the recorder (3.2).

Hamlet's images are never hackneyed, never imitative or repetitive; they are always genuine, coined at the moment of speaking and carrying in their core the major preoccupation of that moment. When he remembers his father's loving care for his mother, he conveys the sense of that delicacy by saying that the murdered king "might not beteem the winds of heaven/ Visit her face too roughly" (1.2.141–42). Later he objects to his old friends' imputation of ambition as the cause of his discontent with the words: "O God, I could be bounded in a nutshell and count myself a king of infinite space" (Appendix (1), (16–17). While imagining his ultimate revenge on his father's murderer, the Prince would like to "trip him that his heels may kick at heaven/ And that his soul may be as damned and black/ As hell whereto it goes" (3.3.93–95). Thus, through the intercession of imagery, states and motions of the soul acquire with him the materiality and the vehemence of urgent physical actuality—a transformation typical of lyrical opsis.

Every kind of intellectual or spiritual activity in which the protagonist engages explodes into images. Let us take, for instance, his dispute with Gertrude in her closet (3. 4). Hamlet can develop a whole argument in the form of an extended metaphor, while focusing on a psychological issue—

                    Mother, for love of grace
        Lay not a flattering unction to your soul
        That not your trespass but my madness speaks.
        It will but skin and film the ulcerous place
        Whiles rank corruption mining all within,
        Infects unseen

                                                    (142–47)

—or while generalizing about humanity, as he does directly after that:

        That monster Custom, who all sense doth eat
        Of habits devil, is angel yet in this,
        That to the use of actions fair and good
        He likewise gives a frock or livery
        That aptly is put on.

                                                    (159–63)

—or even in an apparently "actional" speech, uttered a little later as
a warning to his mother of dangers to come if she is not circumspect
enough:

        No, in despite of sense and secrecy
        Unpeg the basket on the house's top,
        Let the birds fly and like the famous ape
        To try conclusions, in the basket creep
        And break your own neck down.

                                                    (190–94)

—and, finally, turning to his own plans of action against the designs
on his life:

        For 'tis the sport to have the enginer
        Hoist with his own petard, and't shall go hard
        But I will delve one yard below their mines
        And blow them at the moon.

                                                    (204–7)

Most of the hero's longer speeches, even when they form part of
the dialogue, are packed with striking metaphors, which in their extreme bustle convey the restlessness of his excited mind. The effect is
to blur the edges of drama with its concrete situation and action and
to open up wider vistas of the imagination.

But Hamlet's vision is never vaguely poetic. It is always rooted in concrete observation. Shakespeare's ability, noticed in earlier plays, to transmute a trivial detail of ordinary experience into an immortal metaphor finds an even fuller realization here. To know how to express the passage of time and its connection with the life of a human being by focusing on the state of wear of the widow's shoes after her husband's funeral (1.2.147–48) is the exclusive prerogative of a born poet. To suggest the overhasty succession of the widow's remarriage after that funeral by saying that the leftovers of the food baked on the first occasion were served cold on the second (1.2.179–80) is a similar feat of keen imagination. The "vicious mole of nature" that compromises the otherwise perfect life of "particular men" (1.4.23–24), and its ensuing amplification in "the dram of eale [that]/ Doth all the noble substance of a doubt/ To his own scandal—" (36–38), are figures of no lesser distinction, demonstrating the acuteness of poetic observation and the lyrical ability to raise the most mundane details of life to universal significance. [68]

Needless to say, Hamlet is by far the major source of imagery in his play, but it would be wrong to ignore some other interesting contributions to its store. Horatio, a man of few words, has a couple of unforgettable glimpses to offer in 1.1, when he says of the apparition of the dead king: "A mote it is to trouble the mind's eye" (111), and when somewhat later he humanizes the sunrise in a strikingly vivid way: "But look, the morn in russet mantle clad/ Walks o'er the dew of yon high eastward hill" (165–66). Even the much more peripheral Barnardo and Marcellus have by then paid their less noticeable dues. Laertes, who is generally bland in his adherence to social custom, can occasionally surprise us with some bright sparks, as in his instructions to Ophelia (1.3.32–43). His sister is also capable of expressing herself figuratively long before she goes mad. Polonius, we know, is an unredeemable babbler, whose rare moments of mental wakefulness show him as a collector of conventional saws. Most of his cues are trite or downright foolish. When he resorts to a metaphor, it is usually pathetically mixed and confused. However, Polonius is not only "the father of good news" but also of a few fine images. Among these are the love vows/ unholy brokers (1.3.125–30), of which he warns his inexperienced daughter, a couple of suggestions he makes to Reynaldo before sending him on his spying mission to France: to besmear Laertes's character only lightly—"As 'twere a thing a little soiled with working" (2.1.40)—so that with this "bait of falsehood" he can obtain from his associates the "carp of truth" (60), etc. From time to time fresh poetic imagery is produced, as we have seen, by a number of other characters too, including the Ghost, Rosencrantz and Guildenstern, Fortinbras and Gertrude. Even outside her inspired monologue about Ophelia's idyllic death, the Queen's language can be genuinely metaphorical. Here is, for instance, how she describes to Hamlet his appearance during the Ghost's visitation in her closet:

> And as the sleeping soldiers in th'alarm
> Your bedded hair, like life in excrements
> Start up and stand an end.
>
> (3.4.116–18)

But if any other character in *Hamlet* could be compared, even at a distance, with the hero as a generator of lyrical language, that is again his chief antagonist. As we saw, from their first encounter the King and the Prince are sharply contrasted. The one speaks formally and volubly, the other probingly and laconically. Claudius's language is not deprived of figurative expressiveness, but his tropes, unlike Hamlet's, are mostly conventional. They frequently reflect the body-politic doctrine of the time, expounded by Laertes in 1.3.22–23. It is curious how many of the King's images are drawn from human anatomy. In his first public speech (1.2.1–39) he suggests that the whole mourning kingdom ought to be "contracted in one brow of woe" and then emblematizes his ambivalent position as a bereaved bride-groom by picturing himself "With an auspicious and a dropping eye." Turning to Laertes, Claudius assures him that "The head is not more native to the heart,/ The hand more instrumental to the mouth,/ Than is the throne of Denmark to [his] father" (47–49). In his great soliloquy in 3.3 he focuses on his blooded hand (43–46), and then on the symbolical "gilded hand" of crime (57–60), continuing with the bitter observation that "we ourselves [are] compelled/ Even to the teeth and forehead of our faults/ To give in evidence" (62–64), in order to conclude with an appeal to his "stubborn knees" to bow in prayer and to his hardened heart to thaw (70–72). A tendency that we noticed in Richard II's speeches as the construction of the monarch's self-image—the sublimation of his natural body into body politic—has now come to a head. Appropriately, it is not to Claudius's person but to his ears and mouth that the English Ambassadors and Horatio refer metonymically after the King's death (5.2.353, 356).

Conventional limitations notwithstanding, the prayer speech in 3.3, as already pointed out, is abundant in genuine metaphors, revealing imaginative powers not inferior to Hamlet's. Even traditional anatomical symbolism here is raised to lyrical revelation. This new tone is already set at the moment when the King's conscience is first awakened in the revelatory comparison of his face to the "harlot's cheek" (3.1.49–53), but it is in the fourth act that Claudius's language becomes truly impressive by sustaining the high quality of visionary reflection. His momentarily freed imagination proves capable of bodying forth the bodiless inner world with a remarkable intensity:

> But so much was our love,
> We would not understand what was most fit,
> But, like the owner of a foul disease,
> To keep it from divulging, let it feed
> Even on the pith of life.

(4.1.19–23)

> Come, Gertrude, we'll call up our wisest friends
> And let them know both what we mean to do
> And what's untimely done. [   ]
> Whose whisper o'er the world's diameter,
> As level as the cannon to his blank,
> Transports his poisoned shot, may miss our name
> And hit the woundless air.

(4.1.38–44)

To these could be added a couple of Claudius's figurative generalizations about the human predicament, similarly not far removed from Hamlet's philosophical conclusions:

> There lives within the very flame of love
> A kind of wick or snuff that will abate it,
> And nothing is at a like goodness still,
> For goodness, growing to a pleurisy
> Dies in his own too much.

(4.7.112–16)

> That we would do
> We should do when we would, for this 'would' changes,
> And hath abatements and delays as many

As there are tongues, are hands, are accidents,
And then this 'should' is like a spendthrift sigh,
That hurts by easing.

(4.7.116–21)

Such materializations of the invisible seem to lead directly to Macbeth's inimitable artistic insights into the mysteries of a universe in which even the most abstract things acquire disturbingly palpable substance. At such moments Claudius may strike us as a fairly advanced draft for that later and much more impressive regicide and usurper.

It could be concluded at this point that Shakespeare's use of the lyrical mode in *Hamlet* and, particularly, of its opsis aspect is by and large tied down to psychological characterization. The King's way of speaking, though not devoid of figurative expression, is conventional enough to define him as a fairly unimaginative person. But as soon as his conscience is stirred, his language changes and becomes amply capable of conveying complex attitudes and visions in a memorably original form. The difference between him and Hamlet is that, whereas the Prince's lyrical "wakefulness" is permanent, Claudius's is accidental and fleeting—a latent potentiality of human nature rather than a distinctive state of an individual mind. Even so, it contributes to the complex conception of the character as a whole, as well as to the overall impact of the tragedy.

The King's attachment to a particular class of figures, related to the clichéd body-politic conceit, is also indicative of the dramatist's interest in individualization. Two parallel cues in act 4, one belonging to him and the other to the Queen, testify to the author's interest in psychological makeup, Claudius's metaphor for the accumulation of misfortunes being rightly of a military kind while Gertrude's is not:

When sorrows come they come not single spies
But in battalions . . .

(4.5.78–79)

One woe doth tread upon another's heel,
So fast they follow.

(4.7.161–62)

At the same time, if we exclude the protagonist and the antagonist of the tragedy, its poetic imagery is evenly, though more thinly, spread over the remaining dramatis personae, rendering it impossible to argue that their characterization depends on the use of tropes to any significant extent. On this level we come across occasional figures that could be spoken at random by anyone and can hardly be said to offer a glimpse of the characters' inner worlds. Their cumulative effect is lyrical in a generally atmospheric, unspecified way. So high a concentration of poetic imagery—more often than not unhackneyed and powerfully evocative, pointing toward the hidden depths of being—is unprecedented in Shakespeare's work. Its accumulation creates the impression that, instead of the dramatic principle assimilating occasional lyrical intrusions, in this play the pervasive lyrical principle assumes control over the dramatic material. And the lyrical principle's unchallengeable pivot is, of course, Hamlet.

Hamlet's sensitivity to words and to their expressive potential is indeed immense. What he finds hard to tolerate is unnatural, parasitic, insincere, hollow speech. Claudius's formal public oration makes the Prince switch at once to enigmatic language in 1.2. In a letter sent to the usurper after his enforced sea voyage (4.7.43–46) and also in the substituted royal missive to the King of England (5.2.38–47), he parodies the formulae of officialese. But his derision is especially strong when he mimics Osric's courtly artificiality in the course of their conversation in 5.2. Thus, all forms of automatized public language are found wanting. Language in general is suspect, as it tends most often to obscure reality rather than reveal it. The hero's last word is, significantly, *silence*—perhaps that pregnant silence to which lyric tends, but also the silence in which the sound and the fury of life find their final consummation.

Like most lyrical poetry, *Hamlet* too offers elusive glimpses of the truth rather than an overall vision. The final utterance of its fascinating hero, accepting the triumph of silence, comes all too soon—like the last poetic revelations of Keats or of Wilfred Owen. Or—of Shakespeare himself. The most important thing has remained unsaid, unformulated to the end. "Hamlet," as Harold Bloom remarks, "tantalizes us with what he has not the time to divulge."[69] Or maybe the problem is not just the shortness of time. It is the very nature of the poemly theme that drives its expression closer and closer to the edge of silence—beyond even that ultimate brevity, which, Polonius tells us, is the soul of wit and which in a world of words the Prince has so fully mastered on his poetically heroic journey to the impossible goal.

Yet, it has not all been for nothing. Poetry is unable to replace life. It does not have the ultimate solution to all problems of existence, but it can ask the pertinent questions and open the vistas that unthinking action tends to blur. *Hamlet* is very much a play about the inner resources of the self, for which the reality of life is so inadequately narrow. These hidden depths strive to express themselves in language. But as language has become so crassly trivialized and stultified through excessive automatic use, we have to keep testing its relation to truth by examining every word and phrase. Whether in contemplative seclusion or in conversation, Hamlet is busy doing just that most of the time. This is, of course, the task of lyric. As Jan Mukařovský points out, "poetry in the course of its development constantly, and always in new ways, confronts the vocabulary of the given language with the world of things which this vocabulary is supposed to reflect and to whose changes it is continuously adapting itself."[70] And as M. M. Mahood appropriately adds: "The poet has not only that power over words, abused by Shakespeare's villains, of playing upon the associations they hold for other people. He has also power to restore the truth of words, to ensure that where there is a word there is a thing."[71]

Hamlet's role is above all that of the poet, the lyric agent, who explores language and strives to restore its relation to reality. The visions that this work opens up and the vastness of sensibility which it reveals dwindle the hero's specific dramatic task to something unworthy of his natural powers. "Mad or sober," Rosalie Colie writes, "Hamlet's deliberate word-play demonstrates his exceptional agility of mind, reminding us, in another way, that a man with talents like his is wasted by the assignment of revenge."[72] Thus, through the poetic cast of its hero, the lyrical principle in Shakespeare's first great tragedy takes precedence over the dramatic.

The presence of the lyric in the text of this play, however, is difficult to locate and excerpt. It does not, as a rule, reside in isolated insets. Though Hamlet is the most expert soliloquist, his speeches are seldom of a piece. Their strong lyrical infusion is usually intermixed with other generic modes and is seldom cut off from the encompassing dramatic action. On the other hand, the dialogue of the play is again and again "lyricized" chiefly by the Prince's participation. For, he refers everything back to his own person and, in the final analysis, converses with himself rather than with anybody else. It could be argued then that Hamlet imposes the lyrical mode on the very stronghold of the dramatic, the *azione parlata*. His lyricism is not the monologic one of the Navarran lords, of Romeo, Richard II, and Orlando, but of a different, dialogic kind—even when he talks to himself within himself. This peculiarity alienates it from the rhetorical and gives it a richly ironical, punning, ambiguous coloring.

As a lyrical persona, Hamlet is perhaps closest to two of his female predecessors: Juliet and Rosalind. In some ways he is more of a kin with the latter than with any other dramatic creation of Shakespeare's on at least two counts: (1) in that they are both suspicious of all conventional expression, therefore prone to veer away from formal verse toward supple prose, and (2) in that they are both intensely interpersonal. There is, however, a marked difference between the two, for the Prince, unlike Rosalind, is anything but collectivistic in the realization of his lyrical impulses. While she projects her inner nature on her surroundings, he, conversely, draws the whole of the outer world into the throbbing center of his own vibrant being. While she molds the entire drama in her lyrical fashion, he absorbs the whole drama in his lyrical self. The result in both cases is a lyrodramatic generic hybrid, each of whose components is raised to a higher power by their integration.

4

Conclusion

SUMMING UP

THE INROADS OF LYRIC IN SHAKESPEARE'S DRAMATIC WORK ARE MANY and various. What first meets the eye is the fairly widespread tendency of inclusion, which produces easily recognizable self-contained insets. Among these, the songs are perhaps the most obvious kind. Their function, especially in the comedies, seems to be primarily thematic and atmospheric: i.e. they formulate in a lyrical way some central ideas or concerns of the respective play, and they contribute markedly to the creation of that play's characteristic mood or emotional atmosphere. Such are the songs of Ver and Hiems at the end of *Love's Labour's Lost*, as well as—in different ways—those of Lord Amiens and the two clowns in *As You Like It*. Ophelia's flurry of country ditties, however, appears to work in a less obvious way. As they cause a general consternation on the stage, they draw the attention of the audience to an important turn of the plot and its effect on a no less important, hitherto subdued character, closely related to the protagonist. Only in this roundabout, or more organic, way do they direct us to the heart of the tragedy. While the first kind of songs halts the dramatic action, the second would seem to fuse into it, highlighting a crucial moment and thus securing its exceptional prominence.

Inset poems come very close to the songs, yet, in contrast to the songs' focus on communal attitudes, they are almost invariably intensely personal—created by individual characters and airing their particular preoccupations. In the plays considered here, poems are even more numerous than songs. They are, first of all, the effusions of romantic lovers such as the Navarre academicians in *Love's Labour's Lost* and Orlando in *As You Like It*. By definition, these texts

245

are self-centered and, even though some of them are meant to reach their particular addressees and establish actual communication with them, for the most part they fail to do so and remain chiefly an expression of inner states for the sake of the expression. Their function is atmospheric and characterizational.

However, we should not overlook the less purely lyrical contributions of Holofernes, Moth, and Armado, and then, certainly, those of Hamlet. All of these gravitate towards the parodic, the ironic and the satirical. Their generic character is most often epigrammatic and, while they do reflect the psychological makeup or the momentary state of mind of their authors, they are also aimed outwardly—at other personages and at specific developments of the plot, thus coming to grips with the dramatic action in a more immediate way.

Parodic elements can, in fact, be also discerned in the "straightforward" lyrical poems, for, in spite of their personal orientation, they reflect rhetorical fashions of the time, whose affectations are amply displayed and magnified in their texts. The difference between the two kinds of parody is that in the "straightforward" poems the mockery is not specifically dramatic—it comes not from a character but directly from the author and is usually more subtle and veiled.

A feature that often accompanies the lyrical insets—be they songs or poems—is an ensuing critical commentary or a spoof, relativizing their impact, depriving them of the aesthetic autonomy characteristic of that genre, and drawing them into the dramatic environment. The role of the ironical commentator and parodist in *As You Like It* is divided between the witty heroine (who, by the way, happens to be the addressee of some of these texts), the melancholy malcontent Jaques and the professional jester Touchstone. In *Love's Labour's Lost* it is shared between practically all the producers of the texts, the Navarre lords, as they mock one another, but is above all performed by Berowne and, outside this circle, by Holofernes. Hamlet, the tragic hero notoriously doubling as jester, becomes the critic of his own poetic stuff, as demonstrated by the letter accompanying his amorous rime sent to Ophelia. It is indicative that so many characters should be entrusted with the task of disfranchising the textual immigrants of lyric in drama. The containment of these intruders is obviously an urgent necessity. Their extradition, however, is out of the question. They are welcome aliens that may be usefully employed, especially if they are naturalized as law-abiding citizens of the host genre they have entered.

Soliloquies can be of various kinds. The lyrical ones or the extensive lyrical sections of mixed soliloquies may be quite similar to the inset poems, though they are seldom as easy to extract from the play and enjoy in isolation from it, for their connectedness with the whole is much more organic. Consequently, they should be considered as examples not of generic inclusion but rather of lyrical modulation of dramatic texts. Many soliloquies are composite structures combining oratorical, narrative, argumentative and overtly actional parts with their lyrical components. Thus the lyric impulse in them is felt to erupt—sometimes only momentarily—in the midst of a generic medley.

Also, the lyric in the soliloquies rarely acquires the form of Burke's "ordered summation of emotional experience."[1] If we exclude Richard II's inimitable feats of the fusion of lyric and rhetoric with an eye on its public effect, most of Shakespeare's soliloquies present what Una Ellis-Fermor called "an image of the mind as yet in chaos," trying hard to define a truth that escapes linguistic formulation and so keeps disturbing a mind that is a priori sorely disturbed.[2] If they do partake of the lyrical, such speeches illustrate the lyrical process rather than its crystallized final product. More often than not they reflect an inner drama that is no less formidable than the outer one and may be even rendered by specifically dramatic means such as a heated dialogue between the speaker and his public identity or his inner self, etc. What makes the inner drama different from the outer is its being invisible and contained in a single self, thus partaking of the lyrical.

Finally, such a soliloquy does not necessarily arrive at a definitive answer to the painful questions it has raised, thus remaining open to the ensuing action, where the answer will eventually be attained by a resolution impossible to predict. So, however withdrawn from the ceaseless dramatic flow, the intensely lyrical soliloquies may be seen as nodes of accumulated energy making the further vigorous development of the plot possible. Moreover, some of them grapple with an ongoing action even in the process of being uttered. This curious merger of actual physical theater and the imaginative flights of lyric locution is demonstrable in Romeo's and then in Juliet's last speeches in the charnel house. Richard II's observant use of stage props, stage set, etc., like the base court, the royal crown, the mirror, his prison and the music he can hear from afar, to weave out his moving imagery, is also worth noticing. Hamlet follows suit with his memorable disquisition on the similarity between him and the recorder he is handling in the company of Rosencrantz and Guildenstern.

Each of these developments can be traced through most of the plays considered in our study, but they all come to their fruition in the tragedy of the Prince of Denmark. To a much higher degree than the inset songs and poems, the lyrical soliloquies in Shakespeare's plays integrate with their encompassing dramatic element and help it attain its true significance by elevating it from mere intrigue to the heights of momentarily intuited philosophy, which can be offered to us in the "speaking picture of poesy" recommended by Sidney.[3] In the process they themselves acquire a generic form that transcends not only inclusion, but modulation too, and, in spite of the quantitative incommensurability of the two kinds, becomes a hybrid (or crossbreed) of the lyric and the dramatic, so organic that it could be called *lyrodramatic*.

At this point the question naturally arises: how can we tell a lyrical speech from a nonlyrical one outside the formally defined inset songs and poems? First of all, let us reiterate that even the songs and poems are not necessarily "purely lyric" in all cases. The rhymed verse in which they often appear is not a sufficient and unequivocal sign of lyricism. There are other, more essential if more elusive signs, like evocative poetic imagery, supple phonetic orchestration, syntactic patterning, etc. It is the accumulation of such opsis and melos features that betrays the existence of the lyrical impulse, and that can persuade us to class as "lyrical" a prose speech like Hamlet's Picoesque oration in 2.2.259–76.

Yet even when these features are all there, together with the metric and rhyming scheme, we cannot assume that the piece is lyrical, for it can very well be an exercise in public rhetoric, striving to persuade others to embrace your truth, rather than striving to express it and formulate it to yourself. The tone of the one kind of utterance, however, is markedly different from that of the other and we should prick up our ears to catch its revealing accents. Of course, there are some tangible marks of the lyric differentiating it from public oratory. Although both kinds use the same instruments of rhetoric, the lyrically tinged metaphor is fresh, unexpected, startling, and so are the other devices used in the service of lyric: alliteration, antithesis, enjambment, repetition. They do not appear to be deliberately and carefully arranged to make a point forcefully—they rather seem to spring up under the urgent pressure of a strong emotion and to disrupt all predetermined order. Having said that, it must be conceded that there are all sorts of intermediate shades between the two modes, and in some cases classification may be better left in the balance. John Gaunt's and some of King Richard's monologues are good illustrations of such generic indeterminacy. But, far from undermining the typological distinction, they make it all the more subtle and interesting.

The distinction between lyrical and essayistic speeches is even more difficult to make, since the contemplative essay comes very close to the lyric poem as a thematic type of literature and its stricter logical organization provides the only distinguishing characteristic. Borderline examples in this area, as we have seen, are indeed quite frequent in all extensive utterances, irrespective of whether they are addressed outwardly or inwardly.

A similarly blurred divide is that between soliloquy and interpersonal communication. It has been shown again and again on our material that, while the solo speech, the fairly extended self-addressed utterance delivered on an empty stage is the most congenial noninset form of lyric expression, lyric incursions into Shakespearean drama are not at all confined to such passages but spread out boldly across tracts of interaction between two or more characters. Publicly-orientated monologues are the next area of dramatic text in which one should look for traces of lyrical modulation—and indeed such traces are easy to detect in most of these longer contributions to interpersonal exchange.

An especially interesting variety of monologue is constituted by the numerous narrative reports about plot events. The messenger (nuntius) relating a story usually lives himself/ herself into it to such an extent that the account becomes intensely lyrical. Examples can be culled from every play, but York's report on the arrival of Bolingbroke and Richard in London after the deposition and, especially, Gertrude's description of Ophelia's death are masterpieces of generic interplay producing a powerful artistic effect. Narrative essayistic monologues can suddenly betray the speaker's strong empathy with the subject of his/ her narration and develop a shorter or longer lyrical section within the matter-of-fact report. Thus we are offered the result of a triple generic interaction—a lyrically modulated epic inset in the dramatic text.

Other types of prolonged utterances are also capable of such transformation. Compulsive soliloquists tend to forget that they are in the midst of people and withdraw into themselves from the ongoing conversation, often turning a regular monologue into a quasi-soliloquy. Sometimes such switches are quite brief, sometimes they can even spring up in a single-line self-addressed cue, as demonstrated more than once by Hamlet's manner of "communication."[4] But before turning to this minimalist form of lyric intrusion we should pay attention to some of the ways in which lyric endeavors to modulate entire tracts of dialogue.

Love's Labour's Lost offers many interesting examples of dialogue patterned by a variety of rhyming schemes that tend to convert it into a compact lyrical text, a quasi-poem. The technique of playing on a word or a phrase or expanding a poetic image through a number of cues is frequently practiced throughout the play, and the usual set of rhetorical devices on the phonetic, lexical, and syntactic levels of language structuring are employed to reinforce the impression of lyrical locution, especially when the dialogue has to do with the topic of love, which is almost always the case. Rhyming, on the other hand, can be subtly used to underscore dramatic relationship and character, especially in the games of power or preeminence. Thus a traditionally lyrical formal feature, without being deprived of its original function, is appropriated by drama for its specific purposes. But it must be made clear that rhyming in Shakespeare's earlier plays, even if fairly pervasive, is rarely automatic and unrelated to the meaning of the text—a mere formal shell—as it often is in older dramas. Its functionality is manifold, and it provides a useful interface between the two generic components in the playwright's first attempts to create poetic drama, relying chiefly on the mechanism of formal hybridization.

This insistent lyrically tinged patterning of dialogue in *Love's Labour's Lost* can occasionally create fairly self-contained formations which could be called *lyrical modules*. A case in point is the playful exchange between the four Navarre would-be scholars in 1.1.94–97. If this quadruplet, ending with Berowne's green-geese taunt, is no more than a teasing game, based on stichomythic parallelism and excessive identical rhyming, in *Romeo and Juliet* the method is elaborated to produce the inimitable tour-de-force of the protagonists' shared sonnet in 1.5, encasing their "dialogue-of-one." Sophisticated lyrical modules of a formally more relaxed kind, yet employing the full paraphernalia of Petrarchan rhetoric, recur at several crucial points in the further development of the Verona play to punctuate the progress of its love story. And while the prosodic definiteness of its first appearance is later exchanged for greater flexibility, the intricacy of its figurative language is emulated again and again in no less forceful rhythmic structures. Thus a general movement is manifested away from the outer lyrical feature of rhyming and toward the more substantive parts of its generic repertoire, which will allow it to merge more fully into the dramatic. A dialogical module of the transitional kind envelopes the royal couple's parting scene in *Richard II* (5.1). *As You Like It*, however, creates a radically novel type of encapsulated dialogue construction, based on parallelism and repetition, in which the polysemy of language is liberated by its reference to a variety of characters, yet firmly held together by the centripetal compactness of minimalist lyrical locution. It informs the ritualistic game of ascending from individuality to archetypal identity in love, without which the completion of the plot is unthinkable, as is the achievement of its infectiously sparkling mood and atmosphere.

The apogee of the lyrical module as a formal crystallization of dialogue and its subsequent relaxation in *Romeo and Juliet* is a straw in the wind. This development is indicative of the tendency of Shakespeare's dramaturgy in the longer term to dissolve the hard-and-fast inclusion formations in the general dramatic medium of azione parlata, thus permeating the whole with the lyrical mode. The process is accompanied by an important evolution of the figurative language, which frees itself of the poetic cliché and its ingenious derivatives, in order to grapple with the palpable reality of the actual world and probe through it to the underlying significance of being, making the latter no less palpable. The images emerging from this new orientation acquire the unprecedented power of cognitive revelation.

Poetic revelation can at times occur in the midst of quick repartee. Most of the quibbles Mercutio and Romeo exchange in their matches of ready wit, being extremely volatile and centrifugal, have little to do with inwardness or even with a thematic orientation. However, there are crucial dramatic moments, when punning gets right to the heart of the matter, thus gathering considerable lyrical power.[5] We have observed how Mercutio, after being fatally stabbed by Tybalt, answers Romeo's supposition that his "hurt cannot be much" with the words: "No, 'tis not so deep as a well, nor so wide as a church door, but 'tis enough, 'twill serve. Ask for me tomorrow and you shall find me a grave man" (*Romeo and Juliet*, 3.1.97-99). The irony, expressed through the hyperbolical similes and crowned by the paronomastic use of the word "grave" with its foreknowledge of what is imminent, this time is *dead* serious in spite of its playful pose. Mercutio reflects momentarily on the poemly theme of life and death—and he does that in an intensely personal way. One feels that the emotion that brings these words forth is not allowed to burst out and is kept under the control of a superior reason. Sentimentality is suppressed, and the fact that we are not flooded by the passion but only given a hint that it is there, makes it all the more effective.

Rosalind will adopt a similar manner in her dealing with the passion of love, which struggles to conquer her. The heroine's recurrent ironic trumpeting of her partial victory over this passion betrays an inner tumult, and it is our recognition of this precarious balance between reason and emotion that makes her presence so strongly lyrical. The mechanism of its realization is clearly dramatic, for the revelation of Rosalind's unquiet state of mind unfolds exclusively in the interactive medium of dialogue, which is her natural element. But this method will reach its consummation only in Hamlet's cues. The Prince's profound interest in language and its knack of concealing the truths of existence, coupled with his determination to rend this pernicious veil of deception, makes almost every utterance of his a poetic revelation. He picks up each suspicious word from the flow of conversation and subjects it to the test of its own polysemous potential. Thus he becomes an agent of the essential function of poetry, that of confronting "the vocabulary of the given language with the world of things which this vocabulary is supposed to reflect."[6]

It should be noted that Hamlet's keen sense of how things are named and the relation of linguistic labels to the truth of ontological reality is preceded by Juliet's lyrophilosophical question "What's in a name?" (*Romeo and Juliet*, 2.2.43), and also by Richard II's sudden attraction to a word dropped by Bolingbroke: "Say that again!/ The shadow of my sorrow? Ha, let's see" (*Richard II*, 4.1.293–94), leading to a thorough investigation of the suggestions this word, "shadow," has for the understanding of his true being. Yet, while Juliet's interest in the power of words is only occasional and Richard's is sentimentally theatrical, Hamlet's is continuous and profoundly internal. It finds expression chiefly in the brief but incisive spurt of a pun that can suddenly throw an orderly conversation off balance and expose to the view the abyss of uncertainty, which gapes underneath our thin cover of delusive security, made up of conventional assumptions.

Like Rosalind before him (perhaps like Juliet too), Hamlet would never think of himself as a poet, he would never brood with Richard II on the problem "how I may compare/ This prison where I live unto the world." The pedantic inventories of allegory are alien to his nature. He would rather hit on an unexpected association and probe to its utmost depth, instead of spreading out to its periphery. On occasion he may indeed elaborate on a figure that he has stumbled upon, as he does in the case of the Denmark's-a-prison conceit (*Hamlet*, 2.2 [Appendix 1, (1)]. But he would not carry such explorations to extreme lengths, cracking the wind of a poor phrase. His usual way with words and images is brisk, explosive and energizing rather than insistent and laborious.

It is true that, unlike Rosalind, Hamlet is given to soliloquizing. But his soliloquies do not offer us a better insight of his inner world than does his generally laconic participation in dialogue. Both characters are extremely reticent, even secretive. But again and again they betray their true feelings almost in spite of themselves, inadvertently and infectiously. Rosalind does that by being overly excited and vividly imaginative while expanding on the interplay of the sexes—love, marriage, etc., and Hamlet by every now and then retiring into an inner space to make a mental note about life in the course of conversation, leaving his interlocutors in the lurch. His mental notes carry a degree of seriousness much higher than that of the shallow conversation from which they depart.

If we can venture, then, on the limited material of our sample of Shakespeare's dramatic work, to outline the development of his method of introducing lyrical elements into it, the following parameters may be isolated. What predominates in the earlier plays is generic inclusion effected through a variety of poetic insets and fairly autonomous soliloquies, as well as the imposition of lyrical forms on parts of the dialogue. Gradually, this, sometimes rather mechanical, combination of genres is superseded by their more organic integration on a larger scale. On the one hand, longer speeches tend to acquire a hybrid character, resulting in the creation of the lyrodramatic soliloquy and other monologic pieces gravitating towards it. On the other hand, the lyric permeates the entire element of dramatic dialogue along the lines of generic modulation, no longer through the imposition of rhyming but through the saturation of the text with more essential features of the lyric repertoire. As a mixer of genres, Shakespeare seems to be moving from formal to substantive hybridization, gradually attaining what is inconceivable in Fowler's theory, the blending of two kinds incommensurable at the level of historical genres but equal at the higher level of theoretical kinds.

This movement culminates in the emergence of a type of central character partaking of the nature of the lyrical persona in nondramatic poetry and, like that figure, coming close to monopolizing the point of view—a centralization problematizing the very essence of drama as a kind of literature. Both Rosalind and Hamlet are striking manifestations of this development. With them we are made to feel that the actual core of reality is inside the protagonists rather than without. Thus they establish a pervasive atmospheric presence, without which their plays are unthinkable. This presence is lyrical rather than dramatic, though its lyricism is generated as much by the way they interact with the others as by what they say to themselves.

To a greater or smaller extent, some lyrical presence has been established by poetically minded protagonists in earlier plays too, but it is never so absolute. And then, lyricism can be of different kinds. Juliet's (and Silvius's) variety comes closer to the genuine type of Rosalind and Hamlet without being as indirect, reticent and ironical as theirs; the Navarre academicians' version is clearly imitative, conventional, and so are those of Orlando and of Romeo, especially in the initial phase of his development; whereas Richard's kind is theatrically self-conscious. On other grounds, Juliet, Hamlet and Claudius could be grouped together in contradistinction to the rest as prone to turbulent outbursts indicative of inner drama.

In at least one of our plays, *Richard II*, the dramatist sets in marked opposition to each other two central characters who could be seen to represent in pure form the Novalis/ Todorov types of Poet and Hero: King Richard and Henry Bolingbroke. Similar, though less clearly pronounced oppositions can be detected in both tragedies discussed in our sample: Romeo versus Tybalt or Hamlet versus Claudius, Laertes, and Fortinbras. More often than not the Hero manages to destroy the Poet through his determined action, but his plans tend to backfire, drawing him too into the whirlpool of general destruction. In the final analysis, the Poet invariably wins our sympathies and captivates the imagination, thus securing the ultimate aesthetic triumph for himself. This, I believe, is due above all to the fact that he has the privilege of opening up his soul to us in soliloquies and other textual formations, whose lyricism compels us to identify and empathize unreservedly with this character. For we are obliged to see everything through his eyes, just as we do when we immerse ourselves in a lyrical poem.

Of course, a Poet, especially, though not exclusively, in the comedies, can at times be treated ironically. Berowne, Romeo and Silvius, each in his turn, become alternatively exulted paragons of lyricism and caricatures of its ludicrous affectations and dissociation from the realities of existence. A mature perspective on life seems to replace the somewhat facile fantasies of lyricism towards the end of *Love's Labour's Lost, Romeo and Juliet* and *Hamlet.* Yet it remains undeniable that the charm and power of these dramas reside above all in their lyrical vision, no matter how impractical it may have proved for its bearers in dramatic terms.

What does quite often become the butt of criticism and irony in play after play is in fact not so much lyricism as such, not lyric as a literary kind, but its historically established realization in the Renaissance genre of Petrarchan love poetry. The extremely hyperbolized and hackneyed poses, locutions and images of this tradition are criticized and parodied time and again by the French Princess and the ladies of her retinue, and even by the penitent Berowne in the latter part of *Love's Labour's Lost,* by Mercutio and Juliet in *Romeo and Juliet,* by Touchstone, Phoebe and Rosalind in *As You Like It.* Its affectations are exposed most effectively by the device of literalization, which exposes the unrelatedness of Petrarchan conceits to actual life.

Yet this pervasive negativism is effectively countered by Silvius's eloquent defense of the truth that the unrealistic language of lyric can best convey the inner truth of a lover's soul. And as soon as the critics of the lyrical jargon feel the pangs of love, they resort to that language—Phoebe's case is particularly indicative, but even Juliet's development offers interesting material for discussion. Thus, in a truly dramatic way, the ironic deflation of Petrarchan lyricism and its enthusiastic apology are finally held in balance. It is obvious that lyric is an antidiscourse and that its utterances have to be translated into plain speech if they are to be applied to the needs of practical life (as happens in every play), but, as we learn through our theatrical experience, it offers a uniquely effective instrument for the expression of the hidden self, whose reality in the context of Renaissance humanism is no less important than that of the outside world.

Moreover, our plays present a display of other fashionable uses of language, which are held up to ridicule and serve as a foil rather than parallel to lyric in that the poet is not as willing to reprieve them in a similar way. In the first place, that is a kind of idle verbosity—practiced by semi-buffoons like Don Armado, or Juliet's Nurse, or Polonius—which shares with lyric the quality of antidiscourse, but is only a mockery of that mode, since it is absolutely hollow and, instead of exploring the riches of language, parasitizes on them. Holofernes's pedantic formalism, Touchstone's imitation of the dueling technical language, Osric's weaponry jargon and his artificial courtly way of speaking—all these and more are exposed as being resorted to for no other purpose but to satisfy the vanity of their users. Thus these characters are only similar to the imitative practitioners of lyric, who would like to impress the others with their skills, rather than probe into the truths that are inaccessible to other kinds of language and that lyric alone can strive for. The brunt of the attack, then, is against affectation in lyrical expression and not against the expression as such.

The sonnet is, beyond doubt, the staple form and the chief glory of Petrarchan love poetry. This is the genre created explicitly for the expression of intensely personal emotions and concerns, shackled in a rigorous metric and stanzaic mould, as well as in a no less rigorous publicly attested language, consisting of emblematic images. Here, in the intricate configuration of fourteen five- or six-foot lines, packed with a complex of thoroughly tried-out poetic conventions, we have the epitome and the perfect emblem of the humanist ideal: passions controlled by reason. It is not surprising, therefore, that the sonnet figures as such an important form in Shakespeare's plays, especially in the earlier ones, rising from a mere juvenile word game in *Love's Labour's Lost* to the status of a module, which is called upon to encapsulate not only the first dialogue of Romeo and Juliet, but also, it would appear, their entire universe of love, so alien to the surrounding world of rivalry and hate. The sonnet in this romantic tragedy is constructed by the two young lovers as a space of their private happiness walled in by its ideal structure. But only too soon it is forced to open up to the dramatic medium and let the outer reality permeate it. This signals the eventual defeat of the lyric as a self-contained element in drama, but not before it has managed to shape several of the most important dramatic scenes in its own image and likeness.

What is more, the entire Verona play is molded by the principles of the sonnet and, in a more general way, by the principles of the lyrical poem. Over and above the linear drive of the plot we have discovered a number of concentric structures turning upon themselves. First of all, that is the system of recurrent images, but on the more fundamental architectonic levels of the drama there are the recurrent scenes, mise-en-scènes, gestures, etc.—a many-layered pattern of "rhyming" structures, which highlights the thematic aspect of the tragedy, relating this essentially fiction (mythos) type of literature to that of theme (dianoia). We should also include here the unmetaphored conventions of Petrarchism evolved into entire episodes like the balcony scene. The method is at work in other plays too. An interesting example is the wooing of Phoebe by Silvius in *As You Like It*. Static dianoic elements are thus imported into the core of drama. In some of the cases the ironic mode of parody returns us to the critique, or subversion, of the then dominant lyrical vogue; in others, we are faced with lyrical single-mindedness.

The concentric model in the patterning of plot, characters and setting has been detected by us in most of the plays under review. The impulse of their lyrical heroes to discover or create their exclusive timeless space, not unlike the shared sonnet of Romeo and Juliet, is responsible for the emergence of the Navarre academy, Richard's prison and, above all, the magic Forest of Arden. These are all lyrical loci of the mind, purlieus of the imagination, for awhile uninvaded by the imperfect world of drama, nay, almost immune to the onrush of time, for which Hamlet seems to yearn when he exclaims: "O God, I could be bounded in a nutshell and count myself a king of infinite space" (*Hamlet*, 2.2. [Appendix 1, (1)]). The trouble with such nutshells is that sooner or later they get cracked by the pressures of the larger reality outside them or by their own need to open up to that reality. Lyrical isolation cannot last. It is engulfed by the dramatic flow that thunders all around it, yet it does not vanish without a trace. The drama as a host genre infiltrates the lyric, which has entered into it. By depriving the lyric of its self-contained and static autonomy, the drama modifies it into an integral part of its own organism. In the process, of course, the drama in its own turn is modified by the lyric. For drama knows that the lyric can never fully replace it but can enlarge it infinitely. Or if it did not know that previously, Shakespeare has persuaded it that in this marriage it has nothing to fear and everything to gain.

EPILOGUE

Written as they were at the turn of the century, *As You Like It* and *Hamlet* became but the prelude to their author's crowning achievements in the genre of poetic drama. To analyze these in the same detailed way in which their precedents have been dealt with would take another volume, but the present study should not close without casting a glance at further developments of the important tendencies it has traced. Three great tragedies—*Othello, King Lear,* and *Macbeth*—will provide the material for this brief survey. In all of them the full register of methods and techniques employed in the earlier plays is at work, with a marked preference for an even greater pervasiveness and organicity. Thus the interaction of the dramatic and the lyric is carried on to a more advanced stage of integration. Some of its features present themselves readily to the naked eye.

To start with, the inset verse pieces continue to punctuate the plays. Iago's cynically sarcastic epigrams on women in 2.1 tell us a lot about the villain's mind and the philosophy behind his directorial control of the plot; his rowdy drinking songs in 2.3 reveal the primitive impulses of his nature, as well as his ability to manipulate the others by role-playing; Desdemona's gently sorrowful willow ballad, sung before her execution in 4.3, reaffirms our sympathy for this unfortunate young woman, and the fact that Emilia borrows the same tune for her "swansong" in 5.2 clearly signals her complete reformation from her husband's accomplice into her mistress's soul mate.

When King Lear begins to face the consequences of his tragic error in 1.4, the Fool becomes surprisingly "full of songs"—for the most part, aphoristic couplets that alert his royal master to the actuality of his situation and precipitate his spiritual self-crucifixion. Without this convex mirror held up to him again and again, the tragic grandeur of Lear's regeneration would have been unthinkable. It is also important to notice that, while the Fool's rimes are largely coolly ironical allusions to the hero's foolishness, by the same token they satirize the absurdity of the world and thus offer a glimpse of their presenter's humanity, which elevates him above the mere functionality of a stock character. The Fool continues to pour out epigrammatic poetry well into the climactic scenes of act 3 and then, after his crowning piece of Merlin's prophecy, makes room for another songster, Edgar in the guise of Poor Tom, who intersperses his confused speeches in 3.4

and 6 with short ditties filled with gibberish or fragments of similarly desemantized folklore. One way or another, these metric insets are used for the creation of Edgar's assumed character—that of the deranged "noble philosopher"—and of the overall topsy-turvidom that engulfs Lear in this part of the tragedy.

In *Macbeth,* the rhymed insets are of a slightly different kind. Jingling tetrametric iambic or trochaic couplets, brimful with seamy creatures, severed limbs and other unpleasant details (1.3, 3.5, and 4.1), they all belong to the Weird Sisters and their awe-inspiring goddess, Hecate, and are related to the tradition of magic charms and spells. Besides the rhyme, these verses rely on the regular employment of parallel constructions and refrains. They are obviously designed to accompany the witches' ritual dances around the boiling cauldron. An important function of theirs is to underline atmospherically the part played by metaphysical evil powers in Macbeth's life and to foreground the enchanting capacity of these powers by subjecting the audience to their own rhythmic influence.

All in all, the verse insets in the great tragedies are less autonomous than those used in the earlier period. There is hardly anything now that could be set beside the summer and winter songs winding up *Love's Labour's Lost* or Lord Amiens's and the two pages' tunes in *As You Like It*. Instead, most of the new insets seem to derive from Hamlet's biting epigrams or Ophelia's mad balladry. For, while many of them are again contributive to the general atmosphere of the respective play, their first affiliation now is to character and plot. In other words, by advancing further in the direction worked out in *Hamlet,* they are drawn deeper into the drama's architectonics and are not allowed to just shed their light on the play from afar. Moreover, as in *Hamlet,* their lyricism is often subdued and replaced by satire and grotesquery, providing a necessary foil for the immense lyrical upheaval of heroic tragedy in its climactic sections. It could therefore be argued that such insets are largely delyricized and decentered.

The satirical vein is even more salient in such self-contained thematic insets as the essayistic treatise: Iago's orations on virtue, women and reputation in the early parts of the play, as well as Emilia's disquisitions on jealousy and women in wedlock in the later ones. In *King Lear* it is the Fool again who draws a more elaborate parallel between men and beasts in captivity and preaches social prudence. The only contribution of this kind in *Macbeth* is the Porter's lecture in response to Macduff's question: "What three things does drink especially provoke?" All these speeches seem to take their origins from Touchstone's and Rosalind's playful arguments in *As You Like It*. If anything, the new "essays" are more acerbic, and some of them are perhaps too short to qualify as monologic utterances. They gravitate towards the generalizing aphorism or the adage.

In the inception of *Othello* we are faced with a set of such pointed gnomic pronouncements, made by the Duke of Venice (1.3.200–210) and then subverted by their parodic mirror image in Brabantio's speech (211–21). *King Lear* supplies a considerable number too, its last two acts being jam-packed with them: half a dozen belong to Edgar and a similar amount is shared between Lear and Gloucester. Albany, Kent, and Cordelia also have something to offer. And the Fool's many parables frequently come to an unexpected paradoxical *sententia*. In our third play, it is Macbeth and his wife who are privileged to draw and formulate the important conclusions about the universe and human predicament.

Sometimes this philosophic propensity becomes so overwhelming that the aphorism expands back to a thoughtful monologue or soliloquy. Edgar in *King Lear* offers good examples of this method after his experience in the lower depths of existence. One of his arresting speeches starts with the lines: "When we our betters see bearing our woes,/ We scarcely think our miseries our foes" (3.6.99–100); another opines, in consonance with the Arden exiles: "Yet better thus, and known to be contemned/ Than still contemned and flattered" (4.1.1–9). These tries at definitive wisdom are invariably exploded by the subsequent action revealing new depths of complexity and misery and are thus deprived of finality. Drama is not only capable of relativizing the products of the imagination (i.e. lyrical poems set in it) but those of judgment too. One and one only, utterly negativistic, kind of philosophy seems to survive it. Its succinct expression belongs to Macbeth and fills his last memorable soliloquy, which could be ascribed to the ratiocinative variety:

> To-morrow, and to-morrow, and to-morrow,
> Creeps in this petty pace from day to day,
> To the last syllable of recorded time;
> And all our yesterdays have lighted fools
> The way to dusty death. Out, out, brief candle!
> Life's but a walking shadow; a poor player,
> That struts and frets his hour upon the stage,

And then is heard no more; it is a tale
Told by an idiot, full of sound and fury,
Signifying nothing.

                                                    (5.5.19–28)

This vein of homologizing about life thoughtfully yet feelingly can be traced back to Richard II and, above all, to Hamlet, but it comes to a head in the soliloquies of their successors. In it an impulse of rational generalization from accumulated personal experience betrays its strongly emotional underpinning and thus imperceptibly raises the essayistic towards the lyrical.

Lyrically tinged soliloquies are easy to find in every one of the great tragedies. They are almost always marked by a passionate apostrophe. Such is the appeal to Patience Othello makes in 4.2, those to Nature in King Lear's wrathful curse on Goneril in 1.4 and to the disturbed elements in his paroxysm of howls in 3.2 and 4, subsiding to the prayer: "Poor naked wretches, wheresoe'er you are" (3.4.28–36), as well as, with some qualifications, Macduff's impatient summons of Macbeth on the battlefield, eventually transformed into an appeal to Fortune (5.7). Some of these, it will be noticed, erupt again and again from the midst of dialogue, which is incapable of containing them within the frame of interpersonal communication. Others intertwine with it to such an extent that they become almost imperceptible as compact utterances. Such are Othello's passionate series of short contradictory reactions to his situation, cunningly steered by Iago's insistent promptings in 4.1, and Lear's numerous outbursts amidst the storm in 3.2, alternating with the cues of the Fool and Kent.

An extreme variety of the lyrical soliloquy, cropping up in most of these plays, is the deranged utterance of a hero whose sanity has been shattered by a traumatic experience. Othello demonstrates that in "Lie with her? lie on her?" (4.1), when "chaos is come again" for him. Lear rages in an even more violent fashion through long stretches of text in 4.6: "Nature's above art in that respect," "Ha! Goneril with a white beard?" "Ay, every inch a king," "Thou, rascal beadle, hold thy bloody hand," etc. His enunciation at this stage is even less clear and continuous than the Moor's, torn to rags as it is by an unbearable passion. And yet, as Kenneth Muir observes, "Lear's mad speeches have an undertone of meaning, and although he leaps from one subject to another it is often possible to see that there is a subconscious connection between them."[7] Replete with seeming hallucinations and wild waywardness, they are nonetheless consistently focused on a central preoccupation of the speaker, expanding a personal problem to the outermost limits of its social and cosmic repercussions through a welter of striking images. An internal commentator precedes Muir in pointing out this deeper-lying organization of the King's seemingly berserk outpourings—Edgar, like Polonius in *Hamlet,* detects the method in them: "O matter and impertinency mixed,/ Reason in madness" (170–71). Some of this soliloquizing likewise emerges intermittently from the flow of dialogue only to dive back into it again.

The synthetic lyrodramatic type of solo speech is even more widespread with its foregrounding of the inner conflict undivorced from the outer action. It is indeed at the very heart of the great tragedies, springing from the unbearable torments of their heroes. A good example is Othello's "It is the cause, it is the cause, my soul" speech, marked by disturbed vacillation between affection and bitterness and replete with elaborate imagery, at times merging with elements of stage business (5.2.1–22). Another illustration is provided by Macbeth's "To be thus is nothing, but to be safely thus" (3.1.47–71), which does not for a moment loosen its grip on the exigencies of the plot but keeps soaring into higher regions of lyrical turbulence.

An interesting offshoot of the lyrodramatic kind is the soliloquy accompanying action at an even closer range, when the performer of the act verbalizes it and thus enlarges its meaning—a phenomenon already noticed by us in the closing scenes of *Romeo and Juliet* and then in the later plays. A most strikingly effective development of this intergeneric symbiosis occurs at the end of *Othello,* when the protagonist instructs the emissaries of the Duke of Venice to Cyprus how to report to their sovereign about what they have witnessed there:

> And say besides that in Aleppo once,
> Where a malignant and a turbanned Turk
> Beat a Venetian and traduced the state,
> I took by th' throat the circumcised dog
> And smote him—thus!

> (5.2.350–54)

With these words the Moor stabs himself and dies, having augmented the meaning of his self-execution by forging an impressive metaphor at the interface of an emotional narrative and the uninterrupted dramatic action.

In the earlier plays we have witnessed more than one case of the relativization of lyric, including critical commentaries, parodies and other techniques exposing its excesses. In *Othello* this method is carried to the point at which a lyrical utterance can be seen as spurious, being motivated not by an emotional upheaval but by Machiavellian scheming. In 3.3 Iago enters his mock-lyrical role twice, first in response to Othello's suspicion that he may be slandering Desdemona—

> O grace! O heaven forgive me!
> Are you a man? have you a soul, or sense?
> God buy you, take mine office. O wretched fool
> That lov'st to make thine honesty a vice!
> O monstrous world! Take note, take note, O world,
> To be direct and honest, is not safe.
> I thank you for this profit, and from hence
> I'll love no friend, sith love breeds such offence
>
> (376–83),

—and then in a pretence of joining the Moor's solemn vow of revenge—

>   Do not rise yet.   *Iago kneels.*
> Witness, you ever-burning lights above,
> You elements that clip us round about,
> Witness that here Iago doth give up
> The execution of his wit, hands, heart,
> To wronged Othello's service. Let him command,
> And to obey shall be in me remorse
> What bloody business ever.
>
> (465–72)

These extreme examples of duplicity seem to pose the question: is there a way of distinguishing counterfeit lyric from genuine lyric? Much of the rhetoric in both kinds is the same: vehement apostrophes, exclamations, imperatives, repetitions, climaxes, adding up to a breathless rhythm—yet they remain different in their impact and that difference consists in the lack of a true lyrical vision in the imitative variant. The figurative paucity of Iago's speeches, as compared to the imaginative torrents in the outbursts of Othello, King Lear, and Macbeth, is revealing. The melos, after all, seems easier to ape than the opsis. In the final analysis, however, it is the encompassing drama with its action defining each character that helps us to find our bearings and draw the line between authenticity and pretence in any speech.

One way or another, the compact soliloquy has become suspect in the new period. Soliloquizing now is often intermixed with running dialogue and not so readily isolated in inset-like chunks. Sometimes the lyric impulse may make itself known in an unexpectedly fresh, evocative poetic image springing up from a fairly bland actional speech, as the case is towards the close of Montano's short monologue wishing his general safe arrival in Cyprus:

> Let's to the sea-side, ho!
> As well to see the vessel that's come in
> As to throw out our eyes for brave Othello,
> Even till we make the main and th'aerial blue
> An indistinct regard.

$$(2.1.36-40)$$

A speech of quite practical intent can thus suddenly—and often only momentarily—turn lyrical, as can be shown by many examples from the mature tragedies. Did not Emil Staiger say that true lyric cannot last longer than a moment?[8] Clear lyrical notes pierce some largely essayistic monologues too. Among these are Gloucester's "These late eclipses" (1.2.103–17) and "I have no way, and therefore want no eyes" (4.1.20–26), as well as Lear's "Why, thou wert better in a grave" (3.4.99–107), but most of all his anguished social satire poured out profusely in 4.6.

Narratives of different hues form an integral part of the heroic tragedies. Here, as in the earlier plays, the nuntii's epic interventions bring in a strong lyrical infusion through the speakers' empathy with their subjects. Of particular interest are the accounts of apocalyptic upheavals in nature on the night of the regicide in Inverness (Macbeth, 2.3, 4). In an infectiously imaginative way these speeches link the human world to the vast cosmos around it. The sea storm in Othello, as witnessed by a few gentlemen of Cyprus on the eve of the Moor's arrival (2.1) is similarly portentous and so is the storm on the heath that torments King Lear. All these disturbances of the larger sphere seem to be as exceptional and shocking as those in the smaller inscribed one. The observers refer to them in an almost identical bewildered way. The effect of their vision and the accents of their enunciation are powerfully lyrical. But again—like the other monologic forms considered above—such reports are frequently so intermixed with dialogue and deprived of continuity that they are hard to extract.

The lyricized narrative comes truly into its own in *King Lear*. The climactic third act of the tragedy opens with a portrait of the protagonist "Contending with the fretful elements," sketched by an anonymous Knight (or Gentleman). This is a most necessary introduction to Lear's own appearance in the next scene. That the old man "tears his white hair,/ Which the impetuous blasts with eyeless rage/ Catch in their fury and make nothing of" is an evocative detail that spectators could perhaps capture visually in the close-up of a modern cinematic production but not in the theater—unless they are compelled to see it with their inner eye, which must have been Shakespeare's hope. The accumulation of references to "The to and fro conflicting wind and rain," "the cub-drawn bear," "The lion and the belly-pinched wolf" does set the stage for the homeless king's tragic entrance by intensely lyrical means. Kent's similarly tuned speech contributes to the same effect. Another deft use of the narrative may be observed in 4.6.11–24, where Edgar describes to his blind father the imaginary scene of the precipitous cliffs of Dover, making him— and us too—believe that he does stand on the very edge of the abyss. The description is so vivid and sketched out in such conjuring detail that it could serve as a perfect illustration of the method which made it possible to perform the Renaissance plays on a bare stage and yet fill the "empty space" with visions to the brim.

But the most remarkable example of the employment of lyrically modulated narrative in this tragedy belongs to the Gentleman, who in 4.3 appears to apprise Kent of Cordelia's reaction to his message concerning her father's sorry plight. By the time the Gentleman shares his impression of Lear's youngest daughter as she is affected by the news of his ordeal, we have already had an opportunity of getting acquainted with her uncompromising honesty and her aversion to sycophancy. We have also learned that she is a woman of few words. Now, through his description, we see this reticent character deeply moved by grief and love and struggling to control her strong passion in the way the Renaissance admired and recommended. It is again due to the theatrically impossible close-up of the narrative that we get to see how, on her reading Kent's letters, "now and then an ample tear trilled down/ Her delicate cheek," and how her smiles and tears were like "Sunshine and rain at once," only "a better way" as "patience and sorrow strove/ Who should express her goodliest," how "Those happy smilets/ That played on her ripe lip seemed not to know/ What guests were in her eyes" and how these "guests" "parted thence,/ As pearls from diamonds dropped." In silence, at a distance, in a non-dramatic passage, a central dramatic character makes her most indelible impression on the audience, which has been instructed, together with Gloucester, to look with its ears.[9] From this narrative passage, in Cordelia's absence, we get to know more about her true self than from her (scanty) participation in the action. This powerful effect is due to the lyrical empathy and eloquence of the speaker. Need it be insisted that, as has now become usual, the Gentleman's monologue is not allowed to drift away from the dialogue and is repeatedly interrupted and directed by Kent's queries and commentaries.

On the material of *King Lear*, we can observe not only how monologic speech in Shakespeare's mature drama tends to dissolve into dialogue, but how dialogue in turn may approach monologic unity of impact. This, however, is no longer achieved by the dialogue-of-one technique practiced in the earlier plays, but rather by the opposite method, that of *discordia concors*, if I may use the familiar phrase in a slightly different context. It all starts in 1.4, where the Fool begins by riddles and parables to open his master's eyes to the position Lear has willfully brought himself into, thus prompting him to express openly his pain and anathematize his ungrateful daughters. This duo of two seemingly incompatible voices—one tragically self-centered and the other comically derisive—reaches its fortissimo in 3.2, as a raving Lear "Strives in his little world of man to outscorn" the wind and the rain, while the Fool's songs become more and more caustic. The discontinuity between the two opens the gaps necessary for the voltaic arc of lyric to ignite. And the polyphony is further complicated when the duo grows into a trio with the addition of Poor Tom's voice in the hovel (3.4). Here they all appear to speak at cross-purposes, or even in different languages, yet it all adds up to a poetically enlarged realization of the enormity of Lear's tragedy. In 3.6 the wild trio is moved into the larger space of a farmhouse and at once turns it into an imaginary courtroom, where words can be converted into action at the height of a passionate mayhem. The action is plainly as fictitious as its setting: it all takes place in Lear's disturbed mind, which draws into itself other, disparate madnesses, correlating with it contrapuntally. The overall effect is overwhelming in its lyrodramatic complexity and force. Shakespeare has traveled a long way from the earlier formalized lyrical modules to this in-depth permeation of dramatic interaction by lyricism.

What makes such dialogic scenes unmistakably lyrical is above all their complex vision of reality, which rises to the heights of cosmic generalization without losing its grip on the situation at hand. The only way to achieve such transition is through poetic imagery. And the nature and use of imagery in the great tragedies are indeed raised to a markedly higher power. Macbeth's first soliloquy, "If it were done, when 'tis done" (1.7.1–28) demonstrates this advance most impressively. From its opening lines it resembles quite closely Hamlet's meditative speeches, but as we move deeper into it we are made aware of an imaginative vehemence that would have been beyond the scope of even the most outstanding of Shakespeare's earlier heroes.

The distinctive characteristic of this speech is that the abstract notions in it are made to act as if they were physical entities. The boundary between the invisible world of ideas and the world of sensuous reality is obliterated, being and becoming are fused into one single universe of immensely increased significance. If this method comes close to the rhetorical figure of personification, it does not fully merge with it, for the abstract retains its bodiless quality. Its denizenship in the lands of material action does not deprive it of its superior, spiritual essence. Among Shakespeare's nondramatic poetry, his sonnet 66 is the one filled with such half-transformed abstracts. They do appear in some of his earlier dramas too, especially in Hamlet's soliloquies. But the concentration of this technique in the later tragedies has taken a quantum leap. I have counted dozens of examples, most of all in *King Lear*. Sometimes they are momentary but arresting; sometimes they are heaped up in monologic speeches, such as Brabantio's in *Othello* (1.3.95–107) or Malcolm's in *Macbeth* (4.3.114–37); and sometimes again they are indiscriminately mixed with elements of physical reality to form a common space.

But to return to Macbeth's great soliloquy, the exceptional character of its poetic images—and hence of its lyrical impact—does not at all consist only in its tackling of the abstracts. The erasure of the borderline between concepts and things is but one aspect of its overall strategy of aesthetic transgression, reflecting the moral one that is at the very core of the tragedy. Another, no less striking revolution is the shattering of the self-contained form of the image and its opening up to complex interrelations and hybridizations with other adjacent images raising exponentially the expressive temperature of the utterance. The speech's last two sentences (16–28) present a veritable whirlwind of forms, stirred up by an enflamed imagination. There is one single tempestuous drive through this tumbling multitude: Duncan's virtues blow the angelic trumpets of their tongues, and Pity in the shape of a newborn infant strides their thundering sound. To the above image is joined the alternative—and complementary—vision of the cherubins riding on the winds and making them blow the "horrid deed" into all eyes, so that they fill up with tears, capable of drowning the winds. The idea of impetuous motion, concretized as horse riding, continues through the next sentence, in which the speaker imagines himself mounted on his criminal intention, but lacking the spurs (of the will?) to prick its sides (the horse-vehicle of the image surfacing again). The ambition that is in his heart, however, cannot be controlled: it will leap, no mater what, and fall (fatally) on the other (side of itself?).

All riders of this apocalyptical scene are more material than their coursers: Pity has acquired the form of an infant, but it is riding on a mere sound; the cherubins have also been traditionally visualized as young children, but they are mounted on the invisible ("sightless") air currents; and, lastly, Macbeth himself has straddled something no more solid than an intention. Such mounts are indeed precarious and the rider is bound to fall "on th'other—." The vision of the soliloquy is dazzlingly multifarious, yet unitary. The pity/babe transforms into the cherubin-babes and then into the speaker, insecure as a babe on horseback. Duncan's angelic virtues flow into the cherubins. The blast of their trumpet tongues merges into the winds. These are "sightless" (invisible and unseeing) but will blow the foul murder into every seeing eye, whose tears will be so plenteous as to drown them. Nothing in this torrent of images is static and isolated from the rest. They pour their impetus into one another, thus gathering a tremendous visual and emotive momentum, further reinforced by emphatic alliteration, sharp enjambments and other hurtling rhythmic devices. The hitherto compact atoms of language have been fissioned, releasing their incredible nuclear energy.[10]

An overall tendency of development seems to inform Shakespeare's dealing with his ever more complex generic material. Not only has the largely mechanical method of inclusion through the self-contained inset been outgrown at the macrolevel of dramatic speech forms, but a parallel process has taken place at the microlevel of poetic imagery too. At both levels the component units of the respective structures have foregone their isolationist separateness and have fused into the larger organically unified whole. The continuing tensions of this merger only contribute to the inner vigor of the text.

Some of the new vehemence in the treatment of imagery, informing Macbeth's great soliloquy, can be also discovered in Othello's troubled lyrodramatic utterances and, especially, in Lear's volcanic orations on the heath. This unprecedented dynamism is due to the more pervasive spread of the dramatic element through the lyric incursions in Shakespeare's peak period, injecting added vitality into poetic locution and considerably enhancing its impact. Imagery is now used in increasingly closer connection with the exigencies of drama, the construction of plot and character and the foregrounding of their most significant aspects.

An entire scene or episode can be suffused in a particular kind of figures to suggest the implications of its events, thus welding action to atmosphere. Such is, for instance, the case with the first 81 lines of *Macbeth* 2.3, where the Porter's monologues and the ensuing dialogues are saturated with allusions to hell, turning Inverness castle into an emblem of the inferno. A similar demonic effect is achieved by Edgar's deranged speeches and songs in the hovel and "courtroom" scenes of *King Lear* (3.4, 6). This architectonic use of figurative language has little in common with the allegorical method of the garden scene in *Richard II*. Its relation with the aubade episode in *Romeo and Juliet* may be a little closer, though even there the structuring of tropes around the polar opposition of day and night is neatly symmetrical and open to the view, whereas here it is much more diffuse and buried in the depths of the dramatic text.

Recurrent images in the great tragedies have become a commonplace of criticism since the pioneering studies of scholars like Caroline Spurgeon and Wolfgang Clemen, and, as they were referred to in passing already in the introduction, we can afford not to discuss them here.[11] I am tempted, however, to highlight at least one important interrelation of plot and imagery, resulting in their recurrent transformations into each other, as the different structures continue to open up and flow into each other. *Macbeth* is particularly rich in such examples. In 5.1, Lady Macbeth enters with a taper in her hand—sleepwalking. The following dialogue between onlookers ensues:

> DOCTOR. How came she by that light?
> GENTLEWOMAN. Why, it stood by her: she has light by her
>   continually; 'tis her command.
>
> (20–22)

Four scenes later, on hearing of his wife's suicide, the protagonist concludes emotionally:

> And all our yesterdays have lighted fools
> The way to dusty death. Out, out, brief candle!
>
> (5.5.22–23)

Another, much more versatile image in the same play, materializing again and again in the action, is that of the young child, usually referred to as a babe. Its debut is in Macbeth's first soliloquy, where pity is compared to a "new-born babe,/ Striding the blast" and hurtling over the world (1.7.21–22). Next it crops up in a blooded shape in Lady Macbeth's resolute speech:

> I have given suck, and know
> How tender 'tis to love the babe that milks me:
> I would, while it was smiling in my face,
> Have pluck'd my nipple from his boneless gums
> And dash'd the brains out, had I so sworn
> As you have done to this.
>
> (1.7.54–59)

On the eve of Macbeth's second meeting with the witches, their magic incantation contains a reference to a "birth-strangled babe" (4.1.30). Then the apparition of "a bloody child" is conjured up to assure him that "none of woman born" can harm him (80–81). Another child apparition follows with a tree in his hand to boost his confidence by another equivocal promise. In the meantime Banquo's son Fleance has narrowly escaped death at the hands of Macbeth's mercenaries, but Macduff's little boy is less fortunate, and in 4.3 his father is informed by Rosse that his "wife, and babes" are "Savagely slaughter'd" (204–5). In 5.8, before their last fight, Macduff reveals to

Macbeth the shattering truth that he "was from his mother's womb/ Untimely ripp'd" (15–16) and is therefore not included in the number of those "of woman born" who cannot destroy the tyrant. Thus a series of metaphors, symbols, apparitions, etc. come to a focus in the form of a dramatic character destined to bring the tragedy to its end.

Conversely, the bloodstained hands of the Macbeths become the source of a long string of hallucinations and visions turning into a system of figures. The recurrent images of eyesight in *King Lear*— running from Kent's "See better, Lear, and let me still remain/ The true blank of thine eye" (1.1.159–60) through the Knight's reference to the "eyeless rage" of the storm (3.1.8) to Edgar's concluding statement, "we that are young/ Shall never see so much, nor live so long' (5.3.324–25)—acquire stark materiality in the gouging out of Gloucester's eyes and his subsequent tortuous progress to death.

Anatomical imagery is as pervasive in the great tragedies as it is in *Romeo and Juliet*, *Richard II* and *Hamlet*. Only, now parts of the body get detached from each other and start floating in a fragmented universe, entering new disturbing alliances. The most striking example of this change are the ritual chants of the Weird Sisters in *Macbeth*, but many other instances can be culled from the delirious speeches of a number of characters in all great tragedies and, certainly, from the Fool's gnomic ditties in *King Lear*. A close study of these figures would offer useful insights into the process of disintegration of the mimetic (fictional) vision of drama and the new preeminence of the imaginative (thematic) reshaping of experience, energized by the emotional vehemence of lyric.

Shifty instability of meaning informs a number of devices related to imagery and often resorting to its services but extending far beyond its boundaries. The instruments of polysemy continue to be employed in the new period of Shakespeare's creative career, infusing an ever greater lyrical intensity into his dramatic work. Punning is as plentiful now as it was in the earlier plays. Its lewd farcical variety is omnipresent in the clownage scenes in *Othello* and *Macbeth*, as well as in the Fool's speeches in *King Lear*. The sarcastic (sometimes malicious) pun is almost exclusively the speciality of villainous characters like Iago, Goneril, and Edmund. But the most important kind of paronomasia in the new drama is the serious (or tragic) one, which is not associated with giggling or sniggering, but with the appreciation of events or problems of great consequence. Though the first remarkable achievements in the use of this register could be detected in *Hamlet*, in the later tragedies it becomes especially central. Thus Donalbain's puzzled query after his father's murder, "What is amiss?" elicits an ominous aside from the murderer: "You are, and do not know't" (*Macbeth*, 2.3.97), and when, a little later the young man has sized up the situation and decides to flee, he puts his realization in a no less pregnant paronomastic formula, reminiscent of Hamlet's aphorisms: "the near in blood,/ The nearer bloody" (140–41).

Macbeth is a play, whose action is largely motivated by the equivocation of the dark forces. The double meaning of words and phrases is essential to its conception of the universe. One such word is *man*, suggesting both nobility and courage, a moral and an amoral quality, the former denoted by the noun *virtue* and the latter by its Italian variant, *virtù*, as used in the Machiavellian discourse (both deriving from the Latin *vir* for man). The semantic bifurcation of this word in the Scottish tragedy permeates it from beginning to end, starting with the altercation between the Macbeths after the thane's decision to call off the planned regicide in 1.7, and continuing through his dialogue with the murderers hired to kill Banquo in 3.1, to find its definitive conclusion in that of his antagonists preparing to strike back:

> MALCOLM. Dispute it like a man.
> MACDUFF.   I shall do so;
>   But I must also feel it as a man:
>   I cannot but remember such things were,
>   That were most precious to me.
>
> (4.3.220–23)

It could be argued that this tragic quibble in a way informs the entire play, superimposing an important thematic structure over the fictional one of its plot. So the lyric penetration into the complexity of language is not just an overlay added to drama—it goes deep into the work as an important ordering factor.

Equivocation can have different employments. After the discovery of King Duncan's murder Macbeth makes the following speech to Lenox, who does not know anything about the thane's role in it:

Had I but died an hour before this chance,
I had liv'd a blessed time, for, from this instant,
There's nothing serious in mortality;
All is but toys: renown, and grace, is dead;
The wine of life is drawn, and the mere lees
Is left this vault to brag of.

                                                            (2.3.91–96)

This monologue has two alternative addressees: one is Lenox, whom it is spoken to, and the other is Macbeth himself. In its first aspect, then, it is a face-saving hypocritical lament over somebody the speaker has just slaughtered with his own hands. In its second one, however, it turns into a soliloquy of regret for what he has done and of a tragic realization of its irreversibility and its dire consequences. The tone of the speech is sincere and deeply serious—very much in tune with Macbeth's other lyrodramatic soliloquies and in consonance with their preoccupations. Its conclusions lead directly to the hero's final great utterance, "She should have died hereafter" (5.5.17–28). This fundamental duality of the monologue—its integration in the dramatic action and its simultaneous departure into solipsistic lyricism—is immensely interesting in the context of the newly achieved complexity of genre interplay. Such pregnant ambivalence stems from Hamlet's "wild talk," but here it acquires new intricacy and continuity.

The other name of equivocation is irony. And irony's most fundamental variety in this genre, dramatic irony, establishes its full sway in the great tragedies, relying mainly on poetic locution—metaphors and puns—and its polysemantic potentials. Thus the language of lyric molds the dramatic action, turning characters into simultaneously the subjects and the objects of this action. The device is particularly prominent in the First Act of *Macbeth*, where it impregnates almost every cue of King Duncan, intent on the advancement of his cousin by conferring on him the titles of an executed traitor and appearing unwittingly to pass on to him the caitiff's perfidy too. This richly suggestive series of utterances attains its climax in the following monologue addressed to the ambitious protagonist, whose mind's eye is already on the speaker's crown:

                    Thou art so far before,
        That swiftest wing of recompense is slow
        To overtake thee: would thou hadst less deserv'd,

That the proportion both of thanks and payment
Might have been mine!

(1.4.16–20)

Duncan does not suspect how fatally true his words are in a sense that he does not intend. For he means them as a courteous recognition of desert and not as an anticipation of Macbeth's bloody rush towards the throne.

But there is hardly any other play in which the incidence of dramatic irony and its importance for the overall conception of the tragedy would be as high as in *King Lear*. Its "alarum bell" starts ringing already in the induction with Gloucester's introduction of his illegitimate son to Kent: "this knave came something saucily to the world before he was sent for" (1.1.20–21). Just like Macbeth, Edmund has no patience when it comes to fulfilling his unlawful dreams. Thus his father's figurative description of his unwanted birth will in the context of the ensuing dramatic action acquire much greater significance as symbolic of his overall philosophy of life and its realization. Kent's courteous address to the bastard, "I must love you, and sue to know you better" (1.1.29) again seems to convey more than the speaker puts into it, for Edmund indeed should be known better to be dealt with properly, and Kent's "old course in a country new" will necessarily involve him in such a study. When Lear makes his first appearance on the stage later in the opening scene, he declares to all: "Meantime we shall express our darker purpose" (1.1.35). His own meaning is, of course, that he will reveal his hitherto secret plans about the division of his kingdom, but the entire tragic plot, which he sets into motion now and which brings about total destruction, opens up the epithet *darker* to other, ominous meanings latent in it. Something similar happens with Lear's next announcement that he has decided to delegate all cares and business to younger and stronger people, so that he can "Unburdened crawl toward death" (1.1.40). The verb *crawl* in this metaphor is obviously meant to suggest a slow, unhurried movement, but, with the hindsight of what the king goes through afterward, we cannot help returning to it and detecting its other connotations of a movement that is painful and weary—like that of a wounded creature. The complex paradoxical mechanism of radical reversals, contained in dramatic irony, has replaced in the mature tragedies the more straightforward chains of premonitions and their eventual materialization, detected in *Romeo and Juliet* remaining the chief stylistic mechanism of tragic suspense even in *Hamlet.*

Peripeteia, which sets dramatic irony into motion, is, of course, part of the workings of plot ever since Aristotle's time. Here, however, it is effected through the inextricable fusion of language and action into a single entity. And the language used for the purpose has all the characteristics of poetic locution. Its figurative units are liberated from the constraints of concrete discourse and allowed to promote this fusion with their infinitely augmented denotative and connotative volume. In the polysemy of a metaphor we sense at once the delusion of a dramatic character and the actual reality that this character is fatally incapable of grasping. By its focus on a figure of speech, Shakespeare's dramatic irony draws attention to an important thematic preoccupation of the play. As for its relation to the fictional structures of the drama, besides exposing the ambivalent relation between character and plot action, it also highlights the peripeteia, thus connecting two moments of the action, that of the delusion and that of the revelation.

Recurrent actions in the development of plot, as we saw on the material of the earlier plays, can in turn foreground thematic elements in the basically fictional construction of a drama. Such circular forms continue to be utilized, often producing an effect analogous to dramatic irony. Thus, Macbeth's preparation for the coronation ceremony in Scone in act 2 is echoed in Malcolm's similar plans in act 5; the original Thane of Cawdor's ignominious death in the inception of the tragedy seems to foreshadow his successor's no less grim end in its catastrophe; the witches' punishment of a disrespectful sailor with insomnia in 1.3.19–20 ("Sleep shall neither night nor day/ Hang upon his penthouse lid") presages the mysterious curse laid on Macbeth after the murder of Duncan in 2.2.34–35 ("Sleep no more!/ Macbeth does murther Sleep") but, obviously, also on his wife, who regurgitates their shared crime in her sleepwalking in 5.1.

Such "refrains" can throw light on a character and its development, sometimes revealed through the repetition of a single gesture, which imprints itself in the visual memory of the spectator. Something like stage imagery is thus created, capable of forming its own meaningful chains through the development of the drama and combining with those of verbal (poetic) imagery. Lear's kneeling in front of his daughters is a case in point. It first takes place as a mockery of the act, when the king tries to show Regan how unseemly it would be for him to humiliate himself in front of her sister:

>   Ask her forgiveness?
> Do you but mark how this becomes the house?
> [*Kneels.*] Dear daughter, I confess that I am old;
> Age is unnecessary. On my knees I beg
> That you'll vouchsafe me raiment, bed, and food.
>
>   (2.2.341–45)

Two acts later, a changed, considerably humbler and wiser Lear lowers himself in all earnestness and of his own accord in front of his third daughter, whom he has unjustly spurned. "No, sir, you must not kneel," exclaims Cordelia (4.7.59). And, as he imagines their happy isolation from the evil and vain world on the eve of the tragic catastrophe, he says to her:

> When thou dost ask me blessing I'll kneel down
> And ask of thee forgiveness.
>
>   (5.3.10–11)

Though these "refrains" are not solely linguistic but, chiefly, visual, their circular structure tends to relate the drama to the thematic, concentric literary kinds. In the above-considered case, the refrain of Lear's kneeling before his daughters—which is very central to the thematic preoccupation of the tragedy—imposes its static, antithetical form on the whole, while also underlining the dynamism of the protagonist's radical development between its two occurrences. Interestingly, a similar, and even more persistent, "kneeling" refrain has been traced by E. A. J. Honigmann in the "stage imagery" of *Othello*.[12]

Statically conceived antithetical schemes of other kinds detected in the earlier plays are also employed in the great tragedies with an increased complexity and integration. Characters at this later stage are paired off all the time, revealing significant layers of thematic similarity or contrast. The most important binary opposition continues to be that between the contemplative and the active type, the Poet and the Hero. From the old pairs (Romeo–Tybalt, Richard–Bolingbroke, Hamlet–Claudius, etc.) we pass to new, more complex and less clear-cut ones: Othello–Iago, Lear/ Cordelia–Goneril/ Regan, Gloucester/ Edgar–Edmund, Macbeth–Lady Macbeth. The left-hand members of these dichotomies are invariably endowed with the gift of poetic self-expression, while the right-hand ones are largely deprived of it and forced to speak in an unimaginative actional way, but the contrast is not as sharp as before. Iago, though a scheming villain, is not denied the use of figurative language, though his metaphors are of a kind and quality different from those of Othello, a difference that becomes crystal clear from the very beginning. The ancient's mind is immersed in images of dark animal concupiscence. In the middle of the night he wakes up Desdemona's father with a slandering report on Othello, presenting his love affair in the only way his filthy mind is capable of conceiving it:

> Even now, now, very now, an old black ram
> Is tupping your white ewe!
>
> (1.1.87–88)

In the next scene the besieged Othello flashes at his assailants an impromptu image of the diametrically opposite type—pure, clear, and sparkling like his true nature:

> Keep up your bright swords, for the dew will rust them.
>
> (1.2.59)

Further on in the play Iago's soliloquies are as many as those of Othello, but they are all devoted to scheming and biting satire, while the Moor's speeches are invariably reflective and lyrically tinged, replete with evocative imagery, even when his vision is sadly contaminated by Iago's.[13]

It is instructive to set side by side Edmund's appeal to Nature in 1.2.1–22 and King Lear's in 1.4. 267–81, both starting in an almost identical way, but sustained in markedly different registers, the former relying on rhetorical repetition and the latter tossed gravely by a passion erupting in tumultuous visionary metaphors.

Macbeth, who captivates our minds with his great first soliloquy in 1.7 and takes his leave from us with his last, no less moving though deadly tired one in 5.5, crowns the Poets' sequence with the explosively compressed wealth of his uncanny imagination. His wife's speech, pales by comparison, though it is not at all devoid of figurative expression: it would suffice to remember her unsex-me-here soliloquy in 1.5.38–54. The difference between the Macbeths or between Othello and Iago is measured by the choice of imagery each of them makes and the manner each deals with it rather than by a sharp contrast between poetic and prosaic languages.

At this new stage of Shakespeare's career, then, the poles of Poets and Heroes are no longer kept at such a howling distance from one another. While earlier most of the "Heroes" (Tybalt, Bolingbroke, Claudius, and Laertes) were the more or less open adversaries of the Poets (Romeo, Richard II, Hamlet), now they are usually the Poets' manipulators. The interaction of the two categories is more intimate, less mechanical than before. Iago, Edmund, Goneril and Regan, and Lady Macbeth draw close to, respectively, Othello, Gloucester and Edgar, Lear, and Macbeth, attempting to subvert their noble nature and thus driving them to the brink of total destruction. For this purpose, they are compelled to adopt some sort of evocative language. "Heroes" have to pretend they are Poets to the extent of even partly becoming Poets. The Poets themselves are in fact Heroes not only by occupation, like Richard II, but by nature too: Othello is a resolute military leader of the highest rank, Lear is the imposing king of a vast realm, Macbeth is both in succession. They may all be prone to reflection and endowed with the rich imagination of Poets, but their active and domineering characters are not in the least diminished by these propensities. They seem to combine both natures in their complex selves to an extent that their predecessors were incapable of doing in such an integral way. Thus the seemingly incompatible worlds of lyric and drama finally close up.

Generalizations are perhaps even more odious than comparisons, but a few closing words at the end of this survey cannot help taking a step away from the object of study and casting a last glance at it from a greater distance. The tendency of lyric's thorough integration into the dramatic environment continues in Shakespeare's mature period, resulting in the latter's complete transformation and the rise of the full-fledged intergenre of poetic drama. Its organic character, attained at every architectonic level of the plays and also in the fusion of all these levels into an indivisible unity, testifies to the triumph of what constitutes one of the most significant aesthetic transformations in the history of world theater. It would be, of course, wrong to view Shakespeare's endeavors as lonely and isolated. No doubt, he drew on precedents both in pre-Renaissance and early Renaissance dramatic practice. His achievements, however, seem to be more thorough and more far-reaching than all others. They must be rooted above all in the unusual magnitude of his lyrical talent, plunged into drama in an age when both kinds had risen to dominance and were ready to merge. Not a small part of Shakespeare's artistic glory lies in that he managed to effect this merger without impairing either component but, on the contrary, intensifying and developing both to the fullness of their potentials by making them feed their strengths into each other.

Notes

CHAPTER 1. INTRODUCTION

1. T. S. Eliot suggests that Marlowe's *The Jew of Malta* would make more sense as a dramatic work if treated not as a tragedy but as a farce, but "the farce of the old English humour, the terribly serious, even savage comic humour which spent its last breath in the decadent genius of Dickens" ("Christopher Marlowe," *Elizabethan Dramatists*, 63–64). The unlikely dramatic hybrid of "tragic farce" can be illustrated on the example of at least two of Marlowe's plays: *The Jew of Malta* and *Doctor Faustus*.

2. Evans, *Osier Cage*, 8.

3. Gérard Genette refers to *poésie pure* in "Genres, 'types,' modes," 416; later included in *Introduction à l'Architexte*, 1979 (64). John Stuart Mill writes: "Lyric poetry, as it was the earliest kind, is also, if the view we are now taking is correct, more eminently and peculiarly poetry than any other" (*Essays on Poetry*, 36).

4. See Croce, "Criticism of the Theory of Artistic and Literary Kinds," in *Modern Genre Theory*, ed. Duff, 25–28.

5. See, for instance, Genette, "Genres, 'types,' modes," 392–93.

6. "How many parts, then, has poetry?—Broadly speaking, three: one is called *epica*, the second dramatic [*scenica*], the third melic or lyric, as you prefer." (Minturno, "L'Arte Poetica"), 99.

7. "Naturformen der Dichtung" (1819), in "Noten und Abhandlungen," 187–89.

8. Thus Karl Viëtor writes: "The epic, the lyric, and the drama, after all, are not artistic structures, or works, or creations, but are, so to speak, ultimate creative fundamental attitudes. . . . The three great areas of literature, they are rooted in three natural and basic fundamental attitudes of the poet: attitudes not toward the aesthetic object and the public, but of a more basic nature: fundamental human attitudes to reality, to the mastering of reality in their effect and countereffect" ("Probleme der literarischen Gatungsgeschichte," *Deutsche Vierteljahresschrift für Literaturwissenschaft und Geistesgeschichte*, 1931, 9:425f.; quoted in Strelka, *Theories of Literary Genre* 8: 81).

9. Fowler, *Kinds of Literature*, 106–11.

10. Hartmann, *Philosophie des Schönen, Grundriss der Ästhetik*, 1924. See Gérard Genette's presentation of his classification in "Genres, 'types,' modes," 411).

11. Ibid., 409, 410. Genette displays this relative agreement in the following two tables:

Genres / Auteurs	Lyrique	Épique	Dramatique
Humboldt		passé	présent
Schelling	présent	passé	
Jean Paul	présent	passé	futur
Hegel	présent	passé	
Dallas	futur	passé	présent
Vischer	présent	passé	futur
Erskine	présent	futur	passé
Jakobson	présent	passé	
Staiger	passé	présent	futur

Temps / Genres	Passè	Présent	Futur
Lyrique	Staiger	Schelling Jean Paul Hegel Vischer Erskine Jakobson	Dallas
Épique	Humboldt Schelling Jean Paul Hegel Dallas Vischer Jakobson	Staiger	Erskine
Dramatique	Erskine	Humboldt Dallas	Jean Paul Vischer Staiger

It is apparent that there is a considerable divergence of opinions, especially in the case of drama, which necessitates the continuation of this discussion. The present study will also try to contribute to it.

12. Langer, *Feeling and Form*, 307.

13. Azione parlata (It.)—spoken action, Luigi Pirandello's phrase referring to dialogue in drama, coined in an essay of 1899, "L'azione parlata."

14. In "The Art of Fiction" Henry James writes: "What is character but the determination of incident? What is incident but the illustration of character?" (*Literary Criticism* 1:55).

15. Hegel, *Aesthetics*, 2:1038–39.

16. Wellek, *Discriminations*, 252.

17. Olson, "Lyric," 60.

18. Mandelstam, *Collected Critical Prose and Letters*, 67 (from an early essay, "On the Addressee," 1913). Mandelstam quotes a poem by Aleksandr Pushkin.

19. Staiger, *Basic Concepts of Poetics*, 71.

20. Hegel, *Aesthetics*, 2:1121.

21. Shelley, "A Defense of Poetry," in *Shelley's Prose*, 281.

22. Staiger, *Basic Concepts of Poetics*, 81.

23. Ibid., 80.

24. Ibid., 76.

25. Mandelstam, "On the Addressee," in *Collected Critical Prose and Letters*, 68.

26. "Eloquence is *heard*, poetry is *overheard*. Eloquence supposes an audience; the peculiarity of poetry appears to us to lie in the poet's utter unconsciousness of a listener. Poetry is feeling conferring itself to itself, in moments of solitude" (Mill, *Essays on Poetry*, 12). The idea has been repeated or quoted by a number of later writers, notably by T. S. Eliot in his essay "The Three Voices of Poetry": "But my opinion is that a good love poem, though it may be addressed to one person, is always meant to be overheard by other people"(Eliot, *On Poetry and Poets*, 97), and also in "Poetry and Drama": "part of our enjoyment of great poetry is the enjoyment of overhearing words which are not addressed to us" (ibid., 109).

27. Staiger, *Basic Concepts of Poetics*, 146.

28. Paul Valéry (*Tel quel*, 1941); quoted in *Dictionnaire des genres et notions littéraires*, 447.

29. Quoted in Preminger and Brogan, *New Princeton Encyclopedia of Poetry and Poetics*, 3rd ed., 715.

30. Hardy, *Advantage of Lyric*, 15.

31. Hegel, *Aesthetics*, 2:1114.

32. Ibid., 2:1135.

33. Langer, *Feeling and Form*, 219.

34. See Hardy, *Advantage of Lyric*, 16.

35. Staiger, *Basic Concepts of Poetics*, 62.

36. Hernadi, *Beyond Genre*, 164.

37. Even when we have to deal with a poem that envisages some change of the status quo—as the case is, for instance, with W. B. Yeats's "The Lake Isle of Innisfree"—the gist of the message is not that the speaker is indeed going to take the course he is imagining, of leaving the city and settling down on the idyllic shore of the "water lapping" (something that he most probably will never do) but,

rather, that he feels within himself this strong desire to exchange the mindless bustle on "the pavements grey" with the inspiring peace of nature. "The Lake Isle of Innisfree" is not a plan for decisive action but a sweet dream that has come upon the poet's soul now and needs to be verbalized in order to express his present state of mind: his frustration with urban life and his yearning for a change. In a similar way, another of Yeats's most popular early poems, "Down by the Salley Gardens," conveys a memory about a love tryst in the distant past, whose intimations at the time the speaker, to his grief, failed to grasp, and although the ballad is full of enticing glimpses of that distant moment still lingering in his mind, its focus is not on what happened long ago but on the loss that it has entailed in the present. It is indicative that "now" is a key word in both poems, opening the one and concluding the other and thus fixing the diversity of times in the exclusive emotional reality of *this* moment: "I will arise and go now"; "and now am full of tears."

38. Kridl, "Obsevations sur les genres de la poésie lyrique," 149.

39. Hegel, *Aesthetics*, 2:1115.

40. Langer, *Feeling and Form*, 268.

41. Culler, *Pursuit of Signs*, 150.

42. *Dictionnaire des genres et notions littéraires*, 447.

43. Quoted in Genette, "Genres, 'types,' modes," 403.

44. Calderwood, *Shakespearean Metadrama*, 92.

45. Burke, *Grammar of Motives*, 246.

46. Langer, Feeling and Form, 249, 230.

47. Olson, "Lyric," 64.

48. Hegel, *Aesthetics*, 2:1136.

49. This view is expressed by Culler (*Pursuit of Signs*, 149) in his discussion primarily of apostrophic poetry, but it could be extended to most kinds of lyric. His conclusion about the temporal characteristics of the genre is as follows: "This is a time of discourse rather than story. So located by apostrophes, birds, creatures, boys, etc., resist being organized into events that can be narrated, for they are inserted in the poem as elements of the event which the poem is attempting to be."

50. Frye, "Approaching the Lyric," in Hošek, *Lyric Poetry*, 35.

51. Quoted from Ronsard's preface to the posthumous edition of the *Odes* by Mathieu-Castellani, "Les Modes du discourse lyrique au XVIe siècle," in Demerson, *La Notion de genre à la Renaissance*, 130.

52. *Dictionnaire des genres et notions littéraires*, 447.

53. Culler, *Structuralist Poetics*, 178.

54. Fussell, *Poetic Forms and the Lyric Subject*, 5.

55. "Concentric" is Hernadi's term for thematic literary genres (see Hernadi, *Beyond Genre*, 182).

56. Burke, "Three Definitions," 126.

57. Quoted in Hardy, *Advantage of Lyric*, 2.

58. See Nardo, "Submerged Sonnet as Lyric Moment in Miltonic Epic," 24.

59. Frye, *Anatomy of Criticism*, 244.

60. Pound, *Literary Essays*, 25–27.

61. Mukařovský, *Word and Verbal Art*, 14.

62. Hirsch, *Validity in Interpretation*, 121.

63. Ibid., 120.

64. Frye, *Anatomy of Criticism*, 278, 280.

65. Mukařovský, *Word and Verbal Art*, 15. Langer, *Feeling and Form*, 258.

66. Scholes, *Elements of Poetry*, 7.

67. Frye, *Anatomy of Criticism*, 281.

68. Welsh, *Roots of Lyric*, 64.

69. Burke, *Grammar of Motives*, 243.

70. In his *Discriminations*(341) Wellek reminds us of Roman Jakobson's persuasive argument that poetry can, on occasion, dispense with "metaphoricness" or replace it with metonymic relations, grammatical echoes, and contrasts. Jakobson has referred to Pushkin's poem "Ja vas ljubil" as an example of imageless poetry, and Wellek adds to it Wordsworth's "We Are Seven" and Robert Bridges's "I Love All Beauteous Things." He proposes that this kind of poetry be called "poetry of statement," but then he half-concedes that, if we extend the notion of "metaphor," we could see such metaphor-free poems as turning into an overall metaphor or image in their entirety, a view propounded by William K. Wimsatt and Cleanth Brook in their *Literary Criticism*.

71. Shurbanov, "Shakespeare's Sonnet 126 as *Envoi*: the Test of Imagery," *Poetics of the English Renaissance*, 292–93.

72. Welsh, *Roots of Lyric*, 245.

73. Barber, *Shakespeare's Festive Comedy*, 102.

74. Frye, *Anatomy of Criticism*, 271.

75. E.g. Staiger, *Basic Concepts of Poetics*, 62; Langer, *Feeling and Form*, 249; Cameron, *Lyric Time*, 207; Hegel, *Aesthetics*, 2:1134–35.

76. See Culler, *Structuralist Poetics*, 170.

77. Staiger, *Basic Concepts of Poetics*, 54; Smith, *Poetic Closure*, 38.

78. Day Lewis, *Lyric Impulse*, 39. Though the writer considers the lyric in the narrow sense of the word as referring to texts for songs only, his list of repetitions is certainly valid for any sort of lyrical poetry, comprising as it does their phonetic, lexico-semantic and syntactical varieties. The only missing kind in the inventory would probably be the morphological one: root and other syllable repetition.

79. Bahti, *Ends of the Lyric*.

80. Coleridge, *Biographia Literaria*, chap. 14 (quoted in Culler, *Structuralist Poetics*, 171; Zumthor, *Toward a Medieval Poetics*, 146.

81. Culler, *Structuralist Poetics*, 170.

82. Ibid., 162.

83. Langer, *Feeling and Form*, 252; Mathieu-Castellani, "Les Modes du discourse lyrique au XVIe siècle," in Demerson, *La Notion de genre à la Renaissance*, 131.

84. Paul Valéry, *Oeuvres*, 1:500; quoted in ibid.; Culler, *Structuralist Poetics*, 183.

85. Barthes, *Le degré zéro de l'écriture*, 69–70.

86. Hardy, *Advantage of Lyric*, 17.

87. Genette, "Genres, 'types,' modes," 419.

88. Hegel, *Aesthetics*, 2:1147.

89. Lindley, *Lyric*, 89.

90. Miller, *Lyric Texts and Lyric Consciousness*, 127.

91. Ibid., 48.

92. Burrow, *Medieval Writers and Their Work*, 61.

93. Zumthor, *Toward a Medieval Poetics*, 47.

94. Ibid., 355–56.

95. Genette, "Genres, 'types,' modes," 401–2.

96. Miller, *Lyric Texts and Lyric Consciousness*, 126–27.

97. Hegel, *Aesthetics*, 2:1124.

98. Quinones, *Renaissance Discovery of Time*, 3–4.

99. Ibid., 413.

100. Sidney, "Defence of Poesy," in *Selected Prose and Poetry*, 110.

101. Evans, *Osier Cage*, 25.

102. The origin of this idea might be found in some speculations in Hegel's *Aesthetics*, dealing with the relations between the members of the generic triad and their hierarchy.

103. Hegel, *Aesthetics*, 2:1134.

104. Kridl, "Observations sur les genres de la poésie lyrique," fasc. 2–3, 153.

105. Staiger, *Basic Concepts of Poetics*, 53.

106. Hernadi, *Beyond Genre*, 164.

107. Mathieu-Castellani, "Les Modes du discourse lyrique au XVIe siècle," in Demerson, *La Notion de genre à la Renaissance*, 146.

108. Hamburger, *Logic of Literature*, 293–94.

109. See Culler, *Pursuit of Signs*, chap. "Apostrophe."

110. Olson, "Lyric," 64–65.

111. Abad, *Formal Approach to Lyric Poetry*.

112. Zumthor, *Toward a Medieval Poetics*, 135.

113. Guillén, *Literature as System*, 114.

114. See Hernadi, *Beyond Genre*, 129.

115. Ibid., 150–51.

116. Scholes and Klaus, *Elements of the Essay*, 4.

117. Ibid., 7.

118. See Todorov, *Genres in Discourse*, chap. "The Origin of Genres."

119. Colie, *Resources of Kind*, 36.

120. *Dictionnaire des genres et notions littéraires*, 268.

121. See Snyder, *Prospects of Power*, 151.

122. Musil, *Man without Qualities*, 1:301.

123. *Dictionnaire des genres et notions littéraires*, 268–69.

124. Dominique Spiess-Faure, "L'essai," in Bessiére, *Littérature et genres littéraires*, 164.

125. Ibid.

126. A further proof of the kinship of the lyric and the essay can be found in the existence of famous essays in verse, such as those written by Pope and Cowley in the eighteenth century.

127. Scholes and Klaus, *Elements of the Essay*, 9–10.

128. Ibid., 22, 36.

129. Frye, *Anatomy of Criticism*, 52.

130. Ibid., 52–53.

131. Scholes and Klaus, *Elements of Drama*, 19.

132. Frye, *Anatomy of Criticism*, 271–72.

133. Hernadi, *Beyond Genre*, 163–64.

134. See Weinberg, *History of Literary Criticism*, 2:702; Peletier du Mans, *L'art poëtique*, 61.

135. Colie, *Resources of Kind*, 105.

136. Fowler, *Kinds of Literature*, 108–9.

137. Marino, "Toward a Definition of Literary Genres," in Strelka, *Theories of Literary Genre* , 49.

138. *Kinds of Literature* is Alastair Fowler's most important contribution to the subject.

139. See Colie, *Resources of Kind*, chap. "Small Forms: Multo in Parvo," 32–75.

140. Fowler, *Kinds of Literature*, 179–81.

141. Colie, *Shakespeare's Living Art*, 15.

142. Dubrow, *Genre*, 60.

143. Ibid., 58.

144. Zumthor, *Toward a Medieval Poetics*, 120; Colie, *Shakespeare's Living Art*, 7; "It is difficult to underestimate the connection between the theoretical restlessness of the sixteenth century, in the area of poetics, and the ability to start anew, to confront boldly expanding circles of experience, on the part of the greater writers of the period" (Guillén, *Literature as System*, 109).

145. Sidney, *Defence of Poesy*, in *Selected Prose and Poetry*, 127.

146. Weinberg, *History of Literary Criticism*, 2:661.

147. Opacki's example is drawn from the history of Polish literature and it has to do with the preeminence of lyric in the Młoda Polska period ("Royal Genres," in Duff, *Modern Genre Theory*, 118–26).

148. The view of Renaissance humanism as an age molded by the principle of dialogism—a Bakhtinian variant of dialectics, in which the elements of thesis and antithesis coexist without being resolved in a final synthesis—has been substantiated on the material of Italian intellectual history by Russian critic L. M. Batkin in his book *The Italian Humanists: Style of Living and Style of Thinking* (1978). It is possible, I feel, to consider both the structure of thinking and that of artistic expression of the age on a number of levels as evincing the same tendency.

149. Mukařovský, *Word and Verbal Art*, 152.

150. Francis Berry, *Shakespeare Inset*, 7.

151. Colie, *Shakespeare's Living Art*, 137.

152. Olson, "Lyric," 65.

153. N. Brooke, *Shakespeare's Early Tragedies*, 192.

154. See Erskine, *Elizabethan Lyric*, 2:303.

155. Day Lewis, *Lyric Impulse*, 12. As with many other things, Coleridge was again the first to notice the relevance of Shakespeare's songs to the unfolding of his plays and their functioning "not only with the dramatic, but as a part of the dramatic" (Hawkes, *Coleridge on Shakespeare*, 116).

156. See Genette, "Genres, 'types,' modes," 403; Johnson, *Idea of Lyric*, 152.

157. Pfister, *Theory and Analysis of Drama*, 286–87.

158. Ibid., 110.

159. Ellis-Fermor, *Frontiers of Drama*, 108.

160. Hernadi, *Beyond Genre*, 159.

161. On an occasion of this kind, Kenneth Burke makes the following significant distinction between the two generic types: "Mr. Houston Peterson hit upon the happy idea of assembling in an anthology (*The Lonely Debate*) some typical moments of the dramatic arrest. . . . Yet the very isolating of such momentous soliloquies, and their publication somewhat like a book of lyrics, makes us realize all the more clearly how essentially different they are from lyrics. In fact, we might call them the depiction of such personal situations as *most acutely need* resolution in the lyric state, but drive to action precisely because such resolution is missing." (*Grammar of Motives*, 245–46).

162. Olson, "Outline of Poetic Theory," in Crane, *Critics and Criticism*, 565.

163. Quoted in Hernadi, *Beyond Genre*, 38.

164. Ellis-Fermor, *Shakespeare's Drama*, 33.

165. Pfister, *Theory and Analysis of Drama*, 130. Mukařovský theorizes upon this phenomenon in his discussion of the close links between monologic and dialogic speech in literature: "The relation between the 'I' and the 'you' on which dialogue is based does not require two individuals for its activation but only the internal tension, contradictions, and unexpected reversals provided by the dynamics of every individual's psychic life. The apparent and potential dialogic nature of utterances thus has its root in the hidden "dialogic nature" of the course of mental life" (*Word and Verbal Art*, 58).

166. Pfister, *Theory and Analysis of Drama*, 134.

167. Ibid., 136–37.

168. Wolfgang Clemen's *Development of Shakespeare's Imagery* (first published in English in 1951) is still the most concentrated study of this aspect of the construction of Renaissance poetic drama. Its indebtedness to Caroline Spurgeon's *Shakespeare's Imagery and What It Tells Us* (first published in 1935) is as obvious as is its own significant contribution to the topic.

169. Staiger, *Basic Concepts of Poetics*, 157.

170. Langer, *Feeling and Form*, 307.

171. Todorov, *Genres in Discourse*, 50–51.

172. Ibid., 51.

173. Woolf, *English Mystery Plays*, 113.

174. Ibid., 312.

175. Johnson, *Idea of Lyric*, 146–51.

176. Ibid., 152.

177. "Even Shakespeare did not completely outgrow his taste for it, though he, almost alone, managed to countervail the tendency to random dramaturgy which this style seems to encourage" (ibid., 151).

178. Calderwood, *Shakespearean Metadrama*, 21.

179. Eliot, "Poetry and Drama," in *On Poetry and Poets*, 93.

180. Eliot, *Selected Essays*, 52 (quoted in N. Brooke, *Shakespeare's Early Tragedies*, 86).

181. Hamburger, *Logic of Literature*, 199.

182. Colie, *Shakespeare's Living Art*, 24.

183. Ibid., 145.

184. Dubrow, *Genre*, 116.

185. Hernadi, *Beyond Genre*, 75.

Chapter 2. Generic Mixture

1. Calderwood, *Shakespearean Metadrama*, 56.

2. Barber, *Shakespeare's Festive Comedy*, 95.

3. See note 17 of chap. 1 above.

4. Calderwood makes the connection between the recital of love poems in *Love's Labour's Lost* and Mill's definition of the specificity of lyric in *Shakespearean Metadrama*, 72–73.

5. It is, of course, impossible to know whether *Love's Labour's Lost* did not antedate Donne's "Valediction," for the year of composition of the pieces eventually collected in *Songs and Sonets* remain uncertain, but judging by the texts we can compare, it seems more likely that Shakespeare wrote a spoof on the poem (or on this kind of poem) rather than that Donne decided to perfect a text from somebody else's comedy.

6. See Catherine McLay's analysis of the songs in "The Dialogues of Spring and Winter," concluding that "Like the Song, the play too moves from spring to winter, from art to nature, from illusion to reality" (Londré, *Love's Labour's Lost*, 215).

7. F. Berry, *Shakespeare Inset*, 110.

8. Ibid., 114.

9. Coleridge, "Love's Labour's Lost," in *Lectures and Notes on Shakespeare and Other English Poets*; reprinted in Londré, *Love's Labour's Lost*, 60.

10. Pater, "On *Love's Labour's Lost*," in ibid., 67.

11. Bradbrook, *Shakespeare and Elizabethan Poetry*, 215.

12. Moncure-Sime, "*Love's Labour's Lost*," in Londré, *Love's Labour's Lost*, 79.

13. Barber, *Shakespeare's Festive Comedy*, 100.

14. Pater, "On *Love's Labours Lost*," in Londré, *Love's Labour's Lost*, 66.

15. Colie, *Shakespeare's Living Art*, 31; Calderwood, *Shakespearean Metadrama*, 72.

16. Barber singles out this moment for a special praise: "Perhaps the most delightful touch in the whole play is the exchange that concludes Berowne's reformation, in which he playfully betrays the fact that his mockery of sophistication is sophisticated, and Rosaline underscores the point as she deftly withdraws the hand he has taken" (*Shakespeare's Festive Comedy*, 108).

17. N. Brooke, *Shakespeare's Early Tragedies*, 80.

18. Ibid.

19. Introduction, *Romeo and Juliet*, ed. Gibbons, 42–43.

20. Might one not surmise that Shakespeare's original design was to prefix the remaining three acts of *Romeo and Juliet* the same way as he did the first two? This would certainly have been a neater arrangement, and Shakespeare did provide prologues to each act in at least two other plays: *Henry V* and *Pericles*.

21. See Shakespeare's sonnets 65 and 116.

22. In a footnote to 1.5.106–9 in his edition of the play for the Second Arden series, Brian Gibbons suggests that "A fresh sonnet begins" in these lines, "but is interrupted by the Nurse" (*Romeo and Juliet*, ed. Gibbons, 119).

23. Bakhtin defines poetic language as unaffected by heteroglossia in "Word in the Novel," included in the collection of his theoretical essays *Problems of Literature and Aesthetics*, 98.

24. MONTAGUE. Who set this ancient quarrel new abroach?
　　Speak, nephew, were you by when it began? (1.1.102–3)
25. ROMEO. ... O me! What fray was here?
　　Yet tell me not, for I have heard it all. (1.1.171–72)
26. PRINCE. Benvolio, who began this bloody fray? (3.1.153)
27. Caroline Spurgeon includes the lightning images among the larger group of figures of light and darkness she discovers in *Romeo and Juliet* (*Shakespeare's Imagery*, 310–16).
28. After a survey of the opening episodes of *Romeo and Juliet*, M. M. Mahood (*Shakespeare's Wordplay*, 61) concludes that "all the Petrarchan and anti-Petrarchan conventions are thus presented to us in this first scene: love as malady, as worship, as war, as conquest. They are presented, however, with an exaggeration that suggests Romeo is already aware of his own absurdity and is 'posing at posing.'"
29. Robert Evans classifies this speech as "a list of schoolboy examples" (*Osier Cage*, 23).
30. Clemen, *Development of Shakespeare's Imagery*, 68.
31. Calderwood, *Shakespearean Metadrama*, 88.
32. Ibid., 89.
33. All quotations to the end of the paragraph are from Marlowe's "Hero and Leander," 1.197, 330, in *Complete Plays and Poems*, 405, 408.
34. Mahood, *Shakespeare's Wordplay*, 63.
35. See 53–54 in chap. 1 above.
36. "*La creatura bella bianco vestita*" is Dante's memorable phrase for the Angel of Humility in his *Purgatorio*, later used by Hugo and other writers to denote romantic femininity.
37. W. Clemen offers an insightful analysis of Shakespeare's anchoring of poetic clichés in the dramatic scenery of this episode and thus giving them a new lyrical legitimacy (*Development of Shakespeare's Imagery*, 66–68).
38. Sidney, "Defence of Poesy," in *Selected Prose and Poetry*, 118.
39. See 83–85 in chap. 2 above.
40. "*O lente, lente currite, noctis equi!*" (*Doctor Faustus*, 5.2.143, adapted from Ovid's *Amores*).
41. Such glimpses of actual experience, unaffected by courtly poetic conventions and therefore strikingly fresh and memorable, crop up again and again in Shakespeare's work, repeatedly enhancing its lyrical character. A close parallel to Juliet's image of the child's longings can be found, for instance, in Sonnet 143:

> Lo, as a careful huswife runs to catch
> One of her feathered creatures broke away,
> Sets down her babe and makes all swift dispatch
> In pursuit of the thing she would have stay,
> Whilst her neglected child holds her in chase,
> Cries to catch her whose busy care is bent
> To follow that which flies before her face,
> Not prizing her poor infant's discontent [etc.]

42. Robert Evans contrasts Juliet's to Romeo's oxymora and remarks that hers

are all "fresh, original figures, not schoolbookish examples. Under the stress of great emotion Juliet becomes a masterful rhetorician" (*Osier Cage*, 36).

43. Interestingly, Shakespeare appears to parody this theatrical combination of dramatic action and lyrical speech in the "Pyramus and Thisbe" play performed by the clumsy mechanicals in *A Midsummer Night's Dream*, which was probably written directly after *Romeo and Juliet* and poked fun at the heroization of love informing this tragedy.

44. Colie, *Shakespeare's Living Art*, 23.

45. F. Berry, *Shakespeare Inset*.

46. Introduction, *Romeo and Juliet*, ed. Gibbons, 67.

47. Drayton, "To my Most Dearly-loved Friend, Henry Reynolds Esquire, of Poets and Poesie" (1627), in *Works*, 3:228.

48. Eliot, "Christopher Marlowe," in *Elizabethan Dramatists*, 66.

49. Mahood, *Shakespeare's Wordplay*, 56.

50. Evans, *Osier Cage*, 8.

51. See 104 in chap. 2 above.

52. N. Brooke, *Shakespeare's Early Tragedies*, 82.

53. Ibid., 83.

54. Harry Levin interprets this development at the core of *Romeo and Juliet* as the outgrowing of comedy and a transition to the aesthetics of tragedy: "[Shakespeare's] innovation might be described as transcending the usages of romantic comedy, which are therefore very much in evidence, particularly at the beginning. Subsequently, the leading characters acquire together a deeper dimension of feeling by expressly repudiating the artificial language they have talked and the superficial code they have lived by. Their formula might be that of the anti-Petrarchan sonnet: 'Foole said My muse to mee, looke in thy heart and write.' An index of this development is the incidence of rhyme, heavily concentrated in the First Act, and its gradual replacement by a blank verse which is realistic or didactic with other speakers and unprecedentedly limpid and passionate with the lovers" ("Form and Formality in *Romeo and Juliet*," Shakespeare Quarterly 11 (1960); reprinted in Cole, *Twentieth Century Interpretations of "Romeo and Juliet*," 89).

55. Introduction, *King Richard II*, ed. Wells, 9.

56. Pater, "Shakespeare's English Kings," in *Appreciations*, 203.

57. Introduction, *King Richard II*, ed. Wells, 7.

58. Introduction, *King Richard II*, ed. Forker, 57–58.

59. Piper, *Heroic Couplet*, 204.

60. Baxter, *Shakespeare's Poetic Styles*, 157–58.

61. One of these is Albert Feuillerat, whose hypothesis has been summarized in Matthew Black's *Life and Death of King Richard the Second*, 398–400.

62. A badly mixed metaphor at the throbbing center of this outburst, compromising what is perhaps the most striking image in praise of the beloved native land ("This precious stone set in the silver sea,/ Which serves it in the office of a wall/ Or as a moat defensive to a house/ Against the envy of less happier lands" [46–49]) can hardly be a deliberate drop from poetic sublimity pointing to a sudden rhetorical ineptitude on the part of the speaker. This blemish on an otherwise impressively accomplished oration is probably due to authorial oversight. But then, it can hardly be noticed in the heat of a theatrical performance.

63. This speech's lyrical orientation is as clear as that of Yeats's poem "The Lake Isle of Innisfree," which we glanced at above (see note 37 to chap. 1). Its contemplation of future action is as fantastic and as remote from actual planning as the case is with that lyrical piece. Both texts are concerned with expressing a state of mind rather than a firm intention of molding the course of events.

64. Introduction, *King Richard II*, ed. Wells, 25.

65. For a very different commentary on the contrast between Gaunt's and Richard's patriotic orations, see Baxter, *Shakespeare's Poetic Styles*, 68–69.

66. The technique is isolated and discussed in "Donne's 'Dramatic' Imagery," included in Shurbanov, *Poetics of the English Renaissance*, 383–99.

67. Of course, unlike Hamlet, Richard, as we have seen, is very much given to the show of externalities, but in spite of that we have no reason to doubt the reality of his inner self.

68. Pierre de Ronsard, "Quand vous serez bien vieille," *Sonnets pour Hélène* (1578), 2:24.

69. The similarity between the two highly formalized amorous dialogues is noticed in passing by John Baxter (*Shakespeare's Poetic Styles*, 118).

70. See, for instance, Introduction, *King Richard II*, ed. Wells, 34.

71. Knight, *Imperial Theme*, 351.

72. See Introduction, *King Richard II*, ed. Ure, lxix.

73. Clemen, *Shakespeare's Dramatic Art*, 149.

74. Clemen, *Development of Shakespeare's Imagery*, 55.

75. "The conception of Richard as a wilting poet," N. Brooke remarks, "is completely out of place in act 1, which opens in terms of high rhetorical splendour" (*Shakespeare's Early Tragedies*, 110).

76. Chambers, *Shakespeare*, 91.

77. See Introduction, *King Richard II*, ed. Wells, 34.

78. Mahood, *Shakespeare's Wordplay*, 83.

79. Chambers, *Shakespeare*, 90.

80. See 50–51 in chap. 1 above.

81. Charles Forker makes the following observation about the latter part of *Richard II* in a section of his introduction to the play, entitled "Characterization: Attitudes towards Richard and Bolingbroke": "Attack from without has sparked dividedness within. And the result is a protagonist of greater capacity for self-understanding and emotional depth than has yet been disclosed. Meanwhile, Bolingbroke has remained a close book—a figure whose inner self has been carefully screened from our gaze. Paradoxically, the ineffectual King appears to be a more interesting, interior and multifaceted human being than the figure who threatens him" (*King Richard II*, ed. Forker, 31–32).

82. See 25 of chap. 1 above.

83. Prior to Shakespeare such concentric repetitions in the action were methodically used by Marlowe in *Dido Queen of Carthage*. Precedents could in fact be sought as far back as *Secunda Pastorum*.

84. Altick, "Symphonic Imagery in *Richard II*."

85. Introduction, *King Richard II*, ed. Forker, 64–83.

86. See note 168 to chap. 1 above.

Chapter 3. Generic Integration

1. See Young, *Heart's Forest*, 55–56.

2. On dueling and other such handbooks fashionable in Elizabethan England, see Keir Elam, "English Bodies in Italian Habits," in Marrapodi, *Shakespeare, Italy, and Intertextuality*, 32–44.

3. The closing lines of Jaques's speech—

> Give me leave
> To speak my mind, and I will through and through
> Cleanse the foul body of th'infected world,
> If they will patiently receive my medicine—

are strongly reminiscent of Ben Jonson's thundering invective through his dramatic alter ego Asper in the Prologue to *Every Man Out of His Humour*:

> Well, I will scourge those Apes,
> And to these courteous Eyes oppose a Mirrour,
> As large as is the Stage whereon we act;
> Where they shall see the Time's Deformity
> Anatomiz'd in every Nerve and Sinew,
> With constant Courage, and contempt of Fear.

There are, of course, many signs that Jaques lampoons some of Jonson's characteristics as a major satirist to such an extent that *As You Like It* can be considered part of the War of the Theaters. Juliet Dusinberre lists a number of possible allusions in Shakespeare's comedy to Jonson's *Every Man In His Humour* (see *As You Like It*, ed. Dusinberre, 368). However, maybe due to her conviction that *As You Like It* was written before *Every Man Out of His Humour*, she makes no mention of the striking similarity of the two speeches considered here.

4. See on 36 of chap. 1 my presentation of Scholes and Klaus's definition of this variety of the essay in their *Elements of the Essay*.

5. Rosenmeyer, *Green Cabinet*, 220.

6. David Young expatiates on the manifold thematic and attitudinal relations between the pastoral and the lyric in his *Heart's Forest*, 30–32.

7. See 20 in chap. 1 above.

8. For an excellent critical survey of the various facets of the time theme in this play, see Jay Halio's "'No Clock in the Forest': Time in *As You Like It*."

9. See 30–31 in chap. 1 above.

10. Quinones, *Renaissance Discovery of Time*, 4–5.

11. Introduction, *As You Like It*, ed. Latham, xlvi.

12. Ibid., xxiii.

13. Ibid., lvi.

14. See reference to Mandelstam's notion of the odd communication act of lyric poetry on 19 of chap. 1 above.

15. Morgan, *Preface to Shakespeare's Comedies*, 220.

16. The parallels between this section of Orlando's poem and Shakespeare's sonnet 53 ("What is your substance, whereof are you made") are quite striking.

17. See 59 in chap. 2 above.

18. Introduction, *As You Like It*, ed. Latham, xix.

19. See, for instance, Morgan, *Preface to Shakespeare's Comedies*, 221.

20. Rosalind's exclamation in the next act, "O coz, coz, coz, my pretty little coz, that thou didst know how many fathom deep I am in love!" (4.1.193), will come suspiciously close to Silvius's, to establish one of the important half-concealed links between these two characters.

21. See 24–25 in chap. 1 above.

22. Welsh, *Roots of Lyric*, 165, 172.

23. Colie, *Shakespeare's Living Art*, 260.

24. A milder version of this recurrent Shakespearean construct was Berowne's beloved Rosaline in *Love's Labour's Lost*.

25. Dubrow, *Genre*, 116.

26. Rosenmeyer, *Green Cabinet*, 207.

27. Langer, *Feeling and Form*, 275.

28. See 17 in chap. 1 above.

29. Erskine, *Elizabethan Lyric*, 2:26.

30. Introduction, *As You Like It*, ed. Latham, xviii–xix.

31. Shaftesbury, *Soliloquy, or Advice to an Author* (1710); reprinted in *Characteristicks of Men, Manners, Opinions, Times* (1711); quoted by Harold Jenkins in "'Hamlet' Then till Now," 18.

32. R. Berry, *Shakespearean Metaphor*; reprinted in Muir and Wells, *Aspects of Hamlet*, 75.

33. Bloom, *Hamlet*, 60.

34. Wright, *Poet in the Poem*; reprinted in Calderwood and Toliver, *Perspectives on Poetry*, 110.

35. Bloom, *Hamlet*, 2.

36. Newstok, *Kenneth Burke on Shakespeare*, 53.

37. Quoted in Jenkins, "'Hamlet' Then till Now," 20.

38. Coleridge, *Lectures and Notes on Shakspere*, 531.

39. Burke, *Grammar of Motives*, 247.

40. Ibid., 441. In other references to *Hamlet*, Burke defines the play as "essayistic" too. One way or another, its unusually strong thematic orientation is obvious to him.

41. Frye, *Anatomy of Criticism*, 67.

42. Culler, *Structuralist Poetics*, 178.

43. F. Berry, *Shakespeare Inset*, 8.

44. Introduction, *Hamlet*, ed. Jenkins, 124.

45. Clemen, *Shakespeare's Dramatic Art*, 160.

46. Ibid., "Shakespeare's Soliloquies," 147.

47. Ibid., 160.

48. R. Berry, *Shakespearean Metaphor*, 76.

49. N. Brooke, *Shakespeare's Early Tragedies*, 165.

50. Colie, *Shakespeare's Living Art*, 16–17.

51. Even in its earlier position, in which it appears in Q1 and which some commentators and theater directors consider more appropriate, the "To be, or not to be" speech is fairly detached from the surrounding action.

52. Introduction, *Hamlet*, ed. Thompson, 18.

53. Of course, Tamburlaine's—and Marlowe's—magniloquence is of a different order from Claudius's, but the famous Marlovian phrase seems appropriate as a reference to the latter's inflated use of language.

54. See 167–68 in chap. 3 above.

55. R. Berry, *Shakespearean Metaphor*, 76n.

56. Mahood, *Shakespeare's Wordplay*, 113.

57. For an explanation of my choice of the last word's spelling, see note 59 below.

58. Mahood, *Shakespeare's Wordplay*, 114.

59. See Dover Wilson, *Works of Shakespeare. Hamlet* (quoted in *Hamlet*, ed. Jenkins, LN, 435). The Third Arden edition of the play adopts the spelling *son*, thus making Hamlet's message more explicit but depriving it of its paronomastic ambiguity. I have taken the liberty of retaining Harold Jenkins's choice of this key word, which I find more apposite. Of course, spelling is irrelevant in performance, but it can prompt directorial decisions and actorial interpretation.

60. Mahood, *Shakespeare's Wordplay*, 112.

61. See note 85 to chap. 1 above.

62. On the different kinds of punning, see 120–21 above.

63. *Hamlet*, ed. Jenkins, 246n.

64. This sentence refers to an interesting passage of some thirty lines to be found in the Folio text of *Hamlet* only (2.2.238–67) and so relegated to an appendix in the Third Arden edition of the play, ed. Thompson, 466–67. I find it too important in the development of 2.2 to ignore. Among other things, the passage contains several pregnant images and ideas, which we have learnt to associate with *Hamlet*: "Denmark's a prison," "there is nothing either good or bad, but thinking makes it so," "I could be bounded in a nutshell and count myself a king of infinite space—were it not that I have bad dreams," "the very substance of the ambitious is merely the shadow of a dream," etc.

65. The image of the beggars is first introduced by Hamlet a little earlier in the conversation with Rosencrantz and Guildenstern with the cue "Then are our beggars bodies, and our monarchs and outstretched heroes the beggars' shadows" (*Hamlet*, Arden Shakespeare, ed. Thompson, Appendix 1, 467, lines 25–26).

66. *Hamlet*, Arden Shakespeare, ed. Jenkins, 293n.

67. Mahood, *Shakespeare's Wordplay*, 30.

68. Sadly, the last of these figures remains tantalizingly obscure, due to a truncated sentence or to imperfect text.

69. Bloom, *Hamlet*, 120.

70. Mukařovský, *Word and Verbal Art*, 72.

71. Mahood, *Shakespeare's Wordplay*, 184.

72. Colie, *Shakespeare's Living Art*, 238.

CHAPTER 4. CONCLUSION

1. See note 56 to chap. 1 above.

2. See note 164 to chap. 1 above.

3. Sidney, "Defence of Poesy," in *Selected Prose and Poetry*, 110.

4. These cues are different from the aside in that they form part of the ongoing interactive dialogue, yet manage to redirect their central message to the speaker, depriving his interlocutor of the fullness of communication.

5. Burke must have been thinking of a somewhat similar distinction when he wrote: "Had [Shakespeare] not sometimes 'punned atrociously' in his blunt jingles, he could not have punned subtly in his most delicate, metaphorical leaps. The blunt tonal pun and the subtle metaphorical pun are merely opposite ends of a single 'graded series'" (Newstock, *Kenneth Burke on Shakespeare*, 224).

6. Mukařovský, *Word and Verbal Art*, 72.

7. *King Lear*, ed. Muir, 174n.

8. See 32 in chap. 1 above.

9. The effective tears-and-smiles portrait of a lyrically conceived character has already been attempted in two draft versions in *Richard II* discussed earlier: first, in 3.2, where Richard draws his own theatrical picture of his reunion with England—"As a long-parted mother with her child/ Plays fondly with her tears and smiles in meeting,/ So weeping, smiling, greet I thee, my earth" (8–10), and then, in 5.2, in York's nuntius report about the deposed king's progress through the streets of London with "His face still combating with tears and smiles,/ The badges of his grief and patience" (32–33). In both cases the speakers attempt to achieve the endearing effect witnessed in *King Lear*.

10. Even William Blake's inspired illustration of this speech, which does its best to overcome the static character of the visual arts, is incapable of conveying its breathless dynamism. An adequate representation of this form-smashing energy would perhaps become possible only within a more radical artistic method, like the one used by Picasso in his "Guernica."

11. See note 168 to chap. 1 above.

12. Introduction, *Othello*, ed. Honigmann, 89.

13. According to an authoritative count, Iago's role has, in fact, more lines than Othello's (1097 to the hero's 860) and is second only to Hamlet's in the entire canon of Shakespeare's drama (see McDonald's *Bedford Companion to Shakespeare*, 77–78). The interesting phenomenon of linguistic contamination in *Othello* was first studied by Mikhail Morozov in "Individualization of Shakespeare's Characters through Imagery," and, in an apparently independent way, by Wolfgang Clemen in his *Development of Shakespeare's Imagery*, 125–26, whose first English-language edition came out in 1951.

Bibliography

Shakespearean and Renaissance Texts

Shakespeare, William. *As You Like It*. Arden Shakespeare. Edited by Agnes Latham. London: Methuen, 1975.

———. *As You Like It*. Arden Shakespeare. 3rd Series. Edited by Juliet Dusinberre. London: Thomson Learning, 2006.

———. *Hamlet*. Arden Shakespeare. Edited by Harold Jenkins. London: Methuen, 1982.

———. *Hamlet*. Arden Shakespeare. 3rd Series. Edited by Ann Thompson and Neil Taylor. London: Cengage Learning, 2006.

———. *King Lear*. Arden Shakespeare. Edited by Kenneth Muir. London: Methuen, 1969.

———. *King Lear*. Arden Shakespeare. 3rd Series. Edited by R. A. Foakes. London: Cengage Learning, 1997.

———. *King Richard II*. Arden Shakespeare. Edited by Peter Ure. London: Methuen, 1970.

———. *King Richard II*. New Penguin Shakespeare. Edited by Stanley Wells. Harmondsworth: Penguin Books, 1969.

———. *King Richard II*. Arden Shakespeare. 3rd Series. Edited by Charles R. Forker. London: Thomson Learning, 2002.

———. *Love's Labour's Lost*. Arden Shakespeare. Edited by Richard David. London: Methuen; Cambridge, MA: Harvard University Press, 1963.

———. *Love's Labour's Lost*. Arden Shakespeare. 3rd Series. Edited by H. R. Woudhuysen. London: Cengage Learning, 1998.

———. *Macbeth*. Arden Shakespeare. Edited by Kenneth Muir. London: Methuen, 1969.

———. *Othello*. Arden Shakespeare. Edited by M. R. Ridley. London: Methuen, 1965.

———. *Othello*. Arden Shakespeare. 3rd Series. Edited by E. A. J. Honigmann. London: Thomson Learning, 1997.

———. *Romeo and Juliet*. Arden Shakespeare. Edited by Brian Gibbons. London: Methuen, 1980.

———. *The Tragedy of King Lear*. New Cambridge Shakespeare. Edited by Jay L. Halio. Cambridge: Cambridge University Press, 2005.

————. *The Poems.* Arden Shakespeare. Edited by F. T. Prince. London: Methuen, 1969.

Vendler, Helen. *The Art of Shakespeare's Sonnets.* Cambridge, MA: Harvard University Press, 1997.

Brooke, Arthur. *Romeus and Juliet.* Edited by J. J. Munro. New York: Duffield; London: Chatto and Windus, 1908.

Dante Alighieri. *Vita Nuova.* English and Italian. Edited by Stanley Appelbaum. Mineola, NY: Dover Publications, 2006.

Donne, John. *"The Elegies" and "The Songs and Sonnets."* Edited by Helen Gardner. Oxford: Oxford University Press, 1965.

Drayton, Michael. *The Works 1931–41. 2nd ed.* Edited by J. William Hebel et al. Oxford: Blackwell, 1961.

Elizabethan Sonnets. Edited by Maurice Evans. London: Dent, 1977.

Elizabethan Critical Essays. Edited by G. Gregory Smith. Oxford University Press, 1904.

Jonson, Ben. *The Complete Plays.* Edited by Felix E. Schelling. London: J. M. Dent; New York: E. P. Dutton, 1915.

Marlowe, Christopher. *Complete Plays and Poems.* Edited by E. D. Pendry. London: Dent, 1983.

Minturno, A. S. "L'Arte Poetica," 1564. In *Poetiken des Cinquecento,* vol. 6. Munich: W. Fink, 1971.

Peletier du Mans, Jaques. *L'art poëtique de Jaques Peletier du Mans,* 1555. Paris: Société d'édition Les Belles lettres, 1930.

Sidney, Sir Philip. *Selected Prose and Poetry of Sir Philip Sidney.* Edited by Robert Kimbrough. New York: Holt, Rinehart and Winston, 1969.

Spenser. *Poetical Works.* Edited by J. C. Smith and E. de Selincourt. London: Oxford University Press, 1916–66.

Wyatt, Sir Thomas. *Collected Poems.* Edited by Joost Daalder. London: Oxford University Press, 1975.

Critical and Theoretical Works

Abad, Gémino. *A Formal Approach to Lyric Poetry.* Quezon City: University of Philippines Press, 1978.

Altick, R. D. "Symphonic Imagery in *Richard II.*" *PMLA* 62 (June 1947): 339–65.

Bahti, Timothy. *Ends of the Lyric: Direction and Consequence in Western Poetry.* Baltimore, MD: The Johns Hopkins University Press, 1996.

Bakhtin, Mikhail. *Speech Genres and Other Late Essays.* Edited by Caryl Emerson and Michael Holquist. Austin: University of Texas Press, 1986.

————. *Voprosy literatury i estetiki* [Problems of Literature and Aesthetics]. Moscow: Hudozhestvennaya literatura, 1975.

Baldwin, Charles Sears. *Renaissance Literary Theory and Practice.* New York: Columbia University Press, 1939.

Barber, C. L. *Shakespeare's Festive Comedy.* Princeton, NJ: Princeton University Press, 1972.

Barthes, Roland. *Le Degré zéro de l'écriture.* Paris: Éditions du Seuil, 1953.

Batkin, L. M. *Italyanskie gumanisty: stil zhizni i stil myshleniya* [The Italian Humanists: Style of Living and Style of Thinking]. Moscow: Naouka, 1978.

Baxter, John. *Shakespeare's Poetic Styles: Verse into Drama.* London: Routledge and Kegan Paul, 1980.

Beebee, Thomas O. *The Ideology of Genre: A Comparative Study of Generic Instability.* University Park: The Pennsylvania State University Press, 1994.

Berry, Francis. *The Shakespeare Inset. Word and Picture.* London: Routledge and Kegan Paul, 1965.

Berry, Ralph. *The Shakespearean Metaphor.* London: Macmillan Press, 1978.

Bessière, Jean et al., eds. *Littérature et genres littéraires.* Paris: Librairie Larousse, 1978.

Black, Matthew. *The Life and Death of King Richard the Second.* A New Variorum Edition of Shakespeare. Philadelphia: J. B. Lippincott, 1955.

Bloom, Harold. *Hamlet: Poem Unlimited.* New York: Riverhead Books, 2003.

Bradbrook, M. C. *Shakespeare and Elizabethan Poetry.* London: Chatto and Windus, 1951.

Brooke, Nicholas. *Shakespeare's Early Tragedies.* London: Methuen, 1968.

Burke, Kenneth. *A Grammar of Motives.* Berkeley: University of California Press, 1969.

———. *The Philosophy of Literary Form.* Baton Rouge: Louisiana State University Press, 1941.

———. "Three Definitions." *The Kenyon Review* 13 (Spring 1951): 173–92.

Burrow, J. A. *Medieval Writers and Their Work: Middle English Literature and Its Background, 1100–1500.* Oxford: Oxford University Press, 1982.

Calderwood, James L. *Shakespearean Metadrama.* Minneapolis: University of Minnesota Press, 1971.

Calderwood, James L., and Harold E. Toliver, eds. *Perspectives on Poetry.* New York: Oxford University Press, 1968.

Cameron, Sharon. *Lyric Time: Dickinson and the Limits of Genre.* Baltimore, MD: The Johns Hopkins University Press, 1979.

Chambers, Edmund. *Shakespeare: A Survey.* London: Sidgwick and Jackson, 1925.

Clemen, Wolfgang H. *The Development of Shakespeare's Imagery.* London: Methuen, 1966.

———. *Shakespeare's Dramatic Art.* London: Methuen, 1972.

Cohen, Ralph, ed. *The Future of Literary Theory.* New York: Routledge, 1989.

Cole, Douglas, ed. *Twentieth Century Interpretations of Romeo and Juliet.* Englewood Cliffs, NJ: Prentice-Hall, 1970.

Coleridge, Samuel Taylor. *Lectures and Notes on Shakspere and Other English Poets.* London: George Bell and Sons, 1904.

Colie, Rosalie L. *The Resources of Kind: Genre-Theory in the Renaissance.* Edited by Barbara K. Lewalski. Berkeley: University of California Press, 1973.

———. *Shakespeare's Living Art.* Princeton, NJ: Princeton University Press, 1974.

Crane, R. S., ed. *Critics and Criticism: Ancient and Modern.* Chicago: The University of Chicago Press, 1952.

Culler, Jonathan. *The Pursuit of Signs.* London: Routledge and Kegan Paul, 1981.

———. *Structuralist Poetics.* Ithaca, NY: Cornell University Press, 1975.

Dallas, E. S. *Poetics: An Essay on Poetry.* 1852. London: Smith, Elder, and Co., 1972.

Danson, Lawrence. *Shakespeare's Dramatic Genres.* Oxford: Oxford University Press, 2000.

Day Lewis, Cecil. *The Lyric Impulse.* Cambridge, MA: Harvard University Press, 1965.

Demerson, G., ed. *La Notion de genre à la Renaissance.* Genève: Éditions Slatkine, 1984.

Dictionnaire des genres et notions littéraires. Paris: Albin Michel, 1997.

Dimock, Wai Chee, and Bruce Robbins, eds. "Remapping Genre." Special Topic. *PMLA* 122, no. 5 (October 2007).

Donohue, James J. *The Theory of Literary Kinds: Ancient Classification of Literature.* Dubuque, IA: The Loras College Press, 1943.

Duarte, João Ferreira, ed. "Reconceptions of Genre." Special Issue, *European Journal of English Studies* 3, no. 1 (April 1999).

Dubrow, Heather. *Genre.* London: Methuen, 1982.

Duff, David, ed. *Modern Genre Theory.* London: Longman, 1999.

Eliot, T. S. *Elizabethan Dramatists.* London: Faber and Faber, 1963.

———. *On Poetry and Poets.* New York: Farrar, Straus and Cudahy, 1957.

Ellis-Fermor, Una. *The Frontiers of Drama.* London: Methuen, 1964.

———. *Shakespeare's Drama.* London: Methuen, 1980.

Erskine, John. *The Elizabethan Lyric.* Columbia University Studies in English 2. New York: Columbia University Press, 1903.

Evans, Robert O. *The Osier Cage: Rhetorical Devices in Romeo and Juliet.* Lexington: University of Kentucky Press, 1966.

Fohrmann, Jürgen. "Remarks towards a Theory of Literary Genres." *Poetics* 17 (1988): 273–85.

Fowler, Alastair. *A History of English Literature.* Cambridge, MA: Harvard University Press, 1987.

———. *Kinds of Literature.* Oxford: Clarendon Press, 1982.

Frieden, Ken. *Genius and Monologue.* Ithaca, NY: Cornell University Press, 1985.

Frye, Northrop. *Anatomy of Criticism.* Princeton, NJ: Princeton University Press, 1971.

Fussell, Paul. *Poetic Forms and the Lyric Subject.* The John Coffin Memorial Lecture. London: University of London, 1992.

———. *Poetic Meter and Poetic Form.* New York: Random House, 1965.

Gass, William H. *Finding a Form.* Ithaca, NY: Cornell University Press, 1996.

Genette, Gérard. "Genres, 'types,' modes." *Poétique* 32 (November 1977): 389–421.

———. *Introduction à l'Architexte.* Paris: Éditions du Seuil, 1979.

Genette, Gérard, and Tzvetan Todorov, eds. *Théories des genres.* Paris: Seuil, 1986.

Georgiev, Nikola. *Analiz na liricheskata tvorba* [Analysis of a Lyrical Poem]. Sofia: Prosveta, 1994.

Goethe, Johann Wolfgang. "Noten und Abhandlungen zu besserem Verstandnis des West-östlichen Diwans." *Goethes Werke* 2. Munich: Beck, 1981.

Guillén, Claudio. *Literature as System: Essays toward the Theory of Literary History.* Princeton, NJ: Princeton University Press, 1971.

Halio, Jay L. "'No Clock in the Forest': Time in *As You Like It.*" *Studies in English Literature, 1500–1900* 2, no. 2 (Spring 1962): 197–207.

Hamburger, Käte. *The Logic of Literature.* Bloomington: Indiana University Press, 1993.

Hardison, Jr., O. B. *Prosody and Purpose in the English Renaissance.* Baltimore, MD: The Johns Hopkins University Press, 1989.

Hardy, Barbara. *The Advantage of Lyric: Essays on Feeling in Poetry.* Bloomington: Indiana University Press, 1977.

Hawkes, Terence, ed. *Coleridge on Shakespeare.* The Penguin Shakespeare Library. Harmondsworth: Penguin Books, 1969.

Hegel, G. W. F. *Aesthetics: Lectures on Fine Art.* Oxford: Clarendon Press, 1975.

Hernadi, Paul. *Beyond Genre: New Directions in Literary Classification.* Ithaca, NY: Cornell University Press, 1972.

Hirsch, Jr., E. D. *Validity in Interpretation.* New Haven, CT: Yale University Press, 1967.

Hošek, Chaviva, and Patricia Parker, eds. *Lyric Poetry: Beyond New Criticism.* Ithaca, NY: Cornell University Press, 1985.

Ing, Catherine. *Elizabethan Lyrics: A Study in the Development of English Metres and Their Relation to Poetic Effect.* London: Chatto and Windus, 1951.

Jakobson, Roman. *The Framework of Language. Michigan Studies in the Humanities,* no. 1, Ann Arbor: Graduate School of University of Michigan, 1980.

———. *Izbrannye raboty* [Selected Writings]. Moscow: Progres, 1985.

———. *Language in Literature.* Edited by Krystyna Pomorska and Roman Jakobson. Cambridge, MA: Harvard University Press, 1987.

James, Henry. *Literary Criticism.* New York: Viking Press, 1984.

Jenkins, Harold. "'Hamlet' Then till Now." In *Aspects of Hamlet.* Edited by Kenneth Muir and Stanley Wells. Cambridge: Cambridge University Press, 1979.

Johnson, W. R. *The Idea of Lyric: Lyric Modes in Ancient and Modern Poetry.* Berkeley: University of California Press, 1982.

Kleiner, Juliusz. "The Role of Time in Literary Genres." *Zagadnienia rodzajow literackich* 2 1959: 5–12.

Knight, G. Wilson. The Imperial Theme. London: Methuen, 1965.

Kohler, Pierre. "Contribution à une philosophie des genres." *Helicon* 1 (1938): 233–44; and *Helicon* 2 (1939–40): 135–47.

Kridl, Manfred M. "Obsevations sur les genres de la poésie lyrique." *Helicon* 2, 2–3 (1940): 147–56.

Langer, Susanne K. *Feeling and Form: A Theory of Art.* New York: Charles Scribner's Sons, 1953.

Lewalski, Barbara Kiefer, ed. *Renaissance Genres: Essays on Theory, History, and Interpretation.* Cambridge, MA: Harvard University Press, 1986.

Lindley, David. *Lyric.* The Critical Idiom. London: Methuen, 1985.

Londré, Felicia Hardison, ed. *Love's Labour's Lost: Critical Essays.* New York: Garland Publishing, 1997.

Mahood, M. M. *Shakespeare's Wordplay.* 1957. London: Methuen, 1968.

Mandelstam, Osip. *The Collected Critical Prose and Letters.* Edited by Jane Gary Harris. London: Collins Harvill, 1991.

Marrapodi, Michele, ed. *Shakespeare, Italy and Intertextuality.* Manchester: Manchester University Press, 2004.

McCann Boulton, Maureen Barry. *The Song in the Story: Lyric Insertions in French Narrative Fiction, 1200–1400.* Philadelphia: University of Pennsylvania Press, 1993.

McDonald, Russ, ed. *The Bedford Companion to Shakespeare: An Introduction with Documents.* 2nd edition. Boston: Bedford / St. Martin's Press, 2001.

Mill, John Stuart. *Essays on Poetry.* Edited by F. Parvin Sharpless. Columbia: University of South Carolina Press, 1976.

Miller, Paul Allen. *Lyric Texts and Lyric Consciousness: The Birth of a Genre from Archaic Greece to Augustan Rome.* London: Routledge, 1994.

Molino, Jean. "Les Genres Littéraires." *Poétique* 24 (1993): 3–28.

Morgan, Michael. *A Preface to Shakespeare's Comedies, 1594–1603.* London: Longman, 1996.

Morozov, Mikhail M. "The Individualization of Shakespeare's Characters through Imagery." *Shakespeare Survey* 2 (1949): 83–106.

Muir, Kenneth, and Stanley Wells, eds. *Aspects of Hamlet.* Cambridge: Cambridge University Press, 1979.

Mukařovský, Jan. *Structure, Sign and Function: Selected Essays.* Edited by John Burbank and Peter Steiner. New Haven, CT: Yale University Press, 1978.

———. *The Word and Verbal Art: Selected Essays.* Edited by John Burbank and Peter Steiner. New Haven, CT: Yale University Press, 1977.

Musil, Robert. *The Man without Qualities.* Translated by Eithne Wilkins and Ernst Kaiser. New York: Capricorn Books, 1965.

Nardo, A. K. "The Submerged Sonnet as Lyric Moment in Miltonic Epic." *Genre* 9, 1 (1976): 21–35.

Newstok, Scott L., ed. *Kenneth Burke on Shakespeare.* West Lafayette, IN: Parlor Press, 2007.

Olson, Elder. "The Lyric." In *Poetic Theory/ Poetic Practice.* Edited by Robert Scholes, 59–66. Iowa City, IA: Midwest Modern Language Association, 1969.

———. "An Outline of Poetic Theory." In *Critics and Criticism, Ancient and Modern*. Edited by R. S. Crane et al., 546–66. Chicago: University of Chicago Press, 1952.

Pater, Walter. *Appreciations: with an Essay on Style*. London: Macmillan, 1889.

Pfister, Manfred. *The Theory and Analysis of Drama*. Cambridge: Cambridge University Press, 1988.

Piper, W. B. *The Heroic Couplet*. Cleveland, OH: Case Western Reserve University Press, 1969.

Pirandello, Luigi. "L'azione parlata." *Pirandello* http://www.pirandelloweb.com/scritti/scritti_l'azione_parlata.htm.

Popivanov, Ivan. *Problemi na literaturnya zhanr* [Problems of Literary Genre]. Sofia: Nauka i izkustvo, 1972.

———. *Zhanr i zhanrova spetsifika* [Genre and Genre Specifics]. Sofia: Nauka i izkustvo, 1984.

Pound, Ezra. *Literary Essays*. Norfolk, CT: New Directions, 1954.

Preminger, Alex, and T. V. F. Brogan, eds. *The New Princeton Encyclopedia of Poetry and Poetics*, 3rd ed., Princeton, NJ: Princeton University Press, 1993.

Quinones, Ricardo J. *The Renaissance Discovery of Time*. Cambridge, MA: Harvard University Press, 1972.

Rogers, William Elford. *The Three Genres and the Interpretation of Lyric*. Princeton, NJ: Princeton University Press, 1983.

Rosenmeyer, Thomas G. *The Green Cabinet: Theocritus and the European Pastoral Lyric*. Berkeley: University of California Press, 1969.

Rosmarin, Adena. *The Power of Genre*. Minneapolis: University of Minnesota Press, 1985.

Scholes, Robert. *Elements of Poetry*. New York: Oxford University Press, 1969.

———, ed. *Poetic Theory/ Poetic Practice*. Papers of the Midwest Modern Language Association, no. 1. Iowa City, IA: Midwest Modern Language Association, 1969.

Scholes, Robert, and Carl H. Klaus. *Elements of Drama*. New York: Oxford University Press, 1971.

———. *Elements of the Essay*. New York: Oxford University Press, 1969.

Shelley, Percy Bysshe. *Shelley's Prose*. Edited by D. L. Clark. Albuquerque: University of New Mexico Press, 1954.

Shurbanov, Alexander. *Poetika na angliyskiya renesans* [Poetics of the English Renaissance]. Sofia: St. Kliment Ohridsky University Press, 2002.

Smith, Barbara Hernstein. *Poetic Closure: A Study of How Poems End*. Chicago University Press, 1968.

Snyder, John. *Prospects of Power: Tragedy, Satire, the Essay, and the Theory of Genre*. Lexington: The University Press of Kentucky, 1991.

Spingarn, J. E. *A History of Literary Criticism in the Renaissance*. 1908. New York: Columbia University Press, 1963.

Spurgeon, Caroline. *Shakespeare's Imagery and What It Tells Us*. Cambridge: Cambridge University Press, 1935.

Staiger, Emil. *Basic Concepts of Poetics*. University Park: The Pennsylvania State University Press, 1991.

Strelka, Joseph P., ed. *Theories of Literary Genre*. Yearbook of Comparative Criticism 8. University Park: The Pennsylvania State University Press, 1978.

Tennenhouse, Leonard. *Power on Display: The Politics of Shakespeare's Genres*. New York: Methuen, 1986.

Tiegheim, Philippe van. "La Question des genres littéraires." *Helicon* 1 (1938): 95–101.

Todorov, Tzvetan. *The Fantastic: A Structural Approach to a Literary Genre*. Ithaca, NY: Cornell University Press, 1973.

———. *Genres in Discourse*. Cambridge: Cambridge University Press, 1990.

———. "Literary Genres." In *Current Trends in Linguistics*, vol. 12. Edited by Thomas A. Sebeok, 957–62. The Hague: Mouton, 1974.

———, ed. *French Literary Theory Today*. Cambridge: Cambridge University Press, 1982.

Viëtor, Karl. "L'histoire des genres littéraires." *Poétique* 32 (November 1977): 490–506.

Weinberg, Bernard. *A History of Literary Criticism in the Italian Renaissance*. Chicago: The University of Chicago Press, 1961–63.

Wellek, René. *Discriminations: Further Concepts of Criticism*. New Haven, CT: Yale University Press, 1970.

Welsh, Andrew. *Roots of Lyric*. Princeton, NJ: Princeton University Press, 1978.

Wimsatt, William K., and Cleanth Brook. *Literary Criticism: A Short History*. New York: Knopf, 1969.

Woolf, Rosemary. *The English Mystery Plays*. London: Routledge and Kegan Paul, 1972.

Wright, George T. *The Poet in the Poem*. Berkeley: University of California Press, 1960.

Young, David. *The Heart's Forest: A Study of Shakespeare's Pastoral Plays*. New Haven, CT: Yale University Press, 1972.

Zumthor, Paul. *Toward a Medieval Poetics*. Minneapolis: University of Minnesota Press, 1992.

Zutschi, Margot E. *Literary Theory in Germany: A Study of Genre and Evaluation Theories 1945–1965*. Berne: Peter Lang, 1981.

Index

305